Christmas in the Crosshairs

Christmas
in the
Crosshairs

Two Thousand Years of Denouncing
and Defending the World's Most
Celebrated Holiday

GERRY BOWLER

OXFORD
UNIVERSITY PRESS

OXFORD
UNIVERSITY PRESS

Oxford University Press is a department of the University of Oxford.
It furthers the University's objective of excellence in research, scholarship,
and education by publishing worldwide. Oxford is a registered trade mark of
Oxford University Press in the UK and certain other countries.

Published in the United States of America by Oxford University Press
198 Madison Avenue, New York, NY 10016, United States of America.

Library of Congress Cataloging-in-Publication Data
Names: Bowler, G. Q., 1948– author.
Title: Christmas in the crosshairs : two thousand years of denouncing and
defending the world's most celebrated holiday / Gerry Bowler.
Description: New York : Oxford University Press, 2016. |
Includes bibliographical references and index.
Identifiers: LCCN 2016005102 (print) | LCCN 2016031263 (ebook) |
ISBN 9780190499006 (hardback : alk. paper) | ISBN 9780190499013 (updf) |
ISBN 9780190499020 (epub)
Subjects: LCSH: Christmas—History.
Classification: LCC BV45 .B684 2016 (print) | LCC BV45 (ebook) | DDC
263/.91509—dc23
LC record available at https://lccn.loc.gov/2016005102

1 3 5 7 9 8 6 4 2
Printed by Sheridan Books, Inc., United States of America

Contents

Acknowledgments

I WOULD LIKE to thank the staffs of the libraries of the University of Manitoba and Duke Divinity School for their assistance in providing the raw materials for this book. Thanks also to the students of my University of Manitoba Social History of Christmas class for their lively feedback. I am most grateful, however, for the wonderful teachers I have had in my life. This book is humbly and happily dedicated to Mrs. V. Hogg, Miss C. Kortes, Mr. W. Clark, Miss Robinson, Mr. K. Sauer, Mr. R. Rashley, and Professors M. Hayden, J. Fry, R. Grogin, L. Kitzan, G. Porter, and H. G. Koenigsberger. My gratitude comes too late on this mortal path for some of these worthies, but I hope to thank them personally in the Great Library beyond. Thanks also to Cynthia Read and Gina Chung, of Oxford University Press for their encouragement and deft editing, and to Martha Ramsey for her copyediting.

Introduction

IS THERE A war on Christmas? Of course there is. Bill O'Reilly says so, and John Gibson agrees. The Catholic League for Religious and Civil Rights says so, and the American Family Association does too. It is a calculated and pernicious attack not only on the holiday but on Christianity itself.

Is there a war on Christmas? Of course not. Michelle Goldberg at *Salon* says it is a canard, and the *New Yorker* agrees. Jon Stewart mocks the notion, and the *Guardian* calls it nonsense. To claim there is such a war is an example of "Christonormativity," a right-wing plot to bolster the ratings of Fox News and disguise the drive for Christian theocracy.

Is there a war on Christmas? Yes, indeed. In fact, there is a history of almost two thousand years of opposing, controlling, reforming, criticizing, suppressing, resurrecting, reshaping, appropriating, debating, replacing, and abolishing the world's most popular festival. It continues to this very day, and that is what this book is about.

Christmas in the Crosshairs

I

The Inventors

In which the idea of celebrating Christmas is debated,
agreed upon, argued over, regulated, abolished, and then
restored in a diminished state

IN THE TWENTY-FIRST CENTURY, Christmas is a worldwide phenomenon observed in a million ways every year by billions of people. But it was
not always that way—it took centuries before Christians were convinced it
should be observed at all. Though its origins lie in marking the Nativity of
Jesus of Nazareth, whom Christians honor as God come to our planet in
the form of a human baby in a Bethlehem manger, the early Church seems
to have had little interest in celebrating the events of this birth. The first
generations of believers concentrated on the death and resurrection of
Jesus and lived in profound expectation of his imminent return. What
need was there to make a fuss over his humble origins when he would
soon return again in glory to judge the living and the dead and to usher in
a new heaven and a new earth?

As the years went by and Christ seemed to be tarrying, the circumstances of his birth attracted more interest. Pagan critics of the new religion, such as Celsus, made mock of the claims of a virgin birth and asserted
that Jesus was the illegitimate product of an adulterous union. Rather than
bearing a child in a stable surrounded by hosts of angels, adoring shepherds, and wandering astrologers, Mary the mother of Jesus, he said, had
been turned out of doors by her husband and forced to live a disgraceful
life of itinerant poverty.[1] Certain second-century Christians, influenced by
Greek Gnosticism, were skeptical of the idea of a god dwelling in human
flesh—this was a repellent notion to the philosophers; the very purpose of
the soul was not to become trapped in a body but to escape its earthly
prison of meat and bone. Such criticisms prompted the second-century
Church to emphasize the truth of the Nativity stories told in the Gospels of
Matthew and Luke and even to add to them in pious fictions, for example

The Protoevangelium of James, which invented details about the youth of Mary and introduced the character of Salome, a midwife, to the events in Bethlehem.[2]

By the year 200, Christian writers had begun to speculate about when the birth of Jesus had taken place. Clement of Alexandria noted that some in his city had calculated that Jesus had been born in the twenty-eighth year of the reign of Caesar Augustus, 3 B.C. by our calculation. As for the exact date, there were said to be those who favored May 20 and others either April 19 or 20. January 6 was deemed to be the critical date by local Gnostics who, despising the world of the flesh, were not interested in the date of Jesus's birth but rather the date of his baptism in the Jordan River, when God announced that he had chosen him as his Son. In Carthage, Tertullian placed the time of the year as either December 25 or January 6. The widely traveled Julius Africanus stated that the conception of Jesus took place on March 25, making a late December birth likely, and in his *Commentary on Daniel,* Hippolytus, writing in Rome early in the 200s, pinpointed December 25. In 243 an anonymous document produced in North Africa, known as *De pascha computus,* linked the birthday of Jesus to an analogous date in the creation of the world. As God was thought to have begun Creation on March 25 (the first day of spring), the birth of Jesus corresponded to the appearance of the sun and moon on the fourth day, thus making the Nativity March 28. "O how admirable and divine is the providence of the Lord, that on that day on which the sun was made on the same day was Christ born, the fifth of the kalends of April, the fourth day of the week, and so rightly did the prophet Malachi say to the people: 'the sun of righteousness shall rise upon you, with healing in his wings.'" (This would not be the last time solar imagery would play a part in the calculation of the date.)[3]

This does not mean that Christians were seeking to know the date of the birth of Jesus in order to celebrate it. The theologian Origen declared that only pagan rulers had their birthdays trumpeted and, indeed, King Herod Antipas had given birthdays a bad name in the Christian community when he had used the occasion of his celebration to order the execution of John the Baptist.[4] Despite such a view, believers were growing fonder of recounting the story of the birth of Jesus. In Rome, where Christians gathered to worship in the funeral caves outside the city, they decorated a wall with a picture of the Nativity scene. The catacomb of St. Priscilla, which dates to about 250, bears an image of three Magi advancing toward the seated Virgin and Child; a man standing beside her (probably meant to represent an Old Testament prophet) points to the guiding star in the heavens. Second- and third-century pseudo-Gospels such as *The Revelation of the Magi* were particularly interested in the appearance of the Wise Men who, guided by this miraculous star, became the first Gentiles to worship the Christ Child.[5]

With the accession of the emperor Constantine in 312, Christianity became a legal religion, free to marks its holy days publicly, and the celebration of the Nativity soon was celebrated joyfully. Maximus, bishop of Turin at the beginning of the fifth century, contradicted Origen's anticelebratory attitude and proclaimed:

> You well know what joy and what a gathering there is when the birthday of the emperor of this world is to be celebrated; how his generals and princes and soldiers, arrayed in silk garments and girt with precious belts worked with shining gold, seek to enter the king's presence in more brilliant fashion than usual. . . . If, therefore, brethren, those of this world celebrate the birthday of an earthly king with such an outlay for the sake of the glory of the present honor, with what solicitude ought we to celebrate the birthday of our eternal king Jesus Christ. Who in return for our devotion will bestow on us not temporal but eternal glory![6]

The exact moment when the birth of Jesus became a feast in the Christian calendar remains a subject of some uncertainty. The earliest reference to it being settled on December 25 comes from an odd document known as the *Philocalian Chronograph*, a sort of almanac produced in 354, which contained lists of martyrs and bishops, birthdays of emperors, illustrations of capital cities, and a method to calculate the dating of Easter. It makes reference twice to the birth of Christ. In a list of Roman consuls it states "I p Chr. Caesare et Paulo sat. XIII Hoc. Cons. Dns. His. Xpc. Natus est VIII Kal. Ian de ven. Luna XV": "Christ is born during the consulate of C. Caesar Augustus and L. Aemelianus Paulus on the 8th of the Kalends of January [December 25], a Friday, the 15th day of the new moon." And in the list of martyrs it says "VIII Kal. Ian natus Christus in Betleem Iudae": "Christ is born on the eighth of the Kalends of January in Bethlehem of Judea."[7] Since the *Chronograph* refers to events in 336 it can be assumed that by that year the Nativity was celebrated in Rome on December 25. There is some evidence, however, that the hard-line sectarians known as the Donatists had marked the event earlier (beginning sometime between the years 243 and 311) in North Africa.[8]

Why was the December 25 date chosen by the Church in Rome?[9] Some historians have sought the answer to that question in the proliferation of Roman holidays in late December. The popular feast known as Saturnalia, a time of merry-making and social inversion, began on December 17 and lasted until December 23. This was traditionally followed by Brumalia, dedicated to Saturn and Bacchus, on December 25, and by the Kalends of January, the Roman New Year, with its gift-giving, dancing in the streets, and taking of omens. Was it not likely, many thought, that the Church chose December 25 either to appropriate the date from pagan influence or to capitalize on the winter solstice and its theme of the conquest of darkness and renewal of the light—highly appropriate to the birth of a god? This argument seemed particularly strong when considering that in 273 the emperor Aurelian had instituted a new holiday on December 25, Dies Solis Invicti, the Birthday of the Unconquered Sun, in an attempt to unite citizens in a cult that linked the supremacy of the sun god with imperial rule and military success. Many pointed to December 25 as the birthday of the Iranian deity Mithra, also associated with the sun and with the Roman military class. Moreover, it was noted that Constantine, the early-fourth-century emperor who was the first to allow the public observance of Christianity and who later became an adherent of the new religion, had always been a devotee of the sun god, placing the image of Sol Invictus on his coinage and making Sun Day a day of rest, decreeing "All judges, townsfolk, and shops of all crafts are to rest on the venerable Day of the Sun."[10]

It was also suggested that Christians, by choosing a time when their neighbors were engaged in celebration, might hold their own festivities unremarked by hostile authorities, an important consideration around the year 300, when their religion was under intense government persecution. There is no contemporary evidence to support this, and the earliest assertion of this argument comes from a Syriac manuscript dating from the twelfth century:

> The Lord was born in the month of January, on the day on which we celebrate the Epiphany [January 6]; for the ancients observed the Nativity and the Epiphany on the same day, because he was born and baptized on the same day. Also still today the Armenians celebrate the two feasts on the same day. To this must be added the Doctors who speak at the same time of the one and the other feast. The reason for which the Fathers transferred the said solemnity from the sixth of January to the 25th of December is, it is said, the

following: it was the custom of the pagans to celebrate on this same day of the 25th of December the birth of the sun. To adorn the solemnity, they had the custom of lighting fires and they even invited Christians to take part in these rites. When, therefore, the Doctors noted that the Christians were won over to this custom, they decided to celebrate the feast of the true birth on this same day; the 6th of January they made to celebrate the Epiphany. They have kept this custom until today with the rite of the lighted fire.[11]

On the surface this explanation seems quite reasonable, but there are a number of difficulties with it, and the current trend in historical research now looks elsewhere for the origins of the celebration of Christmas on December 25. Historians of the reign of Aurelian and his solar cult are now skeptical about its influence on the dating of the Nativity, and some go so far as to suggest that it may not have preceded the Christian observance at all; in fact, they say, the pagan celebrations may have begun as a reaction to the Christian claims on December 25.[12] The long-held association of December 25 as the birthday of Mithra (often said to be a virgin birth in the presence of shepherds) has now been contradicted by recent research that claims that there is no evidence that the date in question had any Mithraic significance and was certainly not celebrated as the god's birthday.[13]

Another objection is that the association of a Christian festival as important as that of the Nativity with paganism would have been completely antithetical to the mindset of believers at the time. Countless sermons and books by preachers and leaders of the young Church stressed the need to avoid any association with the world of idols and state cults.[14] Their desire to abstain from attendance at the games and the sacrifices that were so much a part of Roman life was noted by their fellow citizens and gained the new religion an unsavory reputation for atheism. It seems unlikely, then, that the Church would have countenanced deliberately associating a Christian festival with pagan celebrations. It is also noteworthy that no contemporary explanation for the dating of Christmas uses the Roman holiday setting as a reason. Rather, people of the time explained the decision with a set of arguments that might seem strange to modern ears.

Take, for example, the notion current in the ancient world that great men invariably lived lives of complete years: that they were born and died on the same date. Since Jesus was deemed to have been crucified in late March, he might have been expected to have been born at that time—as some had earlier suggested. But perhaps it was more appropriate to consider his conception rather than his birth as the starting point in calculations: therefore, his earthly birth would have been in late December. A fourth-century tract, *On the Solstice and Equinox Conception and Nativity*, stated: "Therefore our Lord was conceived on the eighth of the kalends of April in the month of March [March 25], which is the day of the passion of the Lord and of his conception. For on that day he was conceived on the same he suffered."[15] Consider also the idea that the first day of our planet's existence saw the world born in springtime and since Jesus's conception was an analogue to the creation of the universe, the angel's appearance to Mary to herald her pregnancy must have taken place on March 25 and the birth of her child the usual nine months later. These theories of calculation were bolstered by reference to the first chapter of Luke, which describes the earlier miraculous conception of Elizabeth that would result in the birth of John the Baptist. This conception took place when her husband Zechariah's tribe was serving its period in the Temple, and by examining the tribal duty roster many concluded that John's birth was on June 25, as close to the summer solstice as was Jesus's to the winter solstice. Since Mary had visited Elizabeth in the sixth month of the older woman's pregnancy, the date December 25 again fits the time chosen as the date of the Nativity. Finally, John's remark about Jesus that "he must increase but I must decrease" was interpreted as a reference to the waxing and waning of the daylight that followed the solstices.[16]

For whatever reason the Roman Church chose December 25 as the date on which to celebrate the Nativity, it was a momentous decision that would cause centuries of controversy and conflict. The first problem was that other Christian churches in the empire had settled on another date on which to mark Christmas—January 6, or "Epiphany." The term means "manifestation," and the January 6 date celebrated not only the birth of Jesus as his first earthly appearance but also the arrival of the Magi, the manifestation to the Gentile world, his first miracle at the wedding in Cana, and his baptism as an adult in the Jordan River, when his divinity was publicly proclaimed from on high. It was true that this date was originally chosen by radically dissident Christian groups such as the Basilideans and the Marcionites—clearly people not to be listened to—but the official church of the great cities in the East, including Constantinople, Jerusalem, and Antioch, also had established a January tradition, based, it seems, on the calculation of a different date for Easter.[17] From then on, the battle was to persuade Easterners that December 25 was the correct date. This was not a quick process. In the mid-fourth century, January 6 was still the date in the eastern end of the Mediterranean of the joint celebrations of the various manifestations. John Chrysostom, the greatest preacher of his day, gave a sermon in 386 in Antioch pleading the case of the churches in the West and arguing for a separation of Epiphany and Christmas. "A feast is approaching which is the most solemn and awe-inspiring of all feasts. . . . What is it? The birth of Christ according to the flesh. In this feast namely Epiphany, holy Easter, Ascension and Pentecost have their beginning and their purpose. For if Christ hadn't been born according to the flesh, he wouldn't have been baptised, which is Epiphany. He wouldn't have been crucified, which is Easter. He wouldn't have sent the Spirit, which is Pentecost. So from this event, as from some spring, different rivers flow—these feasts of ours are born."[18] December 25, he said, was chosen in Rome because it was believed to be the authentic date of the Nativity; indeed Christians from Spain to Greece had been keeping that day for some considerable length of time—"a day of great antiquity and long continuance," he called it—and he himself had been trying to win over the Antiochene church for a decade. It was, moreover, verifiable by calculating the date of the service of Zechariah in the Temple. Finally, as his trump card, he asserted that the Roman census records that testified to the appearance of Joseph of Nazareth and his wife Mary in Bethlehem on December 25 were still preserved in the imperial archives. Though Chrysostom was successful in persuading the churches in Antioch and Constantinople, notable holdouts resisted changing from January 6 and mocked proponents of the December date as being unduly influenced by sun worship.[19] It was not until 431 that Alexandria abandoned January for December 25; Jerusalem held on until the sixth century; and the Armenian church never yielded—to this day that country celebrates Christmas on January 6.

From the 300s on, the observances surrounding the celebration of the Nativity became more laden with ritual, art, and music, until it grew into the second holiest day on the Christian calendar. Christmas liturgies expanded; Christmas hymns were written; pilgrimages were made to the sites connected to the holy birth. In Bethlehem, Helena, the mother of Emperor Constantine, built a basilica over the cave that had been identified as the birthplace of Christ. Churches sought out relics from the Holy Land that were connected to the Nativity—the church of Santa Maria Maggiore in Rome, for example, claimed to possess wooden slats from the cradle in which the Baby Jesus had lain, and a church in Milan said it held the bones of the Magi. In 529 the emperor Justinian made December 25 a national holiday, and over the next few centuries the period from December 25 to January 6 became known as the Twelve Days of Christmas. Since the most solemn date on the calendar, Easter, had a preparatory fast, Christmas was given one as well, and so developed the season known as Advent.

But while Christmas was growing in stature, its setting during the traditional pagan festive season would cause trouble that lasted for centuries. Because the Nativity was celebrated during a time traditionally marked by popular festivities such as feasting, gift-giving, and decorating homes with greenery, those activities would inevitably affect Christians and their new holiday. Gregory Nazianzen, the archbishop of Constantinople, sounded a warning note in a sermon of 380. He praised what he called "the feast of the Theophany," when God appeared to humans in the form of a baby in order for us to "journey toward God." This was worthy of celebration—but in a godly way, not like a pagan festival. He begged his listeners to avoid imitating their worldly neighbors.

> Let us not put wreaths on our front doors, or assemble troupes of dancers, or decorate the streets. Let us not feast the eyes, or mesmerize the sense of hearing, or make effeminate the sense of smell, or prostitute the sense of taste, or gratify the sense of touch. These are ready paths to evil, and entrances of sin.... Let us not assess the bouquets of wines, the concoctions of chefs, the great cost of perfumes. Let earth and sea not bring us as gifts the valued dung, for this is how I know to evaluate luxury. Let us not strive to conquer each other in dissoluteness. For to me all that is superfluous and beyond need is dissoluteness, particularly when others are hungry and in want, who are of the same clay and composition as ourselves. But let us leave these things to the Greeks and to Greek pomp and festivals.[20]

Gregory left the offensive heathen holiday unnamed, but other Christian critics were not afraid to tackle the festivities surrounding the Kalends of January, the Roman New Year, head on. John Chrysostom compared the revels of the season to an invasion, not of barbarians but "of demons leading a procession in the forum. For the diabolical night-festivities that occur today, the jests, the abuse, and the nocturnal dances, and this comedy, absurd and worse than every enemy, took our city captive."[21] Asterius of Amasea criticized the pagan holiday in ways that will seem very familiar to those who view with a jaundiced eye Christmas in the twenty-first century.

In his Christmas sermon of the year 400, Asterius bewailed the expense and the hypocrisy that went hand in hand during this season: "All stalk about open-mouthed, hoping to receive something from one another . . . the mouth indeed is kissed but it is the coin that is loved." Money is demanded for gifts to one's superiors and to annoying vagrants and buskers on the street. Even children are corrupted by the practice: "This festival teaches even the little children, artless and simple, to be greedy, and accustoms them to go from house to house and to offer novel gifts, fruits covered with silver tinsel. For these they receive in return gifts double their value, and thus the tender minds of the young begin to be impressed with that which is commercial and sordid." Honest folk end up in debt while the unworthy and tawdry grow rich. It is not the poor who benefit from this largesse, complained Asterius; it is the mob of hangers-on, entertainers, and dishonest officials—and all for vanity and the hope of gain. Rather than indulge in this sleazy social bargaining, Asterius urged his listeners to spend their money on Christian charity:

> Give to the crippled beggar, and not to the dissolute musician. Give to the widow instead of the harlot; instead of to the woman of the street, to her who is piously secluded. Lavish your gifts upon the holy virgins singing psalms unto God, and hold the shameless psaltery in abhorrence, which by its music catches the licentious before it is seen. Satisfy the orphan, pay the poor man's debt, and you shall have a glory that is eternal. You empty a multitude of purses for shameful pastime, and ribald laughter, not knowing how many poor men's tears you are giving, from whom your wealth has been gathered; how many have been imprisoned, how many beaten, how many have come near death by the halter, to furnish what dancers to-day receive.[22]

These warnings continued through the centuries. In North Africa in 404 Saint Augustine preached a three-hour sermon against the revels of the New Year and their connections to paganism. He pleaded with his listeners: "When [the pagans] give gifts; do you give alms. They are called away by songs of license; you, by the discourses of the Scriptures. They run to the theatre; you, to the church. They become intoxicated; do you fast."[23] The bishop of Ravenna, Petrus Chrysologus, complained in the 440s that the leading citizens of that imperial capital paraded during the Kalends through the city's hippodrome, dressed as Roman planetary gods.[24] In 575

Bishop Martin of Bracae warned his more humble flock against the dangers of the Kalends, among which he numbered decorating the home with greenery.[25] The Council in Trullo of 692, a gathering of the top two hundred churchmen of the Byzantine Empire, which met in Constantinople to bring canon law up to date, condemned those who participated in the festivities of the Kalends. They were particularly anxious that women not fall prey to unseemly public entertainments involving dancing and crossdressing.[26]

> The so-called Calends, and what are called Bota and Brumalia, and the full assembly which takes place on the first of March, we wish to be abolished from the life of the faithful. And also the public dances of women, which may do much harm and mischief. Moreover we drive away from the life of Christians the dances given in the names of those falsely called gods by the Greeks whether of men or women, and which are performed after an ancient and un-Christian fashion; decreeing that no man from this time forth shall be dressed as a woman, nor any woman in the garb suitable to men. Nor shall he assume comic, satyric, or tragic masks; nor may men invoke the name of the execrable Bacchus when they squeeze out the wine in the presses; nor when pouring out wine into jars [to cause a laugh], practising in ignorance and vanity the things which proceed from the deceit of insanity. Therefore those who in the future attempt any of these things which are written, having obtained a knowledge of them, if they be clerics we order them to be deposed, and if laymen to be cut off.[27]

The Council of Trullo also took time to denounce another custom associated with the Nativity. On the day after Christmas, Byzantine women were following the secular tradition of making a certain kind of cereal in celebration of a safe delivery and offering this to the Virgin Mary. The Council condemned this because the Blessed Virgin was not any ordinary mother and had given birth in a miraculously pain-free fashion.[28]

These constant condemnations of pagan practice had to continue because of the obstinate attachment of people to traditional practices. In the mid-seventh century, near Paris in the kingdom of the scarcely civilized Franks, a bishop who had castigated pagan festivities was answered by his flock: "No matter how often you rebuke us, Romans, you will never succeed in tearing out our customs. We will rather perform our rites as heretofore, and always and forever gather for them; nor will there be a man ever to prohibit our ancient and dearest festivals."[29] In the next century the missionary St. Boniface complained to the pope about the deleterious effect the celebration of the Kalends was having on his work among the Germans. When tribesmen visited Rome and saw—near the church of St. Peter itself!—"throngs of people parading the streets at the beginning of January of each year, shouting and singing songs in pagan fashion, loading tables with food and drink from morning till night," they believed that this sort of seasonal behavior was sanctioned by Christian priests and thereby fell prey to these bad examples.[30]

It is not surprising that the traditions of the old cultures continued to permeate the new and that the Christmas season was influenced by pagan forms of midwinter celebration. In the Middle Ages it was a time of the year that cried out for festivity. Food was wonderfully abundant, and in the absence of modern storage techniques, had to be eaten. The harvest was in, which meant that there were grapes for wine and grain for baking and for brewing beer; the livestock that could not be wintered over had to be slaughtered and made into sausages or hams; the fish pens and eel pens had to be emptied. These were the shortest days and longest nights of the year, which called for fire and light and the hope of the return of the sun's warmth in the spring. It was the most barren time of the year, and folk clung to the greenery that was left to them: the conifers and plants like the holly. Little wonder that almost every culture in our planet's temperate zones has midwinter celebrations that emphasize celebratory excess and hopes for renewal of life.[31]

In the face of such a reality, the Church considered changing its mind about resisting every element of pre-Christian manners, especially on the frontiers of Europe, where the vital job of evangelizing the barbarian peoples was being carried out. In 597 Pope Gregory the Great sent out a group of missionary monks to southern Britain, where a Germanic tribe known as the Angles had settled. A letter of instruction, meant for Augustine, the leader of the expedition, who would become the first archbishop of Canterbury, revealed that a policy of cultural assimilation was now considered appropriate by Rome.

> When Almighty God shall have brought you to our most reverend brother the bishop Augustine, tell him that I have long been considering with myself about the case of the Angli; to wit, that the temples of idols in that nation should not be destroyed, but that the

idols themselves that are in them should be. Let blessed water be prepared, and sprinkled in these temples, and altars constructed, and relics deposited, since, if these same temples are well built, it is needful that they should be transferred from the worship of idols to the service of the true God; that, when the people themselves see that these temples are not destroyed, they may put away error from their heart, and, knowing and adoring the true God, may have recourse with the more familiarity to the places they have been accustomed to. And, since they are wont to kill many oxen in sacrifice to demons, they should have also some solemnity of this kind in a changed form, so that on the day of dedication, or on the anniversaries of the holy martyrs whose relics are deposited there, they may make for themselves tents of the branches of trees around these temples that have been changed into churches, and celebrate the solemnity with religious feasts. Nor let them any longer sacrifice animals to the devil, but slay animals to the praise of God for their own eating, and return thanks to the Giver of all for their fullness, so that, while some joys are reserved to them outwardly, they may be able the more easily to incline their minds to inward joys. For it is undoubt- edly impossible to cut away everything at once from hard hearts, since one who strives to ascend to the highest place must needs rise by steps or paces, and not by leaps.[32]

This change in attitude would not end the Church's war against common people's desire to continue enjoying their ancient traditions; churchmen would long continue to battle against paganism infiltrating the Christian calendar. Time after time, century after century, clergy would warn against unseemly folk rituals being practiced by Catholic believers; Christmastide was not the only battlefield but was a particularly contested one. Church councils, papal decrees, and penitential handbooks that provided priests with lists of sins and their appropriate penances all mandated against enormities such as crossdressing, dancing in the churchyard, decorating the house with vegetation, or wearing the guise of an animal. However, the Church gradually took Gregory's advice and accommodated the cus- toms they deemed more harmless by constructing pious legends and Christianizing them.

An example of this is the custom of leaving out food for the gods at midwinter. As endless prohibitions seemed to have no effect, the clergy learned to put a Christian spin on the practice. In fifteenth-century Bohemia, the monk Alsso declared that it was wrong to put out bread for pagan deities, but it was "a laudable custom to make great white loaves at Christmas as symbols of the True Bread [Jesus]."[33] Across Europe food left out on Christmas Eve was said to be meant for the Holy Family as they trudged toward Bethlehem or the spirits of the family dead who would return on this most sacred of nights to the ancestral hearth.[34] Every European nationality came to have Christmas traditions woven around the use of grain, a traditional pagan symbol of fertility. Whether in bread form, like the Greek *christopsomo*, or as the Twelfth Night Cake of England, the *kutya* porridge of the Slavs, the *oplatek* wafer resembling the Host of the Mass in Poland, the *Christollen* of Germany made to resemble the swaddling clothes, or the sheaves tucked under the tablecloth on Christmas Eve in Ukraine, grain was sanctified with one form of Christian symbolism or another.

Heathen processions during the Kalends in which folk carried about images of their pagan gods were also safely Christianized: throughout the Christmas season, parades of clergy and choirboys clad in white sang joyful songs about the Nativity. In Germany and Spain folk processed through the streets reenacting the search of Mary and Joseph for lodgings; in eastern Europe troupes of Star Boys disguised themselves as Wise Men journeying to see the infant king.

The expulsion of demons at midwinter as homes prepared to make all things clean for the New Year easily found Christian equivalents. We can see this during the period between Christmas and Epiphany, which Austrians term Raunächte, the "Rough Nights," or "Smoke Nights," when the house and farm must be cleansed of evil spirits. Across central Europe processions of masked figures armed with brooms paraded to sweep away the bad influences; some homes were purged using holy smoke from a censer. On January 6 dwellings were visited by men dressed as the Magi, and a seasonal ceremony took place; carrying a representation of the crib and accompanied by a servant with a censer, the Three Kings moved through the house blessing it and its inhabitants. As they left they chalked a mark on a doorpost with the year of their visit and their initials, as in "14 K + M + B 99."[35] In Greece priests blessed the house against the appearance of subterranean monsters known as Kallikantzaroi, who would otherwise come down the chimney to torment the family.[36]

Decorating the house with greenery, which so enraged the churchmen of late antiquity, who saw it as a pagan remnant of the Kalends, became a means of not only brightening the home in the dark of winter but also a way to tell a hundred little pious stories about the Nativity or foreshadowings

of the Crucifixion. Fragrant rosemary was said to be the plant on which
Mary had hung her cloak to dry (or, some say, the baby's swaddling clothes).
Holly with its sharp-edged leaves and red berries was seen as a symbol of
Christ's crown of thorns and the blood he shed. Christmas wreaths of
holly or evergreen were said to symbolize eternal life. Ivy was said to be a
female plant and a symbol of the human weakness that clings to divine
strength. Even mistletoe, long associated with the pagan Druids, could
find a place in church. In York Minster during the Middle Ages, a branch
of mistletoe was laid on the altar during the Twelve Days of Christmas,
and a public peace proclaimed in the city for as long as it remained there.
Even vagabonds and "unthrifty folk" were welcome to the town "in rever-
ence of the High Feast of Yule." In southwestern England a particular
hawthorn bush became known as the Glastonbury Thorn, whose origins
were said to lie in the legendary voyage of the young Jesus and Joseph of
Arimathea to Britain. When Joseph plunged his staff into the earth it
miraculously produced white flowers, and the bush was said to burst into
blossom every Christmas Day.[37]

The giving of gifts at the Kalends had also long been criticized by the
Church, which thought it hypocritical and a form of social extortion in
which money passed from the poor to their superiors and which smacked
of lingering paganism.[38] Gift-giving had also been excoriated for the part
it played in fortune-telling and luck-seeking as people laid wagers to tell
the future or opened their purses so as to let good fortune in. Gradually
the Church was able to sanctify these activities as well, partly by continuing to emphasize charity in giving to the poor but also by using them to
celebrate the human nature of Jesus. Europe from the thirteenth century
on was taught by the Church to regard Christ as a kind of loving older
brother instead of the stern judge depicted in earlier eras. Therefore, just
as the birth of a baby brother called for gifts, so did the birthday of Jesus.
In late medieval Germany such gifts were termed "child's-foot," a name
also used to denote the extra helpings of fodder the livestock were given at
Christmas.[39] The Church further sanctified the delivery of presents to children during the Christmas season by explaining they had been left by various saints on the eves of their holy days. Saints Barbara, Martin, and Lucia
and the Wise Men were all portrayed as miraculous Gift-Bringers; but by
far the most popular was Saint Nicholas.

In the Middle Ages, Nicholas was the most powerful male saint on the
Church calendar: the patron of sailors, Vikings, Russians, Normans, barrel-
makers, thieves, perfumers, picklers, florists, haberdashers, and many

more—but especially of children. He was credited with having saved the daughters of a poor man from lives of prostitution by secretly delivering bags of gold at night, and at some point, beginning in the twelfth century, he was deemed to be the magical deliverer of small gifts to children on the eve of his day, December 6. Soon children were praying to Saint Nicholas and leaving out their shoes to be filled with treats; adults patronized doll- and toy-makers, bakers were baking cookies in the shape of the saint, and St. Nicholas markets were springing up in December to provide the ingredients for feasting, play, and merry-making that the season had come to demand.[40]

By the late Middle Ages the celebration of Christmas had adopted a large number of traditional midwinter customs, many of which had once been condemned by the Church, and had successfully blended them with Christian teachings about the Nativity to create a holiday that was the high festive point of the year. Round-dance music had become Christmas carols, which put sacred words to popular music; midwinter feasting had been sanctified by teachings of fellowship and insistence on charity; gift-giving had lost some of the overtones of extortion, and the late December period of agricultural idleness had become the Twelve Days of Christmas, each day of which both marked a Christian saint and was dedicated to some traditional folk activity that bound the community together.

Though the Church had ceased to struggle against the idea of merriment at Christmas and seemed to be happy with the blended celebration that mixed theology and mirth, it did not mean that there was an end to vigilance or censoriousness. Clergy were ever alert for excesses that signaled a descent into orgiastic behavior during the holiday season. Take for example the scandalous behavior over Christmas at the court of the Emperor Michael III (r. 842–867) in Byzantium, who brought down the wrath of the Church by dressing himself as an archbishop and his companions as clergy, all the while mocking the patriarch of Constantinople and conducting a parody of the Mass.[41] (A church council condemned Michael's behavior, though it had to wait until after his death before it was safe to do so.) The fourteenth-century English reformer (or heretic, depending on your point of view) John Wyclif, or one of his supporters, deplored the debased state of popular entertainment at Christmas, complaining that he "that kan best pleie a pagyn of the deuyl, syngynge songis of lecherie, of batailis and of lesyngis [falsehoods], & crie as a wood man & dispise goddis maieste & swere bi herte, bonys & alle membris of crist, is holden most merie mon & schal haue most thank of pore & riche; & this is clepid worschipe of the grete solempnyte of cristismasse; & thus for the grete kyndenesse & goodnesse that crist dide to men in his incarnacion we dispisen hym more in outrage of pride, of glotonye, lecherie & alle manere harlotrie."[42] A century later the Croyland Chronicle deplored the shameful activities—the dancing, the extravagant costumes, and the riotous merriment—at the court of the doomed Richard III, who was celebrating what would be his last Christmas as king of England in 1484. Even his supporter Bishop Thomas Langton noted that "sensual pleasure holds sway to an increasing extent."[43]

But it was unseemly behavior inside the Church itself that exercised ecclesiastical authorities most gravely. In the Christian East, clergy were misbehaving during services at Christmastime. In the Byzantine Empire of the 900s, there were complaints of priests dancing, yelling, laughing, and singing brothel songs in the midst of sacred celebrations, and a century later Christmas and Epiphany services in Christendom's greatest edifice, Hagia Sophia, the Church of Holy Wisdom in Constantinople, were marred by clerics dressing as women, soldiers, and animals, inducing mirth among the congregants. The celebration at Christmastime of festivals with pagan roots continued in the East for some time, despite repeated Church condemnation. This seemed to many to be a suitable period for the emperor to hand out largesse and for everyone to exchange gifts and to consider wiping the slate clean and starting things anew. Patriarchs of Constantinople, starting around 1100, began to take these excesses more seriously and attempted to crack down on these festivities, which threatened to turn places such as Hagia Sophia "into places of business and a den of thieves and the holy festivals into outrageous gatherings." Though the Church authorities were clearly interested in trying to impose a tighter moral discipline on society, they were never completely successful in extinguishing popular culture's hold on Christmas celebrations.[44]

In the Latin-speaking West, the Christmas season, particularly those days between December 25 and January 6, had become the time for younger clergy to indulge in raucous shenanigans that would not have been tolerated at any other point in the year. The feast of St. Stephen, who had served as a deacon before his martyrdom, December 26, was considered the day for the deacons to act up; December 27, St. John's Day, was given over to the priests; the Feast of the Holy Innocents, December 28, was the climax of activities for the choirboys, which began on December 6, St. Nicholas's Day; the subdeacons took center stage on the Feast of the Circumcision, Epiphany, or the Octave of Epiphany (January 1, January 6, or January 13).

It was the behavior of the subdeacons that most caused superiors to tear their tonsures out in rage and frustration throughout the late Middle Ages.

One of the chief spiritual lessons of Christmas for Christian believers is the notion of social inversion, the world turned upside down. We can see this in the appearance of the incarnated God in a manger—an animal feeding trough—rather than a palace, and in the angelic first announcement of this miraculous birth to lowly shepherds rather than princes. The reaction of the peasant girl chosen to bear the Messiah was the Magnificat, a celebration of the last becoming the first: "My soul doth magnify the Lord. And my spirit hath rejoiced in God my Saviour. Because he hath regarded the humility of his handmaid, . . . He hath scattered the proud in the conceit of their heart. He hath put down the mighty from their seat, and hath exalted the humble. He hath filled the hungry with good things; and the rich he hath sent empty away."[45]

In this topsy-turvy view of the world, two curious ceremonies developed in medieval churches, particularly in France but also elsewhere in Europe: the Feast of Fools and the Feast of the Ass. In the former, subdeacons elected a mock leader called the "Bishop of Fools" and engaged in spirited hijinks inside the church and through the neighborhood. Theologians of the University of Paris lamented:

> Priests and clerks may be seen wearing masks and monstrous visages at the hours of office. They dance in the choir dressed as women, panders or minstrels. They sing wanton songs. They eat black puddings at the horn of the altar while the celebrant is saying Mass. They play at dice there. They cense with stinking smoke from the soles of old shoes. They run and leap through the church, without a blush at their own shame. Finally they drive about the town and its theatres in shabby traps and carts, and rouse the laughter of their fellows and the bystanders in infamous performances, with indecent gesture and verses scurrilous and unchaste.[46]

In the Feast of the Ass, the rowdy young clerics honored the donkey who carried the Virgin Mary by bringing a real animal into the church while singing a hymn of praise:

> *From Oriental country came*
> *A lordly ass of highest fame,*
> *So beautiful, so strong and trim,*

No burden was too great for him.
Hail, Sir Donkey, hail!

At various points during the Mass the priest and congregation brayed like donkeys.

Historians are divided over the meaning of these antics, some seeing them as pagan leftovers, others as a kind of rough but pious liturgy.[47] But high-ranking churchmen of the Middle Ages were of one mind in wanting to suppress this form of Christmas merriment. Bishops, archbishops, popes, and councils all inveighed against the violence and mockery that they saw in these ceremonies. Finally the king of France was moved to act. In 1445 Charles VII declared:

> It has been brought to our notice by Our beloved and loyal coun-sellor the Lord Bishop of Troyes, in a complaint made by him, that notwithstanding the decree [of the Council of Basel, 1436] by which servants and ministers of Holy Church are expressly debarred from celebrating certain derisive and scandalous cere-monies which they call the *Feast of Fools,* which it has been the custom to hold in several cathedrals and collegiate churches dur-ing the Feast of Christmas, in which ceremonies the aforesaid ser-vants of Holy Church have been accustomed to commit irreverence and disloyalty towards Almighty God our Creator and His divine and holy service, to the great shame and scandal of the whole ecclesiastical state, making the churches like public places and performing even during the celebration of Holy Mass divers inso-lent and derisive mockeries and spectacles, disguising their bod-ies and wearing habits indecent and not pertaining to their state and profession, as the habits of fools, of men-at-arms, and of women, with the wearing of masks, etc., all of which abuses, and others customary at this season have been forbidden on pain of penalties, nevertheless in this present year at the said feast of Holy Innocents and the Circumcision these ceremonies have been carried out at Troyes with such excess of mockery, disguis-ings, farces, rhyming, and other follies as has not been known within the memory of man.
>
> All these things having been made known to the Faculty of Theology of Our University of Paris, the Masters of the said Faculty, after ripe deliberation, have composed a certain notable letter to

be dispatched to all the prelates and chapters of Our Realm, detesting and condemning the said damnable Feast of Fools as superstitious and heathen, and declaring its introduction to be the work of pagans and unbelieving idolaters, as Monsieur Saint *Augustine* expressly sheweth.[48]

Despite papal and royal disapproval, the Feast of Fools survived the medieval period, both on the streets and in the churches. As late as 1645 such ceremonies could be found occurring during the Christmas season.[49]

Early Modern Christmas

By 1500 the celebration of Christmas was solidly entrenched in western European cultures and the bearer of multiple meanings. As the second most important feast on the Christian calendar, it was the occasion of special religious ceremonies, sermons, liturgical dramas, glorious music, and high art. It was the season of charity, with licensed begging by marginalized groups including old women, children, prisoners, and the lower levels of the urban working class. It was the time for giving gifts, especially to children and to social superiors. It was the time of hospitality in rural regions, when the country poor might expect their landlords to offer free food and alcohol. The Twelve Days of Christmas, stretching from December 25 to January 6, were also a welcome break in the agricultural year when idleness was tolerated in the countryside and country folk celebrated with a myriad of raucous festivities, dances, and games. At royal courts expensive masques were staged to entertain the high and mighty, regulations against gambling were relaxed, and lords of misrule, abbots of unreason, or *les abbés de liesse* directed the revels. In the city, greenery decorated homes, streets, and churches; seasonal dishes were prepared with rare ingredients bought at Christmas markets; wandering musicians sang carols in the streets. Among the clergy it was the time for social inversion, with boy choristers serving as bishops and lower clergy electing fools' abbots or simpletons' bishops to mock their superiors and staging ceremonies like the Festum Asinorum, the Feast of the Ass, that sailed near to blasphemy.

Such reservations as were expressed about Christmas concerned excesses of celebration that might become abuses. Servant demands for Boxing Day tips had to be kept within proper bounds; going about in the streets in holiday masks was forbidden lest it lead to crime; the behavior of the junior clergy and their subversive hijinks resulted in restrictions by Church authorities; unseemly capering and dancing in churches and churchyards was the subject of legislation—but it had been ever thus.[50] Centuries of official cautions had moderated but never curbed the outbursts of midwinter misrule.

The sixteenth century saw a marked increase in authorities' desire to crack down on popular customs that had the flavor of disorder or lacked the sanction of the ruling classes in the Church or government. Some of these customs were religious in nature: mystery plays, processions, festivals; some were secular: bear-baiting and bull-baiting, apprentice riots, plays and ballads, and witchcraft. Social historians have called this phenomenon "the Triumph of Lent."[51] We can see this in action in the moves by the government of Henry VIII to suppress the celebrations of the boy bishop, a practice whose origins go back at least to the tenth century, when the Emperor Conrad found it celebrated in a monastery he was visiting. Every December 6 (the feast of St. Nicholas, patron of children and students) a cathedral choirboy was chosen to preside over activities until December 28, the Feast of Innocents, when his term ended. The lad would be given a cut-down version of episcopal robes and miter, and he would process with his followers through the church and town. He was given permission to collect donations for the boys' revelries and in some cases was even allowed to give a sermon. As boys will ever be boys, things sometimes got out of hand, with urban violence occasionally erupting—in 1367 a boy bishop in Paris was murdered in a street brawl, and in Salisbury an act had to be passed "to restrain the insolence of choristers."[52] The authorities, touchy about misrule and parody of their power, gradually snuffed out the custom over the centuries. During the reign of England's Henry VIII, a royal decree banned the practice whereby "children be strangelye decked and apparelid to counterfaite priestes, bysshopps and women, and so ledde with songes and daunces from house to house, bleasing the people and gatherynge of monye."[53] His oldest daughter, Mary (known to history as Bloody Mary for her ruthless persecution of Protestants), renewed the practice when she ruled in the 1550s, but during the reign of her successor, Elizabeth I, the boy bishop custom vanished.[54] Henry VIII also forbade the traditional custom of masked revelers going door-to-door presenting Christmas mumming plays in return for a donation or hospitality; this was framed as an anticrime measure. The government of Mary Queen of Scots abolished the post of abbot of unreason, which had traditionally been responsible for guiding the court mirth and merriment during the year-ending festivities, along with other seasonal celebrations that involved large gatherings of common folk.

The "Triumph of Lent" was rooted in a vaster movement of the sixteenth century that was going to revolutionize Western civilization, and Christmas practices would not escape the consequences. The Protestant religious reformations begun by Martin Luther in 1517 and the Catholic responses to them engendered considerable debate about how to mark the Nativity of Christ and the array of days surrounding it, or indeed, whether it should be celebrated at all.

The Protestant reformers attacked an entire way of religious life that had developed over a thousand years in Europe. They criticized what they called the idolatry of the Mass, indulgences, belief in Purgatory, papal supremacy, the role of the priesthood, fasting, clerical celibacy, the monastic system, and the medieval notion of sainthood. Protestant reformers universally despised the medieval cult of saints, which had claimed that some Christian souls had more influence in heaven than others and were therefore worthy of devotion and prayers. Across northern and western Europe, where Protestants came to rule, saints' days were abolished, their statues were pulled down, their images were smashed, their feast days went unmarked, prayers to them ceased, and a host of social customs underwent change.[55] Caught up in this was the magical Christmas Gift-Bringer, St. Nicholas, who by rights ought to have been tossed on to the sacred scrap heap along with the rest of his celestial companions.

There were certainly those who sought to see any veneration of Nicholas obliterated. The sour English poet Barnabe Googe linked the traditional December 5 gift-giving custom to the excessive veneration of saints and other evils, saying: "Thus tender mindes to worship Saints and wicked things are taught." The Calvinist theologian Walich Sieuwerts cried: "It is a foolish and pointless custom to fill children's shows with all sorts of sweets and nonsense. What else is this but sacrifice to an idol? Those who do it do not seem to understand what true religion is." The attack on Nicholas was particularly important in the Netherlands, which was in the midst of a religious civil war and rebellion against its Spanish overlords. This area had a long history of devotion to the saint, but in the town of Grave the authorities complained that the practice of St. Nicholas Eve giving put "many decent people to great expense and stimulates the youth in superstition." They forbade all citizens from observing the early December celebration or allowing their children to put out shoes in the hope of expected presents. In Amsterdam iconoclastic patriots melted down the silver statue of Nicholas in the Old Church (itself dedicated to him) to pay for the war against the Spanish and banned the traditional St. Nicholas market that had provided toys and goodies for the season. Bylaws banned anyone bringing edible treats to the town square during the traditional time of his festival. Frisian towns forbade the practice of youth going door-to-door in search of confections on St. Nicholas Eve. In Arnhem they banned the famous cookies baked in the shape of the saint, even those made in the home.[56]

This war on Nicholas was only partially successful. His devotion continued in eastern Europe, where the appeal of the Protestant reformations was weak and, remarkably, in Holland, with its population split between Catholics and Protestants. (The cult of Nicholas would come to North America via the Dutch colonization of the eastern seaboard of the New World.) In England we hear no more of St. Nicholas's nocturnal visits after the accession of Elizabeth I in 1558. There and in Scotland, gifts were henceforth reserved for New Year's Day, and there are no records of presents for children for a long time. In many areas of Germany, both Protestant and Catholic parents retained the desire for a Christmas Gift-Bringer but chose to replace the now controversial Nicholas with a new figure.[57] Protestant clergy had warned that parents ought not to give presents in the name of a discredited saint. "This is a bad custom," they said, "because it points children to the saint, while yet we know that not Saint Nicholas but the holy Christ Child gives us all good things for body and soul, and He alone it is whom we ought to call upon." For Protestants the Christ Child, or *das Christkindl*, as he was known in German-speaking lands, was an excellent theological substitution: since it was God who brought all things bright and beautiful, there was no better Gift-Bringer than the baby-god himself. This replacement would also serve to move the celebrations away from the saint's day in early December to Christmas Eve, thus focusing more clearly on (as later centuries would say) the reason for the season. So sensible a custom was this that *le petit Jésus* or Ježíšek or Jézuska began to appear on December 24 in many other Catholic areas as well.

The shift to the new-born Jesus was, however, not without problems. In the family economy of 450 years ago, St. Nicholas was a superb aid to strict parenting. Though he brought presents to good children, he could be a terror to those who had misbehaved or refused to learn their catechism. Not only did he bring switches to fill the stockings of the naughty, he (or the disguised adult impersonating him) was known to enter the house, quiz the children, and thrash those whose morality or obedience was found wanting. This intimidation was, no doubt, a spur to good behavior, but it was clearly not a pose the Baby Jesus could adopt—what is less frightening than a babe wrapped in swaddling clothes? Nor could the Christ Child, with his infant limbs, be imagined trudging door-to-door carrying bags or baskets (customs varied regionally) of goodies.

These problems were met by the creation of a number of new supernatural creatures who were expected to appear during the Christmas season. Henceforth the Christ Child, when his physical presence was required, would be represented by a young adolescent female dressed in white. The tasks of frightening and carrying were delegated to a host of lesser bogeymen (or -women) who would accompany the heavenly Gift-Bringer—shaggy, sooty, and dark presences whose names were often linked to the previous administration: Aschenklaus (Nicholas in Ashes), Pelznickel or Belsnickel (Nicholas in Furs), and Ru-klaus (Rough Nicholas), along with an assortment of devils, witches with iron teeth, female disembowelers, monstrous goats, or monks armed with switches. European children in the north and west of the continent learned to dread the arrival of Père Fouettard, Berchta, Cert, Krampus, Hans Trapp, Klabauf, Joulupukki, and Knecht Ruprecht, who might wave whips, shake chains, or threaten to spirit away bad little boys and girls in their packs. (Children in Catholic southern Europe tended to receive their gifts on Epiphany and were serviced by Befana, a kindly witch, the Three Kings, or, in some cases, a pooping log.)[58]

Though they deplored many Christmas superstitions, even many of the strictest of European Protestants did not wish to eliminate the observance of Christmas altogether. The authoritative Second Helvetic Confession of 1561, drawn up by Swiss reformers and widely adopted by Calvinists in other countries, allowed the celebration of "the festivities of our Lord's nativity, circumcision, passion, resurrection, ascension and the sending of the Holy Spirit upon his disciples."[59] This was not the case, however, in Scotland, where an English-backed coup had put a Calvinist regime in power. There clerics, led by the fiery John Knox, felt that the creeds proposed by their continental correligionists did not go far enough in cleansing the Church of "popish dregs." They adhered closely to the regulative principle that held that all forms of worship not specifically mandated by God were idolatrous and to be eliminated; Calvinists in mainland Europe feared to tread on the traditional holidays, but the Scots had no such fears. Their 1560 Book of Discipline stated:

We understand whatsoever men, by Laws, Councils, or Constitutions have imposed upon the consciences of men, without the expressed commandment of God's word: such as be vows of chastity, foreswearing of marriage, binding of men and women to several and disguised apparels, to the superstitious observation of fasting days, difference of meat for conscience sake, prayer for the dead; and keeping of holy days of certain Saints commanded by men, such as be all those that the Papists have invented, as the Feasts (as they term them) of Apostles, Martyrs, Virgins, of Christmas, Circumcision, Epiphany, Purification, and other fond feasts of our Lady. Which things, because in God's scriptures they neither have commandment nor assurance, we judge them utterly to be abolished from this Realm; affirming further, that the obstinate maintainers and teachers of such abominations ought not to escape the punishment of the Civil Magistrate.[60]

And, indeed, such abominations that marked the Christmas season were the subject of the Scottish civil magistrate's (and churchmen's) stern glare during the early modern period. Scots had hitherto been wont to make merry at Christmas; there is much evidence of feasting, caroling, snowballing, masking (including festive crossdressing), door-to-door begging, dancing, and piping. Folk played football through the town or gambled or drank to excess, while bakers baked huge Yule loaves. Under the new Protestant dispensation, however, local kirk officials and town governments began to crack down on such mirthful pastimes. In 1574 fourteen women of Aberdeen were charged with "playing, dancing and singing of filthy carols on Yule Day."[61] Those who opened their houses to give hospitality to holiday singers were to be fined 5 pounds. In 1581 Perth bakers who observed St. Obert's Eve (December 10) with its dances and plays, their traditional festival of their patron saint, were jailed until they paid 20 shillings to the poor and were made to sit in the public seat of repentance in the church during the next Sunday sermon. These scofflaws were also censured in 1597, when they baked "great loaves at Yule, which was slanderous and cherishing a superstition in the hearts of the ignorant." The Glasgow kirk in 1583 ordered excommunication for those who kept Christmas, and in 1593 the minister at Errol equated carol singing with fornication. The commission of such sins at Christmas need not even have been public. In a number of Scottish towns ministers were known to go door-to-door on Christmas Day to ensure that families were not feasting.

In England few voices were raised in opposition to Christmas. Protestantism's arrival in England with the accession of the boy king Edward VI brought significant changes to that country's religious life: the destruction of images and the abolition of the Mass, church guilds, and the cult of saints, and the appearance of new prayer books, married clergy, and a vernacular liturgy. As part of this reformation from the top, Protectors Somerset and Northumberland attacked the customs of the old ritual year in England, discouraging such traditional activities as midsummer bonfires, Plough Monday festivities, Corpus Christi processions, church ales, maypoles, the ringing of bells for the dead on the feast of All Saints, creeping to the cross, and St. George ridings; but with the exception of continuing the abolition of the boy bishop that Henry VIII had begun), Edward's government left most of the Christmas traditions unscathed.[62] In fact the Edwardian court continued to employ a lord of misrule to direct the expensive seasonal festivities meant to amuse the young king during the Twelve Days. During the years 1553–1558, when a short-lived Catholic revival under Bloody Mary was undertaken, no moves against holiday traditions were made, and the boy bishop was even briefly revived.

It was at the Christmas Mass in 1558 that Elizabeth I signaled her intention to follow Protestantism and the Church of England in the style her brother, Edward VI, had established. This meant, among other things, that during the Elizabethan era (1558–1603) Christmas was kept lavishly at court, where the Virgin Queen maintained a sharp eye on the value of gifts given her and gambled with her courtiers using loaded dice; in the lawyers' chambers, where dramas were performed and cats were set upon by dogs for sport to the sound of hunting horns; and in homes decorated with greenery and redolent of the odor of roast goose and gingerbread. Those who objected to Christmas tended to be the hotter sort of gospeler, those who would come to be known as Puritans, marginal voices during the reign of Elizabeth but destined to become louder in the seventeenth century. One such was the pamphleteer Philip Stubbes, who in his 1583 Anatomie of Abuse moaned that

in Christmas time there is nothing els used but Cards, Dice, Tables, masking, mumming, bouling, & such like fooleries. And the reason is, for that they thinke they haue a Commission & prerogatiue that time, to do what they list, & to follow what vanity they will. But (alas) do they thinke that they ar priuiledged at that time to do euil?

the holier the time is (if one time were holier then another, as it is not) the holier ought their exercises to be. Can time dispence with the, or giue the liberty to sin? No, no: the soule which sinneth shal die, at what time soeuer it offendeth. But what will they say? Is it not Christmas? must we not be merry? Trueth it is, we ought both then, & at all times besides to be merie in the Lord, but not otherwise, not to swill and gull in more then will suffice nature, nor to lauish forth more at that time, then at any other times. But the true celebration of the feast of Christmas is, to meditate (and as it were to ruminate in the secrete cogitations of our mindes) vpon the incarnation and birth of Iesus Christ, God and man: not only at that time, but all the times and daies of our life, & to shew our selues thankful to his blessed maiesty for the same. Notwithstanding, who knoweth not, that more mischief is that time committed then in all the yeare besides? what masking and mumming, wherby robbery, whoredome, and sometime murther is committed: what Dicing and Carding, what eating & drinking, what banquetting and feasting is then vsed, more then in all the yeare besides? to the great dishonour of God, and impouerishing of the Realme?[63]

Stubbes introduced here two of the principal criticisms of Christmas that would underpin the radical Protestant critique in the years to come: the observation that the holiday is the occasion for riotous behavior and the assertion that Christians should not regard days other than the Sabbath as special.

Elizabeth was unmoved by such criticisms. The royal court continued to be the site of merriment and play at Christmas, and in fact the queen acted to reinforce traditional attitudes toward the holiday among her subjects. Poets such as Thomas Nashe had complained of a decline in customary seasonal hospitality and fellowship and of a world where Christmas had become lean and mean:

> Christmas the one, a pinch-back, cut-throate churle,
> That keepes no open house, as he should do,
> Delighteth in no game or fellowship,
> Loves no good deeds, and hateth talke,
> But sitteth in a corner turning Crabbes,
> Or coughing o're a warmed pot of Ale[64]

Nashe's complaint had some merit. Landlords of the late sixteenth century felt less of the feudal *noblesse oblige* that had motivated their medieval ancestors to see Christmas as a charitable season that bound servant and master together. The culture of the elites was becoming increasingly separated from that of the lower orders, and the nobility were being increasingly accused of abandoning their rural holdings—and traditional hospitality—during Christmas to spend their time and money in the capital. Asserting that the nation's aristocracy had neglected their customary seasonal obligations, Elizabeth ordered her nobles and gentry to abandon London at Christmastime and return to their manors in the countryside. There they were to strengthen social ties by opening their homes in the good old-fashioned way and to feast their neighbors.

The maintenance of traditional Christmas observances was a concern of James I when he succeeded Elizabeth in 1603 and inaugurated the Stuart dynasty. While king in Scotland he had maintained a festive atmosphere despite the criticism of the Edinburgh presbytery, which twice attempted to curb the Yuletide merriment at his court.[65] In *Basilikon Doron*, his book of advice to his son on successful kingship, he advocated a national policy of seasonal merriment:

> In respect whereof, and therewith also the more to allure them to a common amitie among themselues, certaine dayes in the yeere would be appointed, for delighting the people with publicke spectacles of all honest games, and exercise of armes: as also for conueening of neighbours, for entertaining friendship and heartlinesse, by honest feasting and merrinesse. For I cannot see what greater superstition can be in making playes and lawfull games in Maie, and good cheere at Christmas, then in eating fish in Lent.... And as this forme of contenting the peoples mindes, hath beene vsed in all well gouerned Republicks: so will it make you to performe in your gouernment that olde good sentence, Omne tulit punctum, qui miscuit vtile dulci.[66]

He also had rebuffed Puritan attempts in 1604 at the Hampton Court Conference to abolish those holy days remaining on the Church of England's calendar. James, therefore, was inclined to view an attack on merriment as an attack on the solidarity that should exist between ruler and subject and, indeed, on royal authority itself.

The short play entitled *Christmas His Masque* written by Ben Jonson for King James I and played at court on Christmas Day 1616 is a politically charged defense of the traditional English Christmas and an attack on Puritans and the government of the City of London who have slighted the old-fashioned ways. (James's administration viewed London as a stronghold of Puritanism, religious nonconformity, and cheeky defiance of royal power.) In the masque the figure of Old Christmas defends his Protestant leanings from the accusation that he is a popish innovation and intimates that Londoners have insulted their king and abandoned their national traditions by their Calvinist opposition to mirth and the celebration of Christmas.

> Why, gentlemen, do you know what you do? Ha! would you have kept me out? CHRISTMAS!—Old Christmas—Christmas of London and Captain Christmas! Pray let me be brought before my Lord Chamberlain; I'll not be answered else. "'Tis merry in hall, when beards wag all."[67] I have seen the time you have wished for me, for a merry Christmas, and now you have me, they would not let me in: I must come another time! A good jest—as if I could come more than once a year. Why I am no dangerous person, and so I told my friends of the guard. I am old Gregory Christmas still, and though I come out of the Pope's Head-alley, as good a Protestant as any in my parish.[68]

James fought back with a series of measures. In 1618 the Five Articles of Perth overrode Scottish church legislation against the celebration of Christmas and four other traditional religious observances. (The Scottish response was lukewarm at best. An observer reported of church attendance on December 25: "The great Kirk was not half-filled, notwithstanding the provost, bailies and council's travels... the dogs were playing in the flure of the Little Kirk, for rarity of people, and these were of the meaner sort.")[69] That same year in *The Book of Sports* the king listed the pleasurable pastimes that were permissible on Sunday and challenged the Sabbatarianism of "Puritans and precise people," whom James termed "contemners of our authority and adversaries of our Church" who had attempted to persuade Englishmen "that no honest mirth or recreation is lawful or tolerable in our religion, which cannot but breed a great discontentment in our people's hearts."

The ballad "Christmas His Lamentation for the losse of his acquaintance; showing how he is forst to leave the Countrie and come to London," which appeared during James's reign and again under Charles I, complained:

Christmas is my name, far have I gone, without regard
Whereas great men by flocks there were flown,
There to be flown, to London-ward;
Where they in pomp and pleasure do waste
That which oulde Christmas was wonted to feast,
Welladay!
Houses where music was wont for to ring
Nothing but bats and owlets do sing.
Welladay! Welladay! Welladay!
Where should I stay?
Christmas beef and bread is turn'd into stones
and silken rags;
And Lady Money sleeps and makes moans
in miser's bags;
Houses where pleasure once did abound
Nought but a dog and a shepherd is found,
Welladay!
Places where Christmas revels did keep
And now become habitations for sheep.
Welladay! Welladay! Welladay!
Where should I stay?[70]

Heeding such voices, James also took pains to imitate Elizabeth and disperse the nobility from London in December to spend Christmas in customary hospitality. (According to Francis Bacon, James was wont to say to his country gentlemen: "At London you are like ships at sea, which show like nothing; but in your country villages, you are like ships in a river which look like very great things.")[71]

By the time of Charles I's accession in 1625 the warriors eager to fight over Christmas had only fired a few opening salvoes, but the ammunition each camp was using had become clear. On one side were the claims to authority, tradition, and popular amusement—defense of time-honored festivities had become a litmus test in which supporting the right to be merry was to support the Stuart Church and polity. Arguing against Christmas seemed to proclaim adherence to Puritanism and an oppositionalism that bordered on treason.[72] On the other side was a reforming zeal that saw only idolatry, licentiousness, and popery in customary observances.

It was in 1633 that the battle was waged in a more menacing manner, when William Prynne, a lawyer, produced the massive tome *Histriomastix*.

Chiefly aimed at the evil he perceived in stage plays, his book also marshaled a number of Puritan-style attacks on the celebration of the Nativity. Christmas, he said, was generally spent in "reveling, epicurisme, wantonnesse, idlenesse, dancing, drinking, Stage-plays, Masques, and carnall popmpe and jollity" to the peril of one's soul. The celebration of Christmas was but an imitation of Saturnalia brought into Christianity by "the paganizing Priests and Monks" of the Roman Church, who had embarked on Pope Gregory's ill-advised policy of assimilating pre-Christian customs.[73] The government responded brutally. Prynne, this monster of men and nature, was said to have "spit his venom against the people in general, the magistrates and his majesty's house and household"—indeed against the throne itself. He had "railed, not only against stage plays, comedies and dancings, and all other exercises of the people, and against all who such as behold them, but further and particular against hunting, public festivals, Christmas-keeping, bonfires and maypoles," and even "against the dressing up of a house with green ivy." The hapless author was placed in the pillory, his ears were cropped, his cheeks were branded with "SL" (seditious libeler), and he was sentenced to life in prison. Partly in response to Prynne, Charles I reissued his father's *Book of Sports,* with an addition that linked opposition to traditional entertainments with opposition to royal authority.[74]

In 1642 England erupted into a civil war that pitted royalist supporters against Parliament, a war in which the struggle over Christmas became part of the national debate. Parliament was in the hands of the godly party (as they called themselves), aided by an alliance with the Christmas-hating Scots (who had repudiated the Five Articles of Perth and Christmas observances in 1638), who demanded church reform as the price of their help.[75] With the example of their northern neighbors before them, legislators moved in 1644 to encourage preaching against the holiday and then to bury its observances in a mandatory fast on December 25. In the next year the authors of the *Directory of Public Worship,* the replacement for the Book for Common Prayer, urged the discontinuance of Christmas and all other church festivals. In 1646 Parliament concurred and announced: "Be it ordained, by the Lords and Commons in parliament assembled, that the Feast of the Nativity of Christ, and all other festival days commonly called Holy-days, be no longer observed within this kingdom of England."[76]

This was easier said than done. Most churches seem to have ignored the decree in 1646; 85 percent of parishes surveyed had purchased the Communion elements for Christmas and Easter. Pro-Christmas riots occurred in country towns, and shopkeepers who tried to stay open on December 25 were abused and their goods scattered about. It was worse in 1647; despite armed vigilantes gathered to keep church doors open, the government had to arrest a number of ministers attempting to preach on Christmas Day. The lord mayor of London went about with his men trying to tear down seasonal greenery and was roundly abused for his efforts. (A royalist poet mocked this sort of anti-Christmas effort: "Their madnesse hath extended itselfe to the very vegetables, the senselesse Trees, Hearbes and Weedes....Holly, Ivy, Mistletoe, Rosemary, Bayes, are accounted ungodly Branches of Superstition.")[77] There were serious disturbances, with dead and wounded, in Canterbury, Ealing, Ipswich, and Oxford.

Such violence never reached that level again, though shopkeepers over the next decade still sought protection from thuggish apprentices who resented their Christmas commerce. Parish snoops made themselves nuisances by trying to catch housewives in the act of making Christmas pies (easily spotted because they were traditionally in the shape of a crib), and churches wishing to hold services on the holy days had to do so underground. Troops were on occasion called in to break up these clandestine services.

The battle for Christmas then became a war in print, with both sides setting out their cases for the public. Dozens of publications, ranging from single-sheet ballads to short satirical tracts to lengthy learned texts, provide the Christmas historian with a full range of arguments for and against observing all of the customs, religious and social, that surrounded Christmas. Both viewpoints were trumpeted with vigor, but it is fair to say that the wittier and more alluring material came from the friends of Christmas; its opponents often adopted a hectoring tone that seemed to express more interest in scoring debating points than winning hearts and minds.

The chief argument against Christmas, invariably mentioned by opponents of the feast, was the regulative principle: that worship not specifically commanded by God was therefore forbidden. Time and again supporters of Christmas were asked, "Where does God authorize the observance of Christmas or of any special days in the Gospels?" (It was assumed that Old Testament festivals were not binding on Christians.) A corollary to this was the assertion that December 25 was unlikely to have been the day of the birth of Jesus in any event and thus was even more unworthy of special observance. Perhaps, said the tract *Mercurius Religiosus* of 1651, God kept the true date a secret so as to prevent its idolization—in much the same way the burial spot of Moses had been hidden from the eyes of man. The only day to be kept holy, the Puritans asserted, was the Sabbath.[78]

Having demonstrated to their satisfaction that Christmas had no scriptural warrant, its opponents then turned up the temperature. Not only was the festival not based in Bible teaching, it had not been observed in the early Church, which in fact had inveighed against the celebration of birthdays. But the sin of contemporary Christmas-keepers was even worse—not only was it unscriptural and historically unrooted in Christianity, it was in fact directly derived from pagan festivities. Starting in the fourth century the papacy had foolishly attempted to adopt heathen practices and Christianize them—Pope Gregory's letter to Augustine of Canterbury had made that policy quite clear. Christmas merriment was merely an extension of Saturnalia; carols were an imitation of songs sung to honor Ceres; and the custom of seasonal gift-giving was a hangover from the Kalends of January. What the defenders of Christmas were doing was not keeping harmless old customs but rather perpetuating paganism and idolatry. "And how will you one day acquit yourselves before God for placing and crying up men's inventions instead of the institutions of Jesus Christ?" asked *Certain Quaeries touching the Rise and Observation of Christmas* (1648), one of the more restrained Puritan tracts.[79]

The linkage of Christmas to the papacy, an institution thoroughly discredited in seventeenth-century England among Protestants of all sorts, was a shrewd move. It was well known that Catholics (including Charles I's queen, Henrietta, a Frenchwoman and an open papist!) certainly made much of the feast. If Christmas was popish, surely it was also unworthy of a true Englishman's devotion.

The friends of Christmas used barrels of ink to refute these charges. Christmas, they asserted, had been observed in apostolic times; December 25 was the correct date of Christ's birth; Jesus himself had observed holy days, and as for the regulative principle and denying the magistrate the right to designate certain non-Sabbath days as religiously special, well, why then did the Puritans support the right of the state to proclaim fasts? As for Christmas's popish origins, they were admitted but shrugged off; the early papacy had not been corrupt (unlike its present-day successors), and many valuable things had proceeded from dubious beginnings.

The second line of Puritan attack was always to bring up the bad behavior of Christmas celebration: dicing, carding, sexual incontinence, drunkenness, transvestitism, dancing, gluttony, riot, cats and dogs living together. The vulgarity of Christmas celebrations was equaled only by the baseness of its celebrants—seldom the best sort of person, and those not much overburdened by intelligence or piety: Catholics, the ignorant, and those attracted to the carnal side of the celebration. Were it not for the fleshly attractions of the holiday it would be as little regarded as Easter. "Tis the Butlers boxe, the Cookes fees, the Parsons good cheare, the Sextons vailes, the old mans custom, the plow-mans play dayes, the tenants rost-meate, the Landlords Capons, the School-boys vacation, the Gentryes New-yeers gifts, the Drunkards good Ale, the Gamesters Delight, the Gluttons Mince-pyes, the Fidlers meat, drink and money and the Devils advantage that makes so many cry great is Diana of the Ephesians."[80] Puritans also linked the riotousness of Christmas behavior with idleness, a condition for which the godly had little sympathy. The ancient notion of the Twelve Days of Christmas, established during the reign of Alfred the Great, as an agricultural holiday and the temporary release of schoolboys from the tyranny of their masters, troubled the ultra-Protestant soul. "The least minute...is too much to give to idleness or sin, which is all one, the one is mother, the other the daughter."[81]

While the more learned of the Christmas supporters were embarrassed by this charge and admitted that moderation and sobriety should be the hallmarks of Christmas celebration,[82] the writers aiming at a more popular audience were having none of it. For them excess in celebration was not a bug, it was a feature. That's what Christmas was for, said the authors of such tracts as *A Hue and Cry After Christmas* (1645). Here a town crier is hired to locate Christmas, that good old man, who has gone missing. He sets out through the streets of London calling out whether anyone can

> tell any tidings of an old, old, old, very old gray bearded Gentleman called Christmas; who was wont to be a verie familiar ghest, and visite all sorts of people both poor and rich, and used to appear in glittering gold silk and silver in the Court, and in all shapes in the Theatre in Whitehall, and had ringing, feasts, and jollitie in all places, both in the Citie and Countrie for his comming: if you went to the Temple, you might have found him there at In and In, till many a Gentleman had outed all the mony from his pocket, and after all, the Butlers found him locked up in their Boxes. And in almost every house, you might have found him at Cards and Dice, the very boyes and children could have traced him, and the Beggers have followed him from place to place, and seen him walking up

and downe, and in every house roast Beefe and Mutton, Pies and Plum porrige, and all manner of delicates round about him, and every one saluting merry Christmas.

The crier discovers that Old Christmas has been arrested, to the dismay of many:

> The poor are sory for it, for they go to every door a begging as they were wont to do *(Good Mrs., Somewhat against this good Time)* but Time was transformed, *Away be gone, here is not for you:* and so they instead of going to the Ale-house to be drunk were fain to work all the Holidayes. The Schollers came into the Hall, where their hungry stomacks had thought to have found good Brawn and Christmas Pies, Roast bief and Plum porridge, but no such matter. Away ye prophane, these are superstitious meats, your stomack must be fed with wholesome doctrine. Alas poor tallow-faced Chandlers, I met them mourning through the streets, and complaining that they could get no vent for their Mustard, for want of Brawn.

A tract by theologian Edward Fisher defended every sensual aspect of the holiday, declaring of Yule games that "the body is God's as well as the spirit, and therefore why should not God be glorified by shewing forth the strength, quicknesse and agility of our body," and going on to praise the singing of carols, the eating of mince pies, plum pottage, and brawn, decorating churches and private houses with holly or ivy, playing cards or bowling, and giving gifts to friends and servants during the Twelve Days.[83] Defenders of Christmas also believed that the season was on the side of the poor—the beggars and scholars—and cited the long-established traditions of charity and hospitality. As for the charge that these caused idleness and increase of beggary, it was asserted that while "too much charity hath slain her thousands, too little hath slain her tens of thousands."[84] The long journey of the Magi to bring gifts to the Christ Child showed that God was pleased when the needs of the faithful were relieved for his sake.[85] For this reason, those who condemned Christmas were portrayed as miserly and antisocial.

In *Twelfth Night,* Shakespeare's Sir Toby Belch had asked: "Dost thou think because thou art virtuous there shall be no more cakes and ale?" "Yes," answered the Puritan camp, "that's exactly right!" A number of anti-Christmas writers were happy to move beyond condemnation of excessive celebration; they opposed being merry in principle. For Prynne, laughter was inconsistent with the gravity, modesty, and sobriety that ought to mark a Christian life. Jesus, who himself never laughed, condemned those who did and advised his followers to mourn and weep rather than indulge in unspiritual jollity. In fact, Prynne went on to say, "carnal, worldly pleasures, you know, are no part, no particle of a Christian's comfort; he can live a most happy joyful life without them; yea, he can hardly live happily or safely with them." This spirit of perpetual Lent was echoed by Thomas Fuller; in a Childermas sermon, he advised his listeners not to be carried away in jollity but to mourn while they are in mirth. A tract of 1656 complained: "Bad joy strips God of all. No evil carries the heart so totally from God as evil joy.... A man is very heartily, very totally wicked, every faculty, every sinnew stretch themselves to sin, when sinful in joys."[86]

To the Christmas-lover this mirthless spirit was the least comprehensible argument of his opponents and the one that stirred most resentment in the hearts of ordinary Englishmen. When Christmas was restored in 1660 with the return of the Stuart dynasty under Charles II, the right to be merry and the comfort of long custom were most celebrated. "Can the Black-moore change his skin, or the Sunne alter his continued course? Yet sooner can these things be done then my mind changed, for to keep old Christmas once again," asserted Mrs. Custome in *Women Will Have Their Will*.[87] Far less delight was shown at the return of church services or the right to Christmas charity than at the restoration of good cheer. A ballad "The Merry Boys of Christmas" crowed:

> *Then here's a Health to Charles our King,*
> *Throughout the world admired;*
> *Let us his great applauses sing*
> *That we so much desired,*
> *And wisht among us for to reign*
> *When Oliver rul'd here:*
> *But since he's home returned again,*
> *Come fill some Christmas Beer!*
> *These holidays we'll briskly drink,*
> *all mirth we will devise,*
> *No treason we will speak or think,*
> *then bring us brave minc'd Pies:*
> *Roast Beef and brave Plum Porridge,*
> *our Loyal hearts to chear:*

Then prithee make no more ado,
but bring us Christmas Beer![88]

In the long run this emphasis on the old-fashioned nature of Christmas
and its bacchanalian delights hurt the celebration of the holiday in England
more than the Puritan war to abolish it. By the time the holiday, along with
the monarchy, had been restored, it had lost much of its charm for the
elites of society. Social historians have noted that in these early modern years,

> many games, calendar rituals and other popular customs and beliefs
> were increasingly discountenanced by the ecclesiastical and secular
> authorities and measures taken to reform or suppress them. The
> same period saw a growing divergence between the culture of elite
> groups (nobles, gentlemen, clergy, and some middle-class elements
> in town and country) and that of the mass of the people. The former
> withdrew from, and to an extent became hostile towards, activities
> such as carnivals which they had formerly patronized. In so far as
> they survived repression, many elements of popular culture came
> to be regarded by members of the elites as merely the vulgar pas-
> times of the rude, unlettered masses.[89]

This was certainly true of Christmas, which came to be regarded as a rustic affair, a matter for country bumpkins and those of oafish manners; it
ceased to be the great feast it had been at the royal court.[90] Though it never
suffered as severe an eclipse as in Scotland, where Christmas was almost
utterly ignored until the twentieth century, the English holiday went into
a long, slow decline, kept alive chiefly in the rural areas.

The Christmas wars continued in the colonies Europeans had established in the New World, and as a result celebrations in the Americas varied depending on which nation had colonized an area. In lands acquired by
Catholic powers such as France, Spain, or Portugal—a huge swath extend-
ing from sub-Arctic Canada to the tip of Tierra del Fuego—Christmas continued to be a festive time, marked by processions, Masses, revelry, and an
emphasis on re-creating the scene of the Nativity. In some Protestant areas
it was often a different story. The modern humorist Garrison Keillor has
said of his Puritan ancestors that they came to America "in the hope of
finding greater restrictions than were permissible under English law at
that time." In 1620 in the Puritan colony of Plymouth, in New England, the

new settlers ignored any celebrations on December 25 and spent the day cutting timber and erecting a building. One year later the governor, William Bradford, encountered some newcomers who were unwilling, for conscience's sake, to work on Christmas Day. When he returned from the fields to find some of them "pitching the bar and some at stool-ball and such like sports," he broke up their amusements and declared it was against his conscience that they should play while others worked.[91] Massachusetts Bay Colony, also dominated by Puritans, passed a law in 1659 prohibiting the celebration of Christmas "either by forbearing of labor, feasting or any such other way," on pain of a 5-shilling fine. Under pressure from royalist and Anglican authorities in London the law was revoked in 1681, and a few years later, when the colony's charter was rescinded, the Crown-appointed governor made a point of openly attending Christmas Day services and proclaiming a religious toleration that allowed a number of hitherto forbidden festivals to be celebrated.[92] This was not universally welcomed—the governor had to be accompanied on his Christmas worship by troops. This was a sensible precaution, because even a generation later a Calvinist mob would protest the holding of a Christmas service by smashing the windows of the offending church. For the next century Christmas continued to be a source of controversy and anxiety in New England. The Anglican celebrations began to attract more Christmas-keepers, despite the scorn and hostile preaching of the Puritan-minded. When the Boston minister Cotton Mather discovered that a number of young members of his flock had attended a dance on Christmas Day, he made sure that in the next year the lines were clearly drawn between the godly and the ungodly. His sermon of 1712 is a masterpiece of righteous invective: "Can you in your conscience think," he thundered at his congregation, "that our holy Savior is honored, by Mad Mirth, long Eating, by rude Revelling; by a mass fit for none but a Saturn or a Bacchus or the Night of a Mahometan Ramadan?" Could they possibly, on the anniversary of Christ's birth, "take the Time to Please the Hellish Legions, and to do Actions that have much more of Hell than of Heaven in them?" To do so was to risk the wrath of God.[93] Similar anti-Christmas sentiments were expressed by the Scotch-Irish who penetrated the Appalachian backcountry and brought with them "a fixed aversion to the English government and the English church," among whose ceremonies they numbered Christmas.[94] But other American colonists brought their native Christmas traditions with them and celebrated the season with gusto. In Virginia it was a time of extended merriment marked by balls, feasts, gunfire, and neighborly visits; in Alabama, the costumed Fantastic

Riders; in New Orleans, the King Cake; among the Pennsylvania Dutch, Belsnickling; and in Georgia, Pennsylvania, and North Carolina, where Moravians settled, the first North American Christmas trees and a gentle emphasis on the holiday as a time for children.

In England, though Christmas celebrations were hanging on in rural areas, they were becoming less visible or important in the cities. The 1709 edition of the English annual *Poor Robin's Almanack* said of the holiday "And Christmas scarcely should we know / Did not the almanacks it show." This was the period of the Enlightenment, a self-conscious movement among European social and intellectual elites to reject traditional religion, challenge old ways of politics, and laud advances in science. Many high-ranking church leaders in England and on the Continent came to despise religious enthusiasm, prided themselves in their rejection of divine revelation or miracles, and privately espoused Deism, a nonsectarian belief in an impersonal god who could be equated with Reason or Nature. Churchmen, seeing the prosperity of Protestant communities where saints' days had been abolished, tried to reduce the number of holidays and festivals that required people to cease working for the day. The Italian historian and priest Luigi Muratori asked: "Is not this excess of feasts the reason why our country has the most beggars and mendicants"? What these reformers wanted to accomplish was, in fact, already occurring in Britain, where the onset of the Industrial Revolution was stripping the calendar of holidays. The old agricultural year, with its rhythms of alternating frantic activity and enforced idleness (like that permitted on the Twelve Days of Christmas), was giving way to the machine-driven accounting of time. "We made it a rule," said one mill owner in Lancashire, "that we would not hire any person who would wish to be off his two days [to take part in traditional leisure]. Now the men we employ are as regular as any set of men."[95] In 1761 the Bank of England closed for forty-seven holidays; by 1834 only four days off were observed, and historians have calculated that workers in London increased their hours of annual labor by 40 percent in the years 1750–1830.[96]

The tastes of the age, even among the common people, moved away from the excesses of the baroque and the Counter-Reformation and toward plainness and simplicity; processions became less ornate; the elaborate Nativity scenes of the Christmas season and the decorated sepulchers fell out of favor. Some French churchmen went so far as to discourage the singing of carols at Christmas.[97] Philosophers, for example Voltaire and Jean-François Marmontel, sneered at traditional festivals and ways of celebrating Christmas.[98] Some freethinking Masonic lodges, known for their anticlericalism, treated December 25 as the Roman feast of Saturn.[99] In the Austrian Empire, Joseph II, the quintessential "enlightened despot," embarked on an ambitious program of religious reform that he believed would advance the cause of toleration and modernity. As well as attacking the monastic system and granting religious liberty to Jews and Protestants, he enforced a host of petty regulations on church life. The number of candles was prescribed, directions were given as to the length and content of sermons, and traditional customs of popular religion were banned. Pilgrimages to various statues of the Christ Child were forbidden, as were, in 1782, the large Nativity scenes that were customary ornaments to churches during Christmas season. (The people responded by hiding their crèches until a better disposed ruler might appear and by developing new smaller types of Nativity scenes meant for the privacy of the house.) On December 25, 1789, the US Congress, with more than its fair share of Deists, Unitarians, and Quakers, worked through the day.[100] The public observances of the Feast of the Nativity of Jesus Christ had a hard time thriving in such an atmosphere.

The early modern period took one last kick at Christmas during the French Revolution. When this first of all modern revolutions broke out in 1789 it seemed at first a moderate enough affair, demanding the sorts of rights that Americans or Englishmen would find unremarkable: freedom of the press, freedom from arbitrary arrest, an end to feudal oppression, and a monarchy bound by a constitution. But social upheavals have lives of their own and often cannot be stopped, even when early demands have been realized. The Revolution became increasingly radical, particularly in regard to religion. By 1790, ecclesiastical lands had been seized and the French Catholic Church severed from papal control; priests were forced to swear an oath of loyalty to this new "Constitutional church," though many went underground or into exile; archbishops were deposed; bishops were henceforth to be elected. Churches were vandalized and despoiled of their treasures, and their bells were melted down to make cannon for the revolutionary armies. Religious toleration, which had briefly been the order of the day, gave way to a policy of de-Christianization and a rejection of any worship of the "Jew slave" and his mother "the adulteress of Galilee."[101] In the new state religion, called the Cult of the Supreme Being, churches were turned into Temples of Reason, stripped of crucifixes, and filled with statues to Liberty. Almost all of France's forty thousand churches were closed by early 1794, sold or converted to stables, warehouses, or factories.

Priests were murdered or forced to marry; public Christian worship was forbidden.

Time itself became a tool of the Revolution, with radical reforms to the clock (which now reckoned moments on a decimal basis) and calendar. Months were now deemed to be of equal length (thirty days each, with a five-day holiday at the year end) and were stripped of their traditional names—out went "January" and "February," and in came new labels based on seasonal climatic conditions in Paris: Pluvîose ("the rainy month") or Ventôse ("the windy month"), and so on. Each day in the year was named after an animal, a tool, a mineral, or a plant. Thus December 25 became 5 Nivôse, "dog day." This new calendar erased the old world and along with it Christmas. If Frenchmen wanted to celebrate it, they had to do so in secret. The revolutionary government viewed keeping it as proof of being an enemy of the people and instructed its agents to watch for those who did not show up to work on that day or on Easter. As in the time of the English Civil War of the 1640s, Christmas pastry became a topic of political concern. Puritans had sought to eliminate Christmas mince pies as "idolatry in crust"; the minions of the French Revolution came down hard on bakers who dared term their Epiphany treats "Galette des rois" in honor of the Three Kings. Didn't they know France was now a regicide nation with no time for royalty? "King Cakes" perforce became "Liberty Cakes."[102] A republican liturgy and a reshaping of festivals were proposed: Christmas would become the "Festival of the Birth" if the mother had produced a boy child in the previous year. Good Friday would honour those who had suffered physically or morally.[103]

The rule of the Jacobin clique and the Terror they enforced came to an end in the summer of 1794, and gradually the restrictions on religion were relaxed. The next year saw Christian churches allowed to open again, though they were still restricted in their public observances. By the time Napoleon Bonaparte took power, the energy and fanaticism had been drained from the Revolution. Christmas mangers started to appear in public by 1799; the purchase of New Year's gifts was in full swing by 1800. Christmas midnight Mass was being celebrated openly in Paris by 1802, and before long the holiday was once more on the calendar.[104]

II

The Revivers

In which Christmas is found in a debased and sorry condition but is reinvented by poets, artists, novelists, musicologists, clergymen, and merchants so that the holiday is revived and becomes a global phenomenon

THOUGH CHRISTMAS SURVIVED attempts in Britain, France, and America to ban it, its celebration fell out of favor with the elite classes in much of the English-speaking world. Stripped of its religious significance by Puritans and Enlightenment freethinkers, the holiday came to be dominated by raucous behavior of the lower orders. We can see the state it reached in England by examining a number of satirical late-eighteenth-century prints. A 1794 specimen, "Christmas Gambols, or a Kiss Under the Mistletoe" shows a woman, "Bridget the Cook," violently resisting "Saucy Joe" as he grabs her for an embrace under a branch of mistletoe. Another graphic illustrates a poem, "The Mistletoe. A Christmas Tale," set in a prosperous farmer's kitchen where the neighbors have gathered by the fire to drink ale and share ghost stories. The older farmer looks with dismay on his pretty young wife, who is kissed, not unwillingly and not for the first time, by a handsome swain. An even more jaundiced view of seasonal festivities from 1795 bears the title "Snap Dragon," the name for a popular Christmas game in which a bowl of brandy is set alight and participants try to snatch raisins from the container without being burned. As a group of celebrants laugh, a cat is tortured by holding its paws in the flames. Most disturbing of all is a print bearing the innocent label "Christmas Day," showing how the day is marked in an elegant bourgeois mansion. On the left, a rich family dines in splendor but without any seasonal goodwill; the caption notes that they have quarreled with their parson, who refuses to say grace over their meal. On the right, there is violence and mayhem in the servants' quarters, as the butler plays a cruel trick on the cook, the maid is raped by the groom, food is spilled, and a cat and a monkey run amok. In all of these prints, the core meaning of Christmas seems to be conviviality with a strong current of vulgarity, gluttony, and misrule. Nowhere is there any suggestion in these illustrations that this is a religious holiday or one with many virtues to commend it.[1] *London Magazine*, in a piece of social criticism titled "Christmas: An Essay," noted the games, the overindulgence in food and drink, and the riotousness of the season and remarked sadly: "Here is enough of every thing suitable to the time and occasion—of everything—except *religion*. The most sacred festival of our calendar...is converted into one continuous scene of riot, profligacy, and debauchery."[2]

Outdoor celebration seemed even worse. In many places, the Twelve Days were now marked by drunkenness, street violence, interruption of church services, vandalism, and a general outraging of the sensibilities of the middle class. "It is customary among the common People to sing a Christmas Carol," but it is generally done "in the midst of Rioting and Chambering [sneaking off for illicit sex] and Wantonness...a Scandal to Religion, and a sin against Christ," said Englishman Henry Bourne in 1725.[3] The night air was rent by "Callithumpian Music." Derived from the Greek for "beautiful," "Callithumpian music" refers to clangorous noise made by revelers during the Christmas season in eighteenth-century England, the early United States, and Canada's eastern provinces. "Music" was made by banging on pans, shouting, blowing horns, and making rude noises; it was the brassy voice of defiance from the underclasses aimed at their better-off and more genteel neighbors. Christmas was also the time for brazen demands for money on the street or even door-to-door, as the middle class was harassed for spare change under the cry of "Christmas Box!" In Boston, the Anticks were groups of mummers who formed in the second half of the eighteenth century. During the Christmas season these lower-class males would go in disguise from house to house and perform a version of the English mumming play, which involves broad slapstick humor and a mock death and resurrection. They would expect a gratuity and hospitality for their efforts. By the 1790s their visits were arousing opposition from decent, stay-at-home citizens who had come to resent their intrusions and the street violence that was part of their wanderings. In December 1793 the *Massachusetts Mercury* complained:

> The time will soon arise on which the ANTICKS are wont to assemble. The disadvantages, interruptions and injuries which the inhabitants sustain from these gangs, are too many for enumeration, a few only must suffice.

When different clubs of them meet in the street, noise and fighting immediately commences. Their demands for entrance in [the] house are insolent and clamorous; and should the peaceful citizen (not choosing to have the tranquility of his family interrupted) persevere in refusing them admittance, his windows are broke, or the latches and knockers wrenched from his door as the penalty. Or should they gain admittance, the delicate ear is oftentimes offended, children affrighted, or catch the phrases of their senseless ribaldry.[4]

Nor did the passage of time seem to dampen the enthusiasm of the rougher sort of citizen for his Christmas seasonal sport. The early nineteenth century saw even more end-of-year disorder. In 1806 a nativist mob expressed its anti-immigrant sentiments by trying to break up the Christmas Eve midnight Mass at St. Peter's Church in New York. Though they were unsuccessful, they returned to the area the next night to attack Irish homes; in the ensuing riot a constable was murdered. In 1828, the year of Andrew Jackson's election to the presidency and the fears of an American "mobocracy," the riffraff of New York marked Christmas by assembling a Callithumpian parade and, with the din of "drums, tin kettles, rattles, horns, whistles," and other instruments, moving along the Bowery committing petty vandalism as they went. They then marched to Broadway, where they showed disdain for the city's elites by a demonstration in front of a fancy-dress ball, but they reserved their worst behavior for an invasion of a black neighborhood where believers had assembled in a church for a "watch night" service. In the words of the New York *Gazette,* the mob

demolished all the windows, the doors, the seats, etc. and tied ropes to parts of the building in order to tear it down, but the ropes with which they drew the large wagon not being strong enough, they desisted and poured all their violence against the poor colored people, whom they pursued in all directions beating them with sticks and pieces of rope. The poor preacher was obliged to make his escape through a back window and after running a considerable distance, got clear of the mob by turning into a narrow entry. Are such proceedings to be tolerated in the city of New York? Is not the police of the city strong enough to put a stop to such disgraceful proceedings? If not, it is high time its strength and numbers were increased.[5]

Christmas violence was not just a New York problem. In Philadelphia in 1833 the *Daily Chronicle* complained that "riot, noise and uproar prevailed, uncontrolled and uninterrupted in many of our central and most orderly streets. Gangs of boys howled as if possessed by the demons of disorder." Pittsburgh newspapers protested the number of young men possessed of gunpowder, throwing firecrackers at women and raising a din. In Cincinnati in 1853 an anti-Catholic mob rioted on Christmas Day over the presence of Archbishop Gaetano Bedini, the first papal nuncio to the United States. The Newfoundland custom of masked parades and house invasion (termed "mumming" or "mummering") at Christmas was often the cover for vandalism, riot, and assault. In 1831 the magistrates of one town complained to the governor that "since the commencement of Christmas, many complaints have been made of assaults and batteries as the lower orders of persons are mostly accustomed to spend twelve days in idleness and pastime, that of Mumming has for many years prevailed here ... some persons in Carbonear have had lime or flour thrown on their clothes by such disguised persons when going to attend divine service." When three masked men axed to death newlywed fisherman Isaac Mercer in the Christmas season of 1860, the legislature banned the practice of mumming—a law that remained in force for over a century. Disorder in the streets of Montreal forced the cancelation of midnight Mass in 1848, and a Quebec priest complained of the Christmas season: "this is the time of year when there is greatest dissipation, the most amusements and the greatest disorder." Across the world in Tasmania, Christmas was described "as a period of dark eyes, blood red cheeks, workers lounging about the bars recovering from bouts of dipsomania, occasionally carried off to the '*dead house*' at the back to sober up." In the gold fields of Australia, at "Ballarat, Castelmaine, or rather Forest Creek, and Melbourne, the Christmas and New Year passed in riot and disorder, and every evil thing that accompanies the too easy acquirement of wealth, abounded."[6]

Alcohol, and particularly the custom of distributing free booze, was at the root of much of this disturbance of the public peace. In New York a newspaper editor noted that the "first flash of morning discovered the liquor shops in full operation, with wassail bowls of smoking punch, and 'medicine' of all sorts, free as water. This dangerous and wicked temptation was the means of setting a great many *young men and boys* in a state of crazy intoxication long before noon." Across the Atlantic, an editorial headline in the *Weekly True Sun* of London thundered "*The Evil of Publicans Giving Away Their Liquors on 'Boxing-Day' Was Never More Strongly*

Exemplified; This Office Being Crowded by Persons with Broken Heads, Fractured Limbs, &c. The hearing of the cases occupied the attention of the magistrates until a late hour." The newspaper included, as an illustration of its point, the touching story of Ellen Keeffe, who had appeared in court that week charged with an assault on William Connor. According to the reporter: "The prisoner and complainant met accidentally at a gin palace on 'boxing day' and continued very happy together for several hours, but becoming stupidly drunk, they quarreled, and Miss Ellen Keeffe seizing a poker and crying out *'Its fer love and ould Ireland!'* struck the complainant upon the head, and injured him very much."[7]

Small wonder then that one historian has claimed that for most of the nineteenth century "respectable Philadelphians condemned Christmas as a disgrace" and another that it seemed at the time that the season might die in Protestant Europe and North America. Even folk of the period who loved Christmas thought that it was on its last legs. The musicologist William Sandys lamented: "In many parts of the kingdom...this festival is still kept up with spirit among the middling and lower classes, though its influence is on the wane even with them; the genius of the present age requires work and not play, and since the commencement of this century a great change may be traced. The modern instructors of mankind do not think it necessary to provide for popular amusements." The Episcopalian bishop Philander Chase complained to his wife that "the devil has stolen from us...Christmas, the day of our spiritual redemption and converted it into a day of worldly festivity, shooting and swearing." The English poet Thomas Hervey surveyed his nation's Christmas observances in the 1830s and concluded that it was "alas, but too true that the spirit of hearty festivity in which our ancestors met this season has long been on the decline; and much of the joyous pomp with which it was once received has long since passed away." Many contemporaries echoed his sighs over the waning of festivity and noted that traditional notions of Christmas charity had been eclipsed by modern Malthusian ideas about denying aid to the needy lest it encourage idleness and overpopulation of useless mouths.[8]

Yet Christmas would survive. And thrive. Within a hundred years of its near-extinction, it would recapture all its old strongholds in western Europe and North and South America and be on the way to achieving its present status as the globe's most widely celebrated festival. To understand why this happened, we must examine a number of contributors—some of them dedicated to reviving old myths, old sentiments, and old songs; some of them intent on mending rifts between social classes; and some of them on instilling new ideas about family relations. In addition to these individuals we must also take into account vaster social movements: revolutions in the economy and the intellectual world. These people and phenomena came together in the first half of the nineteenth century to redefine Christmas and, in doing so, save it from neglect and distaste.

The remaking of Christmas in America began with the work of a small group of poets, illustrators, and essayists in New York. Keenly aware of a gap between the lower classes and the elites, a gap that was annually expressed in the vulgarity and violence of the city's end-of-year celebrations, they sought to move Christmas away from its outdoor, proletarian, alcohol-fueled expressions and toward its celebration as a domestic, middle-class, child-centered holiday. Their "Battle for Christmas," as one social historian has memorably termed it, succeeded beyond their wildest imaginings.[9]

The first to enter the fray was Washington Irving. Though today he is mainly known for his tales of Dutch colonial times, including "The Legend of Sleepy Hollow" and "Rip Van Winkle," his effect on the mythology of Christmas was profound. In 1809 he published a satire titled *A History of New-York from the Beginning of the World to the End of the Dutch Dynasty, by Diedrich Knickerbocker*. This mock history introduced to his readers the Dutch love of Saint Nicholas, whose image, Irving claimed, was carved on the very prow of the first ship that brought colonists from the Netherlands to the New World. He further claimed that the children of New Amsterdam yearly awaited the arrival of the saint who would fly over the city in a wagon and drop presents down chimneys on his name day, December 6. For most Americans outside the New York area, this was the first they had heard of any flying, supernatural, nocturnal Christmas Gift-Bringer, but it was not to be the last.

A year later, New Yorkers, or at least some of the city's more respectable citizens, were reminded of St. Nicholas through the efforts of John Pintard. A prominent merchant, Pintard was the founder of the New-York Historical Society, and for its 1810 annual meeting he prepared a handout featuring a picture of the saint. The woodcut that decorated his pamphlet showed Nicholas as a stern figure clad in the traditional robe of a bishop, surmounted by a halo, and holding a rod. Accompanying his portrait is a scene of a home on the morning of his saint's day, December 6. A blazing fire lights the stockings, which he has magically filled, hanging on the mantel and a breakfast of sausages and waffles (always associated in the public mind with Holland). A little girl, whose behavior throughout the year has presumably won her the saint's favor, holds an apron full of goodies; her brother, whom we must conclude has been a naughty child, bawls at discovering the chastising rods that are all that has been left for him. The verse beneath is printed in both Dutch and English and reads:

> *Saint Nicholas, good holy man!*
> *Put on the Tabard, best you can,*
> *Go, clad therewith, to Amsterdam*
> *From Amsterdam to Hispanje,*
> *Where apples bright of Oranje,*
> *And likewise those granate surnam'd,*
> *Roll through the streets, all free unclaimed.*
> *Saint Nicholas, my dear good friend!*
> *To serve you, ever was my end,*
> *If you will, now, me something give,*
> *I'll serve you ever while I live.*

New York seemed to be in the grip of Saint Nicholas fever. Less than two weeks later, on December 15, 1810, another poem, anonymously written, appeared in the *New York Spectator,* praising the "good holy man" for the gifts he brings, asking him to spare the rod and promising him good behavior in return:

> *Oh good holy man! whom we Sancte Claus name,*
> *The Nursery forever your praise shall proclaim;*
> *The day of your joyful revisit returns,*
> *When each little bosom with gratitude burns,*
> *For the gifts which at night you so kindly impart*
> *To the girls of your love, and the boys of your heart.*
> *O! Come with your panniers and pockets well stow'd,*
> *Our stockings shall help you to lighten your load,*
> *As close by the fireside gaily they swing*
> *While delighted we dream of the presents you bring.*
> *Oh! Bring the bright Orange so juicy and sweet,*
> *Bring almonds and raisins to heighten the treat;*
> *Rich waffles and dough-nuts must not be forgot,*
> *Nor Crullers and Oley-Cooks fresh from the pot.*
> *But of all these fine presents your Saintship can find,*
> *O! Leave not the famous big Cookies behind;*
> *Or, if in your hurry, one thing you mislay,*

Let it be the Rod—and ah! keep it away.
Then holy St. Nicholas! all the long year,
Our books we will love, and our parents revere;
From naughty behavior we'll always refrain,
In hopes that you'll come and reward us again.[10]

Note the name used for the saint: Sancte Claus. In the next few years a number of variations on Sinterklaas, the Dutch name for St. Nicholas, will appear in print in America: Santa-claw, Santeclaus, Sandy Claw, Santiclaw, or Sanctus Klaas. This speaks to a long-standing oral transmission of the legend of a Christmas Gift-Bringer, rather than, as some have suggested, the outright invention of Santa Claus by a Knickerbocker literary clique. It seems more reasonable to conclude that writers like Irving and Pintard had capitalized on folk memory in the Hudson River valley in their development of the figure who would in time become the most influential imaginary creature on the planet.[11]

The next addition to the American Christmas literary canon was an anonymous production that was remarkable in many ways. In 1821 William Gilley of New York published *The Children's Friend*, the first lithographed work in the United States and the first to print a picture of Santa Claus. The poem reads:

Old Santeclaus with much delight
His reindeer drives this frosty night,
O'er chimneytops and tracks of snow,
To bring his yearly gifts to you.
The steady friend of virtuous youth,
The friend of duty and of truth,
Each Christmas eve he joys to come
Where peace and love have made their home.
Through many houses he has been,
And various beds and stockings seen,
Some, white as snow, and neatly mended,
Others, that seem'd for pigs intended.
Where e'er I found good girls or boys,
That hated quarrels strife and noise,
I left an apple, or a tart,
Or wooden gun, or painted cart;
To some I gave a pretty doll.

To some a peg-top, or a ball;
No crackers, cannons, squibs or rockets,
To blow their eyes up, or their pockets.
No drums to stir their Mother's ear,
Nor swords to make their sisters fear;
But pretty books to store their mind.
With Knowledge of each various kind.
But where I found the children naughty,
In manners rude, in tempers haughty,
Thankless to parents, liars, swearers,
Boxers or cheats, or base tale-bearers,
I left a long, black, birchen rod,
Such, as the dread command of God
Directs a Parent's hand to use
When virtue's path his sons refuse.[12]

No one knows who wrote the poem or who drew the pictures of "Santeclaus" tiptoeing through the house or sitting in his reindeer-drawn sleigh with its built-in bookshelf, but the creator had more than his fair share of creative genius. *The Children's Friend* wrenches Santa Claus out of his Dutch context and places him in a winter setting appropriate to North America in December. The saint's traditional horse-drawn wagon was replaced by a reindeer and sleigh, and his nocturnal visit was moved from December 6 to Christmas Eve. The Gift-Bringer is no longer the stern bishop of Pintard's woodcut. Now he is a smiling wearer of a tall fur hat (helpfully labeled "Santeclaus") and a fur-trimmed robe that resembles that worn by Old Christmas in seventeenth-century prints. He has not forsaken his judgmental nature though—the poet is quite clear that good behavior will be rewarded with gifts or bad behavior punished by that "long, black birchen rod"—but at least he has abandoned the host of shaggy Germanic helpers, and he seems to need no help in carrying his bags. Though *A Children's Friend* has long been forgotten by all but Christmas historians, its innovations were put to good use within a year in a piece of poetry that became the climax of the literary battle to change the holiday, a poem that has been reprinted more than any other poem of any kind in history.

In the Christmas season of 1822, Clement Clarke Moore, a prosperous New York scholar and landowner, wrote a series of verses in a lively anapestic rhythm for the amusement of his daughters.[13] Legend has it that they were inspired by the portly figure of his fur-clad sleigh driver as he returned home from a shopping trip through the snowy streets. The poem appeared anonymously in the Troy *Sentinel* a year later under the title "Account of a Visit from St. Nicholas":

> 'Twas the night before Christmas, when all thro' the house
> Not a creature was stirring, not even a mouse;
> The stockings were hung by the chimney with care,
> In hopes that St. Nicholas soon would be there;
> The children were nestled all snug in their beds,
> While visions of sugar-plums danc'd in their heads;
> And mamma in her 'kerchief, and I in my cap,
> Had just settled our brains for a long winter's nap—
> When out on the lawn there arose such a clatter,
> I sprang from the bed to see what was the matter.
> Away to the window I flew like a flash,
> Tore open the shutters, and threw up the sash.
> The moon on the breast of the new fallen snow,
> Gave the lustre of mid-day to objects below;
> When, what to my wondering eyes should appear,
> But a miniature sleigh, and eight tiny rein-deer,
> With a little old driver, so lively and quick,
> I knew in a moment it must be St. Nick.
> More rapid than eagles his coursers they came,
> And he whistled, and shouted, and called them by name:
> "Now! Dasher, now! Dancer, now! Prancer, and Vixen,
> "On! Comet, on! Cupid, on! Dunder and Blixem;
> "To the top of the porch! to the top of the wall!
> "Now dash away! dash away! dash away all!"
> As dry leaves before the wild hurricane fly,
> When they meet with an obstacle, mount to the sky;
> So up to the house-top the coursers they flew,
> With the sleigh full of toys—and St. Nicholas too:
> And then, in a twinkling, I heard on the roof
> The prancing and pawing of each little hoof.
> As I drew in my hand, and was turning around,
> Down the chimney St. Nicholas came with a bound;
> He was dress'd all in fur, from his head to his foot,
> And his clothes were all tarnish'd with ashes and soot;
> A bundle of toys was flung on his back,

And he look'd like a peddler just opening his pack:
His eyes—how they twinkled! his dimples how merry,
His cheeks were like roses, his nose like a cherry;
His droll little mouth was drawn up like a bow,
And the beard of his chin was as white as the snow;
The stump of a pipe he held tight in his teeth,
And the smoke it encircled his head like a wreath.
He had a broad face and a little round belly
That shook when he laugh'd, like a bowlful of jelly:
He was chubby and plump, a right jolly old elf,
And I laugh'd when I saw him, in spite of myself;
A wink of his eye and a twist of his head
Soon gave me to know I had nothing to dread.
He spoke not a word, but went straight to his work,
And fill'd all the stockings; then turn'd with a jerk,
And laying his finger aside of his nose
And giving a nod, up the chimney he rose.
He sprung to his sleigh, to his team gave a whistle,
And away they all flew like the down of a thistle:
But I heard him exclaim, ere he drove out of sight—
"Happy Christmas to all, and to all a good night!"[14]

Fifty-six lines constitute a revolution. What Moore had done was to cap the work that Irving, Pintard, and *A Child's Friend* had begun. They had redefined Christmas by moving its focus from the tavern and street to the kitchen and family fireplace, from adult conviviality to the expectant child. Moore went farther. He not only stripped the Gift-Bringer of his bishop's robes but also took away his rods of chastisement: this is a nonsectarian, genial avatar of grandfatherly benevolence that no child need fear. The Gift-Bringer has ceased to be Dutch or Catholic or, indeed, of any particular ethnic or religious affiliation, owing no allegiance to Europe, the pope, or the past. Smiling, and trailing smoke from a pipe, he is neither of one class nor another, successfully bridging the social gap that the Knickerbockers feared. He might be sooty and clench a proletarian stub of a pipe in his teeth (the working man would snap off the long curving stems that the upper classes affected) but he lavished gifts like a rich man. At one and the same time he behaved like a peddler and a lord: the perfect literary creation for a young, self-confident America carving an identity out of the New World.[15]

Moore's poem was quickly reprinted across the northeastern states and became the fountainhead for spreading the Santa Claus legend and domesticating Christmas. Countless storytellers and illustrators leapt into action, eager to capitalize on the new literary sensation and fill in the details of the Gift-Bringer's origins, dwelling, and character that Moore had omitted. For decades there was no one standard version of the nocturnal visitor nor even agreement as to his name. Some of the Knickerbocker school clung to the appellation St. Nicholas, while in Philadelphia he was Kriss Kringle (an oral mangling of *das Christkindl*) or Belsnickel, while others used some variation of Santa Claus. His size was hotly debated. Moore's "right jolly old elf" was small enough to come down a chimney, barely scraping the sides, and was pulled by a "miniature sleigh," but in some stories he was no bigger than a thumb, and in others he was adult-sized. He was a bearded old man; he was a smooth-cheeked youth; he was outfitted like a Dutch peddler; he dressed like George Washington; he was "a little old negro," a "fearful fire-breathing monster," and a "yeoman farmer in the German style."[16] By the late 1850s his home was traced to the Arctic, where he was assisted by a legion of elves, and then in the 1860s, in the work of German American cartoonist Thomas Nast in the pages of *Harper's*, we finally see the jovial, bearded face that became impossible to deviate from when thinking of Santa Claus.

In order to effectively counter the occupation of the Christmas season by the forces of noise, drink, and male bonding, Santa Claus had to be adopted by two elements in American society. The first was parents. Over the next few decades, millions of American men and women, unbidden by any central authority and through a gradual process of diffusion of popular culture, began to reenact in their own homes the myth propagated by Clement Clark Moore's poem. Prompted by articles in women's magazines, children's books, letters from distant family members, or chats with their neighbors, parents began to encourage their children to put up stockings on December 24 by the fireplace or the foot of their beds. They told stories of a supernatural dispenser of gifts who loved little ones, particularly the well-behaved, and who would fill these stockings with treats. They devised means by which children could communicate their wishes to Santa Claus: letters placed in mailboxes or in shoes by the window or in the family's miniature Nativity scene or burnt so that the smoke might be wafted to an icy workshop, shouting up the chimney, or night-time prayers. Through the year parents set aside money to be spent in December or labored in secret to make toys, carving, hammering, knitting. Fathers hauled dead conifers into the house, propped them up, and decorated them with cookies, baubles, popcorn, and paper chains. Mothers baked items not seen in the house the rest of the year and strove to make the Christmas meal a special one. Children were told that they must be asleep lest the Gift-Bringer not come, that they might leave him and his team of reindeer sustenance, and, if they were very lucky, they might hear the jingle of the harness as they drifted off. Every Christmas season across the United States countless parents told fibs, spread pious fables, and acted out little deceptions—tracks of a sleigh in the snow outside or in the ashes of the fireplace, thank you notes from Santa, and gasps of mock surprise as stockings were opened. This was a web of deceit that conspiracy theorists of a later century could only dream about—a massive penetration of the American mind, willingly accepted and renegotiated over each generation. What idea in history has ever spread so quickly, effectively, and gently?

What was going on? Why did parents in the middle of the nineteenth century adopt this idea of Christmas? Certainly there was some self-interest involved. Raising children is the hardest job in the world, and the notion of an all-seeing supernatural figure who could reward or withhold favors, not in some distant afterlife but in the near future, was a wonderful aid to child-rearing. Moreover, by making Christmas the customary time for gift-giving, parents could urge thrift and restraint during other times of the year. Mostly, however, it was about love. An 1856 editorial in *Harper's* knew this: "Love is the moral of Christmas. What are the gifts but the proofs and signs of love?"[17] Christmas gifts bound the generations together; they taught the worth both of saving and generosity and were proof of an incredible altruism—why should parents dodge the gratitude they might have garnered from their children by deflecting it onto a mysterious visitor? Because they realized that in the mythology of Santa Claus they were giving infinitely more than a store-bought trinket or an orange at the bottom of a stocking: they were engendering a sense of magic, anticipation, and joy; a heightened awareness of the passage of time; the possibility of grace and an intergenerational piece of fantasy that the whole family could share, remember, and pass on.

It was not that earlier generations had valued their children less, but certain trends in the nineteenth century contributed to an atmosphere where this new sort of Christmas could thrive in a way that was, perhaps, not possible in earlier centuries. The colonial America of subsistence agriculture and a life spent largely in the countryside had made children an economic necessity and valuable contributors to the family economy from an early age. Even small boys and girls could be set to tending livestock, minding smaller siblings, or laboring in the field. With the rise of the Industrial Revolution and increasing urbanization, attitudes toward children gradually changed. Childhood came to be seen as a separate time of life, precious and fleeting. Techniques of child-rearing were growing less harsh and more tender, more accommodating of a child's natural inclinations. The utterly didactic children's literature of the eighteenth century had given way, as Moore's poem showed, to more fanciful genres. Rote learning, enforced by the cane, was becoming unfashionable. Reformers argued for milder discipline in home and school and praised the influence of Woman, who by "mild and persuasive tones and beneficent countenance, can and does, aided by Divine Revelation, 'win the young hearts of children to duty.'" William Wordsworth's Romantic view of childhood was increasingly influential—children were to be viewed as innately good, innocent, and creative. Play and fantasy were approved methods in parenting the well-developed child. The new industrialized economy had multiplied the number of goods available and lowered their prices so that children's toys were now within the reach of more parents, making mothers and fathers into mass consumers and children into luxury objects on which they were willing to spend money.[18]

By midcentury the American Santa Claus was not only a fixture in the stories told in American homes, he was a positive boon to merchants. Almost as soon as Clement Clark Moore had revealed his peddler-resembling creation, stores saw him as the ideal pitchman for their products. They claimed that Santa had been seen in their establishment choosing their merchandise; they decorated their shops with his image; and before the end of the century he was seen presiding in person in a grotto where he received children and heard their wishes. In 1869 a Fredericton, New Brunswick, merchant announced that "Santa Claus and Sampson's have this day entered into a copartnership in order to more fully meet the demands of parents as well as their children during the coming holiday season.... Parties residing in the city can bring their children's socks to our Establishment Thursday or Friday the 23rd and 24th inst., and OLD SANTA will carefully fill them with the choicest Confectionery, Nuts, Fruits, Toys, etc." A few years later Sampson's was so bold as to guarantee that all goods purchased in their shop would be delivered by St. Nick himself on Christmas Eve. The blessed Gift-Bringer, announced Sampson, would also be scouting his route through Fredericton on the evening of December 22, "probably about nine o'clock, and will drive through the principal streets for a short time to take a view of the chimneys in houses of those who do not wish him to call at the door."[19]

Not for the first time had Christmas become about expense and excess. In earlier, preindustrial centuries the holiday had featured a frenzy of consumption of food and drink, hospitality at all hours, and a sense of plenty that would only last a short while. As industrial and agricultural production increased and Western economies moved farther away from working for mere survival, excess capacity allowed consumers to think about nonessentials. Now Christmas buying and giving was about the acquisition of mass-produced goods, and as such it made the holiday an increasingly important part of the economy. Retail stores, toy manufacturers, bakers, card-makers, jewelers, bookstores, publishers, makers of ornaments and crèches, confectioners, woodsmen, importers, stationers, butchers and poulterers, newspapers, magazines, restaurants, theaters, music halls, furriers, porters, haberdashers, milliners, copywriters, illustrators, carters, taverners, bankers, and so on all prospered at Christmastime. The new railroads opened up the possibility for the first time of reliable winter travel and helped to create the holiday homecoming industry. The newly developed national postal services led to the massive exchange of seasonal cards and the maintenance of family connections. The North American Christmas economy began to make global demands—the toy-makers of Nuremberg, the glass blowers of Bohemia, the paper ornament–makers of Dresden all began shipping their goods across the Atlantic, making glad the hearts of teamsters, steamship owners, and dockworkers.

This sort of Christmas had no time for good old-fashioned riotous assembly, Callithumpian bands, or outraging the decent bourgeois and his family on their way to church. New urban laws cracked down on the rowdiness, professionalized police forces were organized, and the streets of American cities in late December were gradually taken back from the mobs. Middle-class reformers used the season to urge an end to alcohol consumption and its evils. (At the same time in England, temperance societies fought to have liquor taken from the Christmas menu in paupers' workhouses—in some cases unsuccessfully, as the public felt it wrong to deprive the poor of their grog for the holiday dinner, while in other places even the rum in the plum pudding was banned.) One historian has perceptively noted that the holiday had been redefined—reports on balls, church services, Santa Claus, and family merriment were reported in newspapers under the heading "Christmas," and the older sort of disorder now featured in the "Police" columns.[20]

Meanwhile across the Atlantic Ocean

A clergyman in Hertfordshire said in 1844: "The people here seem hardly to feel Christmas Day. I observed that they wore their working-day clothes, and a very scanty attendance at church in proportion to that on Sundays. This seems to be the case very generally throughout the country. The people have utterly lost sight of the great Christian feasts, and with them the knowledge of the mighty events they celebrated. The Popish ways may all be very bad, but at least they teach something of the grounds of our faith and salvation. The religion of the English peasant is confined to generalities." I have shown how the abolition of Christmas by the Puritans in the 1640s started this decline. After Christmas was restored, along with the monarchy, it never quite regained its popularity in the cities and among the middle class. It was felt to be a rural, drunken, and boorish celebration. The leadership of the Anglican Church came to regard Christmas in much the same way. Particularly harmful was the prohibition of carol singing in church and a neglect of ceremony. The Church leadership in the eighteenth century was disproportionately rationalist and Deist in temperament, opposed to popular culture and sentiment. This spurred the growth of the Methodist movement, which preserved Christmas carols—but again this was largely a lower-class phenomenon. Changes in agriculture and a flood of peasants from the country to the city led to a breakdown of the traditional class relationships and the obligations of country hospitality that had been identified with Christmas. New money was buying up estates without understanding of customary obligations. The rise of a new attitude, dictated by the Industrial Revolution, toward time and leisure reduced the number of statutory holidays to fewer than a handful. There was no time or inclination for merriment among a population who were much more mobile and had severed connections with the old seasonal customs of their native heath. It would be going too far to say that Christmas was dying, but for many English people it had lost much of its zest and purpose.

Perhaps surprisingly, one of the first to come to the aid of the belea-guered festivity was an American. Washington Irving was less famous in England for his stories of St. Nicholas among the colonial Dutch and more famous for two collections of essays, one of which, *The Sketchbook of Geoffrey Crayon, Gent.,* contained a number of pieces on Christmas at the home of an old-fashioned English country gentleman. His tales of the

Yule log, the mistletoe, the games, meaty feasting complete with boar's head, wassail bowl, village band, ghost stories round the fire, openhanded feudal hospitality, and deferential tenantry conjured up images of an ideal Christmas of the Elizabethan sort and captured the imagination of readers in Georgian England. This idealization of a past appealed to English people's love of conviviality but also assuaged their fears of class hostility. Irving's country Christmas depicted social harmony: folk of different social groups knew their separate places but could still meet together over a wassail bowl. This sort of Christmas, everyone agreed, was almost dead (if it had ever really existed), but Irving and writers like him touched a chord that many responded to. This was, after all, the time of the Romantic movement and the Gothic revival in England, with their stress on medievalism, drama, emotion, mystery, memory, and sentimentality.

This yearning for the colors of the past had echoes in the Church of England, where the Oxford Movement, also known as the Tractarians, campaigned to restore High Church notions inside Anglicanism and promote an enhanced appreciation of ritual, decoration, and the festive year. John Keble's 1827 book of poems *The Christian Year* celebrated the whole Christian calendar, including Christmas. His work was enormously popular, appearing in 158 editions and selling hundreds of thousands of copies in the next few decades. A particular concern of the Tractarians was the enrichment of the Prayer Book forms of service and a proper observance of the seasons and festivals of the church calendar. The parishes where Tractarians were effective saw the celebration of midnight Eucharist on Christmas Eve and decorations with boughs, banners, flowers, Christmas trees, and Nativity scenes. These examples of attention paid to Christmas services were imitated by other Anglican churches that were not part of the Oxford Movement and by other Protestant denominations in Britain.

Tied in with this movement was the work of a number of collectors of English carols, including William Sandys, Sir John Stainer, and John Mason Neale. The Reformation had put a halt to the religious use of carols in some Protestant countries, including England and Scotland, which had replaced most church singing with the chanting of metrical psalms. (Carols remained popular in Protestant Germany, where Martin Luther himself wrote "Von Himmel Hoch" and translated other Christmas songs from Latin.) Though carols were banned from the church, they continued to be sung at home and by door-to-door carolers on begging visits during the Christmas season, but even this was frowned on in the seventeenth century, when the Puritan revolution took over England in the 1640s. Though the Restoration ended most Puritan anti-Christmas innovations, the Church of England remained opposed to the use of carols in worship. From 1660 to the nineteenth century, the only carols to receive official approval were Nahum Tate's "While Shepherds Watched Their Flocks by Night" and Charles Wesley's "Hark the Herald Angels Sing." Caroling was confined to churches in the north and west of England and to Dissenting and Catholic congregations; many were prepared to declare the carol dead in the early nineteenth century.[21]

The musicologists of the nineteenth century succeeded in rescuing older carols and encouraged the writing of new songs. Sandys, an English lawyer, was an amateur musician, folklorist, and carol collector; his publications helped save important Christmas music from extinction and did much to preserve the observance of the holiday itself. In 1833 he published his *Christmas Carols, Ancient and Modern,* which included thirty-four long-ignored songs, forty contemporary carols from the west of England, and six French songs. Among the carols he helped popularize were "The First Nowell," "God Rest You Merry, Gentlemen," "Tomorrow Shall Be My Dancing Day," "I Saw Three Ships Come Sailing In," and "Joseph Was an Old Man." Sir John Stainer and John Mason Neale also succeeded in rescuing older tunes and encouraged the writing of new songs. In 1853 Neale acquired a rare edition of *Piae Cantiones*, an invaluable sixteenth-century Finnish collection of medieval songs. Thomas Helmore adapted the carol melodies, and Neale either paraphrased the lyrics into English or wrote entirely new ones. Their work, published in *Carols for Christmas-tide* in 1853, gave us such carols as "Good King Wenceslas," "Good Christian Men Rejoice," "O Come, O Come, Emmanuel," "Our Master Hath a Garden," and "Of the Father's Love Begotten," based on a Latin hymn of the fourth century.[22] Another important contributor to the revival of carols was Catherine Winkworth, who specialized in translating German songs, including "All My Heart This Night Rejoices," "From Heaven Above to Earth I Come" (by Luther), and "O Morning Star, How Fair and Bright." In addition to collections of antique carols new songs began to appear, with American composers leading the way, for example Philip Brooks ("O Little Town of Bethlehem") and Edmund Hamilton Sears ("It Came Upon the Midnight Clear"). The Church of England eventually renewed its interest in carols, particularly after Bishop Edward Benson invented in Truro Cathedral in 1878 the form of service called Lessons and Carols, which combined scripture reading with songs.[23]

As in America, literary men helped revive interest in Christmas, and two powerful pieces of writing appeared in 1843 that added a deep moral dimension to the festival in England. The first was Thomas Hood's "Song of the Shirt," which appeared in the Christmas edition of *Punch*. It begins "With fingers weary and worn, / With eyelids heavy and red, / A woman sat, in unwomanly rags, / Plying her needle and thread / — Stitch! stitch! stitch! / In poverty, hunger, and dirt, / And still with a voice of dolorous pitch / She sang the 'Song of the Shirt'." This was a impassioned attack on the sweated labor that produced goods for the upper classes but brought only toil, anguish, and poverty for the worker. The poem was an instant success: it was reprinted many times, sung in the streets, and memorized by schoolchildren, and it aroused indignation in pulpits and editorials over the plight of the poor.[24]

Three days after Hood's poem appeared, Charles Dickens published *A Christmas Carol in Prose, Being a Ghost Story of Christmas,* a publishing sensation that helped turn Victorian Christmas into a crusade against selfishness and greed. In this book and his other seasonal stories he revived the lost medieval link between worship and feasting, the Nativity and Yule, and emphasized the holiday as a time of personal and social reconciliation.

The story of the moral regeneration of financier Ebenezer Scrooge is at the heart of *A Christmas Carol.* Scrooge is visited by a quartet of spirits who confront him with a series of Christmas scenes that make clear his poverty of spirit, the wretchedness of the poor in the great metropolis, and the blessings the holiday confers on those whose hearts are open to it. In the end he is a convert to generosity and forgiveness and an enthusiast for the celebration of Christmas. *A Christmas Carol* proved immensely popular, though literary pirates made more money from it than Dickens, until he hit on the idea of reading tours. His genius was to join the older English idea of Christmas—seen particularly in the Ghosts of Christmas Past and Present: the midwinter jollity and community togetherness—to a number of important additions. The first was the notion of Christmas as the feast of family togetherness, shown in the home of the Cratchits, and forgiveness— Scrooge and his estranged nephew. Second, Dickens accelerated the moral impact by reviving Christmas's connection to charity, especially to the deserving poor, and to religion. Critics who have not looked too carefully at *A Christmas Carol* have claimed that it ignores Christianity, but the book is full of religious sentiment. It does not deal with the Nativity, but it emphasizes other theological points. The historian Geoffrey Rowell has pointed out:

There is no doubt that *A Christmas Carol* is first and foremost a story concerned with the Christian gospel of liberation by the grace of God, and with incarnational religion which refuses to drive a wedge between the world of spirit and the world of matter. Both the Christmas dinners and the Christmas dinner-carriers are blessed; the cornucopia of Christmas food and feasting reflects both the goodness of creation and the joy of heaven. It is a significant sign of a shift in theological emphasis in the nineteenth century from a stress on the Atonement to a stress on the Incarnation, a stress which found outward and visible form in the sacramentalism of the Oxford Movement, the development of richer and more symbolic forms of worship, the building of neo-Gothic churches, and the revival and increasing centrality of the keeping of Christmas itself as a Christian festival.[25]

Thus Dickens reunited the English Christmas with Christianity, overcoming a split the Puritans had succeeded in making two hundred years before.

The resurrection of Christmas also owes much to the example of Queen Victoria and the British royal family as celebrators of a family-centered (as opposed to a traditionally riotous) Christmas. The German background of her husband, Prince Albert, contributed greatly: his importation of the Christmas tree, their adoption of turkey as the seasonal meal, and their emphasis on domestic togetherness proved an enormously attractive model for middle-class folk who now sought to emulate their monarch. After their marriage in 1840 Albert was Victoria's chief adviser and firm supporter. Though never popular with the English people while he was alive, his importing of German attitudes to Christmas did much to lend royal sanction to the holiday in Victorian England. The middle class were quick to adopt novelties such as the Christmas tree and to celebrate the season as they imagined the royal family did. The *London News* in 1848 ran an illustration of the royal tree with the following description:

The tree employed for this festive purpose is a young fir about eight feet high, and has six tiers of branches. On each tier, or branch, are arranged a dozen wax tapers. Pendent from the branches are elegant trays, baskets, bonbonnières, and other receptacles for sweetmeats, of the most varied and expensive kind; and of all forms, colours, and degrees of beauty. Fancy cakes, gilt gingerbread and eggs filled with sweetmeats, are also suspended by variously-coloured ribbons from the branches. The tree, which stands upon a table covered with white damask, is supported at the root by piles of sweets of a larger kind, and by toys and dolls of all descriptions, suited to the youthful fancy, and to the several ages of the interesting scions of Royalty for whose gratification they are displayed. The name of each recipient is affixed to the doll, bonbon, or other present intended for it, so that no difference of opinion in the choice of dainties may arise to disturb the equanimity of the illustrious juveniles. On the summit of the tree stands the small figure of an angel, with out-stretched wings, holding in each hand a wreath.

(This illustration did good service in an American context as well—the regalia that identified the tree-gazing family as royal and Prince Albert's moustache were removed from the picture when it was published in the United States two years later.)[26] The magazine noted that Prince Albert and Victoria each had a personal tree decorated and hung with presents from the other. In a letter sent to his father, Prince Albert described the effect of the tree on his own family: "This is the dear Christmas Eve, on which I have so often listened with impatience for your step, which was to usher us into the present-room. Today I have two children of my own to give presents to, who, they know not why, are full of happy wonder at the German Christmas-tree and its radiant candles." Albert helped the custom spread by sending trees to military barracks, schools, and hospitals, and the example set in Windsor Castle accelerated the trend for seasonal trees in America.

England, having revived its Christmas, made several notable additions to its celebration. Christmas cards were invented in London by Henry Cole in 1843 and spread to the United States in the early 1850s before going global by the end of the century. Christmas crackers, those explosive tubes filled with paper hats or humorous mottoes, were the brainchild of confectioner Tom Smith in 1847. Christmas pantomime grew out of eighteenth-century commedia dell'arte and by the mid-nineteenth century was an indispensable entertainment for the family during the holiday season, especially on Boxing Day.

But if we seek a truly worldwide Christmas innovation we must turn back to the United States and its national Gift-Bringer, Santa Claus. The notion of a kindly, elderly male figure clad in fur making his way over the snows carrying gifts on December 24 for good little boys and girls proved irresistible to much of Europe, even though many countries already had their own magic figures doing the job of Christmas delivery. The problem was that most of these characters were now a bad fit in the family-centered holiday that Christmas was becoming, as they were too medieval, too frightening, too bestial for the gentler methods of child-rearing. The world no longer needed Perchta the Disemboweler, who had frightened generations of central European children with the possibility of having their bellies ripped open; the whip-cracking Père Fouettard of France; the demonic Austrian child-stealer Krampus; Gryla, the cannibal giant of Iceland; or the brutal goat figures of Scandinavia, like Joulopukki. One by one they yielded to a milder Santa imitator—Père Noël, *der Weihnachtsmann*, Bobbo Natale, Samiclaus, or Father Christmas. They might eschew reindeer in favor of walking or riding horses or donkeys, and they might keep their old names even as they changed shape, but in all cases they were now hooded grandfathers looking to bestow gifts rather than rain blows on children who had forgotten their catechisms. These benevolent Gift-Bringers also spelled the end of the millennium-old custom of European children going on their door-to-door quests during the Christmas season demanding treats and threatening curses if they were not forthcoming: now a magical figure brought good things to them under a tree[27]—one more way the holiday was moved from the streets into the parlor.

Who could oppose these changes in the celebration of Christmas or stand against its revival in churches? Concerned parents, clergymen, educators, and revolutionaries, for a start. All of these people saw things in Christmas that threatened the child, the family, the soul, or society; though the celebration of the holiday increased during the course of the nineteenth century, many were willing to mount a rearguard action against it.

The stoutest dissidents were the numerous religious denominations in North America who refused to countenance marking the Nativity of Jesus in their churches. For many of these sects, the fact that Christmas celebrations had been a hallmark of the Episcopal Church, a product of the British Crown, made the holiday seem downright unpatriotic in the days following the American Revolution. Calvinist Presbyterians linked Christmas observances to Roman Catholic superstition, rejecting "the corruptions of popery and of her ape, prelacy." The Society of Friends (Quakers) rejected any formal worship, accepting only those utterances moved directly by the Holy Spirit, and viewed any regular religious holidays as mere human inventions. In 1846, a generation after the beginning of the Santa Claus phenomenon, a Pennsylvania Quaker periodical comprehensively set its face against the celebration of Christmas:

> That particular period of time, especially, called Christmas, viewed as a Religious festival, has, we fully believe tended more to open licentiousness of manners, than to the increase of sound morality and religion. The mummery which takes place in some of the churches, so called, at this season, under the ministration of a class of hireling teachers, and the childish and superficial ideas which are propagated through this corrupt and interested medium, concerning the nature and mode of Christian redemption, are wonderfully calculated to enlarge the sphere of stupidity, and to increase the shades of moral darkness over the minds of mankind. ... We are therefore very desirous that none of our members, while they indulge in innocent acts of conviviality, may give their countenance, in any way, to these anniversary institutions as having any real connection with true piety and religion.[28]

These arguments were echoed by Congregationalists, Baptists, Methodists, Anabaptists, and other Protestant sectarians who revived many of the arguments developed by Puritans during the 1640s: there was no historical backing for the December 25 date; manmade festivals were idolatry; and seasonal merriment was debauchery. In the opinion of a Primitive Baptist of Kentucky: "How groundless and puerile appears the customs [sic] of Romish and English, as well as other communions, in holding sacred the twenty-fifth day of December as the day of Christ's nativity, and adorning their houses of worship with flowers and evergreens as part of their religious devotion on that day. Fallen humanity is prone to worship of 'days and months and years and times' and God has, no doubt, purposely hid the exact time of His Son's advent into the world. Let us worship God alone and esteem every day as a gift from the Lord." To these was added nativist bigotry: because Christmas was popular with the waves of immigrants flooding into the United States in the first half of the nineteenth century—the Irish and Germans in particular—it had to be opposed out of feelings of true Americanism.[29]

As the nineteenth century progressed, Christianity seemed to be taking a greater hold on the American people. These were the days of the Great Revival, which spawned a new vitality in existing denominations and contributed to the creation of novel American-centered sects such as Christian Science, the Seventh-day Adventist Church, the United Society of Believers in Christ's Second Appearing (Shakers), and the Church of Jesus Christ of Latter-day Saints (Mormons). Numberless were the preachers, lecturers, circuit riders, and missionaries combing the continent for converts both in the growing cities and the expanding frontier, and after the 1820s came thousands of volunteers in the Sunday School movement. These men and women, working in the many Protestant sects and in the nondenominational Sunday School Union, sought to reach children with the message of Jesus. As this movement grew, its superintendents and teachers had to confront the problem of Christmas; this became a weighty problem indeed. Churches with a traditional aversion to celebrating the Nativity would naturally want to make no particular mention of the incident during December lessons or, as in the case of *The Sabbath School Visiter* [sic], explain to children why it was not to be made the subject of a festival. "The particular reason why this day was selected seems to have been, that the heathen, among whom the Christians lived, observed it as the birthday of the sun; and the Christians then living, four or five hundred years after Christ, thought it would be well to observe it as the birthday of Christ and so, gradually a heathenish superstition was changed into a Christian festival, by the weakness and folly of blinded Christians. I do not mean that they were true Christians, but only that they were so called, because born in a Christian land."[30] Yet, in the end, Christmas proved irresistible to most Protestants. By midcentury the holiday had largely cast off its associations with male rowdiness and become identified with charity, family togetherness, reunion, and the importance of parental love for children—all of which found religious echoes in the story of the Holy Family and the events at Bethlehem. Moreover, Christmas now had Santa Claus, a figure of tremendous appeal who could attract children (and thus their parents) to Christian worship. Churches, particularly those involved in missions to the urban poor, began to compete with each other in the mounting of December pageants and ceremonies of gift-giving. The Pilgrim Unitarian Church in San Francisco hired a public hall and featured songs, recitations and tableaux, a giant Christmas tree hung with lights and presents, artificial snow falling from the ceiling, and a Santa driven into the room in a sleigh drawn by two real deer. Even on the sparsely settled prairie, Christmas productions were deemed indispensable. In December 1886 churchgoers in Sioux Falls, South Dakota, could choose from the Congregationalists' "Santa Clausville," the Baptists' literary musical entertainment and supper, the Presbyterians' "Gathering of the Nations to Meet Santa Claus," or the Methodist-Episcopal "Christmas House" with Santa.[31] The latter, a playlet by Edward Eggleton, was a popular one in churches and is noteworthy for the character of Santa Claus condemning "Christmas bummers"—children who only made an appearance in Sunday School at Christmas and who often went from one church to another to gather yet more loot in the spirit of Halloween.[32] For a while, there were still holdouts against Christmas in church settings—as late as 1875 the *Evangelical Repository and United Presbyterian Worker* could call Christmas "one of the contrivances whereby Popery holds them fast in her grasp" and rail against Santa Claus and the Christmas tree. The practice of decorating the church with evergreens, it said, was derived from "the ancient Druids, whose gloomy and barbarous rites were regarded with horror by even the heathen Romans." Yet within three years that same periodical was carrying stories of "the glory" of Christmas trees in churches and distributions of gifts to Sunday School attendees.[33] The conclusion of the historian responsible for the definitive assessment of the holiday in nineteenth-century American Sunday Schools is plain: "Christmas returned to Protestant church life because the rank and file of the membership wanted it. It made its way against official opposition in many denominations until there were so many local groups celebrating December twenty-fifth as the birthday of Jesus that opposition was futile and indifference impossible."[34]

In Britain the Victorian Age (1837–1901) was also a period of intense religiosity, an age that took faith very seriously and often in a spirit of "combativeness, aggression and militancy." Opposition to Christmas on religious grounds was waged in nineteenth-century England, as it had been in America, by the more morally rigorous sorts of denominations, the sort who saw in Christmas a festival symbolic of "Catholic idolatry, Anglican hegemony, plebeian revelry and aristocratic vice."[35] Raised in the conservative sect the Plymouth Brethren, the Victorian poet Sir Edmund Gosse remembered the horror with which his father regarded Christmas:

> On the subject of all feasts of the Church he held views of an almost grotesque peculiarity. He looked upon each of them as nugatory and worthless, but the keeping of Christmas appeared to him by far the most hateful, and nothing less than an act of idolatry. "The very word is Popish," he used to exclaim, "Christ's Mass!" pursing up his lips with the gesture of one who tastes

assafoetida by accident. Then he would adduce the antiquity of the so-called feast, adapted from horrible heathen rites, and itself a soiled relic of the abominable Yule-Tide. He would denounce the horrors of Christmas until it almost made me blush to look at a holly-berry.

On Christmas Day of this year 1857 our villa saw a very unusual sight. My Father had given strictest charge that no difference whatever was to be made in our meals on that day; the dinner was to be neither more copious than usual nor less so. He was obeyed, but the servants, secretly rebellious, made a small plum-pudding for themselves. (I discovered afterwards, with pain, that Miss Marks received a slice of it in her boudoir.) Early in the afternoon, the maids,—of whom we were now advanced to keeping two,—kindly remarked that "the poor dear child ought to have a bit, anyhow," and wheedled me into the kitchen, where I ate a slice of plum-pudding. Shortly I began to feel that pain inside which in my frail state was inevitable, and my conscience smote me violently. At length I could bear my spiritual anguish no longer, and bursting into the study I called out: "Oh! Papa, Papa, I have eaten of flesh offered to idols!" It took some time, between my sobs, to explain what had happened. Then my Father sternly said: "Where is the accursed thing?" I explained that as much as was left of it was still on the kitchen table. He took me by the hand, and ran with me into the midst of the startled servants, seized what remained of the pudding, and with the plate in one hand and me still tight in the other, ran until we reached the dust-heap, when he flung the idolatrous confectionery on to the middle of the ashes, and then raked it deep down into the mass. The suddenness, the violence, the velocity of this extraordinary act made an impression on my memory which nothing will ever efface.[36]

Even inside the established Church of England, where Christmas had long been celebrated with enthusiasm and pomp, there were those who resisted what they felt were innovations in seasonal worship. These were antiritualists who felt themselves to be defending their church from creeping "popish" influences. Anglo-Catholicism had been a growing presence in the Anglican Church since the days of the Tractarian Movement; its supporters were committed to doctrines such as the Real Presence in Communion, and many were more than a little hostile to the

Protestant Reformation itself. Antiritualists of the Victorian period wished to block any suggestion that the English Church had taken a wrong turn in the sixteenth century and were quick to spy out anything that smelled of a return to Rome.[37] Such laymen raised objections to overelaborate dress worn by priests ("yellow beaded vestments covering the minister from head to foot"), the use of rites not sanctioned in the Book of Common Prayer, undue veneration of the Virgin Mary, and excessive church decoration. Since Anglo-Catholics had been among those reviving the celebration of Christmas inside the Anglican Church, it is not surprising that zealous proponents of plain worship should find some Yuletide observances and material objectionable. A vicar in Leeds made a young girl remove crosses from some Christmas decorations she had made for the church because other parishioners objected to such "an obnoxious symbol." In 1870, S. P. Andrew, an ultra-Protestant churchwarden in Manchester, organized antiritual disruptions of services and ordered that Christmas decorations erected by a ritualist priest be torn down. The clergyman was warned that "the time is fast approaching when all your foolish things shall be treated as the foolish things of fools and taken away from before the offended eyes of a wise God 'even as dung is taken away.'" The growing popularity of setting up Nativity scenes in the church during Christmas (common practice for centuries among Catholics) and the ceremony of Blessing the Crib were held to be particularly noxious. Such crèches were deemed to "feed the heretical attempt to know Christ after the flesh." Lawsuits, demonstrations, vandalism, and mob violence marked this campaign, and in one church a priest was moved to issue brass knuckle-dusters to his congregation to help them resist the antiritualist zealots of "the Protestant Truth Society."[38]

To be sure, Christmas engendered anxieties even as it became a powerful social phenomenon. An editorial in the *New York Times* spoke of the hedonic dangers that Christmas posed to a child's moral development: "'Jean Paul' says pleasure is inconsistent with happiness. He would have the child disconnect its gratification from any fixed days and seasons; and learn to believe that the current day possesses as abundant means of happiness as any day in the future. The anticipation of Christmas, with its presents and pleasures, he regards as a state of feverish discontent with the passing moment. The brilliant light with which young fancies surround the season, darkens the path leading to it and goes out as soon as the festival is ended, leaving nothing but the cold grey morning air of satiety." Educators worried about the harm that tales of Santa Claus would wreak on young people; even before the Santa craze began, an advocate of fact-based, didactic children's literature bemoaned "false stories...told merely for sport or pastime." Among his targets were tales of ghosts, centaurs, harpies, and "old Santa-claw of whom so often little children hear such foolish stories; and once in the year are encouraged to hang their stockings in the chimney at night, and when they arise in the morning, they find in them cakes, nuts, money and placed there by some of the family, which they are told old Santa claw has come down the chimney in the night and put in." Parents and church officials were concerned that children who learned the truth about Santa Claus might conclude that the religious instruction they had been given was equally false.[39] So frequent were such attacks that one humor magazine penned Santa Claus's suicide note, accompanied by a picture of the Gift-Bringer's corpse pulled on a sled by grieving reindeer and followed by a line of weeping children:

> I die because those who preach the tenderness of Christ to little children say that those parents lie sinfully who mask their own tender impulses under a gentle fable to please their little ones. Santa Claus was always the friend of good and trusting children. That they believed in him was a sign of the goodness of parents who begat them. The children who believed not in him were the children of evil parents, who never cared for the happiness of their offspring.... No discovery of Science has killed me. I was too small a lie to be worthy of the serious warfare of scientific truth. The fine weapons of those who, under the garb of religion, are always looking for wrong in others, have laid me low. Poor Santa Claus departs this earth, not because he did wrong, but because he could not survive the attacks of those who regard happiness as a sin.[40]

Christmas had now reached such a level of popularity and social power that it occupied much of the energy of the populace during December. Its duties, particularly as they fell on females, had become obligatory and onerous. This led to a theme in journalism that has continued unabated from the late nineteenth to the early twenty-first century: Christmas as dysfunctional and in need of serious reform. Perhaps the most famous of the Christmas critics of the period was the Irish playwright George Bernard Shaw:

Like all intelligent people, I greatly dislike Christmas. It revolts me to see a whole nation refrain from music for weeks together in order that every man may rifle his neighbour's pockets under cover of a ghastly general pretence of festivity. It is really an atrocious institution, this Christmas. We must be gluttonous because it is Christmas. We must be drunken because it is Christmas. We must be insincerely generous; we must buy things that nobody wants, and give them to people we don't like; we must go to absurd entertainments that make even our little children satirical; we must writhe under venal officiousness from legions of freebooters, all because it is Christmas—that is, because the mass of the population, including the all-powerful middle-class tradesman, depends on a week of licence and brigandage, waste and intemperance, to clear off its outstanding liabilities at the end of the year. As for me, I shall fly from it all tomorrow or next day to some remote spot miles from a shop, where nothing worse can befall me than a serenade from a few peasants, or some equally harmless survival of medieval mummery, shyly proffered, not advertised, moderate in its expectations, and soon over. In town there is, for the moment, nothing for me or any honest man to do.[41]

Shaw was famously contrarian (not to say crackpot) in many of his public stances, or at least he wished to seem to be, so it is difficult to know how serious he was in opposing Christmas. Nonetheless, he was followed by a crowd of others, each with a bone to pick about the holiday.

Women's magazines, for example, noted with alarm the pressures the Christmas season put on mothers and housewives—what some social historians have termed "the feminization" of Christmas. Shopping, battling crowds, planning, decorating, baking, wrapping, and coping with a lack of money all combined to make the holiday period a time of anxiety for women. For such readers the *Ladies' Home Journal* offered soothing advice: "Perhaps some careworn little mother will say, 'If we could afford it, I could give the darlings a perfect day.' It does not take much to make children happy. The mysteries and surprises which delight their souls can be achieved without the expenditure of much more than time and patience. Some of the best things money cannot buy; and those that they will recollect longest may be the fruit of mother's ingenuity."[42] On the other hand, as women became the dominant seasonal shoppers, men were increasingly portrayed as "emasculated at Christmas, stripped of their authority, publicly humiliated"—and we can see Christmas gender roles becoming entangled in the public mind with the contemporary struggle for women's legal rights and suffrage.[43]

Another common criticism of Christmas was that it made children greedy in ways that previous, unspoiled generations had not been. The weary sophistication and jaded spirit of modern children was a recurring theme in humor magazines, with tots displaying a threatening attitude in their letters to Santa Claus or criticizing their parents for supplying presents that did not match their elevated expectations. Parents, poets, journalists, philanthropists, and churches took great pains by the turn of the twentieth century to balance generosity to one's own family with commitment to Christmas charity for the underprivileged. Fund drives, street-corner collection boxes, banquets, toy distribution, and aid for warm clothing, food, and fuel over the holidays appeared in December, everywhere from the smallest hamlet to the largest metropolis. Cynical souls remarked that this was only capitalism's way of keeping the poor under control with handouts and of assuaging the middle-class conscience.[44]

Other critics focused on the dysfunctional nature of some gift-giving. For a time in the late nineteenth century it was felt necessary to purchase gifts for a very wide range of acquaintances, and thus the "gimcrack" craze was born—a range of cheap and tawdry, ultimately useless objects to satisfy this perceived obligation in the 1890s. One irritated writer noted "that Yuletide has come to be anticipated—with trepidation—is no secret. Each year this becomes more obvious. With midwinter comes the nerve-wrecking realization that before many days all good "Christians" must be prepared somehow to spend money they cannot afford, to purchase "things" the recipients do not want. The horror of appearing mean tempts the wise to become a spendthrift, and the spendthrift to become a fool."[45] By 1910 the gimcrack mania had subsided, to be replaced by the sending of Christmas cards, which, though they had been available for fifty years, now took on the job of acknowledging at the holiday season those not in one's innermost circle and allowing fewer and more expensive gifts to be purchased for one's real intimates.

Gift-giving up the social ladder was also being criticized at the turn of the century as a form of workplace blackmail. Reformers felt that expecting the poorer workers to give to their superiors was a form of corruption, and the Society for the Prevention of Useless Giving was established to shame managers into ending the practice. A similar attempt to shield workers from exploitation at Christmas was the Shop Early Campaign, whose motto was "For the sake of humanity, shop early!." By urging people to make their purchases earlier in December, the American Consumer's League hoped that the last-minute rush and unpaid overtime that was expected of clerks, delivery boys, factory workers, and postal employees would end. The League praised stores who stuck to their normal hours and published a "White List" of shops who required their workers to stay late.[46]

These campaigns did not constitute a war on Christmas. None of the participants wished to see the holiday abolished or privatized or driven underground. Rather they sought to make sure that the season was true to itself, that its deficiencies were corrected, and that it would truly be a time of peace on earth and goodwill toward humanity. This type of reformation of Christmas will provide much material for the chapters to come.

However, a chapter on the revival of Christmas in the nineteenth century would not be complete without reference to another phenomenon that would continue to manifest itself in future centuries—the desire by non-Christian, anti-Christian, and even antireligious groups to stake a claim on the holiday. These movements recognized that Christmas played a number of important social roles and was valued by most of the population; there was, therefore, the possibility that it might, with profit, be co-opted or appropriated in some way to their own values.

I have shown how reforms to Christmas behaviors were in part driven by fear of class conflict and a desire to tame customs that, despite their connection to the birth of the Prince of Peace, had become violent, confrontational, and an excuse for manifesting divisions of religion, ethnic origin, and social status. In New York, Boston, and Philadelphia the wild drinking and rioting that had marked the end-of-the-year festivities and had pitted rich against poor, black against white, and native-born against immigrant were repressed and redefined. Such actions at Christmas and the New Year were no longer viewed as tolerable traditions; they were now crimes or were sublimated as the Callithumpian bands became the socially acceptable mummers' parade. In England the boisterous country celebrations and urban noise-making provoked thoughts of an imaginary English holiday of bygone days when both rich and poor knew their places. Landowners and industrial employers made Christmas a time of class reconciliation, sponsoring events that brought workers and employers together in order to promote "a more kindly sympathy, and warmer concord amongst the various classes of the community." Licensed begging by marginal groups such as children or the elderly, which had been a staple of charity in medieval and early modern times, was now discouraged and survived only in the harmless door-to-door of children.[47]

But there were those groups, in nineteenth-century Europe, who did not care to see class conflicts smoothed over or ameliorated by top-down charity and preferred that the old way of doing things be destroyed and the workers set up as rulers. These were the myriad reformist and revolutionary groups—socialists, anarchists, utopian dreamers—that were attracting a considerable following by midcentury, and among them, perhaps surprisingly, were people who had a place in their thinking for Christmas. In France radical philosophers, including Count Henri de Saint-Simon and Auguste Comte, derived new religious practices based on a firm foundation of reason and science. Unlike many of his contemporaries, Saint-Simon did not see religion and reason as enemies; his particular Positivist religion developed into a full-blown cult, with priests, liturgies, and hymns of its own. Comte, who had served as aide to Saint-Simon, developed what he called the "Religion of Humanity," which had some short-lived success in France and Brazil, where "Temples of Humanity" were established. Both of these men, and those who followed them throughout the nineteenth century, wished to move beyond Christianity as it had been historically presented, particularly its Catholic manifestations, but were unwilling to abandon the advantages a sacred calendar presented. Consequently, festivals were an important part of their plans. Though many followers of the "Religion of Humanity" wanted nothing to do with traditional Catholic holy days, some of them were, as the years went by, moved to develop a "Positivist Christmas."[48]

There were also outright atheists in France who hoped to use the festivities of December 25 to subvert traditional ideas of religion and the Nativity of Jesus. These followers of La Pensée Libre hoped not only to secularize the French state but also to spread atheism into society and the family home. Freethinkers organized Fêtes de l'Enfance on December 25 where children, dressed in costumes of various native provinces or foreign countries, would receive gifts and sing traditional Christmas songs of their area. Also on the agenda were performances of stirring political carols specifically written to celebrate "Noëls républicains." This produced a curious mixture of family celebration and political party rally that occasionally resulted in controversy, as when writer and politician Henri Béranger declared Jesus to be an anticlerical, antimilitarist, and anticapitalist freethinker whose work on Earth, to bring justice and peace, had been brought to fruition by the revolutionaries of France. Even more provocative was the recitation of a poem titled "Le Noël de Pauvre" by Xavier Privas that warned that the moment was coming when the starving beggars would be marching with torches of hate. These socialists and atheists knew the attraction of Christmas and the sensuousness of the holiday's paraphernalia—songs, candles, Yule logs—and thought they knew how to turn them to their political causes. In the end, though, these "Noël Humaine" programs attracted little interest, even among left-wingers, and in fact caused many freethinkers to back away from anything smacking of religion and ancient superstition.[49]

In Britain a similar appropriation of Christmas was undertaken by those who sought a socialist reordering of the world: the Chartist and Owenite movements. The Chartists were political reformers who struggled for decades to garner mass support for their People's Charter, a list of demands that would have won universal manhood suffrage for Britons and an end to much parliamentary corruption. Within their ranks were many opponents of traditional Christianity, which they viewed as oppressive—among other things, the 1834 version of their Charter called for an end to the domination of religion.[50] In 1841 a group of socialists and Chartists attacked a meeting of the Society for the Propagation of the Gospel in Foreign Parts, crying, "We want more bread and less Bibles and more pigs and less parsons.... You are all robbers of the poor!"[51] Nonetheless, in the 1830s and 1840s the Chartists organized themselves in much the same way the original Methodists had, with camp meetings, hymns (suitably altered to express Chartist principles), and sermonizing. This church-like structure allowed them to circumvent the government's ban on mass demonstrations. Chartists also used the Christian church calendar, meeting at Easter or organizing their own Christmas festivities; these were rather sober affairs, with an emphasis on tea-drinking, lectures, and musical recitals. Chartist writers produced their own Christmas carols, short stories, and novels with Christmas themes. "The Labourer: A Christmas Carol," by Ernest Jones, was an 1847 poem that portrayed the barren and freezing cottage whose inhabitants can see the blazing windows of a nearby mansion where the rich are enjoying a lavish holiday meal. In despair the poor father breaks into the Hall to steal food for his starving family and is shot dead.[52] *Christmas Shadows* (1850), a novel by Cautley Newby (publisher of the Brontës and a Chartist supporter), parodied Dickens's *Christmas Carol* with the story of Cranch, an oppressor of needlewomen, who is visited by ghosts who criticize his harsh exploitation.

In the end he triples their wages and introduces benefits such as medical care.[53] For a time, some Chartist writers adopted the "Merry England" approach, which imagined a once-upon-a-time golden era of English liberties and prosperity that was now lost but could be revived. A Chartist hymnbook proclaimed: "The Charter is our aim; / We claim it as our right; / Our ancient sires enjoyed the same. / Nor feared oppression's might."[54] In such a world Christmas represented social solidarity and conviviality. The song "The People Shall Have Their Own Again" proclaimed:

> Time gone the Suffrage was possessed by every man,
> And Old England then was a happy land to see;
> It was joyful in the hall, and in the cottage small,
> And the poorest man could merry, merry be.
> Then gladsome was the sound as the Yule went round,
> Of the song and the glee at Christmas time;
> And happy as the day were our firesides gay,
> For the rich thought the mirth of the poor no crime.[55]

Owenite socialists, followers of Robert Owen, the anticlerical prophet of the cooperative movement, saw themselves as founders of a new set of economic and social relations, and many fancied that their movement could also be the foundation of a new kind of religion. The old churches, they said, were the source of the ills of the world—the competitiveness, selfishness, and private property that marred life in the nineteenth century. Their new cult would be loving and joyous, unburdened by the gloom of those who believed in original sin. Matilda Royle, a female republican and atheist, said approvingly of the Owenites: "they are all anti-Christian and rarely opened their mouths without saying something eminently calculated to bring Christianity into contempt." Nonetheless, even more than the Chartists, the Owenites were systematic in their appropriation of the Christian calendar, hoping to make revolutionary statements: pointedly extravagant during the season of Lenten self-denial, seeking hilarity on Good Friday, and markedly sober during the Christmas revels. Returning home from an Owenite Christmas party, a northern English member concluded that he "could not help contrasting the sobriety and civil manners of those who had participated in our "feast of reason" with the brutal language and bullying conduct of the unfortunates who were reeling from the public houses; and when I considered that those who were now so sober and courteous might, but for the circumstances of our festival, have been similarly situated to the individuals around me, the good moral results of these kinds of institutions, and the general want of them appeared to me clear and self-evident as light amid darkness."[56] The Owenite approach of remaking rather than abolishing Christmas proved popular with other nineteenth-century British freethinking and republican groups, who found it compatible with their beliefs to publish "Christmas" editions of their atheist magazines, to hold dinners and dances on December 25, to call for a semiannual business meeting on that date (in the words of the Leicester Secular Society, "thus consecrating to a good secular service a day which is popularly associated with a theological festival"), or to host a "poor people's dinner"—during which they relaxed their ban on smoking and drinking in their hall. (It must be said, though, that they had their own alternative calendar of holy days, particularly the birthday of skeptic Thomas Paine, which they called a "Festival of Reason.") Nonreligious Christmas music could also be found in their songbooks, for example this 1899 song from *Hymns of Modern Thought*, noteworthy perhaps for the innocence of an age in which the words "thrill and throb" could be adduced in praise of Christmas:

> *"A MERRY Christmas!" how the old words waken*
> *A thrill and throb for many a Christmas fled,*
> *For hopes fulfilled not, that the years have taken,*
> *Into their keeping, like the tears we shed.*
> *"A merry Christmas!" Let the happy chorus*
> *Bring a new thrill, new freedom, new delight;*
> *Past pain makes present joy but sweeter for us*
> *E'en as the dawn of morning after night.*
> *"A merry Christmas!" Be ye thankful ever*
> *For friendship that is left warm, sure and strong,*
> *For love that fills your hearts with high endeavour;*
> *Live life anew; ye do the past no wrong.*
> *"A merry Christmas!" Life has halting-places,*
> *Where ye may pause in all the busy strife*
> *To comfort those whose sorrow-stricken faces*
> *Tell their own story in the book of life.*
> *"A merry Christmas!" Peace and love be stealing*
> *O'er spirits answering to the sound of mirth*
> *And sorrow known shall bring the human feeling*
> *That sheds "good-will" and gladness o'er the earth.*[57]

As the beginning of the third Christian millennium approached, the literary classes turned their minds toward the future, and some of them mused about traditional holidays. Two fin de siècle examples provide an interesting contrast while dealing with the same question: "What will Christmas look like in the year 2000?"

> During the present bi-millennial year 2000, now so near its end, let us imagine, if we can, an American of today caught up by some miracle of translation and set down on Christmas Day among our forefathers a hundred years ago, say in the last quarter of the 19th century. Our contemporary would be astonished to discover that in America a hundred years ago Christmas was remembered.
>
> And this astonishment would certainly be a most rational feeling. To anyone previously ignorant of the real facts, no suggestion would seem more absurd on the face of it than that a society illustrating in all its forms and methods a systematic disregard of the Golden Rule, would permit any notice, much less any open celebration of Christ's birthday.
>
> One would have taken for granted that as December 25th drew near the police would be doubled and detectives in citizens' clothes stationed on every corner to arrest any who should so much as whisper that tremendous name of Jesus. For what treason so black could there be to the social state of that day as any act in honor of the mighty leveler who laid the axe at the root of all forms of inequality by declaring that no one should think anything good enough for another which he did not think good enough for himself, and who struck at the heart of the lust of mastery when He said that our strength measured our duties to others, not our claims on them, and that there was no field for greatness but in serving? It would plainly be the only reasonable supposition that if there were any who loved this revolutionary doctrine, so irreconcilable with the existing order, they must live in hiding.

This was the wondering voice of Edward Bellamy, now almost forgotten, but in the 1890s, a man of wide appeal, the advocate of a uniquely American kind of socialism that prophesied a utopian future and spawned a political movement. Bellamy achieved fame and best-selling status with his science fiction novel *Looking Backward 2000–1887*, the story of a young man of the 1880s who awakes in the twenty-first century to discover the wonderful changes wrought to his country by the abolition of capitalism and the adoption of a cooperative commonwealth called "Nationalism." Poverty had been done away with; crime was now only a medical issue; labor was shared and light. In January 1895 the *Ladies' Home Journal* published the article excerpted above, "Christmas in the Year 2000," in which Bellamy takes a twenty-first-century reader into the past and makes the point that the trouble with Christmas in the 1890s was that no one took its true religious dimension seriously: by concentrating on the supernatural events at Bethlehem, the social message of Jesus was missed. The poor were allowed to starve though the population professed Christianity; competition and avarice had erased the real meaning of Christmas. "In a society such as that of the 19th century," says Bellamy's futuristic interlocutor, "based upon inequalities and existing for the benefit of the few at the cost of the many, it was, of course, out of the question to celebrate Christmas in the way we do [in 2000], as the world's great emancipation day and feast of all the liberties."[58]

Bellamy's concern about poverty and debased social conditions in the late-nineteenth-century United States was echoed in another futuristic look at the holidays. On December 23, 1900, the *Chicago Sunday Tribune* published "Christmas Day: A Hundred Years Hence." Whereas Bellamy's Americans of the twenty-first century cherished Christmas, *Tribune* readers were told a different story about life in the generations to come: "Christmas day in the year 2000 dawned bright and clear over Chicago, only that [*sic*] comparatively few persons were interested in it at that early stage. Santa Claus and St. Nicholas had been myths for 75 years, and the ravages of the 25 years before had stripped the north woods of their evergreens. The reindeer was extinct and the furry robes once accredited to those guardian genii of Christmas were to be found only in museums of natural history." Why had Christmas become extinct? Partly because it had been a time of tension and dysfunction:

> Grandfathers and grandmothers could recall the time when Christmas was something else than it was at this end of the twentieth century. Some of them, indeed, were old enough to remember how they had searched the downtown shops of the city and crowded and fought and jammed through heavy storm doors to the counters, where hundreds of others scrambled for goods hauled down by weary clerks.... Disaffection had arisen with its customs in the

early '20s. As the nineteenth century had progressed in its utilitari-
anism the spirit of Christmas became lost. It came to be a season
for trampling down a thousand fellow-beings in order to give the
trophies of the fight to a dozen. Then, as means of communication
grew, man's circle of acquaintance was enlarged, until the custom
of gift giving became so colossal in dimensions that reform began.

This reform was insidious in the beginning. It was at first an
ethical protest against the juvenile fiction of Santa Claus, Kris
Kringle, and St. Nicholas. Just as insidiously the lovers of the forests
had protested against the destruction of the evergreens. These were
the straws indicating the storm of Christmas reform methods.
Society, which long before had ceased to give wedding presents,
took up the protest. It became vulgar to give presents to acquaintances; then only the children in the family were remembered, and
finally, when mechanical toys became so intricate and so nicely
adjusted that machinists had to be employed for weeks after
Christmas to keep them going, even the children were forced to
drop the holiday expectations.

Christmas had also been consigned to the scrap heap because that was
where all religion had gone—"church creeds were as dead as was Santa
Claus." The twenty-first century was an age of science—underground
trains moved by compressed air, cars on rubber-rimmed wheels, electric
lawn mowers, preventive detention for criminals and civic power utilities;
the only gospel that needed to be preached was the fellowship of man.
Christmas lingered only in the memories of the very old and in the rusting
toys of the Chicago Museum of Christmas Antiquities.[59]

III

The Tyrants

In which dictators learn that Christmas is too big to be ignored

IN AUGUST 1914, much of the planet fell into the greatest conflict that had ever taken place between humans, a conflict so awful that it was known almost at once as the Great War or the World War. Six multicontinental empires battled against each other for over four years, and after an armistice was finally declared and peace treaties were signed, nothing was ever the same again. Trenches full of corpses, the extinction of old nations and the rise of new, ethnic cleansing, hideous developments in weaponry, and a search for meaning among the millions of disillusioned veterans produced not "a world fit for heroes" or "a world safe for democracy" but another age of turmoil and revolution. One of the dominant ideas of that era was the notion of a totalitarian government, one that envisioned, in the words of Benito Mussolini, "everything in the State, nothing outside the State, nothing against the State." This idea thrilled and inspired thousands of would-be revolutionaries of all sorts around the globe, in Munich beer halls, in Mexican prisons, in St. Petersburg worker's committees, and in student discussion groups in Shanghai. The task of creating an all-powerful state that was beyond and above party or class or nation, that could sweep away the old corruption and create new humans who were happy, productive, and united with their fellows, consumed the lives of men like Vladimir Lenin, Adolf Hitler, and Mao Tse-tung, who succeeded in building their new societies, as well as countless failed and forgotten revolutionaries who died on the barricades, in interrogation cells, or in perpetual exile.

The leaders of such totalitarian governments—Lenin, and then Joseph Stalin, in the Soviet Union; Hitler in the German Third Reich; Mussolini in fascist Italy—all faced the challenge of dealing with religion. How could a state govern in a total way if the people owed allegiance to a higher supernatural power, not to mention the deity's earthly cadre of popes, patriarchs, bishops, lamas, imams, mullahs, archimandrites, and abbots? Inevitably, through co-option, coercion, or downright obliteration, the state would have to come to terms with Christmas.

The first successful totalitarianism of the twentieth century was the result of the triumph of the Bolshevik wing of the Russian Communist Party. Led by Vladimir Lenin and Leon Trotsky, the Bolsheviks injected themselves in late 1917 into a Russian revolution that had already overthrown the Romanov tsars and instituted a fledging democracy. Rejecting the results of an election that had not favored them, the Bolsheviks dissolved Parliament at the point of a gun and won power after a four-year civil war. Establishing themselves as the only party in a new Union of Soviet Socialist Republics, the triumphant Communists set out to create a new state and a new sort of human: "socialist man." There was never any question whether this state would take a favorable view of religion. Karl Marx, after all, had termed religion the "opium of the people," a metaphor Lenin echoed: "Marxism has always regarded all modern religions and churches, and each and every religious organisation, as instruments of bourgeois reaction that serve to defend exploitation and to befuddle the working class." On December 25, 1919, Lenin issued the following order: "To put up with 'Nikola' [a religious holiday commemorating the relics of St. Nicholas] would be stupid—the entire Cheka [secret police] must be on the alert to see to it that those who do not show up for work because of 'Nikola' are shot."[1] In the totalitarian USSR, religion would not be allowed to be a "private matter" but would be attacked, degraded, and plowed under in anticipation of the gradual acceptance of atheism by the population. In the early 1920s the Soviet state launched concerted attacks on the Russian Orthodox Church, the nation's biggest faith community, which had deep roots in Russia and was known for its subservience to the tsars. Thousands of priests and monks were murdered; tens of thousands more were condemned to the massive network of slave labor camps that came to be known as the Gulag Archipelago; churches were stripped of their valuables; cathedrals and monasteries were bulldozed or turned into potato warehouses or museums—"The Museum of the History of Religion and Atheism" was set up inside what had been St. Petersburg's Kazan Cathedral. (Similar treatment was meted out to minority Christian groups and to mosques in the Muslim Soviet republics of central Asia.) Of this campaign Lenin said, "The bigger the number of reactionary clergy and reactionary bourgeois we manage to shoot in the process, the better." Lenin was confident that Bolshevism would triumph over religion and prophesied that soon electricity would take the place of God. "Let the peasant pray to electricity," he said, "he is going to feel the power of the central authorities more than that of heaven."[2]

It was one thing to eviscerate the clergy and shut down most of the houses of worship (leaving only the shell of the Orthodox Church with a puppet patriarch); it was something far more challenging to convert a stubborn people with intense spiritual traditions to a new dialectical materialist way of thinking. Consequently, much thought in Communist Party circles was given to how best to root out the daily culture and practice of religion and replace it with atheism. At first the job was in the hands of enthusiastic locals, whose sporadic violence and clumsy public confrontations with believers often backfired, bringing more credit to the side of the religious.[3] Gradually these were discouraged, and the job of eradicating religion was trusted to organized party efforts, often led by the Komsomol, the Communist youth movement.

On Orthodox Christmas Eve, January 6, 1923, activists launched the "Komsomol Christmas."[4] In the new capital city, Moscow, and across the Soviet Union, demonstrators held a series of parades with provocative and often obscene floats designed to denigrate religion. Clowns capered and sang the "Internationale," a figure of God embraced a naked woman, Christmas trees were topped with red stars, staged trials judged Christianity, and mock priests and rabbis intoned lewd parodies of religious services. In a "Carnival of the Gods," Christianity was linked to paganism, and the Moscow parade ended with images of Buddha, Christ, Mohammed, and Osiris all being burned in a bonfire. Komsomol youth went from house to house singing an adapted version of the Christmas Troparion hymn of the Orthodox Church. Here is a verse from the original hymn:

> *Your Nativity, O Christ our God,*
> *Has shone to the world the Light of wisdom!*
> *For by it, those who worshipped the stars,*
> *Were taught by a Star to adore You,*
> *The Sun of Righteousness,*
> *And to know You, the Orient from on High.*
> *O Lord, glory to You!*

This verse became:

> *Thy Komsomol Christmas*
> *Restoring to the world the light of reason*

Serving the workers revolution
Blooming under the five pointed star
We greet thee, sun of the Commune
We see thee on the heights of the future Russian
Komsomol, glory to thee![5]

Activists confronted believers emerging from church services, taunting them. In Odessa demonstrators burnt effigies of Moses and Jehovah in the main square. In Pskov an orchestra was enlisted to entertain while militants buried an effigy of "Counter-Revolution" and immolated the old gods. Antireligious plays such as *The Liberation of Truth* were staged, as were parodies of Orthodox rites where readings from scientific literature replaced the scriptures. In the countryside this sort of behavior often ended in spontaneous violence as offended believers confronted zealous atheist youth. Despite misgivings that these demonstrations were counterproductive, a few months later a Komsomol Easter was organized with more antireligious speeches, charades, and plays with titles like *The Political Trial of the Bible*. In Leningrad, Young Pioneers sang "materialist" songs and displayed slogans such as "The Smoke of the Factory is better than the Smoke of Incense." Over the next few years a series of parallel antifestivals were devised, including Electric Day to replace Elijah Day, Forest Day to replace Trinity Sunday, Harvest Day to replace the Feast of the Intercession, and the Day of Industry to replace the Feast of the Transfiguration. It was felt that as the people were having religion taken away from them, they should be given something healthy in return. Such celebrations would not only displace the old religious meanings but also provide workers with fun and enlightenment.[6] The celebration of traditional saints' days and Christmas was made more difficult by making them ordinary work days and limiting the sale of foods normally associated with these festivities.

The Komsomol Christmas efforts, however, were not deemed a success by the Communist Party leadership, who had received numerous reports of violence, vandalism of churches and cemeteries, and drunkenness on the part of the antireligious youth. Stalin urged that "hooliganish escapades under the guise of so-called anti-religious propaganda—all this should be cast off and liquidated immediately." There were other notable failures at the local level. Like the American educators of the 1820s who saw harm in telling young people the stories of imaginary creatures like centaurs and Santa Claus, early Soviet educational theory took a dim view of fantasy, claiming that fairy tales, toys, and songs were of no use to "children of proletarians." At one school play, members of the Young Pioneers (one of the age groups of the Komsomol), staged a show in which they expelled fictional characters as "non-Soviet elements." They explained that the old stories of princes and princesses glorified oppressors of the poor and that fairy tales were myths to fool children. Cinderella was put on trial for betraying the working class, and Grandfather Frost (Ded Moroz, the Russian Christmas Gift-Bringer) was accused of climbing down chimneys as a spy. The condemned storybook figures were led away to punishment, but the distraught children protested: "Bring them back! Bring them back! Don't shoot them!"[7] During subsequent years the Komsomol Christmas and Easter campaigns were kept on a shorter leash, and the main work of cultivating atheism was turned over to a new group.

In 1924 the Central Committee of the Communist Party set up an "Antireligious Commission." Out of this would emerge a newspaper of atheist propaganda titled *Bezbozhnik* (The Godless), and from the supporters of this effort came the All-Union League of the Godless, better known by the name it adopted in 1929, the League of the Militant Godless. The League ran a publishing empire of journals and newspapers, sponsored lectures, set up museums of atheism, and employed field agents to spur on the drive to eliminate religion from the lives of the Soviet people. (A parallel organization aimed at eradicating Islam from the Soviet Union's central Asian republics was called the Union of the Tatar Godless.) They continued the Komsomol's attack on Christmas, hoping that its message of science and technology would win over believers in a way the teenage bigotry of the Young Pioneers had not. Sponsored by the League, anti-Christmas carols were written and collected in *And Now We Are Building Socialism*, an anti-Christmas album for schools.[8] A striking series of posters and magazine covers decried religion and its encouragement of idleness and drunkenness. "Down With Religious Holidays!" was the title of a poster showing two brutish peasants reeling home drunk after celebrating Christmas or Easter; in the background are images of an abused wife, street fights, and industrial accidents. In 1927 a war scare revived the attack on Christmas, producing articles with titles like "The Christmas Holiday and the Defense of the U.S.S.R." How could good patriots waste time and energy on a decadent festival when the Western enemies of the nation were gathering strength for an attack? The next year, party directives banned the use of the fir tree as a decoration; and Grandfather Frost was unmasked "as an ally of the priest and kulak."[9] In order to discourage the cutting of Christmas trees, Young Pioneers were taught to think of good forestry techniques and to sing:

> *Don't chop down trees without need,*
> *Show respect for the woods.*
> *Instead of showing your greed*
> *Plant a sapling, and do some good.*[10]

In 1931 the League reported, from its spies observing the churches that remained open, that fewer people were celebrating Christmas openly, but activists still complained about the sale of ornaments and festive food.[11]

By the mid-1930s Stalin was in complete control of the Soviet Union, having outmaneuvered his rivals, including Leon Trotsky, in the aftermath of Lenin's death. Shrewd and paranoid, he remained in power by keeping any potential enemies in a state of fear, switching intraparty alliances ruthlessly, and abandoning old ideologies when they became inconvenient. So it was with the war on religion. In the midst of show trials and mass arrests of party officials and military officers in 1935, Stalin felt the need for greater popular support; the result was a slackening of attacks on believers and a curb placed on the Militant Atheists, whose magazine *Godless* was shut down. Voices in the Party had urged the creation of some sort of midwinter festivity, especially for the sake of children—clearly a sort of substitute for the Christian Christmas. New Year's Day was the obvious solution, but there were misgivings about it as a festivity. In the early 1930s it had been highly politicized; it was used as a time to urge workers to boost production, to praise those who had met goals, and to mock those who had fallen short. Stalin overrode those suspicions; he ordered religious repression slackened, blessed January 1 as a holiday, allowed the return of Grandfather Frost. For the first time in years, fir trees were openly on sale in the big cities. As far as the Communist Party was concerned, of course, these were New Year's trees, and an attempt was made to halt their sale after January 1 so that traditional believers could not purchase them for Orthodox Christmas on January 7. As part of the Stalinist personality cult, the dictator was portrayed in the press as the Soviet Grandfather Frost, the source of all good things. Grandfather Frost himself was kitted out in new blue robes, and before long he had two traditional helpers: Snegurochka—the "Snow Maiden"—and the New Year Boy.[12] Children's literature now featured pictures and stories of Lenin anachronistically celebrating with wee ones beside a decorated evergreen tree. Stalin's transfer of winter festivities from Christmas to New Year's Day mirrored that of the Calvinist Scots in the seventeenth century. He extracted religion from the holiday but kept the cheer and merriment and many of the accessories, including the fir tree, ornaments, gifts, greeting cards, and feasting. In significant ways New Year celebrations were more suited to the Communist state than Christmas. Christmas is about memory, cyclicality, and being rooted to important moments in the past; New Year's Day always celebrates the new and being reborn, attuned to the future; it was quite reasonable therefore that in the Soviet era it became a time to celebrate innovative science and technology.[13]

In 1939 Stalin's armies cooperated with Hitler's in the attack on Poland that began World War II, and the two dictators divided the subjugated country between them. In the areas conquered by the USSR, the Soviet version of Christmas was imposed on the Poles. The traditional "Christmas tree" was deemed to be tainted by its association with its pagan origins, and the evergreen was now referred to as "the Soviet tree." This tree, henceforward linked with New Year's celebrations, was free of any religion because religious beliefs, Communist Polish collaborators told their fellow citizens, were "false concepts in contradiction with the fundamentals of materialist thought, as concepts overcome in the epoch of socialism." Children were told that gifts came from Stalin, not God or St. Nicholas; that they should receive them at the New Year, not December 25; and that Jesus was a mythical figure who never existed. In case these truths were not self-evident, 25,000 activists of the League of the Militant Godless were dispatched into the newly conquered territories to spread the glad tidings of the new sort of Christmas.[14]

In December 1949 the *Washington Post* ran this Christmas story:

Santa Claus has been banned from the Soviet zone of Germany, and Jack the Giant Killer and his cohorts are in danger of being liquidated in Communist lands. Though Santa, or Kris Kringle, or Father Christmas, as he is variously called, originated in Germany, he is now an exile. So is the Christmas tree. The organ of the Communist Party, *Pravda*, has assailed a children's magazine for publishing animal stories and fairy tales on the ground that they are "isolated from life." Youth, it says, should be acquainted with true and more thrilling tales of the "full, many-sided life of the Soviet state." ... And who especially is to double for Santa in Eastern Germany? We have a good tip and we'll tell you this much. He hasn't a beard, but he does have a big mustache.[15]

The *Post* was not exactly au fait with the Santa situation in the Soviet zone—the magical Gift-Bringer certainly had not been invented in Germany and was never important enough a figure in that country to be banned in 1949—but the paper was on to something in sensing a cultural change surrounding Christmas. The Red Army tide that swept into Berlin in April 1945, forcing Hitler to suicide and helping bring an end to the war in Europe, did not recede for another forty-four years. The Soviet occupation of eastern Europe resulted in subservient Communist governments being installed in East Germany, Poland, Czechoslovakia, Hungary, Yugoslavia, Albania, Romania, and Bulgaria, and Latvia, Lithuania, and Estonia lost their independence altogether and were absorbed as republics into the USSR. Wherever these "people's democracies" were installed, behind what came to be known as the Iron Curtain, a war on religion was waged, and the repression and mutation of Christmas ensued.

The course this war on Christmas followed varied from country to country. In some places, for example Poland, Christmas was too much a part of the deeply Catholic culture to be extinguished; but elsewhere, where Christianity was a minority religion and the drive to become an atheist state was intense, celebrating the holiday was illegal, and priests who conducted Christmas Mass were shot or imprisoned. Albania seems to have treated religion more harshly than any other Communist country in Europe, forcing Christianity and Islam underground and obliging the faithful to be secret in their religious practices, hiding icons of St. Nicholas, for example, behind official portraits of Communist leader Enver Hoxha. Throughout eastern Europe, the Communist state apparatus, with its monopoly of the news media, publishing houses, educational system, and the police, attempted to muscle religion out of the winter holiday by moving festivities to the New Year, renaming events, making December 25 and 26 work days, and replacing any magical Gift-Bringer who had religious connections (e.g., Saint Nicholas or the Christ Child) with Grandfather Frost. In the German Democratic Republic, Christmas angels were renamed "end-of-year winged figures." There were even attempts to divert the holiday to Stalin's birthday, December 21. In Hungary the festival was called the Feast of Father Winter or Feast of the Fir Tree; December 26, St. Stephen's Day, a traditional part of the Christmas season, became Constitution Day. Romanians, heirs to a rich tradition of Christmas carols, found that they were barred from hearing them performed in public, though their National Chamber Choir, sent abroad to earn hard currency, was allowed to sing them in foreign concerts. Only through smuggled recordings or listening to the forbidden broadcasts of the BBC, Voice of America, or Radio Free Europe could Romanians enjoy their own sacred holiday music. Even singing these songs in a private setting had its dangers. During the Communist era a little girl heard her aunt singing

> *We shepherds three are on our way*
> *To Bethlehem this holy day*
> *With gifts for Jesus Christ our King*
> *O joy! Our Lady, joy we sing*

The child interrupted and announced, "Comrade Teacher said we shouldn't have any of those with religion in them. Sing one without religion." So her aunt was obliged to sing a hymn of praise to the country's dictator:

> *We shepherds three are on our way*
> *To Bucharest this holiday*
> *Gifts to Comrade Ceausescu we bring.*
> *O joy! Our happy joy we sing.*[16]

In Czechoslovakia in 1952, President Antonín Zápotocký told his nation's children that the traditional Gift-Bringer Ježíšek (Baby Jesus) had grown up, grown a beard, and turned into Deda Mráz (Grandfather Frost). In Yugoslavia, translators of foreign books removed references to Christmas and changed them to New Year's Day or omitted them altogether. The Christmas carol scene in *The Wind in the Willows*, for example, was excised, but references to the pagan god Pan were left in. The lameness and artificiality of these efforts can be seen in this 1952 *New York Times* quote from the Czech Communist newspaper *Rude Pravo*: "Dado Moros (Russian term for Little Father Frost) will arrive in Prague Dec. 1. He brings young Czech Communists a message of greeting from the Soviet young pioneers and will tell Prague children about the happy life of young builders of communism in the Soviet Union. That's why adults as well as children await his arrival with great excitement and joy."[17] Control of the economic levers was essential in downgrading Christmas. In Croatia the Ministry of Trade was responsible for ensuring that the shops had sufficient holiday food, and the Ministry of Forestry was responsible for providing the requisite number of fir trees. Both departments took care that neither the treats nor trees were available until after Christmas Day—they were for the New Year celebrations only.[18] (In East Germany the economic approach was different;

there the government attempted to show that Communist Germany could outproduce the capitalist West in terms of living standard and consumer goods for Christmas. Advertisers boasted of "our rich offering of goods, the result of the successful labor of our workers for the victory of social- ism!")[19] East Germany presents an interesting exception to some of the Iron Curtain countries' usual Christmas behavior. Before World War II the German Communist Party had opposed the celebration of Christmas (see below), but after 1945 it had come to see a deep attachment to the holiday among the populace for whom it meant home, normality, and peace after years of suffering. Consequently, the authorities of the German Democratic Republic chose to preserve the holiday, strip it of many (but not all) of its connections to religion, and cast it as a time of peace, free- dom, and a new socialist beginning. Soviet-style Grandfather Frost and the Snow Maiden might make their appearances as *Grossväterchen Frost und Schneeflöcken,* but *der Weihnachtsmann,* the secular German Gift- Bringer who had resembled Santa Claus since the mid-nineteenth cen- tury, would be seen most often, and even Communist Party functions might see folk tearfully singing "Stille Nacht, Heilige Nacht" (the German original of "Silent Night").[20]

In the long run neither European Communism nor its war on Christmas survived, but until the Berlin Wall and the Iron Curtain came down in 1989, the struggle to control the holiday had some disparate effects. At a public level, the state had considerable success in controlling the agenda, secularizing and commercializing the public aspect, and shifting the mer- riment to January 1. This meant that believers were forced to retreat to the domestic sphere in order to celebrate the holiday in a Christian fashion. It also meant that the holiday took on a deeper spiritual significance for those who chose to cling to Christmas.[21] Finally, to celebrate Christmas in traditional ways in eastern Europe was to protest against Soviet influence and Communist rule; old customs that might have died out were main- tained in order to bear witness to a spirit of nationalism or resistance.

Outside of the Soviet Union, Marxist revolutionaries also had to decide what to do about Christmas. In the People's Republic of China, particu- larly during the ultrarevolutionary years of the Great Proletarian Cultural Revolution (1966–1976), the answer was simple: abolish all religion and religious customs. Mao Tse-tung's regime had first narrowly tolerated some expressions of Christianity, trying to control them through the Catholic Patriotic Association or the Three-Self Patriotic Movement com- mittees, which forbade foreign influence or funding. When Mao, in order to solidify his hold on the Communist Party and eliminate opposition to his unpopular policies, unleashed the youth of China against their elders and traditional culture in the Cultural Revolution, his Red Guards closed all places of worship in China and intensely persecuted followers of all religions.[22] Maoist revolutionaries in Peru, calling themselves the Shining Path (Sendero Luminoso), waged an antireligion campaign in the Andes. As part of this violent struggle they forbade the native peasants to celebrate Christmas or any of their pre-Christian festivals—these feudal hangovers had been imposed by "tyrants" and were false beliefs. In their stead they demanded that villagers follow a Shining Path festal calendar: May 18, which marked the beginning of the armed uprising; June 18, the Day of Heroism, commemorating a massacre of their followers; and December 3, the birthday of the movement's founder, Abimael Guzmán.[23] In Cuba the Communist government of Fidel Castro banned Christmas celebrations and public decorations in 1969, ostensibly to keep efforts focused on the sugar harvest. One writer recalls this time: "Of all the naughty words and phrases I remember from childhood, two stand out as being particularly taboo: 'Christmas' and 'Human Rights.'" Christmas was not made legal again until 1997, in honor of an upcoming visit by Pope John Paul II, but officials are still suspicious of the holiday as being open to manipulation by those wanting to express pro-American sentiments. The same hostility to the United States led president Hugo Chavez to ban Christmas trees and pictures of Santa Claus from government offices in Venezuela, a fervently Christmas-loving country. The Sandinista government of Nicaragua, a Marxist regime with strong support from Catholic clergy influenced by liberation theology, made no move to overtly ban Christmas when they took power in 1979, but they did attempt to use the holiday politically and to associate it with their revolution. One Sandinista Christmas carol, "Cristo de Palacagüina," was famous for depicting the Holy Family as local peasants and the boy Jesus as wanting to grow up and become a revolutionary freedom fighter.[24]

In Germany and Italy another sort of totalitarianism arose out of the wreckage caused by World War I: fascism. Like Soviet Communism, it too demanded that the state subsume every aspect of life and that all activity be subservient to the nation or "the People." The first fascist state emerged in Italy, which was demoralized after its experiences in World War I, class-riven, and subject to violent strikes, sabotage, assassinations, and kidnappings. Posing as the one who could end chaos, Benito Mussolini, a fiery ex-socialist, became prime minister in 1922 and ruled unchallenged as Il Duce after 1924. His version of fascism was ultranationalist, anti-democratic, anticommunist, and autarkic, with the state in control of most of the economy. It suppressed oppositional voices in politics, the press, and the trade unions, claiming to transcend old divisions of class and region. Though Mussolini was at heart an anti-Christian—he claimed that Christmas Day only reminded him of "the birth of a Jew who gives the world debilitating and devitalizing theories"[25]—he professed to be a devoted Roman Catholic while neutralizing the political power of the Italian Church through a concordat with the Vatican. His love of spectacle, his emotional oratory, and the black shirts his followers wore all inspired Hitler, who was still an obscure conspirator when Mussolini took power.

Mussolini meant to give his nation new pride in itself, and he made fascist rule popular by launching a series of successful imperialist wars in Africa, suppressing Mafia excesses, and in boosting the prestige of Italian technology and design. As part of the creation of a new national identity, new symbols and activities had to be devised. The royal coat of arms was replaced by the sign of the fasces, an ancient Roman piece of regalia meant to represent unity, strength, and the power of the state. The calendar was altered to make 1922 Year One of the Fascist era; the anniversary of his march on Rome that had vaulted the Fascisti into power became the new Italian New Year. Other prefascist celebrations were eliminated or their meanings changed to portray the values of the new regime. The Christmas season did not escape reform. Though Nazi Germany would later make the evergreen one of its core Christmas images, Mussolini urged that Italians abandon the Christmas tree as a foreign, "northern," or "barbaric" innovation with no roots in Italian culture. (An exception was made for those of German background in the Tyrol, once under the control of the Austrians.)[26] Toys and other presents were to be Italian-made only and to be "at the service of the state." In Balkan territories that Italy had annexed, celebrating Christmas in the traditional ways or language could result in punishment.[27] The greatest fascist appropriation of Christmas for political purposes came at Epiphany, January 6, when Italian children traditionally received gifts from the hand of the kindly Christmas witch La Befana. Under Il Duce, Epiphany became the Befana Fascista, a time of distributing gifts and relief to the poor, in which the role played by Mussolini and his wife was prominent. This made the celebration not only religious and domestic but national and unifying as well, with Mussolini portrayed as a benevolent patriarch.[28] One admiring observer noted in 1932: "How fortunate for the children of Italy that every year their great friend remembers them, that every year, he increases the circle of his dear, faithful 'clients.' The attending adults tweaked the kids' cheeks, asking, 'Now who gave you so many nice things?' pointing out the tiny pants, woolen undershirts, little shoes, hats, illustrated books, toys, sweets...and each of the little lads piped up '*il Duce*.'"

The German variant of fascism called itself National Socialism and was led by Hitler, who was an Austrian-born war veteran. Placing himself at the head of a tiny political group that he named the National Socialist German Workers' Party (Nationalsozialistische Deutsche Arbeiterpartei, whence the derogatory shorthand term "Nazi") Hitler tried first to overthrow the German republic and then to contest elections in it. His party's policies were intensely nationalistic, to the point of racism, and the National Socialists were opposed to both capitalism and communism. They envisaged radical economic and technological change while calling for a return to traditional German values, which they thought were threatened by the licentiousness of the postwar era. It is not surprising therefore that they had strong views on Christmas, whose practices were deeply embedded in the German consciousness.[29]

The constitution of the postwar German government, known as the Weimar Republic, had set up a system of proportional representation in elections and consequently encouraged the proliferation of political parties, many of them quite extreme. The left wing of the electorate was dominated by the German Communist Party and the Social Democratic Party, both of whom staked out opinions on the role of Christmas. For the Communists of Germany, like their Bolshevik comrades in the USSR, religion was a dangerous drug, and Christmas was a sentimental fantasy that should be abolished. The Communists' publications railed against the holiday, and their demonstrators vandalized stores and burnt civic Christmas trees. The Social Democrats chose to use the expectations of Christmas to accuse the middle class of hypocrisy and exploitation, best seen in the parody of the beloved German carol "Silent Night," recast as "Worker's Silent Night":

> *Stille Nacht, traurige Nacht,*
> *Ringsumher Lichterpracht!*
> *In der Hütte nur Elend und Not,*
> *Kalt und öde, kein Licht und kein Brot,*
> *Schläft die Armut auf Stroh.*

Silent night, sad night,
All around glorious light!
In the hovel only misery and distress,
Cold and dreary, no light and no bread,
The poor are sleeping on straw.[30]

With the leftists having set their faces against Christmas, the National Socialists were able to pose as its defenders. Just as they opposed the decadence of modern art, jazz music, and short-skirted women smoking cigarettes, they claimed to be defending the German consumer and small businessman from the rapacious Jewish department store owners. In the 1920s, department stores, like the big-box stores of the twenty-first century, had gained an unsavory reputation for driving the little local shops out of business. Nazis used the Christmas season to advance their anti-Semitic agenda by urging consumers to avoid Jewish businesses, which they surrounded with picket lines, and by vandalizing them where they could, throwing in stink bombs or smashing windows. A 1928 pamphlet by the National Socialist propagandist Joseph Goebbels claimed: "Six hundred small businesses have gone bankrupt due to Jewish department stores this Christmas season in Berlin alone!... Set out the Christmas tree. Daughters of Zion, rejoice! The good Germans are forging their own chains from their hard-earned coins....The Jew will grow fat from the coins you give him, the German will starve."[31] Three years later, when the Great Depression had hit Germany, Goebbels made a similar diagnosis:

> There is little we can buy this Christmas with our limited means. But that which we buy should at least be bought in Germany, from Germans, for Germans. The small merchant is in a desperate situation. We should support him. He must be brought along the path to the coming recovery. He may not be left behind, a victim of the collapse. This year, German men and women will shop only in German shops. They will avoid the Jewish department stores where they formerly gave their hard-earned money for trifles and fooleries, money that flowed into the channels of international Marxism to be used to further enslave German labor. However gray and empty the festival of love may be this year, we should wherever possible light the candle of solidarity and camaraderie in the midst of social darkness.[32]

When the Communist Party's Red Front Fighters marched against capitalism during Christmas, destroying community trees or intimidating churchgoers, the Nazi Brownshirts (aka storm troopers, members of the Sturmabteilung, or SA) poured into the streets to confront them, appearing in the public mind to be the group more respectful of national traditions. Nazis understood much better than the Communists or Social Democrats how deeply embedded Christmas was in the people's understanding of what it meant to be truly German.

The elections of 1933 brought Hitler and his party to power. Their actions up to this time had linked National Socialism with a Christmas that was in no way Christian but rather "national"—anti-Semitic, patriotic, and historically German; once in office the Nazis worked to consolidate their linkage with traditional values of the season by sponsoring a vast program of public welfare every December, the Winterhilfwerke. This winter relief effort saw thousands of volunteers and members of the Nazi youth formations out on the streets or going door-to-door soliciting donations, in return for a little token. Though Germans made the same complaints about the incessant badgering for donations as the early modern Englishmen who complained of servants extorting Boxing Day gifts, the Winterhilfwerke succeeded in helping many destitute Germans during Depression-era Christmases and in associating National Socialism with charity and social solidarity. Other actions after their electoral triumph revealed a more radical approach to the holiday and demonstrated that a Nazi Christmas would be far different from any seen before.

Creating this new vision was the task of Goebbels and his Ministry of National Enlightenment and Propaganda. During the first Christmas under National Socialism, it appeared that the Nazis would merely associate themselves with traditional symbols. In December 1933 at the Christmas celebrations of the national railway, for example, brown-shirted storm troopers accompanied the Holy Family in a Nativity play while the audience sang the Nazi fight song, the "Horst Wessel Lied," along with familiar Christmas carols. A film of that same year depicted a Nativity scene of Mary, Joseph, and the Christ Child beneath a portrait of Hitler and surrounded by SA troops and Teutonic knights. But the Nazis were much more ambitious in their plans for controlling what the German nation would think about the seasons and the marking of time; like the Jacobins of the French Revolution and the Bolsheviks of the USSR, National Socialists wanted to re-create the calendar and the cycle of celebrations. There would be new holidays, including the anniversary of seizing power and Hitler's birthday, and new ways of celebrating rites of passage such as marriages, and old holidays, including Christmas, would be Germanicized and paganized. The party began to issue instructions on how to celebrate Christmas in a National Socialist manner, giving directives not only to party branches such as the Hitler Youth, the SA, the SS (the elite, black-shirted Schutzstaffel), and its Women's League, but also to the school system. The overarching purpose was to eviscerate the Christian element in the holiday and replace it with secular or neopagan elements that served the Nazi racial state.[33]

> *No evil priest can prevent us from feeling*
> *that we are the children of Hitler.*
> *We follow not Christ, but Horst Wessel.*
> *Away with incense and holy water.*
> *The Church can hang for all we care.*
> *The swastika brings salvation in earth.*

So sang the Hitler Youth at Nuremberg rallies. The peacefulness and non-violence at the heart of Christianity had no place in a nation of racial warriors, as testified by Berlin banners that proclaimed "Down with a Christ who allows himself to be crucified! The German God cannot be a suffering God! He is a God of power and strength!"[34]

A totalitarian government can allow no spiritual rivals, no organizations or systems of thought that have a higher allegiance than the state. If Hitler's policy of racial purity and territorial expansion were to be successfully enacted, he would have to neutralize the inevitable objections of the Christian churches. A concordat in 1933 between the German Reich and Catholic authorities traded the political neutrality of the Church for promises of institutional independence (promises the Nazis very soon broke). In that same year the German Christian Movement (Glaubungbewegung Deutsche Christen) took control of the national Protestant Church and attempted to align its teachings with National Socialist principles: Jesus was portrayed as an Aryan victim of the Jews, altars were draped with swastikas, and a pagan ceremonial of "blood and earth" was introduced. This takeover led to dissident pastors like Martin Niemoller being arrested and thrown into concentration camps or, like Dietrich Bonhoeffer, going underground to continue clandestine preaching. The Christmas season became a time of genuine struggle between thoroughgoing Nazi pagans, paganized Christians of the official Church, and mainstream Protestant and Catholic leaders who hoped to use popular attachment to Christmas to defend Christianity. The result, says the most acute observer of German Christmas history, was dismay and turmoil: "Christmas was not fascist enough for Nazi party loyalists but too politicized for Christian believers."[35] With German Catholic leadership locked into a frustrating policy of overt noninterference and Protestants led by ultra-nationalist racialists, ordinary Christians of the 1930s saw Christmas changing before their eyes. "German Christian" hymns were often subtly amended, and new songs with neopagan themes were introduced:

> *Christmas! Christmas!*
> *Blood and soil awake!*
> *Above you God's stars shine.*
> *Below sing the seeds in the fields:*
> *Volk, from God's light and power,*
> *Your honor and heroism come.*[36]

Children were taught a new version of "Stille Nacht" in which Hitler replaced the Christ Child as the object of veneration:

> *Silent night, Holy night,*
> *All is calm, all is bright.*
> *Only the Chancellor stays on guard*
> *Germany's future to watch and to ward,*
> *Guiding our nation aright.*
>
> *Silent night, Holy night,*
> *All is calm, all is bright.*
> *Adolf Hitler is Germany's star*
> *Showing us greatness and glory afar*
> *Bringing us Germans the might.*[37]

Cries of "Hosanna" or "Hallelujah" were edited out of hymns as being Hebrew in origin. The name of the Norse god Baldur replaced that of Jesus in seasonal songs. The beautiful carol "Es ist ein Ros' entsprungen," which speaks of Christ as a flower sprung from a Jewish root, suffered judicious paring.

> *There dwelt a race in German lands,*
> *A strong upright and blue-eyed clan;*
> *The Germans, whose natural traits combined*
> *Heroic spirit and gentle mind.*

One of the worst examples of a mixture of Christian and pagan themes came in the Christmas cantata *Heliand,* which began with the assertion of John 1:1 that "in the beginning was the Word" but went on to liken Christ to the Teutonic god Wotan and then devolved into a mishmash of German myth, dragons, adultery, blood feuds, and racism.[38] Some of this bowdlerizing went too far even for Nazi officials, and in 1937 the president of the Reich Musical Chamber had to protest against an attempt to write new words to Handel's *Messiah,* which was felt to contain lyrics that no longer accorded with the National Socialist soul.[39]

A redacted version of the Gospels excised any Old Testament prophecies mentioned in the Nativity story, though the Wise Men were kept as being too familiar to be removed. In German schools, carols and Nativity plays were banned in 1938; Christmas was celebrated in the absence of the mention of anything Christian, as directives mandated a "People's Christmas, in a consciousness of German tradition." The Advent wreath (invented in the nineteenth century by a Protestant pastor who devised it to make Christmas more real for the children in his orphanage) was termed the symbol of "ancient German longing for light during the winter season." Christmas toys and books for children were increasingly of a military nature: model SA or SS troops, handbooks on pistols and machine guns, child-size tanks, and a picture book titled *Our Army,* which contained the little ditty "What puffs and patters? / What clinks and clatters? / I know what, O, what fun! / It's a lovely Gatling gun!"[40]

"We live in the age of the final confrontation with Christianity. It is part of the mission of the SS to give to the German people over the next fifty years the non-Christian ideological foundation for a way of life appropriate to their own character."[41] A number of the Nazi inner circle, particularly Heinrich Himmler and others in the SS, were genuine pagans, anxious to educate the nation in the ways of the old Teutonic gods and the power of ancient symbols. In order to expropriate the German people's deep investment in the Christmas season without referring to its Christian content, Nazi propagandists and ethnologists took advantage of the holiday's proximity to the winter solstice and attempted to build a new set of behaviors around December 21. A 1939 article in an educational monthly stated baldly: "The real Christmas community celebration...is the winter solstice."[42] An instruction booklet given to SS families on how to celebrate the Julfest (Yuletide) stated that the season began on Wotan's Day (December 6, traditionally St. Nicholas's Day): "In olden days the God of our ancestors drove through the air, visited his people, was friendly to them, and left them little presents. He wanted to announce the start of the Winter Solstice season and the coming of the New Year. The Christian church couldn't suppress these yearly visits of this white bearded, one-eyed leader of the good Spirits. So they put one of its assumed saints, St. Nikolaus, in his place." Every SS family member should have his or her own Jul plate, which was to be left on the windowsill, to be filled with apples, nuts, and biscuits made in pagan shapes: runes, swastikas, solstice suns. On the winter solstice the SS men were to be on the mountaintops, lighting fires and performing "manly dances" with torches, while in town the community was to gather around a massive bonfire, from which children would ignite their candles to "bring home the light" for the candles on their own Jul tree.[43]

When Hitler took Germany into war in 1939 in order to acquire eastern Europe for the expansion of living space for his Aryan master race, the drive to neutralize the Christian content in Christmas continued with even more urgency. A religion that preached "peace on earth" and worshiped one who urged turning the other cheek to an enemy required careful handling. On the one hand there was tremendous emotional capital in the traditional Christmas celebrations that could not be directly attacked without popular resentment and harm to the National Socialist cause. Leveraging this resource could actually turn love of Christmas into a positive good for Nazism if the people could be convinced that the war was being fought to protect the holiday and preserve the good old ways and treasured feelings. On the other hand the churches' constant maneuvers to use the Christian aspects of Christmas as a means of preserving their religion within the National Socialist state had to be resisted. Then there were the hard-core Nazis who despised Christianity and wished to see no evidence of it in public. The solution was to avoid any direct attack on the traditional Christmas but to use the state's power, wherever possible, to promote a non-Christian view of the holiday that emphasized national unity, family togetherness, the role of the mother, and the eternal cycle of the seasons.

We can see this in the flood of publications that emerged from government and party printing houses: women's magazines, children's literature, Advent calendars, and books aimed at the soldier at the front and his family at home. In none of these was there much reference, in prose, verse, or song, to the Christian Nativity or to the message of Jesus, but there was a plethora of symbolism that could pass as vaguely Christmas-y in the dusk with the light behind it. Among the offerings were "Weihnachtsabend 1924 auf Festung Landsberg," a tale of Hitler's Christmas in his jail cell when he was serving time for a failed coup attempt, and *Völkisch* fairy tales and poems like "Das Hohelied der Mutternacht," a hymn to an archetypal Mother that used an old pagan name for Christmas. Any idea that these publications wanted to convey a message of peace and human harmony would have been dispelled by the words of Hitler in a short epilogue to *Deutsche Kriegsweihnacht*, a Nazi handbook of Christmas stories and pictures: "All nature is a tremendous struggle between power and weakness, an eternal victory of the strong over the weak." One of the most revealing of these publications is an Advent calendar that was sent to German families to help them plan activities for the month of December. The solstice symbol on the front cover—a spinning sun—gives a clue that the booklet will include none of the usual Christian elements of the season. In fact the authors repeat the mantra "Weihnachten ist Sonnenwende": "Christmas is the solstice." December 6, once St. Nicholas's Day, is given over to a picture of a shaggy Knecht Ruprecht and his white horse, identified in Nazi lore with the Nordic god Wotan, who was said to have ridden through the winter sky, leaving presents and announcing the winter solstice. The calendar instructed mothers in how to use the image of this "Rider on the White Horse" to decorate trees or be served in pastry form. A page on seasonal symbols includes the sun wheel; the "odalrune," the sign of peasant ties to blood and earth; and the swastika, a symbol of the "struggle of our Greater German Reich for its bright future." The course of the war dictated changes to this Advent calendar that are revealing. The graphic for December 24, 1942, was a picture of German soldiers standing respectfully around the grave of a fallen comrade; surrounding them was a wreath of evergreens intertwined with the names of Nazi conquests: Norway, symbolized by a pair of fish; France, with a cluster of grapes; "the East," with a burning Russian village. The drawing of the soldiers remained in the 1943 edition, but this was the year of German defeats—Stalingrad, the loss of North Africa and of Sicily and southern Italy, the battle of the Atlantic—so the wreath of conquests was edited out. In 1944, as the German armies were collapsing on all fronts and the Allies were driving toward Berlin, the page for December 24 was given over to a chilling "Poem of the Dead Soldiers," wherein readers were told "Einmal im Jahr, in der heligen Nacht, / verlassen die toten Soldaten die Wacht": "yearly on this date the ghosts of fallen soldiers rise to visit their homes and silently bless the living for whom they died." It is noteworthy that by far the most common image of Nazi Christmas cards for the troops was that of a single sentry, outdoors in the bleak wind and snow, standing on guard for the nation.[44]

The fact that these publications were stripped of all Christian content did not go unnoticed by the troops. In December 1943 a Wehrmacht lieutenant on the Eastern Front wrote to the editor of *Soldatenblätter für Feier und Freizeit* to complain that there was nothing in this year's issue, nor in the 1942 volume, of Christmas as traditionally understood by Germans. Where were the carols, the beautiful artwork, the stories of the cradle, the Mother and Child, the shepherds and the Three Kings? There was nothing of the good news of Christ's birth, only vague blather about ancestors, the struggle of light against darkness, and a time of seasonal renewal. Soldiers, the lieutenant complained, would put down the magazine in disappointment, missing the real meaning of Christmas that they were accustomed to sharing with their loved ones. The editor replied, thanking the letter writer but explaining that a deal had been struck between the Army and the Nazi Party that prevented the inclusion of religious material that might be controversial and that, consequently, there were lines that could not be crossed.[45] There were reports in military hospitals of Waffen SS troops objecting to the pious carols sung by the wounded soldiery of other less ideologically militant units. Military and party authorities tended to view overt Christianity at the Christmas season as a sign of defeatism and passivity—thus their suppression of the "Stalingrad Madonna," a touching drawing of the Mother and Child that a Wehrmacht pastor trapped in the Stalingrad cauldron created to cheer his fellow soldiers at Christmas. Though the drawing was flown out of the battle site back to Germany (its creator would be left behind and would die in captivity) it was not allowed to be displayed. Perhaps its captions— "Life," "Light," "Love"—were considered too subversive to be borne.[46]

Morale at the holiday season was carefully monitored by the secret police, who gathered reports from a host of informers; being gloomy at Christmas could be considered "defeatism," and Germans knew that the guillotine had been introduced as a penalty for open opposition to the Reich. The police recorded complaints about the scarcity of toys or holiday food in the shops; they measured attendance at church services and noted that they seemed to be full of weeping women. Christian clergy frequently fell under suspicion of disloyalty (thousands were arrested during the war and sent to concentration camps), and party activists were urged to make note of casualty lists at the Christmas season so as to beat the priest or pastor to the side of grieving families. Even the types of Christmas toys made by Hitler Youth units were subject to official scrutiny: a 1943 directive mandated culturally appropriate gifts but forbade Mickey Mouse characters, jumping jacks of Churchill or Stalin, and "sweetish little Negroes." In order to preempt traditional Christian celebrations, the SS attempted to monopolize the supply of candles, using them instead for their "birth of the light" ceremonies. One National Socialist circular yearned for a day in the not-too-distant future when the war would be over and Christ could be removed from the calendar altogether.[47]

Until that day could come, however, the German populace had to be kept happy at Christmastime. Reichsmarschall Herman Göring deemed it essential that the shops be full of things to buy and plenty of extra food was available for the holiday. But where was the money for these goods and the Christmas provender to come from? From the conquered territories, of course. The gold reserves of occupied nations were stolen, their citizens were taxed to the breaking point, their currencies were debased to make purchase of their goods with German marks extremely cheap, food was shipped from the East regardless of the needs of Poles, Ukrainians, and Russians, Jewish property was seized, and wealth was simply stolen. In 1942 Göring stated baldly: "I intend to loot anyway, and to loot thoroughly.... I will then hang these things in shop windows here at Christmas so that the German people can buy them." Thousands of freight cars and barges carried the plunder into Germany in time for Christmas, the better to distract the people from the fate of their Sixth Army, surrounded and starving at Stalingrad. Göring pronounced his "Christmas project" a success: "The special allocations of foodstuffs have paid off again. My gifts of something extra for old people and large families have worked wonders."[48]

A final note to demonstrate how seriously National Socialism took Christmas as a marker of German identity. When Nazi armies swept toward Moscow, Hitler's plan was to cleanse the conquered lands of Jews and Slavs and replace them with ethnically correct settlers. The settlers were to be found in the *Volksdeutsche*, descendants of German migrants who had moved into eastern Europe hundreds of years before. A million of these were plucked out of Galicia, Bessarabia, Bukovina, and so on and resettled in Poland, where they were expected to "Germanize" the expanded Reich. The problem was that these folk, though they were of the right bloodline, had lost much of their old culture over time and would have to be re-Germanized themselves. That task fell in large part to women sent by the SS and the Reich Women's Leadership to instruct these newcomers in the way things were done in proper National Socialist fashion. An essential part of this drive was the education of the colonists in what constituted a true "German Christmas." In December 1940, 172 women from the German heartland arrived in one of the new settlements in conquered Poland to stage Christmas ceremonies that would divert the transplanted families from a religious version of the holiday. Though the settlers had asked for a church where their children "could pray and hear the word of God," their advisers tried to steer them away from a Christian celebration. Traditional pieties about "peace on earth" were to be replaced by tougher slogans, political skits, and pagan symbolism. Results were mixed and often discouraging; some of the instructors fell back on religious elements that could at least give their colonists "something for the soul." Within a few years German armies were in retreat, and these new settlements would be destroyed. The rottenness at the core of this short-lived experiment, and indeed of the whole Nazi notion of Christmas, can be seen in the Yuletide gifts for the colonists in Lublin sent by Heinrich Himmler, head of the SS—clothing, suitcases, and bedding confiscated from Jews in Auschwitz.[49]

IV

The Godly and the Godless

*In which atheists and believers find plenty to object to
in Christmas*

The Militant Godless Return

The twentieth century was supposed to be the golden age of the godless. Atheist regimes achieved power in Asia, Latin America, and eastern Europe and, as already shown, attempted to eradicate religion and its celebrations and to replace faith with scientific atheism. Secularization theorists predicted that increased modernity and industrialization would make humanity less needful of religion's comforts. Sociologist Peter Berger predicted in 1968 that by the twenty-first century religious believers would be found only in small sects "huddled together to resist a worldwide secular culture."[1] By the end of the twentieth century it was clear that this was not going to be the case and that religion, rather than withering away, might outlive its persecutors. Mexico, which violently persecuted Catholicism in the 1920s in the name of revolution, abandoned its enforcement of anticlerical statutes and eventually changed its constitution to grant legal status to all churches.[2] The Soviet war on religion grew more halfhearted after the 1960s and then collapsed utterly with the end of the USSR and the fall of the Communist governments of eastern Europe.[3] China intensely warred against all varieties of faith during the Maoist years, but many attitudes changed after the death of the Great Helmsman in 1976. Though the Chinese Communist government was still prepared to act without pity against political dissent (as the students in Tiananmen Square discovered in 1989), its new breed of rulers made some space for religion. At the turn of the century it was estimated that there were tens of millions of Christians in China.[4]

But if religion was not going to go away, neither was atheism. The rise of the religious right in the United States and social tensions caused by growing Muslim immigration in Europe seemed to call forth a renewal of public nonbelieving in the 1990s. Termed the New Atheism, this move-ment was led by academics, including the English biologist Richard Dawkins (*The God Delusion*) and the American cognitive philosopher Daniel Dennett (*Breaking the Spell: Religion as a Natural Phenomenon*), and the polemicist Christopher Hitchens (*God Is Not Great*). None of their ideas was particularly novel, but what was unique about the New Atheists was a willingness to be confrontational, mocking, and even openly contemp-tuous of their opponents, a tactical attitude more akin to the Soviet League of the Militant Godless than earlier Western humanists. The American atheist blogger PZ Myers, for example, drove a rusty nail through a conse-crated Communion Host, threw it in the garbage, and distributed a photo-graph of it, remarking that he hoped Jesus's tetanus shots were up to date. An artistic display on Blasphemy Day 2009 featured the work "Jesus Paints His Nails," showing "an effeminate Jesus after the crucifixion, applying polish to the nails that attached his hands to the cross." Hitchens told an approving Toronto audience: "I think religion should be treated with ridicule, hatred and contempt, and I claim that right."[5] Religion, he said in his best-selling book, ignoring thousands of years of church music, art, architecture, and social service, poisoned everything. Atheists began to urge that parents be forbidden to teach their faith traditions to their children; Dawkins termed such transmission of religion "child abuse." Sam Harris, a neuroscientist and author of *The End of Faith*, called raising a child in a religion a "ludicrous obscenity."[6] Atheists started to refer to themselves as "Brights," presumably with the implication that those who opposed them were the "Dims."[7]

The long-standing Western notion that there was virtue in the toler-ance of opposing views took a hit from some atheists. The masthead of the website Newatheism.org reads: "Intolerance of ignorance, myth and super-stition; disregard for the tolerance of religion. Indoctrination of logic, rea-son and the advancement of a naturalistic worldview." The site goes on to boldly proclaim: "Tolerance of pervasive myth and superstition in modern society is not a virtue. Religious fundamentalism has gone main stream and its toll on education, science, and social progress is disheartening[.] Wake up people!! We are smart enough now to kill our invisible gods and oppressive beliefs. It is the responsibility of the educated to educate the uneducated, lest we fall prey to the tyranny of ignorance."[8]

Given such an aggressive, not to say "evangelical," attitude toward sec-ularism, it is no surprise that Christmas has become a target of atheist movements. The season was Christianity's most public annual display and provided a dazzling array of targets and themes for the humanist critic. Nor were atheists shy about their intentions. Tom Flynn, whose jolly bearded face bore more than a passing resemblance to that of Santa Claus, urged Americans to repudiate the celebration of Christmas and in fact to declare war on it as a way of promoting minority rights and religious diversity. Brian Flemming, producer of a movie claiming to prove that Jesus of Nazareth never existed, went so far as to issue an official declaration of war on Christmas, declaring:

> Whereas there has not hitherto ever been a war on Christmas; and
>
> Whereas conservative Christian pundits relentlessly claim there is such a war; and
>
> Whereas nobody would want these pundits to be made liars;
>   Therefore let it be resolved that Beyond Belief Media hereby formally declares War on the holiday known as Christmas.
>   All her resources are hereby pledged until such time as the conflict is terminated.[9]

Flemming, no fool when it came to marketing, used the campaign as part of an advertising strategy to promote his documentary, which he touted as a splendid Christmas present.

The ultimate aim of these attacks was to discredit religion, Christianity in particular, by undermining the supernatural claims of this feast. If one is going to subvert the notion of God, then what better immediate target than that festival, whose central claim is that the divinity came to earth two thousand years ago in human form? Thus the Yuletide message of the Freedom From Religion Foundation: "At This Season of the Winter Solstice, Let Reason Prevail. There are no gods, no devils, no angels, nor heaven nor hell. There is only our natural world. Religion is but myth and superstition that hardens hearts and enslaves minds." The Foundation said its sign reminded citizens of "the real reason for the season"—the winter solstice, which, it said, had long been celebrated in the Northern Hemisphere with presents and feasting. Using the famous 1897 editorial from the *New York Sun* as a talking point, the Foundation bought advertising space on Seattle buses to proclaim "Yes Virginia, There Is No God."[10]

However, many opponents of theism could also point to manifold dysfunctions of the typical Western consumerist Christmas. The most comprehensive catalogue of seasonal sins has been compiled by Flynn, author of *The Trouble with Christmas*.[11] According to Flynn, who boasts that he has been Yule-free since 1984, Christmas is not the ancient festival its supporters make it out to be; in fact, it is all borrowed from the pagans, except those parts that were made up by dead white European males like Dickens in the nineteenth century. (The link to pagan origins is one frequently made by atheists, as it serves to erode Christian truth claims.) Christmas's effects are overwhelmingly deleterious: it creates a system of Insiders (those who celebrate the holiday) and Outsiders (Jews, infidels, Wiccans, etc.). Christmas teaches parents to lie to kids and thus stunts moral development. It harms the family by encouraging parenting through fear; it promotes selfishness; and when all is said and done, the kids don't even enjoy it. Acknowledging that some psychologists had defended the Santa myth, Flynn announced that he found their findings unconvincing.

What should be the public response to such a horrible phenomenon as Christmas? Flynn advises parents to abandon the Santa Claus myth and tell children frankly that the presents under the tree have been provided by parents or friends. Kids should also be inoculated against supernaturalism and be taught why their house has no truck or trade with flying reindeer or their passengers. In a move sure to stir community controversy, Flynn recommends that Jews, newcomers, and infidels rebel against Christmas and demand that religion be privatized; Christmas will be restricted to the homes of those who wished to practice its customs. Public schools will observe no religious holidays of any kind. Religion might be taught in public schools, but only in a nonsectarian way. Religious music might be used to illustrate lessons but only if recorded; students must not be asked to perform faith-inspired pieces. Flynn frowns on the infidel community celebrating Christmas or any "analogue" (such as "HumanLight," below)—celebrations should be of global relevance, marking only human capacities. Perhaps most controversially, Flynn wants to see the anti-Christmas message propagated missionary-style at the elementary school level; he urges atheist parents to "encourage (or at least permit) children to share their Santa skepticism with friends, at school, and during recreational activities. This is vital even if it leads to confrontations with neighbors, relatives or teachers who accuse your kids of 'ruining other children's Christmas.' Should this occur, defend your children's open iconoclasm. Challenge critics who stoop to such negative stereotypes as 'Scrooge' or 'Grinch.' Most important, be sure that children know that— and how—you support them."[12] Earlier anti-Christmas ideologues sought to lessen love of the holiday by inventing new midwinter celebrations. Scottish Calvinists moved merriment from December 25 to New Year's Eve and Hogmanay. Nineteenth-century French secularists promoted a "laic" or "Positivist" Christmas; French leftists of the 1930s opted for "Red Christmas." Nazi Germany hoped to shift holiday focus to the midwinter solstice. The Soviet Union preempted Christmas with New Year's festivities. At the turn of the twenty-first century some lighthearted atheists recommended replacing traditional celebrations with parodies such as Festivus, an invention of the television series *Seinfeld*, which involved ritual feats of strength, airing of grievances, and a bare aluminum pole instead of a decorated tree. Enthusiasts have even written a number of Festivus carols.[13] In England, atheists have sponsored holiday shows called "Nine Lessons and Carols for Godless People," combining comedy, music, and scientific demonstrations.[14] Those hoping to find a holiday in which mixed Jewish-Christian families could participate came up with Chrismukkah.[15] In the United States, more sober-sided secularists have created a new holiday called HumanLight. Rejecting the supernatural underpinnings of Christmas but still eager to enjoy good cheer in late December, they choose to focus on a "humanist's vision of a good future…a future in which all people can identify with each other, behave with the highest moral standards, and work together toward a happy, just and peaceful world." Suggestions for a HumanLight celebration include a meal, short readings from earlier atheists, educational entertainment for the children, a sing-along with humanist songs, and the distribution of "The Affirmation of Humanism for Kids Coloring Book." Candles might be lit as an appropriate song is sung, for example "These Three Flames":

> *This flame shines with the light of reason*
> *May it illuminate the wonders of our world*
> *This flame glows with a warm compassion*
> *May it expand the caring circle of our love*
> *This flame gleams like a hope-filled beacon*
> *May it sustain us through the darkest winter night*
> *These three flames mark a joyful season*
> *May they unite us in a happy HumanLight*
> *And may Reason Compassion and Hope*
> *Light the path of every human life.*[16]

It is safe to say that HumanLight gets full marks for earnestness of intentions but scores poorly in the merry midwinter fun category. Compare the plodding sincerity of "These Three Flames" with the mock holiday songs of other atheists. Catherine Dunphy, a former Catholic turned associate humanist chaplain at the University of Toronto, has penned an atheist version of the "Twelve Days of Christmas" that ends this way:

> *On the 12th day of Christmas, my true love gave to me,*
> *12 happy humanists!*
> *11 atheists doubting,*
> *10 biologist dissecting,*
> *9 agnostics wondering,*
> *8 physicists arguing,*
> *7 poisonous water snakes swimming,*
> *6 fossilized dinosaur eggs,*
> *5 postcards of Dan Dennett dressed like Santa Claus!*
> *4 Galapagos finches,*
> *3 French Noble Laureates,*
> *2 trilobite fossils,*
> *…and Dawkins' Christmas Tree!*[7]

The winner of an online atheist Christmas carol contest is also sung to the tune of "The Twelve Days of Christmas." Its final verses are:

On the tenth day the first priest invented idiocy. Gods everywhere now, they want us dancing, with legs a-hurting, oh, what a shame—aaall without proof! Gods getting pop'lar, weather now warm, lifeforms do pray, no one knows the Big Bang Theory.

On the eleventh day the churches controlled the minds unfree. Just one God, which one is right, they want crusaders, with swords a-slinging, oh, what a shame—aaall without proof! Monotheism, weather quite dark, lifeforms do pray, no one knows the Big Bang Theory.

On the twelfth day the clever ones finally broke free! No more Gods, but atheism, science is right, tell the believers: "No swords a-slinging, no holy war, Naaature is hot!" Jen writes her blog, weather is sunny, lifeforms shall think and we all love the Big Bang Theoryyyyyy!

The second-place finisher, sung to the tune of "Angels We Have Heard on High," summarizes the views of four leading New Atheists and ends with a nod to Christopher Hitchens. "Faith just makes us hateful and small, / We'll start growing strong by knowing / God isn't great at all!"[18] The Reverend Christopher Chris Raible, a Canadian Unitarian minister and author of the Gilbert and Sullivan pastiche "I Am the Very Model of a Modern Unitarian," penned this ditty for his congregation:

> Gods rest ye, Unitarians, let nothing you dismay;
> Remember there's no evidence there was a Christmas Day;
> When Christ was born is just not known, no matter what they say,
> O, Tidings of reason and fact, reason and fact,
> Glad tidings of reason and fact.
> Our current Christmas Customs come from Persia and from Greece,
> From solstice celebrations of the ancient Middle East.
> This whole darn Christmas spiel is just another pagan feast,
> O, Tidings of reason and fact, reason and fact,
> Glad tidings of reason and fact.
> There was no star of Bethlehem, there was no angels' song;
> There could not have been wise men for the trip would take too long.
> The stories in the Bible are historically wrong,
> O, Tidings of reason and fact, reason and fact,
> Glad tidings of reason and fact![19]

Often, the clash of atheists and Christmas takes place in the context of arguments over the division of church and state and the suggestion that Christians are being given constitutionally impermissible privileges in December. The Arkansas Society of Freethinkers has protested public school students being taken to see *A Charlie Brown Christmas* in a Little Rock church. The play itself was deemed dangerously religious, and the setting was particularly problematic. According to atheist critics, the content and venue entirely overstepped the line between church and state.[20] In Chicago, atheists complained that a program to exchange recycling bags for used Christmas trees violated the rights of non-Christians, who would not have such trees to exchange. Irreligion as a principle apparently trumped the practice of human generosity in a number of cases. In Bellevue, Washington, an atheist couple asked the local council in 2004 to have a Christmas tree tossed out of City Hall. They were not moved by the fact that the conifer was called a "giving tree" and was used to raise donations for needy families;

for them it remained a symbol of Christianity and was thus to be evicted. Their position was that City Hall should be "a place where everybody feels welcome. It is impossible for everybody's religious belief to be displayed and non-religious belief to be displayed, so therefore, no religious beliefs [should] be displayed." In 2013 a threatening letter from the American Humanist Association forced a school to drop a Christmas toy drive because it was associated with a Christian group known as Operation Christmas Child. Though the boxed gifts contained no religious materials and participation in the project was voluntary, the atheist organization called it unconstitutional and demanded that the school terminate its part in this charity or risk a lawsuit and punitive damages.[21]

The atheist assault on Christmas has become increasingly public as nonbelievers have begun to invade spaces usually reserved for religious seasonal displays. The Freedom From Religion Foundation has demanded that civic buildings that contain a Hanukkah or Christmas display also carry an antireligious message from the Foundation. Though they have been successful in a number of states, their signs have occasionally been stolen or vandalized.[22] Pennsylvania Nonbelievers, Inc., "Central Pennsylvania's leading organization of atheists, agnostics, and secular humanists," wanted to install a display at the site of the town of Chambersburg's war memorial fountain in 2009. This display was to celebrate the winter solstice and to honor the atheist veterans of the Civil War and other conflicts, but the town council, rather than give way to what they thought might become a free-for-all of groups demanding public space, banned all such manifestations, which meant the traditional Christmas crèche had to go too.[23] In 2011 Santa Monica atheist groups swamped a public area that had traditionally been given over in December to Nativity displays and erected signs bearing images of Jesus, Satan, Neptune, and Santa Claus with the slogan: "37 million Americans know a myth when they see one.... What myths do you see?" The resulting brouhaha led the city council to ban all such religious (and irreligious) exhibitions, a decision that led atheists to triumphantly proclaim: "Reason Has Prevailed." The cofounder of the Freedom From Religion Foundation explained: "The free thinkers ... played the game of the religionists and they outsmarted them. They showed the Christian people of the city what it feels like to have a public park promoting views that offend your personal conscience. These views were on public property that were supposed to be owned equally by everyone."[24] In response to a Christmas crèche erected by a private group at the Wisconsin state capitol, the Foundation in 2011 installed what they termed a "slightly blasphemous" take on the Nativity scene, stating: "There's no war on Christmas, there's a war on the Constitution during the entire month of December." Their display mockingly celebrated the birth of the Unconquered Sun and included cutouts of a naked Venus, an astronaut, Charles Darwin, and Albert Einstein. A Foundation spokesperson remarked, apparently without irony: "In celebrating the Winter Solstice, we celebrate reality."[25]

In 2015, Nebraska atheists succeeded in supplanting the Christian Nativity scene at the state capitol. Realizing that groups could only book the capitol display area for one week, they were quick off the mark and secured the prime Christmas period for their exhibition, "Reason This Season." When December 18 rolled around the crèche that been on view was nowhere to be seen, having had to make way for the lessons the local militant godless had prepared. "It's going to be a big shindig," said Chris Clements of Lincoln Atheists. "Our message is that it's a secular government and religion has to stay separate from that. And it's meant to communicate that atheists are not bad people—we can be good without God."

The pointed message of the exhibit was a table holding a miniature church and mosque and symbols from other religions, with a wall keeping them apart from a tiny White House, Statue of Liberty, and US Capitol—a reminder of the American principle of separation of church and state. Other displays included a pine "reason tree" decked with messages promoting free thought and the "happy humanist," an eight-foot cardboard cutout of Thomas Paine.[26]

Atheists have increasingly used public advertising to make their point during the Christmas season, buying up billboards, advertising kiosks, and the sides of buses. Provocative messages read: "Who needs Christ at Christmas? Nobody"; "Why believe in a god? Be good for goodness' sake"; and "Reason's Greetings." Contrasting a jolly Santa with a crucified Jesus, a sign sponsored by American Atheists read "Keep the Merry! Dump the MYTH"; a Nativity scene accompanied the message "You KNOW it's a Myth. This season Celebrate Reason." In 2014 a five-city billboard campaign throughout the American Bible Belt featured the image of a child's letter. "Dear Santa," it read, "All I want for Christmas is to *skip church*! I'm too old for fairy tales"; a year later the billboards read: "Go ahead and skip church! Just be good for goodness sake. Happy holidays!" The 2014 campaign was justified in interesting new ways by American Atheists president David Silverman: "Millions of American children are forced to go to church under the threat of being denied meals, losing household privileges, having their college tuition cut off, or being kicked out of their homes. Many atheist adults are forced to go to church under threat of divorce or lose custody of their children. We must ask the question, who are the real bullies? Those who are unafraid to stand up for our views on billboards, or those who destroy families from the inside out?" A glimpse of a sense of humor was shown by the Freedom From Religion Foundation folks on their billboard, which read "Keep Saturn in Saturnalia," and by the online wag who begged: "Keep Mithra in the Midwinter Solstice Celebration." Atheists believe that this campaign is good for their image. Says David Silverman: "We are raising awareness, reducing ignorance, and enlightening this country. Atheists are here, atheism is growing, and if you have a silly idea, we are going to challenge you on that. And God is a silly myth." As for choosing religious holidays to pick fights with believers—"We don't go out of our way to avoid these times, and we even have a good reason for occasionally selecting them," Fred Edwords, national director of United Coalition of Reason, has said; "it is during Easter and Christmas that non-Christians become most aware that they don't belong to the dominant faith. They are forced to think about that. So this is an ideal time to let people like us know that they, too, can enjoy the warm fellowship of others who think as they do."[27]

This campaign naturally sparked a Christian fight back. In 2008 Missouri members of the Praise Chapel Christian Fellowship were motivated by atheist anti-Christmas advertising to take to the streets dressed as Jesus. In long flowing robes and crowns of thorns, they appeared at work and in malls, post offices, and restaurants to remind people of the religious roots of the holiday.[28] Billboard retaliations erupted, with pro-Christmas messages in public places, for example "God Is"; "You know it's Real. This season celebrate Jesus"; and "I Miss Hearing You Say 'Merry Christmas'—Jesus." The atheists' letter to Santa from a child complaining about church attendance was countered with the message "Dear Santa, All I want for Christmas is for families to keep Christmas sacred without being attacked on public billboards. Peace, dignity, and respect for all." Other counterattacks read: "Merry Christmas. It's my birthday. Join the celebration December 25. RSVPJesus.org"; and "Jesus Christ is the Reason for the Season." The Catholic League for Religious and Civil Rights sponsors such messages annually in New York but in 2014 chose to erect a pointed attack in Hollywood aimed at those running the American film industry:

Not All Christian Haters Are Equal:
Abroad We're Beheaded
At Home We're Bashed
The Differences Are Profound;
So Are the Similarities
Have a Peaceful and Joyous Christmas

"The Hollywood moguls who disrespect Christians are not the same as radical Muslims who behead us, but both are full of hate. Moreover, both need to be challenged," said the League's press release. "Christians are fed up with the barbarians abroad and the bigots at home. It's time all these bullies learned to practice the virtue of tolerance and the meaning of diversity." When legal threats by the Freedom From Religion Foundation forced the Minnesota town of Wadena to take down its traditional Nativity scene in 2015, disappointed citizens responded by turning the township into an orgy of crèches. A local movement sprang up to replace the single banned Nativity scene with hundreds of them in businesses, offices, and private yards. The mayor, who had reluctantly yielded to the Foundation's demand, put up eight displays in front of his own house.[29]

For those nonbelievers who hate to see the Christmas season pass without mailing out greetings to fellow infidels, merchants have provided a wide range of atheist holiday cards. One such card shows the Holy Family speaking to the Wise Men in the manger. Beneath her halo Mary tells the three visitors: "And remember, the main point of this whole thing is to promote shopping." Another depicts Jesus and the message "Accept God's Love This Christmas or He Will Burn You In Hell"; using the same graphic, another proclaims: "Christmas Is for Christians, Not Unsaved Human Trash Like You." One makes the pertinent astronomical point: "Axial Tilt is the Reason for the Season."[30] Many of these cards are witty; many are obscene. Most proceed from the assumption that religion is harmful or stupid and that atheists may make use of the season to mock the faithful.

In order to bolster their attack on Christmas, atheists now have their own online television channel, AtheistTV, which runs a series of programs to debunk the season. American Atheists president Dave Silverman has said, "Christmas is hard for many atheists, so we will provide programming free from superstition and fairy tales that allows families to watch together and not worry about being preached at." The offerings, though, were more preachy than entertaining, featuring a speech from Flynn, executive director of the Council for Secular Humanism, and shows such as "Is Christmas a Religious Holiday?"; "A Christmas With No Christ"; and "No Mercy on Christmas."[31]

Ultimately, atheists know that Christmas is too big to be destroyed, but waging war on it has benefits: attacking the holiday is a cost-effective way of spreading the atheist message. Engendering controversy during the holiday period against the celebration of the birth of the Baby Jesus is guaranteed to win lots of press coverage and air time. In their dreams, the best the activist atheists might hope for is to drive Christmas out of the public sphere and to privatize its celebration. As Hitchens has said, atheists have no desire to ban Christmas as the Puritan Parliament did. "No believer in the First Amendment could go that far. But there are millions of well-appointed buildings all across the United States, most of them tax-exempt and some of them receiving state subventions, where anyone can go at any time and celebrate miraculous births and pregnant virgins all day and all night if they so desire. These places are known as 'churches,' and they can also force passersby to look at the displays and billboards they erect and to give ear to the bells that they ring. In addition, they can count on numberless radio and TV stations to beam their stuff all through the ether. If this is not sufficient, then god damn them. God damn them everyone."[32]

The Christian Critique

The Puritans succeeded, for a time, in their war against Christmas. The holiday was banned in England from 1645 to 1660; the celebration virtually vanished in Scotland, where seasonal merriment was transferred to New Year's Eve. In New England, prejudice against marking the birth of Jesus either in church or in the family lingered until the late nineteenth century: Christmas was an ordinary working day in Boston until 1856, and schools in that city did not close for a Christmas holiday until 1870. As Christmas observance became wildly popular, the Calvinist objections to Yuletide merriment gradually grew weaker; the issue no longer dominated public debate, and even Presbyterian churches—longtime strongholds of Scottish Calvinist worship in North America—began to celebrate the Nativity.[33]

But the Christian objections to Christmas never completely disappeared, and to this day a variety of churches still wage a determined war against its celebration. Many, probably most, of these groups are rooted in

Calvinist theology, particularly in its Scottish guise, while others are more recent Christian sects that in earlier times might have been termed heretical.[34] Their battle is carried on in earnest debate, witty (and not so witty) parody, and offensive public provocations.

Neo-Calvinist theologians muster a range of arguments against Christmas, and most would be familiar to their coreligionists of the sixteenth and seventeenth centuries (see chapter 2). "Whatever is not commanded by Scripture in the worship of God is forbidden. Anything that the church does in worship must have warrant from an explicit command of God, be deduced by good and necessary consequence, or be derived from approved historical example (e.g., the change of day from seventh to first for Lord's day corporate worship)."[35] This regulative principle, that ceremonies not directly ordained by God are to be considered manmade and idolatry, is as important to modern objectors as it was to the Puritans of King Charles I's time. A twentieth-century Calvinist happily quoted a Scottish opponent of Charles I from the 1630s calling all nonbiblical observances "the wares of Rome, the baggage of Babylon, the trinkets of the whore, the badges of Popery, the ensigns of Christ's enemies, and the very trophies of Antichrist."[36] Even customs such as the giving of gifts or sending Christmas cards with scripture verses on them is forbidden to such believers as "an abomination in the sight of God."[37]

It is vital for these opponents of Christmas to locate the origins of its celebrations not in early Christianity but in pre-Christian paganism. Not content with identifying the usual suspects—Saturnalia, Mithra, the Kalends—they want to unveil even older culprits: the Babylonians and Egyptians. According to one critic, December 25 was the birthday of Tammuz, the Babylonian sun god, and the Egyptians performed a "tree ceremony" on the birthday of their sun god, Ra, who was, not coincidentally, born on December 25.[38] Another noted that Isis the Egyptian "queen of heaven" gave birth near the winter solstice and revealed that "Yule" was Babylonian for "infant." Even the innocent Christmas ham was linked to the killing of Adonis by a wild boar.[39] Where Christmas is not pagan, it is irremediably linked to something almost as bad—papistry, the practices of the Roman Catholic Church. "The Mass of 'Christ' Is Plainly Idolatry: Christmas gets its name from the Latin Christes Masse, or the Mass of Christ.... By celebrating the 'Mass' of Christ, one is openly supporting the authority of the Roman Catholic Church, and its pagan Mass."[40] The blog "Balaam's Ass" is even unkinder:

All Saints Day was fixed on November 1 so that the pagans could come to town, sacrifice a baby to the devil, then the next day they could go to Mass and drop a coin in the collection box in the name of the saints. At the winter solstice, the Roman Catholic Church simply did a "bait and switch" on the pagans. They took Greek Core and Roman Lato away from them, and they gave the pagans a new goddess and son—Mary and Jesus. Thus, the very first Christmas in which Mary and Jesus were involved is clearly a pagan affair. The Mary and Jesus of the Roman Catholic Whore Church are devils from Sumer and Babylon who happen to have the same names as two Bible characters whom we dearly love.[41]

This anti-Catholicism appears frequently in the amended versions of popular Christmas carols that one James Dodson produced in the 1990s. Take, for example, "God Keep of All You Protestants" (sung to the tune of "God Rest Ye Merry Gentlemen"):

> *God keep all of you Protestants*
> *From walking in the way*
> *Of heathens and idolaters*
> *To celebrate this day.*
> *You resurrect this Romish mass,*
> *for you have gone astray.*
> *Chorus: O, I know that its just a popish ploy, popish ploy*
> *Yes, I know that its just a popish ploy.*
> *You celebrate the birth of Christ*
> *Though God did not command*
> *This service of idolatry*
> *Is not part of His plan*
> *You wed the devil to the Son,*
> *when Christ-Mass you demand.*

And who could forget that timeless classic "Banish Christmas," crooned to the tune of Mel Tormé's "Christmas Song," where instead of roasting chestnuts we have the unfortunate Michael Servetus, executed for heresy in John Calvin's Geneva in 1553.

> *Servetus roasting in an open fire*
> *John Knox preaching where he can*

Calvin teaching against every sin
The folk all look so Puritan.
Everybody knows idolatry is wickedness
for papist, Protestant or Jew.
Though some people say,
They got carried away
Banish Christmas here, too![42]

Bad roots produce poisoned fruit, say the neo-Calvinists: Christmas customs are base and vulgar, full of alcohol, prone to violence, and leading to debauchery. The criticisms of excess that began in the fourth century have never ceased. There was even a brief revival of Puritan anti-Christmas sentiment in Boston in 2001, when the Church With the Good News tried to buy transit advertising proclaiming that "Christians in the Bible never observed Christmas" and did not believe in "lies about Santa Claus, flying reindeer, elves, and drunken parties."[43] Other critics asked plaintively:

> What about the parties and revelries and debauchery that take place at this time of year, supposedly in connection with the birth of Jesus Christ. Why is it that liquor flows more freely at this time of year than any other? Why is it that there are more automobile accidents during the "holiday season" than at any other time? We may quibble about the origins of the Christmas tree and manger scene, but one thing is certain: If you use the Incarnation of our Lord as an excuse for revelry and debauchery, you can be sure that you will reap the judgment of God.[44]

These arguments are not new; as the neo-Calvinists would happily assert, they are long-standing in the Reformed Christian tradition. What is new about the neo-Calvinists' attack on Christmas is their sense of humor, something notoriously lacking in the turgid tract wars of previous centuries, coupled with the traditional Puritan indifference to the offense their arguments gave to the general populace. Consider the glee with which some neo-Calvinists demonize Santa Claus, as revealed in this 1990 North Carolina handout that portrays Santa as a devil. A poem titled "Ho! Ho! Ho!" accompanies the illustration. It begins: "The devil has a demon, / His name is Santa Claus. / He's a dirty old demon!"[45] Lest you think that Santa's cry of "Ho! Ho! Ho!" was an innocent expression of Yuletide mirth, consider this: "Every time Santa says Ho-Ho-Ho, he is saying 666. How can a person know this? Each word 'HO' has 6 letters and spaces between the H and the O You get…H i j k l m n O If you write down the number of letters and spaces between each H and O, they add up to 6. HO-HO-HO equals 6 6 6." As if that weren't evidence enough, it can be revealed that another term for Satan (according to the *Oxford English Dictionary*) is "Old Nick." Thus, "every time we refer to good Ole Saint Nick, we are actually referring to Satan!!! And not to be outdone, the Catholic church made him a Saint!"⁴⁶

If Santa is truly demonic, then what should good Christians do about him? Put the jolly old fellow on trial, of course. This was the course adopted in 1980 by the Truth Tabernacle Church of Burlington, North Carolina. A quasi-judicial proceeding charged him with being a "Babylonian inter-loper posing as a Catholic," impersonating a saint, molesting children, appearing in liquor ads, and as a pagan, stealing Christmas from Christ. No one could be found to speak up for Santa; consequently, he was sen-tenced to be hanged in effigy. (Not to be outdone, in 1981 a Truth Tabernacle Church in Niles, Ohio, burnt the Easter Bunny in public.)⁴⁷ It is not known whether the Santa figure that was hanged from a church in Denmark in 2010 was given a fair trial. Pastor Jon Knudsen, of the Løkken Free Church in Vendsyssel, claimed that Santa Claus was a demon who led people into paganism at Christmas. Knudsen strung up an image of the magical Gift-Bringer with a sign that read: "We forsake the devil and all his evil deeds, and all his being." An offended passerby rescued the strangled Santa in order to, as he said, bring joy back to children, and was hailed as a public hero. Undaunted, the brave pastor, who also performs home elf exor-cisms, has hanged Santa Claus every Christmas since.⁴⁸ Back in America, the devilish Santa with his infernal love of Christmas is repelled by a holy command:

The Light Before Christmas

'Twas the night before Christmas; and strange as it seems
I wasn't indulging in covetous dreams;
But reading my Bible, I searched for a clue
Why Christians take part in this holiday too.
I plainly could see that it carried His name,
But the spirit behind it just wasn't the same.
The songs spoke of wise men, of virgin and child,
Of shepherds, of God, and all men reconciled;
But nothing was said of the blood and the cross;

Of repentance, and faith, and of counting the cost.
They sang of the babe, His miraculous birth,
But not of the day when He'll judge the whole earth.
My Bible said nothing of Santa, or toys,
Of Frosty the Snowman, and small drummer boys.
A reference to Rudolph not once did I see.
But it seems Jeremiah did mention the tree.
I sat and I pondered this curious matter,
When out on the roof there arose such a clatter
That I knew in a moment he soon would be here;
So I prayed in the Spirit and stood without fear.
He slipped down the chimney, quick as a flash,
And stepped from the fireplace all covered with ash.
There stood St. Nick with his bag and his beard,
He looked at the Bible I held, and he sneered,
"Another fanatical Christian, I see;
No stockings; no holly, no pictures of me."
I asked him if Jesus was God in the flesh,
He said that was something he couldn't confess.
He said, "I am Santa, I come from afar."
I stood in the truth—"The Devil you are.
That suit and that beard doesn't fool me one bit.
Your jolly deception is straight from the pit.
Beneath all your Ho Ho Ho's Lucifer lurks;
With your all-seeing eyes and your gospel of works
Like a thief in the night you impersonate Christ,
Returning to judge the naughty and nice."
"So call Christmas pagan," he said, "That's O.K.
'Cause that's what my sons at the Watchtower say.
You'll look like a pagan or like a deceiver,
But none will suspect you to be a believer."
I said, "I don't care what your servants will say,
My loyalty lies with the Ancient of Days.
No matter how many abuses are hurled,
My Bible says be not conformed to this world.
You have no power, and no part of me,
So I stand on God's Word, and command you to flee."
He squealed like a pig that was stuck with a knife.
He ran to the chimney and climbed for his life.

And I heard him exclaim, as he drove out of sight,
"Merry Xmas to all, and a long, dark night."[49]

One of the darkest blots on the American landscape in the early twenty-first century was the figure of Fred Phelps, leader of the Westboro Baptist Church in Topeka, Kansas, an independent congregation utterly unaffiliated with, and vehemently repudiated by, every official Baptist denomination. Phelps, born in 1929, came to fame in the 1950s as a civil rights lawyer who defended black clients and successfully fought a number of racial discrimination cases; in the 1980s he was awarded commendations by African American groups for his legal work. He was a registered Democrat who on numerous occasions ran for governor of Kansas; he finished second in the 1992 Democratic primary for the US Senate, receiving over 30 percent of the vote. In the 1980s Phelps began to campaign against homosexuality—politically, by sponsoring referenda against gay rights, and religiously, by sermons and demonstrations. This became his signature cause and vaulted him into international attention. It is Phelps's contention that by refusing to condemn homosexuality America deserved God's wrath and that any disaster befalling the country and its citizens was a "Godsmack"—a divine punishment. The 9/11 bombings were such a punishment, as was the death of any American soldier or indeed of any American child. In order to bring this point home, Phelps and his family (thirteen children, eleven of whom are lawyers) have picketed funerals and mocked the loved ones of the dead. This behavior was so outrageous that numerous state governments passed laws against it, but in 2010 the Supreme Court ruled, eight to one, that it was protected by the First Amendment to the Constitution. The white-hot zealotry of the Phelps clan can be seen in the names of the websites the church's followers maintain: godhatesfags.com, godhatesislam.com, godhatesthemedia.com, godhatesindia.com, godhatesamerica.com, and, lest anyone be missed out, godhatestheworld.com. Hate is Westboro's prime commodity.

Among other targets of Phelps and company have been the Catholic Church, Princess Diana, Mormons, Mr. Rogers, Billy Graham, and Christmas. The attack on Christmas stems from Phelps's Calvinism and takes on the usual Puritan critique of paganness, debauchery, and Catholic links, with the added zest of calculated outrageousness. Among the many provocative signs at Westboro demonstrations—"God Hates Dead Soldiers"; "Thank God for Breast Cancer"; "God Hates Fags" are typical—can be found those aimed at Christmas: not surprisingly, "God Hates Christmas" and a decorated pine tree labeled "Pagan Idol."

Likes James Dodson, the Phelps clan has a large supply of parodic Christmas songs: "Doom to the World" replaces "Joy to the World"; "This Might Be Your Final Christmas" is based on "We Wish You a Merry Christmas"; and this ditty replaces "Santa Claus Is Coming to Town":

Santa Claus Will Take You to Hell.

You better watch out,
get ready to cry.
You better go hide I'm telling you why,
'cuz Santa Claus will take you to Hell
He is your favorite idol,
You worship at his feet,
But when you stand before your God,
He won't help you take the heat.
So get this fact straight,
You're feeling God's hate
Santa's to blame for the economy's fate
Santa Claus will take you to hell.
Don't leave your kids
With this red fright
Just like a priest
He'll rape 'em at night.
You tell the children he is real
You know that's just a lie
To justify your own vile sins
Is the only reason why.
So get this fact straight,
You're feeling God's hate
Santa's to blame for the dead soldier's fate.
Santa Claus will take you to hell.[50]

The message to Americans who celebrate Christmas is clear: "You evil freaks are not content to bring the wrath of God upon your own heads, but you cause your children from the womb to land squarely in the cross hairs of a furious God. YOU—THE PARENTS AND LOVED ONES OF THOSE DEAD SOLDIERS—KILLED THOSE CHILDREN. Every time you put

Christmas in their face, every time you told them it's okay to be gay, every time you told them God loves everyone, you sealed their doom!!!... Your hateful, vicious, murderous, thieving, feces eating, adultery, fornication, idolatry (think Christmas as the mother of all idolatry and branch out from there) has made the deeds of the people of Sodom and Ancient Israel pale, such that God says you have justified them—that is, you make them look good!"[51] Fred Phelps's death in 2014 has done nothing to diminish the zeal of his followers, who have continued his campaign of confrontation.

In June 2015 a service at Houston's Lakewood megachurch was interrupted by members of a radical Protestant sect. Six men, shouting out scripture verses and "Joel Osteen, you're a liar," tried to disrupt the morning sermon but were escorted from the premises and charged with trespassing. Coming less than two weeks after the church massacre in Charleston, South Carolina, the incident made national headlines and drew attention to the hecklers' Church of Wells, an ultrafundamentalist congregation with a reputation for confrontation that, it appears, not only opposes Pastor Osteen's theology but most other churches calling themselves Christian.[52] Naturally, the Church of Wells despises the celebration of Christmas. Their website contains a number of lengthy poems decrying the holiday and an extended rant about the evil of Santa Claus. Elder Sean Morris opines in his online tract "The Abominable Sacrifice to Santa Clause [*sic*]":

Xmas is the heathen's heaven, and their cumulative lust and dream of a Judgment Day with God. Everyone esteems the kindness, care, and love the season brings. However, this "kind and generous" community of families is a grief to God; a mockery of blasphemy that tries the forbearance of a jealous God! I urge you, do not eat and drink in the forbidden, forsaken, land of pseudo-Christianity. The land is defiled with blood. But you will say, "What blood? There is no sacrifice here."

Thus Santa Clause [*sic*] is the spiritual kidnapper of the Western world's children, and America's children are being spiritually given over to the fire of Satan's hell because the professing Christians that are either spiritually destitute, or dull of hearing infants in danger of wrath. But you will say, "What is he talking about?" Come now ye sinners and adulterous Christians, the blood of your children does rise up to God for judgment and wrath. What will ye do in the end thereof when the God of Abel lays hold on judgment? Satan was able to cause those who follow Baal to physically give their children to be burned as a sacrifice to Baal. Satan has craftily accomplished this task in false Christianity by the multitudes on December 25th. The parents may not believe in the reality and existence of Santa Clause, but their children do.[53]

See also Morris's "Xmas Day Wake Up Call," prophesying that those who go to church on Christmas are rotten souls who "will be covered in carnivorous fowls to feast on [their] rottenness like ravening wolves."[54]

Not to be outdone, Elder Jordan Fraker has his own poetic take on the holidays. Riffing on Psalm 50, Fraker asks (entirely rhetorically): "A merry christmas now sanctified? No possibility stands! / For as a whole it hath defied, and broken My commands! / Fear God and do it not, lest I tear [you] in pieces wholly."[55] Like Westboro Baptist Church, the Church of Wells believes in a God who kills people. "Reconcile yourself," they say, "to the fact that the Holy God of the universe, as revealed in the bible, may be willing to riddle your Xmas living room with your carcasses if you do not repent." A unique aspect of their anti-Christmas message is the correlation between the celebration of the holiday and the late-December rise in death rates. In "A Case Against Xmas: A case presented in the light of over 500 verses from Holy Scripture," Morris repeats some of the centuries-old Calvinist objections: Christmas is of pagan origin; Christmas is of Catholic origin; any nonbiblical ceremony is idolatry; marking Christmas is not commanded in the Bible; we do not know the time of the Nativity; Christmastime behavior is unworthy; mirth is suspect; and so on. To these familiar criticisms Morris adds his analysis of medical statistics. He quotes studies purporting to show that cardiac death rates are highest on December 25 and 26, and January 1 and that noncardiac mortality peaks on those same days. This means that from 1973 to 2001, "42,039 more deaths occurred than would be expected if the holidays did not affect mortality." While scientists search for the cause of this seasonal pandemic in explanations such as delay in seeking treatment, Morris is certain "we need more than fallible, man-motivated hypotheses; we need the unalterable, undeniable, infallible, eternal word of God to shine light on the gloom of this situation." In other words, God is to blame. In the eyes of a righteous and wrathful deity, Christmas is an abomination, and its observance must be punished in the way that a long list of Old Testament transgressors were smitten.[56]

Another peculiar stance of the Church of Wells is their objection to the crèche, or Nativity scene, as an instance of idolatry:

> Nearly every form of pagan worship descended from the Babylonian mysteries, which focus attention on the "mother-goddess" and the birth of her child. This was adapted to "Mary-Jesus" worship, which then easily accommodated the multitude of pagans "converted" to Christianity inside Constantine's Roman Catholic Church. If anyone were to erect statues or images of Mary and Joseph by themselves, many within Protestant circles would cry "Idolatry!" But at Xmas time, an image of a little baby is placed with the images of Mary and Joseph, and it's called a "nativity scene." Somehow, the baby Jesus statue "sanctifies" the scene, and it is no longer considered idolatry![57]

Other ultra-Protestant groups have criticized Christmas vegetation such as the evergreen tree and the wreath as pagan, but the Church of Wells may be the only one to place the origins of the mistletoe custom in Celtic homosexuality.[58] They have also discovered what philologists have long puzzled over: the meaning of the word "Yule." Brushing aside long-held academic findings that the term is of Scandinavian descent, this church states that Yule was "a Chaldean word meaning 'infant'"—a clear reference to the ancient sun god Tammuz, child of Semiramis. Their mastery of linguistic anthropology knows no bounds: a page later they reveal that "Jule" was a Scandinavian "sex-and-fertility god" whose worship demanded twelve days (!) of human or animal sacrifice. Can such a holiday be redeemed? Can anyone put Christ back in Christmas? No, says the Church of Wells, it is idolatry. "The 'spirit' of Xmas is a demonic spirit, the reason for the season has become a provision for biblical treason."

"Christianity is based upon pagan LIES and anyone that teaches Christ was born on Christmas day will be found a liar!" This is the opinion of Israel United in Christ, an African American church that believes that the original Twelve Tribes of Israel were black. Those who call themselves Jews in the twenty-first century are merely Caucasian converts—today's Native Americans, Puerto Ricans, Jamaicans, Haitians, and American blacks are the true descendants of biblical Israel. Israel United holds to many Jewish customs, including the Saturday Sabbath, Passover, and the Day of Atonement, but decries Sunday worship, Mother's Day, Easter, and other "false holidays," among which they number Christmas. "Christmas trees, holiday shopping sales, decorations in offices, homes, and storefronts.

These are all signs of the approaching holiday season. Once again, it is the season for Israel to be sober and mindful of the laws, statues, and commandments of the Most High. We should be sober and mindful of the laws always, but in this season of increased pagan worship, we must increase our strength in Christ to fight off the so-called 'Holiday Spirit.'"[59] Today's Christmas tree was clearly foreseen by the Prophet Jeremiah, who said of pagan worshipers: "For the customs of the people are vain: for one cutteth a tree out of the forest, the work of the hands of the workman, with the axe. They deck it with silver and with gold; they fasten it with nails and with hammers, that it move not." As for Santa Claus, Israel United is onto him as well. When Megyn Kelly of Fox News claimed that Santa Claus was white, they retorted: "The imaginary Chris Kringle aka santa clause is actual[ly] based on a real life man named St. Nicholas. A Russian Jew that celebrated the feast of dedication/Hanakkuh. He never celebrated pagan Christmas according to the holy scriptures." In fact, as Russian icons show, St. Nicholas was black.[60]

Israel United in Christ is not alone among "Black Hebrew" groups condemning Christmas. "All Holidays are Evil as well as your Birthday celebration. The Most High doesn't recognize any of these pagan Holidays. Many people across the world celebrate these Evil Holidays, Christians and other so called religions. In fact, the Most High doesn't even care about these Holiday's are blesses them, so why do we? In truth, the Most High curse them rather than honour them. Did you know where the word Holiday comes from? Holiday comes from the word Holy-day. There is nothing Holy about these Holidays in America. I am going to give you proof that we shouldn't celebrate these Evil Holidays." So says Israelites Unite, a church with a similar Judaizing approach; they use many of the same biblical proof-texts as Israel United in Christ and the Church of Wells. Nimrod and his son Tammuz are featured, as are Jeremiah and his dislike of decorated trees; we learn that "Santa is Satan spelled inside out."[61] The Israelite Church of God in Jesus Christ Inc. is also onto the numerous deceptions and impieties of the Christmas season. In "A True Spiritual View," spokesperson Izaraya-Nathan uses biblical calculations to prove that Jesus was born in springtime rather than December and says that "no matter how hard you pray over the ham," you can't justify breaking God's laws and deceiving your children. "Will you continue to lie about Satan Claws coming down the chimney especially when some of you don't even own a chimney? You work hard, break your neck, and don't pay your rent to put toys on layaway for your children, just to tell them that the fat white man you saw in a red suit at the mall gave them those gifts. Now that's really childish." Only Jewish holidays such as Hanukkah should be kept.[62]

Though groups such as Israelites Unite believe that African Americans are the true descendants of the biblical Jews, the British Israelite movement has quite contrary ideas on the subject. It claims that the white inhabitants of northern and western Europe (and those who emigrated to North America from there) are the true children of the Ten Lost Tribes of Israel, who disappeared from history after being taken captive by the Assyrians in the eighth century B.C. One of the offshoots of that movement is the Ohio-based United Church of God, who believe that Christianity has wrongly abandoned many of the Jewish customs that would have marked the primitive Church of the first century. They cling to Saturday rather than Sunday as the Sabbath; they celebrate Jewish holidays and reject those they see as innovations, such as Easter and Christmas. The tract "Holidays or Holy Days—Does It Matter Which Days We Observe?" asks: "what do a bearded man in a red suit, brightly decorated trees, mistletoe, holly and candles have to do with the birth of Jesus Christ? Why is December 25 assumed to be the day of His birth when the Bible itself nowhere gives the actual date and, in fact, gives strong indications that Jesus *could not* have been born at that time of year?"[63] The United Church of God ascribes to the usual set of accusations about the heathen origins of Christmas: its roots in the paganism of Rome and Persia and its situation on December 25 as a response to Saturnalia and the Kalends; Santa Claus as an avatar of Odin, Saturn, or Silenus.

It may be worth noting that the United Church of God rejects the Trinitarian view of the Deity (where the Father, Son, and Holy Spirit are three persons in one God). In fact, it is not uncommon for non-Trinitarian churches to reject Christmas. Jehovah's Witnesses, the Philippine-based Iglesia ni Cristo, the True Jesus Church, which originated in China, and the Church of God (Seventh Day) are alike in their avoidance of the holiday. The United Church of God is also a Sabbatarian organization, preferring Friday evening to Saturday evening as the Lord's Day, rather than Sunday, and this too tends to be a marker for anti-Christmas sentiment. Seventh-day Adventists are perhaps the largest American denomination in this category.[64]

Though few would go as far in opposing Christmas as Fred Phelps, the Church of Wells, and other hyper-Calvinists, many Christians still have bones to pick with the holiday. For them there are lessons to be learned from earlier critiques, lessons that move them in various ways to reform Christmas. In the last half of the twentieth century these reformers have sought to emphasize the spiritual aspect of the holiday and to purge it of its connections to the world of buying and selling. In 1949 American Catholics launched campaigns to reclaim Christmas for the faithful and to refocus attention on the manger rather than the pile of presents under the tree. "Put Christ Back in Christmas" was the slogan adopted by the Milwaukee Archconfraternity of Christian Mothers, whose crusade attracted national attention. The strategy involved a publicity blitz, cooperation with pious laypeople, the Knights of Columbus, clergy, politicians, schools, and local merchants. Its success attracted Protestants to the movement, and throughout the early 1950s it penetrated the public consciousness and, most remarkably, the commercial marketplace. Stores, banks, restaurants, and other popular gathering places began to display Nativity scenes; businesses of all kinds used "Put Christ Back in Christmas" in their advertising.[65] God and Mammon had come together to save the holiday.

Such campaigns naturally had to confront the problem of Santa Claus, the world's dominant fictional character and the one who most successfully bridged the gap between capitalism and Christmas—he was, after all, the first imaginary being from whom humans took shopping advice and the secular spirit to whom millions of children addressed their desires. Parents and clergy had long worried that his popularity was displacing the Baby Jesus at the heart of the season. In December 1949, *Catholic Review,* the magazine of the Archdiocese of Washington and Baltimore, took the gloves off and gave the magical Gift-Bringer a punch on his cherry-red nose. The editor, Reverend John Sinnott Martin, called Santa Claus a "Sugar Daddy," "usurper," and "unholy fraud" who had displaced Christ from the minds of "children who learn about the reindeer but have never heard about the ox and the ass." Santa was a myth "but not half as sensible as Jupiter, Baal, Mr. Elwood P. Dowd's Harvey or Barnaby's fairy godfather." Teaching children to believe in Santa would only lead to the "painful, unnecessary and dangerous disillusionment that, sooner or later, will take from Christmas the cheap enchantment that gave it a hazardous happiness founded upon a lie and ending in the loss of childish confidence and trust and faith." The solution was to banish Santa altogether: "Leave Santa to those who have nothing better. Leave him to those for whom life must end in disillusion and despair. For Christians Christmas without Christ is a blasphemy."[66]

Public relations campaigns to keep Christ and the cradle at the center of Christmas continued throughout the 1950s and 1960s. Perhaps the most spectacular of these took place in Dijon, France. On the day before Christmas Eve in 1951 the public burning of Santa Claus in the confines of the beautiful Gothic cathedral of Saint-Bénigne attracted attention around the world. This was a demonstration of resentment of the French Catholic Church toward the growing influence of Santa in the religious experience of families at the expense of the more traditional seasonal symbols, the Nativity scene, and *le petit Jésus*. Strong flavors of nationalism and anti-Americanism were also involved. (French people's pique simmered over their diminished global influence, their need for massive Marshall Plan aid from the United States, and the appearance of foreign Christmas innovations like large illuminated trees, Salvation Army appeals, and wrapped presents.)[67] The American Santa, said the local Catholic hierarchy, represented the paganization of an important Christian festival and was a myth devoid of religious value; he was a heretic and a usurper. Cardinal Jean-Gérard Saliège, the archbishop of Toulon, accused Santa Claus's supporters of using him as a way to strip Christmas of its religious character; Cardinal Clément Roques, the archbishop of Rennes, denounced the "unreasoning stupidity" behind this imaginary character. They decried the fact that Santa had been received into public schools, where the crèche had been banned by law. So, in front of a crowd of young people, an oversized effigy of the Gift-Bringer was strung up from the railings of the church, and a voice demanded: "Does Santa Claus deserve death?" "Yes, yes!," screamed the mob of children, who pelted the image of Santa with orange peels as he was set alight. After the execution, a manifesto was posted on the church door: "United in all the Christian homes of the parish, 250 children who want to fight against lies have burned Santa Claus. This is not a vaudeville act, but a protest against lies which are incapable of awakening the religious feelings of children and are in no sense a method of education. To a Christian, Christmas is the anniversary of the Savior's birth."[68] Academics, psychiatrists, Marxist theoreticians, and other anti-American elements among the intelligentsia who would normally array themselves against the Catholic Church signaled their agreement with the attack on the transatlantic interloper. (The next day, however, pro-Santa forces rallied, and a demonstration in favor of Père Noël was held in front of the Dijon town hall.) Almost sixty years later, three French Catholic youth belonging to the ultraconservative Fraternity of St. Pius X repeated the Dijon auto-da-fé by setting a Père Noël doll on fire and posting the conflagration on the internet. They called Santa a pagan idol and claimed that "in this time of perdition the enemies of Our Lord attempt to de-Christianize Christmas." Burning Santa was purification by fire and the only appropriate response to an attempt to make a substitute to the true God. They called on French families at Christmastime to "make an example to your neighbourhood of decorating the exterior of your house only with representations of the Nativity." Pope Benedict XVI avoided criticizing Santa Claus openly, but in the Christmas season of 2005 he took aim at the sort of activity Santa is often used to personify. He noted that "in today's consumer society, this period has unfortunately suffered a sort of commercial 'pollution' that risks changing its authentic spirit, marked by recollection, moderation and joy, which is not external but intimate." One solution for this malaise, he suggested, was the tradition of a family Nativity scene. "Putting up the Crib at home can be a simple but effective way of presenting faith, to pass it on to one's children."[69]

For fifteen hundred years Christians have marked the approach of Christmas with a season of spiritual and physical preparation known as Advent. In the early twenty-first century, churches hoped to reemphasize that period as a way to preserve the festival's deeper meanings. Environmentally minded Christians in the United Kingdom recommended that families and churches "reclaim Christmas" and put "the waiting back into waiting." The *Times* reported that the Church of England's new Advent website offered a contrasting response to the economic downturn, compared to the efforts of the chancellor of the exchequer to boost High Street spending. Whywearewaiting.com featured an interview with the archbishop of Canterbury, Rowan Williams. Advocating a more austere approach to the season, Williams critiqued the consumerism of Christmas that easily crowded out the traditional Advent activities of waiting and reflecting: "We don't have quite the sort of quiet we need to think, 'Well what would it be if Jesus really came as if for the first time into my life?'" The website includes a quiz about patience and daily quotations one can open up onscreen. Meanwhile, with the motto "Shop less, live more, save the earth," the team at Operation Noah, anxious about climate change, is promoting a series of events throughout Advent encouraging people to experience Advent in its traditional sense—as a period of "quiet reflection and eager anticipation for the birth of Christ" rather than a time to buy and consume. Among the suggested activities for the Christmas season are meeting at a local landfill site and gathering for a short service of reflection on how humanity is running up ecological debts. One might bring shopping receipts, credit card statements, and other symbols of mass consumption and burn them in a brazier.[70]

Though the evangelical wing of Christianity has been an innovative and enthusiastic user of broadcast media, mainline churches have been more reluctant to take their message on air. One historian of the relationship between advertising and religion has noted that Church of England bishops fretted in 1941 over the first radio broadcast of Dorothy Sayers's pious play *The Man Born to Be King* because it involved listeners hearing the voice of Christ.[71] Eventually, however, churches made the decision to spend money on media campaigns to orient believers to proper attitudes toward Christmas. The United Church of Canada, for example, launched a "Christ in Christmas" initiative—a series of billboard, radio, and television ads that aimed at reducing consumerism and alcohol consumption during the holidays.[72] In 1992 a coalition of American religious leaders launched "A Campaign to Take Commercialism out of Christmas." Leading Catholic, Unitarian, and Protestant clergy criticized the "advertising lords" of Madison Avenue who "had reduced Christmas to a carnival of mass marketing." They called on the faithful to consider how excess spending could lead to debt, harm the planet, and sap the spiritual significance of Christmas, "fostering the belief that the marketplace can fulfill our highest aspirations."[73] This does not seem to have been a successful effort. Merchants, in the midst of a recession, were worried about their bottom lines, and Christian critics noted that despite the plea for more spiritual content in the season, the manifesto lacked a single reference to Jesus, whose birth was the occasion for the celebration of Christmas.[74] It is perhaps the nature of such appeals to the public conscience to generate controversy. That is certainly the case with the long-running series of provocative advertisements by the Christian Advertising Network, a coalition of British denominations who sponsor an annual Christmas ad campaign meant to attract people to churches during the holidays and to focus attention on the figure in the cradle. Their 1996 advertisement depicted the arrival of the Magi with a caption reading: "Bad hair day? You're a virgin, you've just given birth, and now three kings have shown up—find out the happy ending at a church near you." Tackling the problem of misplaced priorities, the 2003 initiative featured a classic painting of the Nativity with a baby Santa replacing the Baby Jesus. The caption read: "Go on, ask him for something this Christmas." In 2010 an ultrasound photograph of a fetus with a halo proclaimed: "He's on his way. Christmas starts with Christ."

Though often encountering resistance and protest, these efforts by the Christian Advertising Network (now going by the name ChurchAds.net) at least offered critiques of modern attitudes to Christmas and emphasized the figure of Jesus. A New Zealand "progressive" church seemed more interested in causing offense for the sake of debate with its own Christmas advertising. In 2009 the rector of St. Matthew-in-the-City, an Auckland congregation of the Church of England, posted a billboard in front of his church featuring a dejected Joseph lying beside Mary in bed, with the headline "Poor Joseph. God is a hard act to follow." This was apparently to challenge the notion of a virgin birth and the literal maleness of God. In 2012 the church erected another poster showing a shocked Virgin Mary reacting to a pregnancy test. Clergy invited commenters to think up captions for the billboard "as a way to promote conversation." Suggestions included: "If I say I'm a virgin, Mum and Dad won't kill me," and, "Now, which way to the abortion clinic?" The sign was torn down by an angry passerby. Undaunted, the bold clergyman doubled down on his provocation the next year by captioning a picture of a manger and child "It's time for Jesus to come out"; the suggestion being that Jesus might have been gay. Reverend Glynn Cardy claimed the sign was meant to "lift the humanity of Jesus." A breathless downtown Auckland awaited Cardy's 2013 outrage, but he disappointed the curious by leaving the Anglican Church and taking a job with a suburban Presbyterian congregation. Needless to say, he produced another sign for Christmas; this time a far less in-your-face message asked: "If God took a selfie—a self-portrait— what would it look like?" The answer was a haloed baby in a manger. Cardy's 2015 Christmas billboard was a dreadfully uncontroversial image equating the Holy Family seeking refuge with the current refugee crisis.[75] The billboard included this passage from a poem by Christina Rossetti:

> *What can I give Him,*
> *Poor as I am?*
> *If I were a shepherd*
> *I would bring a lamb,*
> *If I were a wise man*
> *I would do my part,*
> *Yet what I can I give Him,*
> *Give my heart.*[76]

Also featured was this quote from Bill McKibben: "Christmas is a school for consumerism—in it we learn to equate delight with materialism. We celebrate the birth of One who told us to give everything to the poor by giving each other motorized tie racks."[77] Time and again churches returned to consumerism as a threat to the proper celebration of Christmas. Just as Bishop Asterius in 400 complained about the waste and extravagance of the Kalends, critics bemoaned the fact that Christians had fallen into a new idolatry. For an increasing number of Christians, Christmas had simply become too much about consumption, and they were not going to put up with it anymore. For some this meant using the season as a call to simple living; for yet others it meant that to save Christmas, capitalism itself would have to die.

For years the leading Christian voices trying to reform Christmas by opposing the season's commercialization came from a nonprofit organization known as Alternatives for Simple Living. It was founded in 1973 and for decades churned out books such as *Simplify and Celebrate*, videos like *Break Forth Into Joy!: Beyond a Consumer Lifestyle*, and kits and tools to encourage a more meaningful celebration. Its most influential product was its booklet "Whose Birthday Is It Anyway?" It had wide circulation through churches. The 1999 edition, for example, contained suggestions for suitable charities to make a Christmas donation to, tips for making a ceremony of setting out the family Nativity scene, spiritual and social activities through Advent, and stories and reflections to concentrate on the religious core of the holiday. This is a typical set of suggestions generated by Alternatives:

TEN TIPS FOR A SIMPLER, MORE MEANINGFUL CHRISTMAS

1. Plan ahead. Instead of going on auto-pilot the day after Thanksgiving, hold a family meeting to decide what the group really wants to do and who's going to do what.
2. If you need a symbol for giving (in addition to Jesus and the Three Wise Ones), learn about St. Nicholas. Santa Claus has been completely taken over by commerce.
3. Avoid debt. Refuse to be pressured by advertising to overspend.
4. Avoid stress. Give to yourself. Don't assume that things have to be the same way they've always been.
5. Draw names rather than everyone giving something to everyone else in your giving circle. Set a ceiling for each recipient. Give

children ONE thing they really want, rather than so many gifts. If need be, pool funds.

6. Give appropriate gifts. Get to know the recipient. Give what they want to receive, not what you want to buy. Avoid war toys and violent video games.

7. Give alternative gifts. Give 25% of what you spent last year to the needy…individuals or groups locally, nationally or internationally.

   Buy crafts and clothing from developing countries at alternative gift markets, not from commercial importers, so that the artisans receive a fair price for their work. Give of yourself, not just "stuff"—a coupon book for future services (such as baby-sitting or an "enchanted evening"); something baked, sewn, handmade, composed, etc.; or a family service project, such as working together at a soup kitchen.

8. Celebrate Advent for four weeks before Christmas. Use the booklet "Whose Birthday Is It, Anyway?" or some other appropriate guide.

9. Put the gifts under the tree shortly before opening them. Then take turns opening them around the tree, not all at once, so that each gift can be admired and each giver thanked.

10. Make changes slowly but persistently. Don't try to change everything and everybody all at once. The resistance will make you feel defeated and lonely.[78]

This is the sort of advice on voluntary simplicity that Bill McKibben gave in his very influential 1998 *Hundred Dollar Holiday*. Beginning in rural Methodist congregations, McKibben attempted to persuade friends and churchgoers that Christmas could be spent more meaningfully and with more true pleasure if one reduced one's monetary expenditure and increased one's time with loved ones. For this he was called a "Grinch," after the Christmas-hating Dr. Seuss character, but he took heart in knowing that the Grinch found, in the end, that the holiday was not all about "things" and came from no store.[79] For McKibben the driving force behind this attempt to radically reform the holiday was the threat it posed to the environment. Christmas was the great engine of consumption and ceaseless demands for more material goods, demands that were harming the planet. Carbon dioxide, he claimed, would ruin our ecological niche, and fuel efficiency was insufficient if it simply lead to us driving more. We had to question the need for economic growth and change our behavior. Today's climatologists were merely echoing the words of Christ and his disciples: community and simplicity. "Not because it is good for our souls, or for our right relation with God, but because without simpler lives, the chances of stabilizing the planet's basic workings are slim."[80]

In 2006 five Protestant pastors from churches across the United States banded together to combat the causes of the dread they all felt around Christmastime. They were spending December trying to tell their flocks about the importance of the coming of Jesus—God made flesh—while their congregations were more interested in a flurry of busyness and consumption. Together they formed the Advent Conspiracy, an attempt to remind believers that Christmas is more than a single day, that it is an entire season, and that this season could be made infinitely more meaningful for Christian families. How? By following four simple commands: Worship Fully, Spend Less, Give More, and Love All. The movement spreads by engaging the clergy in thousands of churches to broadcast the message: turn Christmas upside down, consume less, use the money saved to promote a good cause—clean water and antislavery campaigns are particularly promoted—and focus on the love of God and humanity. Sermons, Sunday School curricula, Advent calendars, YouTube videos, and computer apps emerge from the Conspiracy's headquarters, which also shares ideas from local churches.[81]

Since their arrival in North America in the seventeenth century, Mennonites have been known for their love of a simple lifestyle. In 2001 a number of Canadian Mennonites combined that anticonsumerism with a Marxist perspective on the economy to produce the Buy Nothing Christmas movement, which was inspired by *Adbusters'* "Buy Nothing Day," the Center for a New American Dream, and McKibben's *Hundred Dollar Christmas*. Claiming not to wish to abolish Christmas, they aim to "offer a prophetic 'no' to the patterns of over-consumption of middle-class North Americans." Much of their material is phrased in religious terms—a Byzantine icon of Christ with the slogan "Where did I say that you should buy so much stuff to celebrate my birthday?"; a reference to "Mary, the unwed mother of Jesus [who] went against the grain"; a play based on the biblical characters Mary and Martha; and a "Buy Nothing Christmas" liturgy. The group's founder used religious imagery in a piece for the *Washington Post*:

To me, Black Friday is essentially our version of a religious pilgrimage. We worship in the mega stores, make schedules around holiday deals, display allegiance to brands and low prices, offer tithes to the cashiers. Masses of people swarm the stores with hype and fervor. But where's the meaning? The deep meaning?

We know we're placating the gods. Which is why Christians need to pull back from the biggest shopping day of the year. Retail products occupy too much space in our homes and hearts.

It's not that there's something more important than the economy, it's that the economy needs to be re-fashioned. Jesus acknowledged wealth and power (give to Caesar what is Caesar's) and sought to undermine it (woe to the rich, blessed are the poor).

By resisting the impulse to shop for deals on Black Friday we stand at the feet of the retail titans and, with the power of non-cooperation, we challenge the injustices of poor labor conditions, exploitative hiring practices, unfair monopolies, and irresponsible resource extraction.[82]

The Buy Nothing Christmas movement has, inevitably, produced a musical play, *A Christmas Karl,* based on Dickens's *Christmas Carol:* "a tender tale of commercialism, compassion and fruitcake"; they make available gift cards that offer a service or loving gesture instead of a retail product. Their most effective way of gleaning media attention is their street theater and the cheeky invasions of shopping precincts during the Christmas season, singing parodies of Christmas songs and getting evicted by mall security.

> *The tv's on, are you watching?*
> *Another product that they're hawking*
> *one more thing that you need, to make life complete*
> *Welcome to Consumer Wonderland.*
> *In the stores, you will hear it*
> *"Pricey gifts, show holiday spirit"*
> *That's what they call it, to get to your wallet,*
> *Welcome to Consumer Wonderland.*
> *At the mall, we can go out shopping*
> *and buy lots of stuff we can't afford*
> *we'll have lots of fun with our new toys*
> *until we realize that we're still bored.[83]*

Unlike earlier Protestant movements that sought to purge Christmas celebrations of excess, the Buy Nothing Christmas movement is avowedly anticapitalist. By attacking Christmas spending, they hope to bring capitalism to its knees. In reply to the question "If we all buy nothing this Christmas, won't a lot of people lose their jobs?" their website says:

> Yes, and now we're getting close to the core reasons for why Buy Nothing Christmas is necessary in the first place: our economy is based on a consumer driven capitalism. And because it's the only economy we have right now, if we stop shopping we stop the economy.... But the pitfalls of our current economic system (we work too hard to save money to buy things we don't really need, and we endorse a standard of living that reinforces the gap between the rich and poor and ruins the earth) are simply untenable. Once we finally see the retail sector shrivel... we can redirect our efforts to cleaning up our mess and developing more sustainable activities (how we build our homes, transport ourselves, manufacture clothes, and spend our leisure time).

Elsewhere they explain what they "have against capitalism": "In a nutshell, it favours the rich, is heartless and is based upon the assumption that people buy things out of self-interest. WE'RE NOT SAYING THAT COMMUNISM IS A BETTER OPTION. We are in a critical time when economists (e.g. Herman E. Daly and John B. Cobb, For The Common Good, 1994) are working on and proposing new models that assume that people are not only self-interested, but also interested in the common good."[84] Attacking a consumer-oriented Christmas and culture while using Christian imagery is Reverend Billy of the Church of Stop Shopping, "a New York City based radical performance community." Reverend Billy, a flamboyant parody of a southern evangelist, is the alter ego of Bill Talen, writer, producer, actor, and ex-believer. He and his choir have invaded banks and businesses (actions they call "retail interventions"), staged cash register exorcisms, set up mock revivals, belted out cellphone operas, occupied Wall Street, singing and dancing while touring four continents with their anticonsumerism and antimilitarism message. He has been arrested about seventy times. In the movie/book/CD *What Would Jesus Buy*, Talen sings and sermonizes in grand fashion and conveys a deep spirituality, though of a highly unorthodox variety. Just before he was arrested for a protest during Christmastime at Disneyland, his chorus sang a song that reminded listeners that just as humans had invented Mickey Mouse, Christmas, and Santa Claus, they could unmake bad ideas and create good ones: "Let's take back change! / Isn't that the best gift we can give each other this / Christmas? Yes, let's give each other Change! / Merry Christmas!"[85] Dreadful poetry to be sure, but great street theater.

Christians have decried buying and selling commercial gifts as the central acts of a Christmas celebration and sought to resacralize the holiday, to move the focus back to the Nativity and its magical stories. One way they have devised to reinject spiritual content into Christmas is to downplay the importance of Santa Claus. A poll of British young people in 2000 revealed that 67 percent of the sample associated the Christmas season with Santa Claus while only 8 percent linked it to Jesus. As pastors railed in sermons against this false consciousness, the purveyors of American popular religion also took the problem seriously. Toby Keith had a hit with "Jesus Gets Jealous of Santa Claus," and his fellow country singer Ricky Traywick sang of an encounter between the magical Gift-Bringer and Christ in the song "The Night Jesus Met Santa Claus." (Apparently Santa has never heard of Jesus—everyone was too busy asking him for favors—but Jesus explains to him the principles of salvation, fills his toy sack with Bibles, and sends him on his way.) The challenge of manifesting Christ's superiority to Santa is also met in numerous Nativity scenes, ornaments, paintings, greeting cards, and YouTube clips (such as "The Night Jesus Met Santa Claus") where Santa Claus is depicted kneeling beside the manger of the Baby Jesus, baring his head in worship.[86] As one online merchandising site says: "The Kneeling Santa is a wonderful way to teach anyone the true meaning of Christmas. With Santa humbly knelt in adoration and prayer in front of the Christ Child, it helps us refocus our celebrations on God's greatest gift to us—His Son, Jesus."[87]

Another way of dealing with Santa's unwonted preeminence was to replace him as Gift-Bringer with his much more religious predecessor, St. Nicholas. In the same year that the poll revealed the disturbing news of Santa Claus's dominance, a number of Church of England clergy, including George Carey, the archbishop of Canterbury, formed the Saint Nicholas Society. Believing that emphasizing the role once played by the saint would increase public awareness of the holiday's Christian roots and expose the relatively recent, American and secular nature of Santa (or Father Christmas, as he is known in Britain) the society's founder, Jim Rosenthal, said: "We want St Nicholas to replace Father Christmas as the face of Christmas. For centuries, St Nicholas, who wore bishop's robes and carried a mitre, was at the center of the celebration. He was the very reason why people gave gifts. We now feel it is time for Father Christmas to get out of his elf's costume and back into his religious robes." Europeans such as the Dutch and Poles had clung to the good saint as the Gift-Bringer, but it was going to be an uphill battle in the English-speaking world to bring Nicholas back to the preeminence he once enjoyed. Who remembered that Nicholas was once the most powerful and popular male saint of the Middle Ages or that 450 churches were dedicated in his name in Britain alone? (Nor did the actions of the Vatican help in this regard—in 1969 St. Nicholas was downgraded in status by Pope Paul VI; his cult was no longer to be celebrated by the whole church, though local veneration could continue.) In seeking to revive St. Nick the British society was one with a number of national projects with a similar aim. In the United States, for example, the Saint Nicholas Center of Holland, Michigan, aims to "to bring Roman Catholic, Episcopal, Orthodox, and Protestant Christians together in common purpose—to help people understand and appreciate the original St. Nicholas, the only real Santa Claus." They sponsor a traveling exhibition, maintain a very informative website, and cultivate links with similar groups in Europe, including the Sint-Nicolaasgenootschap Vlaandere (Belgium), Centro Studi Nicolaiani (in Bari, Italy, where Italians claim the saint is buried) and Vorfahrt für den Nikolaus (Germany). Interestingly, the desire to bring St. Nicholas to the fore is not seen as an attack on Christmas consumerism; rather the opposite. The Saint Nicholas Society recognizes the value of gift-giving and Christmas generosity and wants to associate the good feeling this generates with the Christian origins of the holiday. Michael Turnbull, the bishop of Durham, has said: "I think restoring the link between Father Christmas and St Nicholas is a very good thing. I think the Father Christmas you see in supermarkets can breed in children a huge commercial selfishness. It makes children think about all the joy that can be found in shops and presents, instead of the fact that a good deal of joy can be found in giving. St Nicholas and Christmas are meant to be about the joy of giving, but many children think it is about the joy of getting."[88]

One place where St. Nicholas is particularly revered is the Netherlands, where for centuries he has been the magical Gift-Bringer. In Holland his appearances are largely in public: he arrives by ship in mid-November; accompanied by his helper, Zwarte Piet (Black Peter, who miraculously appears in hundreds of clones). He will be greeted by camera crews, marching bands, and dignitaries and parade through the streets in full episcopal garb on a white horse. He will visit schools, hospitals, malls, and public events. After his gift-giving is completed on the eve of his saint's day (December 6), he bids farewell to his Dutch followers until next year. This beloved custom was threatened in the last half of the twentieth century by the appearance of Santa Claus, a manifestation that caused confusion among Dutch children and diluted the uniqueness of the country's Christmas celebrations. Lately, however, there has been legal and social pushback against the Americanized intruder. A national St. Nicholas committee was formed to protect the image of the saint. The town of Assen in the northeast of the Netherlands felt that their children were growing up without any knowledge of the native holiday traditions and so has forbidden any public display of Santa Claus, reindeer, or Christmas trees until after December 6. Local police have the right to arrest any interloper dressed as Santa. Said the head of the local St. Nicholas Association: "We don't want the commercialization of Father Christmas and the celebrations of Christmas that you have in America, England and Germany. We want to keep our Dutch celebrations."[89]

French academics have labeled this desire to reassert the value of long-held native traditions in the face of globalizing innovations "patrimonial-ization."[90] The term is applicable to the Dutch movement to cling to St. Nicholas, as well as to certain actions taken by governments that we have seen before: Mussolini's and Franco's distaste for the Christmas tree, for example, or the French clergy's burning of Santa Claus at Dijon. All of these are defensive gestures in reaction to the invasion of a foreign species of Christmas. In this regard, governments in wartime have been quick to use the holiday as a way of associating their brand of nationalism with the sacred season. All European belligerents in World War I were lavish in their use of the images of Santa Claus (or Father Christmas or Père Noël or the Weihnachtsmann) or the Christ Child to bolster the war effort; in World War II, as already shown, the Nazi regime was conflicted in its use of Christmas, though the Allies were unanimous in linking their cause with Santa. When the German forces occupying Norway banned the use of the Norwegian flag, the resistance movement made use of Christmas cards bearing the image of elves wearing the national colors red, white, and blue and the message "God Norsk Jul"—"A Merry Norwegian Christmas." The Germans soon caught on to this subversive use of Christmas and banned the cards.[91]

Sometimes defenders of local culture have attempted to introduce well-meaning synthetic replacements for Santa Claus, with humorous and short-lived results. In the 1930s the Brazilian government, rocked by the impact of the Great Depression and impressed by the seeming success of Mussolini's Italian fascism, turned inward and instituted policies that emphasized national self-sufficiency. Foreign goods and foreign ideas were rejected and replaced with local production and ideology. This encouraged an abortive move to replace Papai Noel, the local version of Santa, with Vovô Índio, or "Grandfather Indian," meant to be an alternative to Euro-American Gift-Bringers and thus to inflate Brazilian patriotic sentiments. Instead of a fat, fur-clad saint from the chilly north, Vovô Índio was the child of a black slave and an aboriginal mother, raised by a white family, and wore only a feather headdress and loincloth. Despite political backing by the president and fascist ultranationalists, Vovô Índio never caught on with the children of Brazil (in fact, he was perceived as rather frightening), and he soon disappeared from public consciousness.[92] About the same time as Brazil's autarkic experiment, Mexico too was in a revolutionary mood, anxious to cast off old ways. In a similar ill-starred move, to boost nationalism and assert Mexican independence of American and Spanish cultural figures, the minister of education proposed replacing Santa Claus and the Three Kings with a pre-Columbian pagan deity. Children were urged to direct their Christmas hopes to the Aztec god Quetzalcóatl; merchants used the god in advertising—GE ran an ad boasting that whether it came from the Magi, Santa, or Quetzalcóatl, there could be no gift like a General Electric refrigerator—and on December 23, 1930, the government constructed a replica of an Aztec temple in the national stadium where the Plumed Serpent himself delivered presents to a crowd of children, watched by an approving President Pascual Ortiz Rubio. Like Vovô Índio, Quetzalcóatl proved to have no popular appeal. Critics pointed out to the ruling regime that an Aztec god, half-bird, half-snake, was as foreign to contemporary Mexican culture as Santa Claus or the Reyes Magos. Before Fidel Castro banned the public celebration of Christmas in 1969, a brief attempt was made to create a Cuban-style holiday free of Yankee influences. Christmas trees and foreign treats were banned; in street art the Three Wise Men were portrayed as Fidel Castro, Che Guevara, and Juan Almeida (the Afro-Cuban army chief); the gifts they brought were Agrarian Reform, Urban Reform, and the Year of Education. José Martí, the writer who had long stood as a symbol of Cuban independence, was artistically rendered in star-like fashion with a light-bulb on his forehead. Santa Claus, as an American invention, had to go. In his place came Don Feliciano, "Mr. Happiness," a straw-hat-wearing, bearded peasant. A new carol to the tune of "Jingle Bells" went "With Fidel, with Fidel / Always with Fidel / Eating Corn or Malange / Always with Fidel."[93] After a decade of this, it was El Comandante's wish that Cubans not celebrate Christmas, and lo, for a generation it was so.

Sometimes a government misjudges the mood of the people and tries to abolish a popular Christmas custom in the name of modernity or respectability. In the Catalonian region of northeastern Spain it has long been the custom to place in every Nativity scene a *caganer*, a figure of a red-capped peasant who has dropped his drawers and is in the act of defecating. This has been the case since at least the sixteenth century and is probably some sort of fertility symbol, though now retailers have got into the act and will happily sell you a figurine of a pooping pope, politician, soccer star, or actress. In 2005 the administration of Barcelona committed an outrage on public decency by failing to include a *caganer* in the city's official Nativity scene. Many saw this an affront to Catalan customs and thus a not-so-subtle attack on demands for greater political autonomy in Catalonia. The government said this was not the case at all but that the city had just passed ordinances banning public urination and defecation, which made the *caganer* a bad example for urban hygiene. A "Save the Caganer" campaign was launched with wide media support, and the next year the traditional pooper was back on the scene.[94]

Lately, however, the demands for a patrimonialized Christmas have more to do with an assertion of the rights of a religious Gift-Bringer and the downgrading of the status of a secularized version. This can be seen in both anti-Soviet and anti-American forms. Starting in 1989 with the fall of the Berlin Wall, massive demonstrations in the Baltic republics, the violent overthrow of the Ceausescu regime in Romania, and President Gorbachev's signal that the Soviet Union would not use force to preserve its hegemony, Communist governments collapsed all across eastern Europe. One by one the various satellite states on which Marxist governments and attitudes had been imposed during the Cold War adopted democratic constitutions and market economies and sought the return of national customs. One of the chief victims of this shift was Ded Moroz, the Grandfather Frost figure who had marched in with the Red Army and who had, for over forty years, replaced local magical Gift-Bringers. He had been regarded in eastern Europe as a symbol of Soviet oppression, and his hold on the hearts of children had always been feeble. When the Red Army pulled back to Russia, the now-disgraced Ded Moroz left with them. In Croatia he was replaced by Sveti Nikola (St. Nicholas); Święty Mikołaj (St. Nicholas), and Dzieciątko (the Baby Jesus) and angel helpers were rehabilitated in Poland; in Hungary Jézuska (the Baby Jesus) reappeared with gifts on Christmas

Eve. Only in Slovenia did Grandfather Frost linger. There artists, preferring a native bearer of gifts to an Americanized servant of Coca-Cola, gave Dedek Mraz a traditional peasant costume and a rustic, round fur hat and began to claim that he lived in Slovenia, under a local mountain. He maintained his role as New Year's Gift-Bringer, one of three magical Gift-Bringers in the country, coexisting with St. Nicholas and Santa Claus.[95]

The unease felt by Slovenians over the intrusion of Santa was widely shared in eastern Europe. The vacuum created by the collapse of Warsaw Pact Communism and the retreat of Grandfather Frost had allowed the importation of novelties such as Santa Claus and American Christmas customs. This engendered resistance in many nations of the former Soviet Bloc. Poles, for example, complain about the commercialization of Christmas, the intrusion of American practices, and the decline of native seasonal traditions such as the display of Krakow-style crèches, the performance of Nativity plays, and the primacy of St. Nicholas. "More than any other single gimmick, Santa has been used by the forces of militant commercialism to take Christ out of Christmas and turn the holidays into a 'Greed Fest' for Yuletide profiteers and spoiled brats alike," said one critic. "Indeed, Santa can be called the 'Grinch' who stole genuine Christmas traditions and replaced them with the goofy, giddy and glitzy."[96] In the Czech Republic in the autumn of 2006, a father reading a Christmas book to his daughter was horrified to discover that Ježíšek (Baby Jesus), the traditional Gift-Bringer, was portrayed as a jolly bearded fat man in a red suit. Santa Claus had stolen not only the Christ Child's role but his very name as well! In response, the Creative Copywriters Club, a group of advertising professionals, fought back against the intrusion of Santa. "Czech Christmases are intimate and magical. All that Santa stuff seems to me like cheap show business," said one of the members. "I'm not against Santa himself. I'm against Santa in my country only."[97] Their reply took the form of an annual ad campaign to push the elf from the North Pole back whence he came—they had not rejected Ded Moroz merely to adopt another invasive species. They quickly generated publicity and support with images such as the Virgin suckling a baby Santa Claus, a Czech lion posing with a Santa-skin rug, and Santa being hauled away in a garbage container. A comic pseudodocumentary posted on YouTube shows Santa presenting his American citizenship in a police office and being declared an undesirable. He ends up on a stairway drinking his blues away with a bottle of cheap vodka proffered by a slovenly Ded Moroz figure.[98] The Club also holds an annual mock award ceremony to shame the Czech company that has failed most conspicuously to keep Christmas in the time-honored fashion. The Club's cry has been taken up by others; members of the "Save Ježíšek" movement, dressed as snowmen, held demonstrations against Santa Claus in a number of cities and collected signatures on a petition to the Czech prime minister to protect traditional Czech Christmas customs. Some department stores aided the effort by refusing to sell any products bearing the image of Santa.[99]

Even in western Europe, where Santa has held sway since the end of World War II, he is not safe from criticism. Like the Dutch who are demanding a return to the good old days of St. Nicholas, many Austrians wish to preserve the rights of the Christ Child, who was once the chief Gift-Bringer in their country. In 2002 they formed the Pro-Christkind Association to resist Santa Claus and the commercialization of Christmas, which they claim he carries in his sack. At first their campaign was rather crude and aggressive: stickers of Santa with a slash mark across his face, images of Santa peeing on a rooftop, or impaled on the front of an airplane. This provoked hard feeling in the United States prompting an apology from the Association for what might have been perceived as an anti-American sentiment; they only wished, they said, to stand against turning Christmas into a buying frenzy. These days the images are lighter in tone—an angelic figure trying to pull off a beard and red hat, or a gingerbread cookie in the shape of the star of Bethlehem. Across the border in Germany the campaign is also waged: Santa is portrayed inside a circle and slash with the motto "Wir glauben ans Christkind. Gebt dem Weihnachtsmann keine Chance"—"We believe in the Christ Child. Don't Give Santa a Chance."

"We're the Three Kings—who the hell are you?" In Spain, defenders of the Wise Men, the Magi, as the native Gift-Bringers launched a no-holds-barred attack on North American Christmas customs, calling for "Una Navidad sin Papá Noel," a "Christmas without Santa Claus." A poster campaign, street demonstrations, and a dark YouTube hip-hop video accused Santa of obesity, exploiting elves, and unremitting greed; finally the rapping Magi gun down Santa Claus in a dark alley.[100] Meanwhile in Mexico, Santa Claus has been castigated by a Catholic journal as "a fat clown, with the chapped cheeks of a heavy beer drinker, the big stomach of a bon vivant, the nose of a drunk," and the "boots of a gendarme." On the eve of St. Nicholas's day the Archdiocese of Guadalajara's *Semanario* newspaper lamented his disappearance from the celebration of Christmas and asked "What happened to the bishop? What happened to his miter...his sacred vestments and his consecrated hands blessing the devoted?" it asked. The article, titled "Santa Claus the Usurper," accused Santa of having "usurped the name and the personality of St. Nicholas.... "Let's not permit him to usurp the place of Christ."[101] The Mexican editorial might as well have been written in Serbo-Croatian, so alike was it to a blast from a Serbian Orthodox priest in 2005: "All European nations, both at the east and the west celebrate Saint Nicholaus. He is the one giving presents to children, like the wise man from the east. Only recently at the west, especially in America, Saint Nicholaus is being replaced by that lying Santa Claus, and they even started celebrating him here. It is an non-existing, lying creature which brings the European nations back to their paganic roots. Santa Claus has nothing to do with the church of Christ."[102]

Across the border in Bosnia, there is no less hostility on authorities' part toward Santa, but there it is not in defense of St. Nicholas, or indeed any Christian custom, but of the country's Islamic heritage. In the wake of the breakup of Yugoslavia in the 1990s and heightened nationalist feelings in the Balkans, Bosnia's Muslim president, Alija Izetbegovic, attempted to declare Djed Mraz, Grandfather Frost, a "fabrication" from the period of Communist rule. Followers of his party beat up in the streets those who championed the presence of the Christmas Gift-Bringer; a mob shouting anti-Serb and anti-Croat slurs and "Kill! Kill!" chased away men who had dressed as Santa Claus for a Sarajevo children's festival. In Bosnia, divided between Muslim Bosniacs, Catholic Croats, and Orthodox Serbs, the year-end Christmas and New Year's period had long been celebrated in a common fashion, one of the few things that national groups could share. But as the twenty-first century opened, the Bosniac majority attempted to increase Islamic education in the Sarajevo school system and eliminate non-Muslim traditions. One of the casualties was a Christmas visit by Djed Mraz, deemed by authorities to be no part of the Bosniac lifestyle. Parents protested: "Grandfather Frost is not a religious symbol. Unlike our politicians who are trying to separate us like sheep, Santa symbolises friendship, joy and contributes to the richness of our city." Ironically, a secular Santa had become the focus of religious friction.[103]

But what of the original Ded Moroz, the Soviet winter figure imposed for forty years on the satellite states? Not the least abashed by his banishment, he is in fine fettle. Russians have taken him to their collective bosom, declaring him to be the one and only Gift-Bringer to be venerated by their nation. It is against the law to deny his existence, and all foreign versions of Santa Claus have been warned off by state officials. The mayor of Moscow has paraded him around in a troika and boasted: "Look at our huge, beautiful Ded. You can't compare him to that puny Santa Claus!" Ded Moroz has established permanent residence in the depths of the Russian north at Veliky Ustyug, where those hoping for a local tourist boom have built him a splendid wooden palace and where the Russian postal service delivers all letters from children addressed to him. Among his annual duties is a peace-making exchange of gifts with the Finnish version of Santa Claus, one Joulupukki by name.[104] And thereby hangs a tale of how nationalism and patrimonialism have turned into an unedifying spectacle of Christmas imperialism.

The Finnish name for Santa Claus—Joulupukki—means "Christmas Buck," a term coined when northern European Gift-Bringers were still conceived of as rough and frightening creatures. Children no longer have to fear "Perchta the Disemboweler" (a notably terrifying German female figure) or a fearsome shaggy goat because the North American Santa Claus succeeded in taming these midnight visitors by the turn of the twentieth century. Scandinavian Gift-Bringers might retain their old names, but they became comfortable grandfatherly characters. However, in a spectacular act of cultural ingratitude, the Finns began to insist that Joulupukki, their newly reformed version of Santa, was the original and only authentic model. They claimed that he lived on Mount Ear in Lapland and that all other versions of the magical Gift-Bringer were phonies. Surprisingly, this claim has been accepted by many in Europe and Asia, who write letters to the Finnish Santa, flock to the Joulupukki theme park above the Arctic Circle, or build similar attractions in China. (No word yet as to the Finnish reaction to the declaration by the Canadian government that Santa Claus is a Canadian citizen.)[105]

Asia Minor provides another instance of patrimonialism, partly religious, partly nationalist, overwhelmingly commercial. St. Nicholas, the patron saint of children and prototype for many of the world's Santa figures, was a bishop of the fourth century whose church was at Myra in what is now southern Turkey. In 1087 an expedition of Normans from the Italian town of Bari sailed to Myra to steal the saint's bones, highly prized for their value as prestigious relics. After torturing the Orthodox monks who safeguarded Nicholas's tomb, the Normans were given some bones that they duly enshrined in the new cathedral at Bari. The monks later boasted that they had foisted some worthless skeleton off on the Normans and claimed that the true saint still resided in the church at Myra. To this day, both churches attract flocks of pilgrims (largely Catholic at Bari and largely Orthodox at Myra); both tombs continue to ooze a sweet-smelling liquid—historically a sure sign of sanctity—which is bottled and sold to tourists. In the twentieth century the Turkish government decided that Myra (or Demre, as the locals now call it) could be profitably promoted as "the birthplace of Santa Claus." In 1981 a donor gave to the church there a bronze statue of St. Nicholas, portrayed as a hooded figure rather like the German Weihnachtsmann or the French Père Noël, surrounded by children. On the base are inscribed Christmas greetings in many languages. To show solidarity with Myra and its ties to the historical saint, a Russian group led by Moscow's mayor, Yuri Luzhkov, gave a statue of Nicholas to the town of Myra, which erected it in its public square in 2000. However, this statue's portrayal of Nicholas as a Christian saint standing on a globe was deemed by some locals to miss the point entirely—it was Santa Claus, not some ancient non-Muslim clergyman, whom they wished to tout—and so the donated statue was removed in 2005 and replaced by a gaudy bakelite portrayal of a red-suited Santa that would not have been out of place in a minor strip mall in North America. Eventually the saintly statue ended up on the grounds of the St. Nicholas Church. The sign for the building also attracted negative attention, so it was changed from "St Nicholas Church" to "Baba Noel Müzesi"—the Santa Claus Museum, despite the fact that the vast majority of tourists were pious Orthodox Christians from Russia. After hearing complaints from Americans and Europeans about the cheesiness of the Santa statue, and mindful of the half million tourists who came every year to pay homage to Nicholas, this statue too was displaced, and a new depiction was erected on Christmas Day 2008. The new fiberglass statue, commissioned by the Turkish Ministry of Culture, was meant to depict a figure unlike the North American Santa and unlike an ascetic bishop; in fact it was to "look like Turks."[106] This effort was not greeted with universal acclaim. Another Turkish sculptor opined that "this sculpture does not suit any style. It looks like 'uncle Nail' of today, not Saint Nicholas who lived in the 6th century."[107] Certainly few previous depictions of St. Nicholas have featured a middle-aged man wearing culottes, sandals, and an embroidered sash, standing on a raft, but it seems to satisfy Turkish nationalist sentiment.

In multicultural democracies, Muslims seldom voice opposition to Christmas, and in fact one often hears them praising Christmas. When a judge banned a Christmas tree from a Toronto courthouse in 2006, the Canadian Muslim National Congress issued a news release calling on

Muslims to "celebrate Christmas with their Christian cousins and light up Christmas trees to send a message to the Ontario judge that she is wrong on all counts." In Britain a Muslim cabinet minister urged others of her religion to enjoy the holiday. "Being brought up—before the politically correct brigade got going—on harvest festivals, maypoles, Nativity plays, Christmas carols and the Lord's Prayer, made me much more sure about my own identity," said Lady Warsi. "I didn't feel it was all watered down to the lowest common denominator."[108] However, where Islam is the majority religion and where radical Islamists flourish in European urban enclaves, a more aggressive attitude is often in evidence. Though both Islam and Christianity revere the figure of Jesus, Christmas is the celebration of the birth of the Son of God, a claim Muslims find incorrect and objectionable. As a Lebanese cleric pronounced in 2011:

> You cannot say: "Merry Christmas." Not even if an alien came and said it to you—you cannot even say it to him, and say: "He's just an alien. I'm never going to see him again. He's not going to tell anyone." No "Merry Christmas"—not from a Muslim and not from a non-Muslim. It's not part of our religion—period! It is the concept that God was born on the 25th of December. That's as polytheistic and heretic as you can get. When you say: "Merry Christmas," you are saying: "Congratulations on your false religion," "Congratulations on your false understanding of life." You are congratulating them on the most evil of polytheism and heresy. As Ibn Qayyim said, this is worse than fornication, drinking alcohol, and killing someone, because you are approving of the biggest crime ever committed by the children of Adam—polytheism.[109]

Much of the Islamic animus against Christmas is the fear that Muslims will participate in it, either because it is part of the surrounding culture or because it represents an attractive element of a globalizing West. In Turkey in 2010 the Anatolian Youth Association at an Istanbul university paraded with an inflatable Santa Claus and delivered a tirade against Christmas as a phenomenon that estranged Muslims from the true religion and seduced them with a corrupt Western imperialism. In front of the plastic Santa were strewn beer cans, a syringe, and a cross to show the danger of allowing Christmas into Turkish homes. The demonstration climaxed with the defacing and stabbing of the effigy. Three years later the group produced a poster showing Santa being punched out and attacked the

Christmas and New Year celebrations in which secular Turks were in the habit of taking part. A very similar poster appeared across the border in Macedonia, a Christian country with a Muslim minority. It quoted Muhammad: "He who is practicing the way and the belief of unbelievers is not part of my people. Do not celebrate; fear Allah." The imam of the Turkish town of Kuzan attacked Santa's character in 2011. Imam Suleiman Eniceri found it suspicious that Santa Claus brought presents by climbing down chimneys. "If he was an honest person he would come through the door as we do," the imam said. The cleric cited a passage in the Koran that calls on the faithful to enter houses through doors and warned Turkish Muslims against drinking alcohol. "Christmas is not our festival," he said. A right-wing nationalist party demonstration featured a man dressed as Santa Claus being chased by another in the costume of an Ottoman soldier. Protests against the growth of Turkish interest in the holiday continued in 2015. Activists from the Fatih Generation Youth Education Association gathered beside a Christmas tree in Istanbul's Maltepe Square, shouting: "That charlatan called Santa Claus is the father of Christians! We're a nation of the Prophet Muhammad" and carrying signs reading: "Musluman Noel Kutlamaz" ("Muslims Do Not Celebrate Christmas"). The youth wing of the ruling Adalet ve Kalkınma Partisi (Justice and Development Party) called a conference to examine "the Christmas threat," presumably the danger posed by an interest in foreign, non-Islamic customs.[110]

Santa came in for some harsh treatment in Tajikistan in 2012 when a mob of Muslim extremists set upon a man dressed as the Russian Grandfather Frost. Crying "You infidel!" they beat him and stabbed him to death.[111] In Indonesia's Aceh province, where sharia law is the rule, the Islamic clergy has instructed its Muslim community not to celebrate Christmas and New Year's. Instead, they want authorities to strictly enforce Islamic law by severely punishing anyone who violates it; for example, Christian ceremonies must not disturb or cause problems for Muslims at work, at home, or even when they are staying in hotels, which are already prohibited from holding holiday celebrations. Just days before Christmas, Muslim clerics decreed that seasonal celebrations were not part of the Islamic tradition but were typical of Western culture; wishing neighbors "Merry Christmas" or participating in holiday dancing, drums, and fireworks were deemed *haram* (forbidden). In Muslim-majority Malaysia in 2011, the police demanded that some Christian churches name and give details of those attending Christmas services, on the grounds that singing carols at church or in homes required police authorization. Iranian Protestants were arrested in 2009 and 2011 for having celebrated Christmas in their legally registered churches or in their homes; the authorities seemed to focus on detaining converts from Islam. "In a hadith narrated by Ibnu Umar (may Allah the Almighty be pleased with him), Prophet Muhammad (pbuh) said, 'Whoever imitates a people is one of them,'" said Brunei imams in a December 2015 sermon aimed at dissuading Muslims there from observing foreign holidays. The sultanate's government followed up by issuing a series of restrictions that limited Christian expression of Christmas and threatened participating Muslims, even those only wearing Santa hats, with five years' imprisonment. Shops and hotels were told to take down Christmas decorations. "These enforcement measures are...intended to control the act of celebrating Christmas excessively and openly, which could damage the faith [aqidah] of the Muslim community," said the Ministry of Religious Affairs. Christians, the government said, could maintain their religious customs among their own community, but doing so in public would violate the penal code, which prohibited propagating religion other than Islam to a Muslim. That same year, Somalia and Tajikstan issued similar edicts forbidding all Christmas and New Year celebrations as contrary to Islamic culture. "We warn against celebration of Christmas, which is only for Christians," said Sheikh Mohamed Kheyrow, director of Somalia's Ministry of Religion. "This is a matter of faith. The Christmas holiday and its drum beatings have nothing to [do] with Islam." Government officials and imams also expressed fear that such festivities might prompt attacks from the jihadist al-Shabaab movement. Muslim-majority Tajikistan, though in law a secular state, has been increasingly enforcing Muslim norms, banning the Soviet-era Grandfather Frost and evergreen tree decorations.[112]

Other Muslims see Christmas itself as a social evil. While the British Christian-Muslim Forum was doing its best in 2010 to promote good feelings by adherents of both religions toward the holiday, some London Islamists launched a poster campaign in London decrying it. "The Evils of Christmas" presented a new version of the "Twelve Days of Christmas" in which the "fruits" of the festival were listed: "On the 1st day of Christmas my true love gave to me an S....T....D." On the second day came debt; on the third, rape; on the fourth, teenage pregnancy; next came an abortion, raves, claiming God has a son, blasphemy, exploitation, promiscuity, night clubs, crime, pedophilia, paganism, domestic violence, homelessness, alcohol, and drugs. The activist behind the posters claimed to be indifferent

FIGURE 1. Some historians believe that the dating of Christmas on December 25 was related to the Roman holiday of the Feast of the Unconquered Sun on that day. This coin minted in Gaul in 313 A.D. shows the first Christian emperor, Constantine, in front of a figure of Sol Invictus, who wears a radiant crown.

FIGURE 2. This representation of the month of December is from the Philocalian Calendar, the earliest document to record December 25 as the date of the Nativity. The calendar, also known as the Chronograph of 354 A.D., was a manuscript prepared for Vitellius, a rich Roman Christian. Note the accessories for the celebration of Saturnalia: the dice and the festival mask. From Codex Vaticanus Barberini latinus 2154.

FIGURE 3. John Chrystostom, patriarch of Constantinople, struggled for years to get the Christian cities of the eastern Roman Empire to accept December 25 as the date of the Nativity of Jesus. From a mosaic in Hagia Sophia Cathedral, Istanbul.

FIGURE 4. The medieval custom of the boy bishop was one of the Christmas practices associated with misrule that governments attempted to suppress in the sixteenth century. This is a drawing of an effigy of a boy bishop in Salisbury Cathedral.

FIGURE 5. One of the fiercest Puritan opponents of Christmas was William Prynne. For his seditious writings he was condemned by the government of Charles I to imprisonment, branding on the face, and the cutting off of the ears. This portrait dates from 1640, after he had been freed from prison by Parliament. Engraving by Wenceslas Holler (1607–1677), date unknown, Wenceslar Hollar Digital Collection, Thomas Fisher Rare Book Library, University of Toronto.

Behold the maieſtie and grace——.
of loueing. Cheerfull, Chriſtmas face.
Whome many thouſands with one breath:
Cry out let him be put to death.
Who indeede can neuer die:
So long as man hath memory.

FIGURE 6. The English government abolished Christmas celebrations from 1645 to 1660. The book *The Examination and Trial of Old Father Christmas* (London: 1658; reprinted 1678) defended the holiday as a boon to the poor and an expression of genuine religious sentiment. This page from the book shows Father Christmas in a fur-trimmed cap and robe that would be the basis of his costume, as imagined by artists, for centuries.

FIGURE 7. Cover illustration of *The Vindication of Christmas*, a tract published in 1652. The English Puritan government had abolished the celebration of the holiday, but this woodcut attempts to show that "Old Christmas" was welcomed by the common man.

FIGURE 8. The figure of Santa Claus was first used to support a war effort in this cartoon by Thomas Nast published in *Harper's Weekly* in January 1863, during the American Civil War. Santa brings gifts to Union troops and dangles a puppet in the image of Jefferson Davis, president of the Confederacy.

FIGURE 9. The League of the Militant Godless was a key part of the Soviet Union's plan to eliminate religion. The cover of the League's magazine, *Bezbozhnik,* from 1929, shows Christ being dumped by proletarians calling for an end to Christian holidays and their replacement with secular celebrations.

Bald tritt Rupprecht in das Haus,
leert mir's volle Säcklein aus !
Seinem Schimmel schütt ich Heu,
Daß er sich darüber freu.

FIGURE 10. Associating Christmas with nationalism was a common appeal during times of war. This is a Canadian card from World War II. Courtesy of the author.

FIGURE 12. The Nazi government of Germany did not attempt to abolish Christmas in the way the Soviet Union had but attempted to paganize it. This Advent calendar illustration replaces St. Nicholas and the Christ Child as Gift-Bringer with the figure of "Knecht Ruprecht," a version of the Germanic god Wotan. Courtesy of the author.

FIGURE 11. Nazi Germany did not abolish Christmas but tried to twist it to its own ends. On this card Adolf Hitler sends its recipient good wishes for both Christmas and the winter solstice. Courtesy of the author.

Einmal im Jahr, in der heiligen Nacht,
verlaffen die toten Soldaten die Wacht,
die fie für Deutfchlands Zukunft ftehen·
Sie kommen ins Haus, nach Art und Ordnung zu fehn,
Schweigend treten fie ein in den feftlichen Raum –
den Tritt der genagelten Stiefel, man hört ihn kaum –
fie ftellen fich ftill zu Vater und Mutter und Kind,
aber fie fpüren, daß fie erwartete Gäfte find·
Es brennt für fie eine rote Kerze am Tannenbaum,
es fteht für fie ein Stuhl am gedeckten Tifch,
es glüht für fie im Glafe dunkel der Wein·
Und in die Weihnachtslieder, gläubig und frifch,
ftimmen fie fröhlichen Herzens mit ein·
Hinter dem Bild im Stahlhelm dort an der Wand
fteckt ein Tannenzweig mit filbernem Stern·
Es düftet nach Tannen und Äpfeln und Mandelkern·
Und es ift alles wie einft – und der Tod ift fo fern. –
Wenn dann die Kerzen am Lichtbaum zu Ende gebrannt,
legt der tote Soldat die erdverkruftete Hand
jedem der Kinder leife aufs junge Haupt·
"Wir ftarben für euch, weil wir an Deutfchland geglaubt."
Einmal im Jahr, nach der heiligen Nacht,
beziehen die toten Soldaten wieder die ewige Wacht·

Noch 1 Tag bis Weihnachten   Thilo Scheller

FIGURE 13. As World War II progressed and German armies were in retreat, official Christmas publications took on a grim hue. This page from a 1944 Nazi Advent calendar presents Christmas Eve as the night when the ghosts of dead German soldiers return to their homes. Courtesy of the author.

FIGURE 14. Governments often use Christmas and its symbols to drum up support for war efforts. On this American card from World War II, Santa Claus is giving the victory sign while Uncle Sam boots the enemy leaders of Germany, Italy, and Japan. Courtesy of the author.

Where did I say that you should buy so much stuff to celebrate my birthday!?

www.buynothingchristmas.org

FIGURE 15. Anticonsumerist groups decry families' excessive expenditures at Christmastime. This 2002 poster was printed by the Buy Nothing Christmas movement. Courtesy of Aiden Enns.

Whose Birthday Is It, Anyway?

IDEAS FOR A CHRIST-CENTERED HOLIDAY 1999

OUR COVENANT WITH STEWARDSHIP GOD

FIGURE 16. Anticonsumerist groups publish extensive material on how to live more simply and profoundly at Christmastime. Here is a version of a popular illustration by Tom Peterson in the booklet *Whose Birthday Is It, Anyway?* (Alternatives for Simple Living, 1999). Used by permission. Creative Commons, administered by SimpleLivingWorks.org.

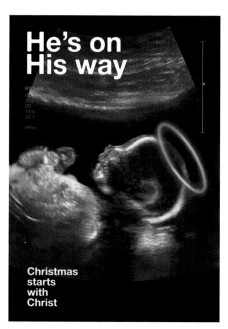

He's on His way

Christmas starts with Christ

FIGURE 17. Every year a coalition of English churches, ChurchAds.net, produces provocative advertisements intended to link Christmas with Christ in the public mind. This image is from their 2010 campaign. Courtesy of ChurchAds.net.

FIGURE 18. Many Europeans resent the invasion of the globalized figure of Santa Claus and prefer their own native Christmas Gift-Bringers with a longer tradition, such as the Christ Child, the Three Kings, or the Befana. Here the Polish artist Łukasz Ciaciuch expresses his preference for Swiety Nikolaj, or St. Nicholas, as the police arrest Santa Claus, a North American interloper. Courtesy of the artist. Copyright Łukasz Ciaciuch.

FIGURE 19. In many European countries a backlash against the globalized Santa Claus is taking place. This 2013 German ad contrasts St. Nicholas as the "original" Christmas Gift-Bringer with Santa, the "forgery." Courtesy of Bonifatiuswerk/Weihnachtsmannfreie-Zone.

FIGURE 20. The celebration of Christmas is opposed by many Christian groups. One of the most notorious of these is the Westboro Baptist Church of Topeka, Kansas, founded by Fred Phelps. Here, members protest Christmas at a demonstration in Massachusetts in 2013. Copyright Westboro Baptist Church.

FIGURE 21. People for the Ethical Treatment of Animals is one of a number of special-interest groups who use Christmas as way of attracting attention to their concerns. Here readers are urged to avoid idly buying animals as Christmas gifts. Illustration by Ken Cursoe. Image courtesy of People for the Ethical Treatment of Animals, www.peta.org.

to the offense he had given. He said: "Christmas is a lie and as Muslims it is our duty to attack it. But our main attack is on the fruits of Christmas, things like alcohol abuse and promiscuity that increase during Christmas and all the other evils these lead to such as abortion, domestic violence and crime. We hope that our campaign will make people realise that Islam is the only way to avoid this and convert." The Muslim mayor of the area said, "The messages on these posters are offensive and do not reflect the views of the Council or the vast majority of residents." That view was not shared by Anjem Choudary, a well-known London Islamist who in 2012 took his confrontation against Christianity to the steps of St. Paul's Cathedral on Christmas Eve. Choudary claimed his group was simply staging a "Christmas Debate" and said they would attack a litany of supposed societal faults, including "bribery, pornography, homosexuality, blasphemy and promiscuity."[113]

Similarly, in India there are those who fear that Christmas customs pose a danger to the Hindu majority. The right-wing nationalist organization Vishwa Hindu Parishad is dedicated to defending the country's religious heritage against foreign influences. According to its founder, the world "has been divided to Christian, Islam and communist. All of them view Hindu society as very fine rich food on which to feast and fatten themselves. It is necessary in this age of conflict to think of and organise the Hindu world to save it from the evils of all the three." Among those evils is Christmas. When a Santa Claus at Christian schools in Chhattigsarh distributed chocolates to children during the 2014 Christmas season, the Vishwa Hindu Parishad responded by making a number of aggressive demands. Santa was to stop trying to convert kids to Christianity through the use of sweets or cash bribes, priests were no longer to be called "Father," and the schools must put up pictures of Hindu deities. The organization, despite pleas from the national government, also chose Christmas Day to host mass "reconversion" ceremonies in which Christian and Muslim families adopted Hinduism. The fact that only weeks earlier the president of India, Pranab Mukherjee, had personally met with the Finnish version of Santa Claus in Lapland enraged Hindu nationalists even more.[114]

Another Asian country where nationalists are made uneasy by Christmas is China. Many in China—despite its being the planet's Christmas factory, annually manufacturing shiploads of ornaments, lighting, gifts, and cards for the world holiday market—are bent on preserving their nation from "western spiritual pollution." As Christmas 2014 approached, the Modern

College of Northwest University in Xi'an hung banners around campus exhorting students to "strive to be outstanding sons and daughters of China, oppose kitsch western holidays," and "resist the expansion of western culture." Officials locked the university's gates to prevent any participation in Christmas activities and instead made students attend a three-hour course of cultural propaganda focusing attention on Confucius. Young people were urged not to "fawn on foreigners" or regard other cultures as more advanced and their holidays "more elegant." In Hunan, students held anti-Christmas demonstrations, carrying signs reading "Resist Christmas." The Department of Education in Wenzhou banned the holding of any Christmas activities in schools or kindergartens. Such celebrations were termed "kitsch" and not in accordance with Chinese traditions. Critics of the move noted that Wenzhou contained a significant Christian minority, already upset by the destruction of a large church earlier that year. These government actions seemed motivated by a combination of national pride and fear of the growth of Christianity in China—Wang Zuo'an, the director of the State Administration for Religious Affairs, visited a Beijing church on Christmas Eve but used the occasion to call for a "firm determination against any foreign influence through Christianity."[115]

In the land where the Nativity of Jesus took place, there are also glimpses of an anti-Christmas animus and calls for rejecting un-Jewish customs. In 2009 a group called the Lobby for Jewish Values and a conference of rabbis tried to persuade the hospitality industry in Jerusalem to refrain from putting up Christmas trees or calling attention to the holiday, despite its attraction to the thousands of tourists visiting the Holy Land. They urged boycotts of hotels and restaurants that did not comply and suggested that the kosher certification of such businesses might be withdrawn. Their pamphlet stated: "The people of Israel have given their soul over the years in order to maintain the values of the Torah of Israel and the Jewish identity. You should also continue to follow this path of the Jewish people's tradition and not give in to the clownish atmosphere of the end of the civil year. And certainly not help those businesses that sell or put up the foolish symbols of Christianity." The campaign attracted publicity but it was mostly unfavorable, and nothing came of the threats; but the topic arose again in 2015 with the provocative words of the Israeli rabbi Benzi Gopstein: "Christmas has no place in the Holy Land," he said, adding: "Let us remove the vampires before they once again drink our blood." Gopstein heads an ultranationalist movement that advocates no dealings with non-Jews and the burning of Christian churches and Islamic mosques. He and his supporters demonstrated outside a Christmas event at Jerusalem's YMCA, protesting the "murder" of Jewish souls and the history of persecution at the hands of Christians. Waving Israeli flags and singing Hanukkah songs, they demanded that all the "impure" Christians leave the Holy Land.[116]

V

The Appropriators

In which a multitude of interest groups, often at the margins of society, attempt to use Christmas to promote their viewpoints

CHRISTMAS IS THE biggest single event on the planet. No sports tournament, war, stadium rock tour, viral media sensation, or global marketing campaign affects as many people around the world every year as Christmas. It is a phenomenon that engages billions of people who are caught up in its commercialism, music, sentiment, travel, and busyness whether they personally celebrate the holiday or not. It is, therefore, not surprising that it has been seized on continually by groups, often at the margins of society, who would like to bring attention to their particular causes. The Christmas season is wreathed in powerful themes that tug at people's emotions—generosity, reconciliation, family, community spirit, connection with a treasured past, and so on—and clever minds have been quick to try to appropriate these meanings in their struggles for public attention. Commercial advertisers are, of course, the greatest force that muscles in on the season and turns it to their own ends.[1] Right behind the merchants and manufacturers come politicians, who may always be found beside the state Christmas tree, sending out tens of thousands of holiday cards, or linking Christmas with the current war, as in the case of post-9/11 America.[2] In the British Commonwealth the annual broadcast message from the ruling monarch has been a Christmas Day tradition since George V first gave it in 1932. A plethora of scholarly work has charted these associations;[3] therefore, this chapter will concentrate on the voices from the margins, eager to be heard amid the seasonal clamor and using the Christmas moment to do it.

Black Christmases

Take, for example, the ever vexed questions surrounding race relations in the United States, a sphere where Christmas has been grasped by both extremes. In the Christmas season of 1874 in Vicksburg, Mississippi, a Santa Klaws parade, organized by the Santa Klaws Klan, processed through the streets of the city, cheered by the white citizenry. The Santa Klaws chief, conveyed in a four-horse chariot, distributed gifts to the happy crowd. Coming only weeks after a massacre of local blacks, this was a display of white triumphalism and a celebration of the end of the Reconstruction era in Vicksburg.[4] The Klan's use of Christmas was meant to convey a return to normality and a world of white supremacy. In the early twentieth century, things had changed; for the new Ku Klux Klan, the goal was respectability and a place in the mainstream of white Protestant politics. During their spectacular revival in the 1920s, they sought to gloss over their terrorist past and present themselves as the voice of the nativist middle class, anxious about immigration from foreign parts, drunkenness and sexual immorality, urbanization, internal migration by blacks into the northern states, and the malign covert influence of the Catholic Church and Jews. They wished to abjure, at least for the most part, their image as violent night-riders and adopt the pose of concerned citizens in a service organization, as valuable to their communities as the Lions Club, the Elks, or the Rotarians. To that end the Klan used the Christmas season to show their charitable side. In Indianapolis during Christmas in 1922 and 1923 they attracted publicity with their distribution of truckloads of food and clothing to poor families, including, they were happy to point out, black and Catholic families. In Atlanta the Klan donated money to the Christmas fund for former slaves; in Richmond they contributed to the upkeep of the African American old folks' home; in Buffalo, the Protestant Home for Unprotected Children received warm clothing for 150 kids. *Time* printed a photograph showing hooded Klansmen and their Grand Dragon, dressed as Santa Claus, presenting an elderly African American couple with a radio as a holiday gesture of goodwill. To demonstrate the contribution of the ladies' auxiliary, hooded and robed Klanswomen held Christmas parties for children and distributed hampers to needy families. In Detroit a masked Santa Claus opened a mass Klan rally, but in Salt Lake City the Klan ran into legal trouble when their masked Santas collecting money for charity violated an ordinance against soliciting while in disguise. The Klan's attempt to make use of Christmas continued even after the sudden collapse of their 1920s influence—in 1993 their bid to erect a cross at the Columbus, Ohio, Christmas display erupted into controversy, leading to a court decision that protected their right of free expression.[5]

The great civil rights struggles in the United States during the 1960s spawned a number of attempts to use Christmas to advance African American rights. The Rosa Parks–inspired boycott by blacks of the Montgomery, Alabama, bus system in 1955–1956 led to the successful desegregation of the city's public transportation system. During this struggle Martin Luther King Jr. suggested a boycott on holiday spending in white downtown stores; the money could be saved or given to charity or the Montgomery Improvement Association.[6] Activists learned that threats to the white establishment's pocketbook were an effective tool, and so were born a number of "Black Christmas" movements in American cities. Milwaukee in 1967 was the scene of intense struggle over the issues of fair housing and black unemployment. Led by radical priest James Groppi and the NAACP, civil rights supporters staged demonstrations, went on marches, picketed judges' homes, and organized a boycott not only of white businesses during the holiday season, but also of the public celebration of Christmas itself. "No housing bill, no dollar bill" was their motto. Demonstrators invaded department stores singing "I'm Dreaming of a Black Christmas" and chanting Black Power slogans. The campaign seems to have been economically effective; retail sales went down in Milwaukee, as did revenue from conventions, restaurants, and theaters. Few in the black neighborhoods decorated the outsides of their homes, either out of support for the movement or possibly out of fear of retaliation from the Young Commandos, an NAACP youth group. Groppi's sermon at midnight Mass on Christmas Eve castigated the opponents of desegregated housing for imitating the innkeeper in Bethlehem who had no room for Mary and Joseph at his inn.[7] In Durham, North Carolina, in 1968 the Black Christmas movement organized for changes in welfare, housing, and employment, staging a "Selective Buying Campaign" that tried to divert African Americans away from certain businesses. It encouraged supporters to take their patronage to Raleigh or Greensboro or to buy goods from church basement sales. Its most visible manifestation was a separate Christmas parade sponsored by the Black Solidarity Committee for Community Improvement, who marched through the streets of Durham at the same time as the usual merchants' association parade. Bands played, beauty queens waved from decorated floats, and a black Santa Claus threw candy to children.[8] Jesse Jackson shot to prominence in 1969 with

Operation Breadbasket in Chicago, an offshoot of King's Southern Christian Leadership Conference but an organization the flamboyant Jackson
soon made his own. Part of its drive was to encourage black business and
entrepreneurialism. Since Christmas was the biggest commercial season
of the year, it fell naturally into Jackson's schemes. He claimed that the
psyches of black children were destroyed by the practices of American
white Christmas and that black families fell into cruel debt to "Saint
Trick," instead of "Saint Nick." The traditional Santa Claus was godless
and irrelevant to black culture, and in his stead Jackson introduced "Soul
Santa," who came not from the Arctic but the southerly "Soul Pole." Soul
Santa was "young, gifted and black," was clad in a dashiki of traditional
African colors, and traveled (as befitted the traditional poverty of black
Americans) in a horse-drawn wagon. His message to African American
children was to open accounts at black banks, buy from black businesses,
and avoid giving white merchants the usual Christmas windfall that kept
black Americans dependent on the white man and his seasonal symbols.
"Black mothers and fathers work too hard throughout the year for their
children to allow their gratitude to be showered on an outside white
figure," said Jackson. He decried the rush to buy at white-owned stores
that allowed their owners to vacation in the Caribbean while black shoppers struggled through the year to pay off their debts. "Black Christmas"
encouraged the patronization not only of black businesses but also of
black periodicals, insurance companies, accountants, and professionals
in general.[9]

While Jesse Jackson was organizing the African American community
in Chicago around his concept of Black Christmas, Maulana Karenga
(formerly Ronald Everett) had different ideas in Los Angeles. In late 1966
he instructed members of Organization US, his black nationalist group,
that they were not to celebrate Christmas that year. There was to be no
December 25 gift-giving, feasting, or Santa Claus; instead he presented
his followers with a replacement for the white man's holiday: Kwanzaa, a
syncretic cultural invention that purported to transmit African values and
symbols. Though many Americans today celebrate both Christmas and
Kwanzaa, it is important to note just how oppositional the new holiday's
organizers meant it to be. Conceived in the red-hot racial politics of 1960s
California, where competing black activist groups shot it out on the streets
(two of Karenga's Organization US murdered two Black Panthers on the
UCLA campus) and the FBI ran its COINTELPRO program to undermine
perceived black subversion, Kwanzaa's inventors placed it deliberately

during the Christmas season to challenge its commercialism, its domination of the holiday calendar, and its connection to the white ruling order.[10] Kwanzaa's early racial aggression can be seen in the way it was promoted by activists, some of whom echoed Jesse Jackson's critique of white Christmas as harmful to the African American spirit: "It's time that we as Black People with Black families put down crazy cracker celebrations for something that is for us. Think about: Easter, Thanksgiving, Passover, Chanukah, X-Mas, Columbus, George Washington, Independence Day, on and on.... Zillions of white holidays and lily white images—but nothing for us. Think of all the negative effects of all these so-called holidays." Kwanzaa could also "break chains"; it could replace capitalism as the heart of the Christmas celebration and abolish the new slavery that held down black people: debt. "Once again it is time for us to PLAY THE FOOL.... MAS-X SEASON is here, better known as XMAS. The time for us to sigh, buy, cry, grin, and PURCHASE, purchase, PURCHASE! All for the hippy-dippey Christ and his OLD new year. TAKE THE CHAINS OFF YOUR BRAIN BLACK PEOPLE!!!" Activist groups called for boycotts of Christmas shopping and the adoption of "the alternative to the Christmas rip off—Kwanza [sic].... Kill Santa Claus, relive Kwanza, bring forth the cultural revolution." Kwanzaa has had its ups and downs over the years. It went into an eclipse when Karenga was jailed during the 1970s for assault; it has been criticized for its racial exclusion and for promoting a kind of fascist groupthink. Today, however, it has achieved a sort of middle-class respectability— recognized on American postage stamps and in presidential greetings— and has moved away from its anti-Christmas origins.[11] The equation of Christmas with white exploitation continues, however. In 2015 the Black Muslim leader Louis Farrakhan renewed the call for an economic boycott over the holidays, claiming that this had once been the wish of Martin Luther King. "We intend to boycott Christmas, but not Jesus. We think that they have taken advantage of us and our consumer dollars by materializing the respect and honor of Jesus and making it a bonanza for white business.... So on Black Friday, we won't be there. We choose not to spend dollars on Black Friday, Black Saturday, Black Sunday, Black Monday. We are not going to spend our money for the rest of that year with those that we have traditionally spent our money on."[12]

The term "Black Christmas" was an apt one for African Americans, signaling both the drive for black pride and ownership of the calendar, as well as its hints at a reversal of expectations, the world turned upside down, an implicit repudiation of "May all your Christmases be white." The phrase took on grimmer meanings in apartheid-era South Africa during the township uprisings of the 1970s and 1980s. There, groups of dissident youth, known as "The Boys" or "The Comrades," enforced joyless Christmases in the communities, letting their people and the world know that as long as racial segregation and inequality continued there would be no celebrations of the Nativity. Rather, people's emotions would be directed toward mourning those who had been killed in the previous year's struggles and a boycott of white-owned businesses. Starting in 1976 and intensifying in the mid-1980s, township youth gangs demanded that there be no parties, seasonal lights, beer halls, or gift-giving during the so-called holiday period, when South Africans were used to celebrating with great gusto. They smashed the lights of householders who put up Christmas decorations, searched the bags of shoppers and threw out suspect goods, and threatened businesses or taverns who did not comply with their campaign. Whites were made keenly aware of the buying power of the black majority and its ability to disrupt the normal economy. There was community resistance at first to these demands, but as time went on and revolutionary ardor grew ever hotter, the new sort of Black Christmas was accepted in the townships. As one supporter of the movement said: "The civic society demand for a 'black Christmas' without any kind of celebration initially proved a difficulty for many of us for whom Christmas was a time of celebration. Celebrating the religious significance of the event without forgetting the many who suffered, however, did not prove as difficult as originally expected. We simply reminded ourselves that Jesus was born into poverty and oppression, that he became a refugee, an exile from his own land, and proclaimed peace in a world not too far removed from our own in terms of oppressive violence."[13]

Race has also become a contested Christmas issue in the Netherlands, where the appearance of St. Nicholas's sidekick, Zwarte Piet, has divided the country in an acrimonious debate. The legends that put Piet at the side of the saint are clouded; for some he is a former devil who was tamed into serving the forces of goodness, in other accounts he was a Moorish slave rescued by Nicholas, and still others see in Piet a remnant of Odin's black ravens in Germanic folktales. For the past 150 years Piet has appeared as a page in the garb of the sixteenth century, hearkening back to the days of the Spanish occupation of the Netherlands, with dark skin and African features. Distributing candies to children and climbing down chimneys to distribute gifts, Piet was a universally beloved character until late-twentieth-century critics, acting in defense of the sensibilities of the flood of Asian,

Surinamese, and North African immigrants, perceived in him a symbol of racism and colonial oppression. They began pressing for alternatives—rainbow-colored Piets, Piets darkened with chimney ash, or (in Gouda) cheese-colored Piets—to the traditional Piet with his frizzy hair, red lips, and earring.[14] Demonstrators took to the streets with tape over their mouths and T-shirts reading "Black Pete is Racism." For most Dutch people these calls for change were not welcome—over 90 percent of those polled supported the traditional Piet; there was resentment of being asked to alter a cherished custom and being accused of racism. The popular discontent accelerated when it became clear that for some innovators, a change in skin tone was not enough: the "power relationship" between Piet and Nicholas had to go, as well as the cross on the saint's bishop's mitre. Then the United Nations appeared to get involved. For some reason, the UN Working Group of Experts of People of African Descent decided to consider the now controversial tradition, and "human rights researcher" Verene Shepherd was sent to the Netherlands to investigate. She was horrified by what she found and could not understand why the Dutch could not see what she saw: that Piet and St. Nicholas were avatars of the slave trade and did not belong in the twenty-first century. Not only did Piet have to be abolished, but she saw no need to keep St. Nicholas around either, when the country also loved Santa Claus.[15] The vast majority of Netherlanders reacted with outrage—protest songs were written; politicians from all across the spectrum stated the obvious, that "Black Peter is black"; a Facebook site defending Piet received a million likes in a single day; and members of the UN team were insulted and threatened. Finally, the United Nations seemed to disavow Shepherd and her working group when a Belgian UNESCO representative undercut her claim to authority. "She's just a consultant who abused the name of the UN to bring their own agenda to the media. All the hoopla that Shepherd has caused with her letter is nothing more than a bad move in the game of pressure groups in the Netherlands," said Marc Jacobs.[16] Piet's future seems assured, but he will almost certainly have more diverse appearances in the years to come. (In a related issue, the city of Madrid recently vowed to stop employing blacked-up white actors to portray Balthazar the Wise Man and will henceforth hire only genuine Africans.)[17]

Christmas in its ideal form is normality. Togetherness, love, and family. Cozy worship and warm fireplaces. Reconciliation and reunion. To attach the adjective "Black" to "Christmas" is to signal a change in meaning, perhaps, but not necessarily for the worse. In the American Black Power appropriation of Christmas beginning in the 1970s, it signaled a more prideful attitude toward blackness and a desire to share more fully in the season's richness. In South Africa it meant anger and mourning, a Lent imposed on what would otherwise have been a time of celebration. To Mexican dissidents in 2010 it meant terror. As a rebel press release explained: "On January 1, the rage of the repressed exploded in coordinated strikes throughout the nation. This rage stormed not simply for better wages and less poverty, but for total liberation of the earth and humyn as well as non-humyn animals." The anarchist group Conspira blew up two ATMs; the Earth Liberation Front and the Animal Liberation Front attacked a construction company; the Unforgettable Vengeance Eco-Sabotage Brigade took on more ATMs, a slaughterhouse, and some car dealerships; while the Propaganda of the Deed Brigade vowed that although they did "not believe in absolute dates," 2010 would be a year of struggle. In Tijuana "an autonomous affinity group of anarchists" attacked police with machine guns, "symbolizing the beginning of their own Black Christmas." The dauntless rebels also robbed seven convenience stores belonging to a chain that sold "commodities gleaned from the earth through slavery and environmental devastation."[18]

If attacking ATMs is not sufficient proof of revolutionary bravado in striking at the very heart of the ruling class, consider the actions undertaken by the Ramshackle Incendiary Gang Punky Mauri of Santiago, Chile, who on December 22, 2009, set fire to a Nativity scene and Christmas tree. Their communiqué went into great detail describing the arsonist device and explained their attack thus:

We attacked the crib and the Christmas tree for being symbols of power that has [sic] religion in its alienating and oppressive work.

We repudiate their disgusting festivities, which are pervading everything over [sic] these days, while the domesticated zombies rush en masse to buy the latest mobile phone, designer clothes, a new tv, the car of the year, the latest videogame, etc.... anything to quell the desire for opulence, feeling good by having something that others don't have. This action is in solidarity with all the imprisoned comrades on hunger strike, showing that prison has not bowed their heads and that the struggle continues and is spreading. This is also greetings of courage for all the comrades that have been struck by power, like in the latest raids against social centres and squats of Santiago, showing the State's desperation at its incapacity to put a stop to the attacks. A salute also to the comrades in Mexico who are accused of actions of the earth liberation front, and the comrade Tamara in Spain, accused of sending a letter-bomb.

For all of you comrades, greetings of strength and conviction, because in the war against power nobody is alone and every blow will be returned.

Genoese activists sabotaged the city's Christmas light display in December 2010, and those sympathetic to their cause also attacked some unspecified "symbols of power" on the following eve of Epiphany. Their manifesto read:

While cities are wearing party clothes with lights and Christmas trees and the people are in the throes of convulsive shopping raptus, there are those from inside the ICE and the prisons, and who in the streets, are fighting to recover what is theirs: freedom, the future.

Freedom and future which this very democracy denies those who do not adapt and wear the guise that it imposes.

Democracy, along with her bridesmaids, pennyaliners and servants in uniform, is trying to focus the gaze of the spectators on the very uncertainties it has created "the security of citizens."

They want to voluntarily distract us from what is the only real problem, namely the spread of a global crisis, whose only causes are the bosses and politicians.

Your authoritarian and repressive project has turned and will turn against you.[19]

Showing that no Christmas tree was safe from the wrath of a righteously aroused people, rioters protesting police actions that had taken place a decade earlier burnt down a government-erected evergreen in Buenos Aires in January 2012. Athenian riot police had to protect a tree in the city's main square in 2008, and Mexican anarchists threw Molotov cocktails in Mexico City at the Christmas tree erected on the Paseo de la Reforma in 2013.[20]

If you cannot advance your political cause by destroying a Christmas tree, you can go after a church during the Christmas season. This was the path chosen by a gay anarchist group in Bristol, England, on Christmas

Eve 2013, when they glued shut the doors of the city's Catholic cathedral, smashed stained-glass windows, and painted antireligious graffiti on the building. This was in aid of a protest against "subservience and patriarchy." A message posted on the internet boasted: "Early morning mass was blackened this Christmas Eve. Overnight we glued locks on their doors, spray-painted 'without God,' 'without law,' and anarchy symbols on the grand exterior and signed 'queers x.' We hate the many forms of churches and priests who work to instil subservience and patriarchy with their wretched morals, when not still with the whip."[21] This sort of mischief, of course, pales beside the annual attack on churches at Christmas in Africa and Asia conducted by hard-line Islamists such as Boko Haram or al-Qaeda, but the similarities are striking—there is no danger to the attackers in choosing such soft targets; and there is, because of the deep symbolic importance of Christmas, always enormous publicity to be gained from such actions—the more outrageous the better.

Correcting Your Vices

If you are a hardworking activist, dedicating your life to alerting society to its sinful ways and prescribing for your neighbors a painful but much-needed remedy, you find yourself desperate for a share of media attention. For a moment in the spotlight, you are struggling against not only the continual commercial blare of advertising on billboards, newspapers, store fronts, computers, televisions and radios, the mindless mumble of "reality" shows, the latest trailers for films based on comic book heroes, and viral YouTube cat-meets-new-baby videos but also public service announcements crafted by every other do-gooder out to save the rainforests, whales, spotted owls, and heat-stressed Gaia herself.

To the rescue of such well-meaning folk comes the Christmas season, occupying 10 percent of the calendar year and receiving massive media coverage. The hunger of journalists, producers, and talk show guest bookers for something new to fill pages and air time during the month of December cannot be overestimated. Every year the same old stories will appear about the seasonal charities, the traditional recipes and the variations on them, celebrities' holiday memories, the school concerts, performances of the *Nutcracker* and *Messiah*, festive light and house decoration tours, how to choose the right tree, government agencies' warnings of fire hazards, salmonella in the eggnog, and alcohol abuse. Every year some poor but deserving family will lose their presents to fire or burglary, and every year their plight will be alleviated when media attention is brought to bear. Every year the pope will issue a plea for world peace and be echoed by every local religious leader whose phone number is in a reporter's digital rolodex. Every year the old myths will be recycled—Santa is an invention of Coca-Cola, Martin Luther invented the candle-lit Christmas tree, "The Twelve Days of Christmas" is really in secret Catholic code, a Japanese department store once featured a crucified Santa, the suicide rate goes up at Christmas, poinsettia leaves are deadly poison—and duly rebutted. So when an antismoking campaigner comes along with a new twist on "'Twas the Night before Christmas," she is immediately booked on morning and afternoon talk shows around the continent to tell people that Santa Claus has to be deprived of his pipe for the sake of the children. Canadian writer Pamela McColl omitted the lines "The stump of a pipe he held tight in his teeth, / And the smoke, it encircled his head like a wreath" in order to "save lives and avoid influencing new smokers."[22] The fact that she was instantly attacked by librarians and foes of censorship made this appropriation of Christmas pure gold for the media—not only could they produce precious column inches out of the bowdlerizer's work but they could report on the controversy. A British public health campaign with the slogan "All children really want this Christmas is their parents to quit smoking" had less impact, probably because it featured earnest children and did not attack the iconic Santa Claus.[23]

This was the worst Santa Claus had ever looked: his beard was gray and disheveled; his red jacket was unbuttoned to show his undershirt. He looked as if he were coming off a long alcoholic bender or perhaps had been beaten up by the secret police. Filmed by flashlight in what appeared to be an underground bunker, he turned to the camera and intoned in a doom-laden voice this message:

Dear children. Regrettably, I bring bad tidings. For some time now melting ice here at the North Pole has made our operations and our day to day life intolerable and impossible and there may be no alternative but to cancel Christmas.

I have written personally to President Obama, President Putin, all world leaders. Sadly my letters have been met with indifference. Needless to say these individuals are now at the top of my naughty list. My home in the Arctic is fast disappearing and unless we all act urgently then I have to warn you of the possibility of empty stockings for evermore. Please help me.[24]

Who are more desperate for public attention these days than those alarmed by climate change? It was almost inevitable, then, that they would turn to picturing Santa and Christmas as endangered species. The foregoing desperate Santa (played by the redoubtable Jim Carter, usually employed as Downton Abbey's butler) was the creation of Greenpeace, seeking to use children's fear of losing Christmas to make their point about global warming. John Sauven, executive director of Greenpeace UK, claimed: "Everyone loves Santa and nobody wants him to lose his home. We should all be worried about the ice melting around the North Pole. If enough people support our campaign to protect the Arctic then the younger generation will be able to sleep well on Christmas Eve, safe in the knowledge that Santa's home will be saved." An Arctic without ice; polar bear extinction; starving reindeer; Bangladesh, London, New York, and Amsterdam sunk beneath the waves—these are the threats exposed in the article "Polar Bears Dream of a White Christmas," another example of Greenpeace's use of Christmas in their fundraising campaigns.[25] In Canada an environmentalist group has echoed fears for Santa in its "Where Will Santa Live?" campaign. On its website, David Suzuki, the ineluctable face of the Canadian green movement, poses as a reporter in a rainy Arctic and pleads for money.

> Climate change is melting the North Pole and it's no longer safe for Santa and his Workshop. So our dear old friend is packing up the sleigh to find somewhere else to live.
>
> You can help! Move your mouse over this website to find gifts you can buy Santa to help him set up a temporary Workshop and protect the North Pole for his return.
>
> Of course, you're savvy enough to know we won't be sending actual gifts to Santa. You will receive a tax receipt for 100% of your purchase and proceeds will be used by the David Suzuki Foundation to support our critical work to protect nature and the environment from threats like climate change.
>
> Buying these green gifts and personalized ecards on behalf of hard-to-buy-for friends or relatives on your holiday list is a great way to show you're thinking of them—and the planet![26]

If you thought that donating to these organizations at Christmastime would help save the planet, the Australian Conservation Association comes along to tell you that that the holiday season itself is a menace to life on earth. Their report "The Hidden Cost of Christmas" informed Australians that their buying clothes for gifts would produce approximately 720,000 tons of greenhouse pollution, use thirty-eight gigaliters of water, and leave more than half a million hectares of disturbed land. Buying appliances generated 780,000 tons of greenhouse pollution, and as for buying books or magazines for your loved ones, well read it and weep: the environmental cost of such gifts demanded "416,100 tons of materials such as waste paper, ink cartridges and packaging; left more than 40,000 hectares of land disturbed; and created 430,000 tons of greenhouse pollution, the equivalent of a year of pollution from 85,000 cars."[27]

Scholars have concluded, somewhat tongue-in-cheek, that in many ways Santa Claus is a "public health pariah." An article in the *British Medical Journal* points to a number of risks the magical Gift-Bringer poses. He is often used to promote unhealthy and dangerous products such as alcohol, and leaving a glass of sherry out for St. Nick clearly sends the wrong message to kids about drinking and driving. Accidents are the leading cause of childhood death, yet Santa is an exponent of "extreme sports such as roof surfing and chimney jumping." His contact with ill children and his wide travels make him a vector in the spread of infectious diseases. And then there is obesity—the article laments that Santa is "a late adopter of evidence based behaviour change and continues to sport a rotund image." The authors note that given his global influence Santa need only "affect health by 0.1% to damage millions of lives." A new positive image was necessary.[28] The American Dietetic Association, "the nation's largest organization of food and nutrition professionals," has enlisted Santa to create awareness of calorie intake and healthy food choices. They calculate that if Santa consumed two butter cookies and a glass of whole milk at each house he visited he would end up absorbing more than seven billion calories and 384 million grams of fat—and that was in the United States alone. (Who could calculate the additional damage from the shortbread left out by Scottish children, the mince tarts in England, or the cold beer provided by thoughtful Australian tots?) In order to spare Santa's waistline from fatal damage, the association recommended offering him skim milk, "skinny nog," and graham crackers.

In pushing opposition to eating meat, the *Vegetarian Times* published a parody of Clement Clarke Moore's classic poem. Friends of political correctness will note that the work also amends certain sexist and antienvironmental elements that had escaped censorship for too long.

> *'Twas the night before solstice; all through the earth house*
> *Not a creature was stirring, down to the Mac mouse;*
> *The stockings were hung by the solar collector with care,*
> *In the hopes that the Nicholases soon would be there.*
> *The children were nestled in snug futon beds,*
> *While visions of organic plums danced in their heads,*
> *And mama and I in our muslin P-jay's*
> *Had just settled down after long busy days,*
> *When out in the garden there arose such a clatter,*
> *That we sprang from our bed to see what was the matter.*
> *Away to the windows we flew like a flash,*
> *She opened the shutters, I threw up the sash.*
> *When what to our wondering eyes should appear*
> *But a recycled sleigh and eight well-fed reindeer,*
> *With two agile drivers, so lively and quick,*
> *That we knew in a moment it must be the "Nicks."*
> *More rapid than eagles their coursers they came,*
> *And they whistled, and coaxed them and called them by name,*
> *"Now, Tofu! now, Tempeh! now Seitan and Couscous!*
> *Come, Pasta!, come Pesto!, come Ginger and Kudzu!*
> *Right up to our front door the reindeer they flew*
> *With a sleighful of presents and the Nicholases, too.*
> *So we flung the door open, and without a sound,*
> *In they both came with a leap and a bound,*
> *They were dressed all in hemp from feet up to head*
> *Vegetable-dyed, hers in green, his in red.*
> *Their eyes—how they twinkled; their dimples, how merry!*
> *His cheeks were like roses, her lips like a cherry!*
> *They were slender and fit from a vegetarian diet,*
> *And as role models, they inspired others to try it.*
> *They spoke not a word, but went straight to their task.*
> *And filled all the stockings, then left in a flash.*
> *But we heard them exclaim ere they drove out of sight,*
> *"Happy Solstice to all, and to all a good night!"*[29]

Turkeys, we are told, are amazing birds. They "have a zest for living and, treated with respect, they become very friendly. Turkeys have large, dark, almond-shaped eyes and sensitive fine-boned faces." So says Viva (Vegetarians International Voice for Animals), a pressure group that uses Christmas dinner to highlight the plight of food animals—one billion of whom are killed each year for the British table, along with 4.5 billion fish and 2.6 billion shellfish. Viva offers vegan alternatives to turkey, including chestnut *pâté en croute* and a "festive roast" made out of nuts and lentils and suggestions on how to persuade your family, friends, and neighbors to "bring peace to ALL animals this Christmas." One of those tools is the heartfelt plea of a doomed turkey in the song "Can You Stop the Carvery?" The caged bird protests: "What is wrong with a great tofu? / Plenty of protein and good for you / My drum sticks are meant to run."[30]

Of all the groups urging us to change our diets, the group least bound by good taste or public decorum in their advertising is People for the Ethical Treatment of Animals (PETA). It would be tedious to recall the litany of their provocative campaigns, except to say that there are few social taboos they have not violated. One must not, therefore, expect them to be circumspect in their appropriation of Christmas to bring their message to public attention. To be sure, they are capable of parading around a female Santa and elves with the signs "Soy to the World. Go Vegan!" and "Peas on Earth," but they can walk on the raunchy side as well. Consider, for example, their graphic of a red-suited gent looking with dismay into his pants with the caption "Santa's not coming this Christmas." "Hey, kids! Is the milk that you're leaving out for Santa sending his 'North Pole' south? It could be that 'Jolly Old Saint Nick' can't get his jollies because milk is bringing him down. The fact is, milk can cause impotence by clogging the arteries and slowing down the blood flow to all organs, and hardening of the arteries can make it a blue, blue Christmas for the 30 million North American men who suffer from erectile dysfunction." Who knew that the consumption of dairy products led to impotence? (Apparently meat does too. The English branch of PETA ran an ad with a busty model holding a hotdog with a drooping wiener. "Eating meat got you down?" it asks; "Fight Impotence. Go Vegetarian.") Showing that the Nativity is as fair game as sexual punning is the campaign that portrayed the Virgin Mary suckling the Baby Jesus with the caption "If it was good enough for Jesus...The Breast is Best. Dump Dairy." In 2015 PETA bought ads on the sides of buses asking: "If you wouldn't eat your dog, why eat a turkey? Go Vegan." In comparison with PETA, Dutch critics of Sinterklaas's fur-trimmed robe are positively genteel, noting only that "removing the fur would make a better, more animal-friendly impression."[31]

And for more linkages of sex and Christmas: "Santa only comes once a year ... but that's all it takes," says an ad featuring a woman wrapping herself around Santa in front of the chimney. The British Pregnancy Advisory Service (the country's biggest abortion provider) recognized that "Christmas is a time when people don't think about contraception as a priority, but accidents still happen" and so offered careless merrymakers a free "Christmas Pack" containing condoms and a "morning-after pill." After all, "in the heat of the moment it's easy to get carried away with the festive spirit." Also in the Christmas spirit were Planned Parenthood and Options for Sexual Health, with their "Twelve Days of Christmas" contraception carols in which one's true love provides his inamorata with sterilizations, abortions, and sundry devices of a latex nature.[32]

And speaking of romance, in Japan, when Katsuhiro Furusawa was dumped by his girlfriend in 2006 he turned for solace, as one does, to *The Communist Manifesto*. In this revolutionary tract by Karl Marx and Friedrich Engels he learned that his loveless plight, and that of so many men, was a class issue. From this discovery came Kakuhido, or the Revolutionary Alliance of Men That Women Find Unattractive, whose first target for protest was that "blood-soaked conspiracy of Valentine's Day, driven by the oppressive chocolate capitalists." Shouting their slogans through bullhorns, waving banners, and wearing T-shirts declaring "Sex is Useless," Furusawa's followers denounced the terrorism of flirting and urged solidarity "in resolute opposition to Valentine's Day and the romantic industrial complex." In time, the group turned its baleful glare on White Day (the equivalent of Valentine's Day for males), cherry-blossom season, and finally Christmas. These gloomy foes of Cupid find Christmas objectionable because in Japan it is less a religious occasion, or even a family-centered holiday, than it is yet another occasion for romantic expenditures on gifts, expensive meals, and hot-tub hideaways. "Kurisumasu funsai!" (Crush Christmas!) their signs read, as these lonely activists marched through Tokyo shopping districts in 2015. "In this world, money is extracted from people in love, and happy people support capitalism," said their spokesman. "Christmas is the most symbolic event for this." In addition to promoting support for an unjust economic system, the holiday also oppresses single males. "Unpopular men, who don't have a girlfriend or are not married, are overly discriminated (against). We want to break this barrier."[33]

Asserting Their Right

If Christmas means love, reconciliation, family, and mass social participation, it must, therefore, equal respectability. Many marginalized groups are quick to use Christmas to apply a secondhand gloss to their issues. If they can claim a place at the Christmas table, who can then deny them the larger social attention that they demand?

> Our Christian friends are often quite surprised at how enthusiastically we Pagans celebrate the "Christmas" season. Even though we prefer to use the word "Yule," and our celebrations may peak a few days BEFORE the 25th, we nonetheless follow many of the traditional customs of the season: decorated trees, carolling, presents, Yule logs, and mistletoe. We might even go so far as putting up a "Nativity set," though for us the three central characters are likely to be interpreted as Mother Nature, Father Time, and the Baby Sun-God. None of this will come as a surprise to anyone who knows the true history of the holiday, of course.[34]

So up step the neopagans, followers of a host of cults claiming to practice a mythical Old Religion, once suppressed by Christianity but now being rediscovered—a religion of many spirits, ecologically sensitive, close to the earth, female friendly. Despite their claims to antiquity, these groups are actually of recent origin and are synthetic in their "customs," the product not of the primeval forests of Bronze Age Europe but of 1950s English drawing rooms. For this reason, touchy Wiccans and other neopagans are quick to claim Christmas itself as one of their inventions, that the Yule of the Nordic tribes and the midwinter festivities of earlier civilizations were the real forerunners of today's holiday.[35] In this, of course, they resemble the fundamentalist Christian critics of Christmas.

Neopagans who have little access to the authentic rituals of those pasts they selectively delight to dip into must invent their own songs, symbols, and ceremonies. Often these inventions are self-conscious parodies of those used by Christians; parodies that we might call blasphemy but are the mirror of the sort of borrowing that Christian missionaries to the West engaged in a millennium ago. Here is a song from a Yule ritual performed in cyberspace in 1994, sung to the tune of "Hark the Herald Angels Sing": Brothers, sisters, come to sing / Glory to the new-born King! / Gardens peaceful, forests wild / Celebrate the Winter Child![36] Or the pagans might borrow from something more secular and sing "It's a Magickal night, we're having tonight, / Dancing in a Wiccan Wonderland."[37] Other appropriated ditties include "We Three Crones," "God Bless Ye Merry Paganfolk," "Hark the Neo-Pagans Sing (Glory to the Holly King)," and "We Wish You a Merry Solstice."[38] One of the odder middle-European Christmas Gift-Bringers is the frightening female Berta, also known as Perchta the Disemboweler, whose bipolar nature leads her to give presents to those she favors while she may cut open the bodies of others, fill them with chaff, and sew them up again with a ploughshare and an iron chain. Some Wiccans have chosen to celebrate this creature in song; to the tune of "Santa Claus Is Coming to Town" they sing: "She carries a sack made out of a skin / She dumps the toys out and stuffs bad kids in. / Mother Berta's coming to town." Those wishing to evoke an even older deity at Christmas might, in the musical manner of "Rudolph the Red-Nosed Reindeer," laud Faunus the Roman Goat-God, who we are told "had a very rigid pr*ck / And if you ever saw it / You would say it's quite a trick."[39]

Those wishing to go beyond appropriating Christmas music for neopagan holiday-making might consider the advice of pagan high priestess Selena Fox: "Yule, the winter solstice, is a festival of peace and a celebration of waxing solar light. I honor the new sun child by burning a[n] oaken yule log in a sacred fire. I honor the great goddess in her many great mother aspects, and the father god as Santa in his old sky god, father time, and holly king forms. I decorate my home with lights and with holly, ivy, mistletoe, evergreens and other herbs sacred to this season. I ring in the new solar year with bells." Her tips on how to "re-paganize" Christmas include:

- If you choose to have a living or a harvested evergreen tree as part of your holiday decorations, call it a solstice tree and decorate it with pagan symbols
- Reclaim Santa Claus as a pagan godform by decorating him with images that reflect his various heritages ranging from the Greek god Cronos (father time) to Odin, the Scandinavian all-father riding the sky on an eight-legged horse
- Place pagan mother-goddess images around your home, possibly including one with a sun child, such as Isis with Horus
- Honor the new solar year with light—light candles, burn a yule log and save a portion for the following year, put colored lights outside your home, and with the popularity of five-pointed stars, consider displaying a blue or white pentagram.[40]

Why do pagans do this? It is clear they are not interested in celebrating Yule as it might once have been—human sacrifice, pig- and horse-slaughtering, and mead binges are no longer spiritually correct—or in simply asserting antiquarian truths. They wish to assume for themselves the legitimacy of Christmas and to claim its power for their own, even though they, like the Nazi fanatics before them, wish to shift seasonal focus from December 25 to the winter solstice on December 21. Says Kate West, high priestess of an English Wiccan coven in Cheshire: "We celebrate the rebirth of the sun, not the son." Her coven marks the turning of the year with a ritual fight between the Holly King and the Oak King followed by drumming and chanting to "bring up the sun."[41] Even Santa Claus gets a pagan makeover. One American witch, when asked whether her family makes use of the legend of the Christmas Gift-Bringer, replied: "My kids believe he is a god of Christmas, you, know, him and his wife. And I have things—I have an altar in my front room which I rearrange with the seasons, and at that point we have a Santa Claus and a Mrs. Santa Claus there, and we put all the bows and ribbons and things around them. They are surrounded by it to imitate the spirit of Jupiterianism, you know, which is really what Santa Claus is, a Jupiter type of god."[42]

There are other groups at the margins who want a piece of Christmas. The priest of the Auckland church suggested that maybe it was time the Baby Jesus "came out," slyly hinting that perhaps Christ was gay. It was only a matter of time before other Christmas icons were treated in a gay fashion. Here is an interview Santa Claus allegedly gave to Laurence Watts that appeared in the *Huffington Post* in December 2011: "I'm gay," he tells me with a festive chortle. "I guess I've always known, deep down. I had a moment of clarity a few years ago when the elves and I were wrapping a consignment of Princess Bride Barbie and Sweet Talking Ken dolls. I've never really cared for Barbie, but I couldn't put my finger on why. Then I looked down at one of the Ken dolls, effortlessly cool in his baby blue T-shirt and denim jeans, and I realised: I wanted to be the one dating Ken."[43] The play *Santa Claus Is Coming Out*, a one-man mockumentary that premiered in 2001 and made it to New York's Off Broadway purports to be the story of "a big fairy" who once hung around gay bars and was known as "Santa Closet." A rather rancid song attempted the same change in orientation: "Butch The Gay Santa Claus, filled with Christmas cheer / Butch The Gay Santa Claus, his beard tickles your ear / All the children at the mall wait for their surprise / It's not just Rudolph's nose that's red when they sit on his thighs," and so on.[44] In its multitude of television and movie treatments of

Dickens's *Christmas Carol*, Ebenezer Scrooge has been cast as English or American, as a white man or a white woman, as a female pornographer and a cartoon Scottish duck, as a black woman, and in Los Angeles in 2010 as "an empty, lonely, loveless, closeted gay man who has been so repressed that he has lost his ability to give and receive love." This was the premise of *A Scrooge and Marley Christmas Carol*, staged by Knightsbridge Theater. A gay cinematic take on the Dickens book appeared in 2012 as *Scrooge and Marley*, billed as "A New Holiday Classic for a New Kind of Family." And for those who feel that traditional Nativity scenes were too reflective of the patriarchy or heteronormativity, manufacturers have responded with a Joseph cast as a rosy-faced female, crafted to appeal to lesbian or single-mother buyers.[45]

"Hit 'em where it hurts this holiday season!" For a few months in 2011 the Occupy Wall Street movement monopolized media attention in the United States and Britain. Beginning in September of that year, crowds of demonstrators with a host of economic, social, and political grievances began to occupy a number of public spaces to air their discontent, chiefly a dislike of Wall Street and the "One Percent" who were said to have "appropriate[d] the wealth of our society."[46] Long on outrage and short on solutions, the movement quickly blossomed and, as quickly, disintegrated. One of its offshoots was Occupy Christmas, a collection of approaches to protesting seasonal consumerism, largely spread by social media. *Adbusters*, the engine of Buy Nothing Day, was quick to suggest some helpful projects for their readers during the runup to Christmas. They could, for example, stage a "Zombie Walk" where the "cheerful dead wander around malls, marveling at the blank, comatose expressions on the faces of shoppers. The zombies are happy to be among their own kind, but slightly contemptuous of those who have not yet begun to rot." If behaving collectively in a brain-dead fashion were not sufficient social protest, one might offer to cut up shoppers' credit cards, thus striking a blow against consumer debt, or engage in a "Whirl-Mart," where "you and nine of your closest friends silently drive your shopping carts around in a long, inexplicable conga line without ever actually buying anything."[47] Fun for the whole family and a crushing rebuke to The Man. Posters generated by the movement included one, headed "WANTED: People to take control of their money," that listed suggested activities to "show the banks who's boss": don't use credit cards, pay with cash; buy from locally owned shops; upcycle; make gifts; and "spend time more than money."[48]

Appropriators of Christmas are drawn to *A Christmas Carol* like elves to gingerbread. The Occupy Chicago folks in December 2011 staged *Occupy*

My Heart, based on the Dickens classic. In this play, ambitious banker Josh rediscovers his old flame, Kay, who is an Occupy protestor. Once a dauntless progressive, Josh's heart has turned flinty, but on Christmas Eve he will be visited by three spirits who "will show him that other world, the one that might have been with Kay, a world of hope and decency and dignity for all." The drama was billed as "a story of the 99%, for the 99% and by the 99%. Occupy My Heart, A Revolutionary Christmas Carol is the story of us."[49] Naturally Santa Claus is co-opted to speak on behalf of the movement. In a tongue-in-cheek Funny or Die video, he explains that the world economy is in trouble and it is time to "Occupy Christmas," which Santa describes as "a new way to celebrate the birth of Jesus who was, after all, a socialist." Vote with your dollars, he tells the audience, by avoiding shopping at big corporate stores and instead patronizing local shops. His elves catch the spirit of the movement and explain that Occupy Christmas "isn't just about camping out in public parks, being a communist hippy or not setting goals for yourself," it's also about ending the Federal Reserve and telling big banks to go [bleep] themselves.[50] As the movement's Facebook page said:

> The only way to send a message to the establishment is through their pocketbooks. We are feeding the very machine responsible for destroying us. In this regard we have no one to blame but ourselves. We can change this by taking our money out of the banks, buying local goods, and living more self sustainable lives in general. We can also participate in events like this. Maybe you can't go and physically occupy your city but you can make the conscious choice to make a difference via an adjustment of your actions. The only thing necessary for evil to triumph is for good men to do nothing. What will you tell your children and grandchildren, from whom we borrow this world, your reasons for sitting idly by while our country was stolen from us? When that time comes, let it not be said that we did nothing.

In a 2011 British poll, 83 percent of respondents agreed that Christmas was about "spending time with family and friends," and 62 percent agreed that "Christmas is a time when we should be generous to people less fortunate than ourselves." However, only 34 percent agreed that "Christmas is a time when we should challenge poverty and economic injustice," and even fewer (19 percent) agreed that "Christmas is a time when we should challenge political oppression around the world."[51] Though apparently not in the majority, there are many who will wish to use the holiday season to challenge the status quo. It is one of the joys of Christmas that anyone feels able to take part in it or to grab a part of it to make a political or social point, and not only in the United States.

In Germany activists have adopted that fine old Teutonic invention the Advent calendar to make a point about housing policy. In Hamburg in 2010 the antigentrification group Komm in die Gänge dressed as elves and Santa to decorate the doors of twenty-four houses with a number and a Christmas decoration, thus forming the world's biggest Advent calendar.[52] Instead of each door opening to reveal a treat as Christmas approaches, these are entrances to unused houses. The group wants these houses and many others opened up to use instead of being stockpiled by developers. A much less genteel German protest took place in Cologne Cathedral during the 2013 Christmas morning service. A woman who had been sitting in the pews suddenly leaped onto the altar, bared her breasts, and revealed a message scrawled across her torso: "I Am God." Closer inspection determined that she was not, as she had claimed, the Supreme Being but was, in fact, a member of the international provocation group FEMEN, upset at the conservative hierarchy of the Catholic Church.[53] The following year saw more bare-bosomed outrage as another topless blonde, inscribed with the message "God Is Woman" and shouting anti-Catholic slogans, tried to steal the image of the Baby Jesus from the Nativity scene erected by the pope in front of St. Peter's Basilica. The act was a protest against "the centuries-old Vatican stance on women's rights for [their] own body and reproductive function." This was part of FEMEN's anticlerical "Massacre of the Innocents" campaign, which called for the theft of Baby Jesus from crèches around the world. "The maniacal desire to control women's fertility is a common trait of many religions, National Socialism, nationalism and other antediluvian, anti-humanist ideologies. Abortion is sacred," said the group. Upping the ante from nudity to self-immolation, a California man set fire to himself, American flags, and a Christmas tree in Bakersfield, California. Third-degree burns were the price of his protest against "the religious establishment" and a decision by a local school board to change the names of winter and spring breaks to Christmas and Easter vacation.[54]

Opponents of the security wall erected on the West Bank by the Israeli government have used Nativity scenes as a means of protest. Bethlehem, site of the Church of the Nativity, built over the birthplace of

Jesus, has been cut off from Jerusalem by the barrier, with a resulting loss of visitors and tourist revenue. In 2006 a Catholic church in England replaced its usual Christmas display with a twenty-four-foot-high replica of the barrier, flanked by protest banners and photographs. The Israeli embassy protested, saying that "in 2005 over half of the Israelis who were killed in terrorist atrocities were killed by terrorists who came from or through Bethlehem." During the Christmas season of 2007, English charities sold olivewood Nativity scenes carved by Palestinian Christians—but these were crèches where "the wise men won't get to the stable" because they were split down the middle by a wall (removable in case peace broke out and the security barrier was taken down). In 2011 the Bethlehem protests were carried out in the town itself, where young activists dressed as Santa Claus and erected a Christmas tree out of barbed wire and decorated with cards commemorating significant moments in the history of the Israeli occupation. Their aim was to alert tourists to their plight and to encourage a boycott of goods produced by Jewish settlers in the Occupied Territories. In England a group called Jews for Boycotting Israeli Goods organized an event titled "Bethlehem Now: Nine Alternative Lessons and Carols for Palestine," involving "traditional carols with untraditional lyrics, interspersed with poetry and prose readings, to highlight current reality in the Holy Land." "The Twelve Days of Christmas" was amended to list "Twelve assassinations, Eleven homes demolished, Ten wells obstructed, Nine sniper towers . . . And an uprooted olive tree." The carol "Once in Royal David's City" was changed to "Once in royal David's city / stood a big apartheid wall / People entering and leaving / Had to pass a checkpoint hall / Bethlehem was strangulated / And her children segregated." Palestinian sympathizers have also used Christmas cards to make their point. Australians for Palestine included a poem entitled "In the Shadow of the Wall" with their greeting card: "In the shadow of the Wall, / 'Peace on Earth' and / 'Goodwill to all people' / are but words / caught and frozen in the web of Occupation." A group of pro-Palestinian artists took a giant step in appropriating Christmas by claiming the Baby Jesus himself as one of theirs. The Ireland Palestine Solidarity Campaign offered a set of Christmas cards depicting Mary and the Baby Jesus in the colors of the Palestinian flag. Another group showed a swaddled infant, presumably meant to be the young Jesus, with the slogan "Made in Palestine"; but their most explicit linkage was the poem "Christ Was a Palestinian," which included the line "and unto us a new era is born."[55]

The central image of the Nativity scene—a young mother and her baby huddling in a stable—has a powerful emotional impact that has been expressed by artists for centuries. In the twenty-first century that image has been appropriated in the debate over admitting refugees from Africa and the Middle East to Europe and North America. In 2013 a life-size figure of Balthazar, one of the Wise Men, was stolen from a Nativity scene in Santiago de Compostela, Spain, and was later found outside the office of the General Secretariat for Emigration with a sign denouncing the use of razor wire to protect the border between Morocco and a small Spanish enclave in North Africa. (Protestors had claimed that the wire harmed those who were trying to infiltrate Spanish territory to seek asylum.)[56] The internet in late 2015 was flooded with memes depicting the Holy Family and finger-wagging captions: "Don't forget to hate refugees as you set up a nativity scene celebrating a Middle Eastern couple desperately seeking shelter," said one; another read: "Remember that Jesus was an undocumented child refugee." In other illustrations of outdoor crèches, one was labeled: "It's nice that people put out these lawn ornaments to signal that their homes have room to take in refugees," while the motto over another read: "If you are refusing to help refugees you may not know what this is."[57] (Critics of the memes retorted that the Holy Family were not refugees, they were merely responding to a census, and their "flight into Egypt" was in fact well funded by the gold brought by the Wise Men.) The other side of the debate was not shy either about using Christmas to argue for an end to migration. In Dresden, Patriotische Europäer gegen eine Islamisierung des Abendlandes (Patriotic Europeans Against Islamization of the West) took to the streets to protest the flood of Muslim immigration into their country. Carrying banners with slogans such as "Against Hatred, Violence, and the Quran," "Against Religious Fanaticism," and "No Sharia in Europe," the marchers carried song sheets that had been distributed online. To assert their Germanness and to equate national identity with Christianity, they sang traditional Christmas carols: "Stille Nacht," "Alle Jahre Wieder," and "O Du Fröhliche."[58]

Christmas cards with a political message have a long history with the radical left. One from late-nineteenth-century Britain contrasts the humble Jesus riding a donkey with the contemporary aristocracy in their elegant coaches: "In days of yore when Divinity rode / On His mission of Love, an ass He bestrode. / But woe for the change! It now takes, alas, / Two men and two horses to carry an ass." During the pre–World War I struggle for women's suffrage, one card showed a smiling suffragette in her prison cell and the caption "Hoping you're in for a good time this Xmas! May Xmas never prove a 'sell', / And naught mar your delights, / For when they give you 14 days, / You'll get your Womens Rights." A 1973 pro–Irish Republican Army card proclaimed, beside a picture of despairing prisoners: "Christmas Greetings. Third year of internment. 1973." The right wing has taken its turn at using Christmas cards to advance their cause, though examples are much rarer. Infinitely more pro-union, pro-Greenpeace, antiwar, prochoice, pro-Castro, and so forth, cards are produced than cards advocating management rights, coal mining, the invasion of Iraq, an end to abortion, or prolonging the Cuban embargo. The National Rifle Association issues annual Christmas cards, but they are greatly outnumbered by its opponents' parody cards—one such featuring the NRA seal showed a little boy asking Santa for "racial purity," which, no matter what some believe, is not known to be on the NRA's wish list. Since the right is often associated with maintenance of the status quo, they are less often involved in social agitation and less likely to use Christmas to shake up the establishment. It seems that only when the right is in an insurrectionary mode are they likely to appropriate the holy season. White Russian émigrés who fled the Soviet revolution produced a card showing a tree decorated with military medals commemorating their fight. The fiercely anti-Communist resistance movement Ukrayins'ka Povstans'ka Armiya (Ukrainian Insurgent Army) issued a card in 1945 showing one of its camouflaged fighters looking at a blazing star in the heavens.[59]

It is far more common for antiwar messengers to use Christmas than those who support a particular military action. In 1969 John Lennon and Yoko Ono attacked the United States' involvement in the Vietnam War when they bought billboard spaces in North America and Europe to proclaim "WAR IS OVER / IF YOU WANT IT / Happy Christmas from John and Yoko." They followed that up in 1971 with the song "Happy Xmas (War Is Over)," which had commercial success when it was released and again in 1980 after Lennon was murdered. In 1987 "All I Want For Christmas Is World Peace," by Timbuk3, asked St. Nicholas "It looks to me like World War III / Underneath the Christmas tree / Please dear Santa, Mr. Santa please / Can't you make the firing cease?" The events of the famous 1914 Christmas truce of World War I have been made into a number of antiwar songs, particularly "Christmas in the Trenches," by John McCutcheon, and a movie with a similar sentiment, *Joyeux Noël* (2005).

Since the 1920s it has been a belief of the antiwar movement that toys and books with a military connection encourage children to think that war is a normal or even praiseworthy activity. Groups such as the Women's International League for Peace and Freedom and the Women's Peace Society tried to discourage manufacturers from making such toys and parents from buying them. In the 1960s, Parents for Responsibility in the Toy Industry protested at annual toy fairs, and in 1982 Blacks Against Nukes (BAN) urged African American parents to avoid buying playthings such as GI Joe. In 2005 the American all-purpose protest group Code Pink launched "Operation Stick It to 'Em," which encouraged its supporters to put stickers on war toy packages stating "Surgeon General's Warning: Violent Toys = Violent Boys." They also proposed a "buy and return" policy in which believers would buy the evil playthings for the purpose of returning them after Christmas, giving them a chance to lodge complaints with store managers while creating longer lines in customer service departments.[60] Australian feminists, including Green politicians and academics, tried to draw a direct line between toy choice and male-on-female violence in the home:

> Insofar as toy guns and soldiers communicate to children that aggression and violence are the natural domain of boys, and Barbies and pink tea sets, that beauty and domesticity are the most appropriate realm for girls, they serve to uphold cultural conditions which facilitate the lesser treatment of women, enacted through behaviour such as domestic violence. . . . Given that intimate partner violence is the highest contributor to death, disability and ill-health for Australian women under 45, Australia needs to move beyond "bad apple" theories of why domestic violence occurs and look instead to cultural and systemic explanations for why this epidemic exists. Maybe Santa should rethink what he's putting in the stockings of our young men.[61]

It's not just children who are deemed at risk from gendered toys. What about the adults? The author of an article in The *New Statesman* found that choosing Christmas gifts for one's office mates created a quandary. What to get for someone one barely knows outside brief comments beside the photocopier? While everyday life for "a feminist mother of three who works in publishing" demanded one take a hard line against sexism, resorting to gendered gifts was in this case almost a necessity. "Just note down whether this person is a he or a she and buy accordingly. . . . Christmas is a time when adults have obvious reasons to treat each other as pronouns, nothing more: For Her (blank-faced woman who likes bubble bath and chocolate), For Him (blank-faced man who likes booze and crap jokes)."[62]

Speaking of appropriators of Christmas shouting from the fringes of society, who is more marginal than a conceptual artist? These plucky observers of the human condition, armed only with government arts grants, have for decades confronted the public with the fruits of their conceptualizing. Striving less for beauty than for provocation, they invariably find Christmas too easy a target to resist. Take Canadian artist Jimmy Wright, for example. Weary of the commercialization of the sacred holiday and wishing to register his opposition to the orgy of consumption that raged about him, he erected a cross in front of his house and placed on it a crucified Santa Claus. Above the bewhiskered victim was a sign reading *Sumptum Fac Donec Consumptus Sis*, which is sort-of Latin for "Shop Till You Drop." Despite pleas by neighbors not wishing to have to explain to their children why Santa was executed on a Vancouver Island lawn and a visit from the pastor of Saint Mary's Anglican Church, Wright refused to remove the effigy, stating that Santa "represents frivolous consumption. He shot Jesus right out of the saddle. He's the focus of Christmas."[63] Then there was English artist Mark McGowan, who, in a holiday season performance labeled "Rollover 2002," rolled across London from the Elephant and Castle to Bethnal Green, a distance of four and a half miles. Dressed in waterproof pants, a parka, a red knit hat, and rubber gloves, he sang "We Wish You a Merry Christmas" during his eight-and-a-half-hour roll, which left him bruised, bloody, and dizzy. He undertook this journey to protest the fact that when he worked as an office cleaner, no one thanked him or wished him a happy Christmas. In 2005 Glasgow art student Darren Cullen planned to splash his Christmas message across billboards; they were to read "Stop Lying To Your Children About Santa Claus" and "Santa Gives More To Rich Kids Than Poor Kids." Cullen denied that he meant to ruin the holiday for children; he was just trying to alert tots to their role as society's victims. "Santa Claus is a lie that teaches kids that products will make them happy," he said. "Before they're old enough to think for themselves, the story of Santa has already got them hooked on consumerism. I think that's more immoral than this billboard." To Cullen's dismay, the owner of the billboard company felt the message was inappropriate and vetoed the plan, but he eventually found a site willing to host his season's greeting.[64] When it comes to conceptual artists getting into the public eye at Christmas, no one does it with more élan than Keith McGuckin of Wellington, Ohio. Over the years, he has graced his community with installations of pyromaniac snowmen, a Santa Claus in an iron lung, a child wetting his pants while sitting on a department store Santa, and a gingerbread re-creation of the murder in a Dallas police station of John F. Kennedy assassin Lee Harvey Oswald. Determining the most offensive of his offerings is difficult; critics are divided between the 2006 diorama of gingerbread men wearing swastikas and giving a Nazi salute and his 2008 display in a public library of a Christmas tree pushing a wheelchair-bound Santa down a flight of stairs. A sign informed library patrons that the homicidal tree would spend the money he had stolen from Salvation Army kettles on a spree in a strip club.[65]

"Zombie Lives Matter," proclaimed a T-shirt slogan in support of another controversial display. Social historians in distant centuries will be doubtless fascinated by our era's obsession with the undead and their taste for human brains or blood. Capitalizing on this fad in 2014–2015 was Jasen Dixon of Sycamore Township, Ohio, who erected the world's first zombie Nativity scene in his front yard. Ghastly lighting illuminated the decomposing Mary, Joseph, Wise Men, and shepherd bending over a demonic Baby Jesus, a tableau that aroused the ire of municipal officials and local Baptists, who leafleted the neighborhood and left an accusing tract in the cradle: "If you read the scriptures closely," the Baptists' letter said, "the God of the Bible is not only a God of love, but also a God of wrath. God never expresses even the slightest inkling of humor towards demons or, in this case, zombies." Dixon, who vows he is not an atheist, claimed that the display was "a wonderful piece of artwork" and not religious commentary. Justin Contre, a developer at an Arizona toy company planning to market a Zombie Nativity kit, felt that his product drew him closer to his Catholic faith and said that his religious parents were pleased that he had finally acquired a Nativity scene, even if it was populated by the undead.[66]

"He probably should've used yellow lights for Santa's urine," said the sheriff. The police official had been summoned by neighbors who were upset by a 2015 Christmas display that seemed to support Islamic terrorism. Spelled out in bright red lights on the side of a home in Limerick, Maine, was "ISIS," the acronym of the Islamic State in Iraq and Syria. What the complainants had failed to discern was the illuminated image of Santa Claus higher up on the roof, peeing down on "ISIS." When the confusion was pointed out to the homeowner, he vowed to change the color of the urine stream of lights to more accurately reflect his Christmas sentiments. His was a pro-American wish, he asserted.[67]

Conceptual art expressed through Nativity scenes is the forte of the Claremont United Methodist Church in California. For years they have used their Christmas display to feature "a piece of art that comments on our times." Over this time they have presented the Nativity in a bombed-out building, a graffiti-covered border wall topped with barbed wire, the Virgin Mary detained in a jail cell, the gunned-down Trayvon Martin gushing blood, and the "suggestion that Jesus could be born in a context of 'equal marriage.'" The church's 2014 offering portrayed a homeless woman and her baby in a bus shelter. The Reverend Mark Wiley was unhappy that more people weren't offended by the latter piece. "Why didn't people get upset at our nativity? I find it horribly disturbing that people didn't get upset that there are so many poor in our country. No one came to the church office to say, 'How can I make a difference?' Was no one morally offended that so many children are born into poverty, and continue to live diminished lives?" Giving offense to passersby is clearly important to Pastor Wiley, who said "I love the idea of making a modern Nativity as provocative as the first Nativity. (In fact, the Nativity was so threatening that Herod ordered the very first Christmas mass killing!)" However, in 2015 his church's Creative Peacemaking committee could not find "the right balance between the witness, the mood, and the visuals." They had wanted to "make a witness about gun violence" but worried about provoking counter-demonstrators and so settled for erecting a banner reading "Peace" in many languages.[68]

A final cry from the margins. In a famous legal case that went to the US Supreme Court, the city of New London, Connecticut, seized by "eminent domain," over one hundred private homes to develop the area for businesses that would "stimulate the economy." Homeowner Susette Kelo fought the project, but even after being evicted, she refused to let her opponents have the last word. In 2006 she sent Christmas cards to the officials involved in seizing her home. The cards showed a view of her property and a heartfelt seasonal greeting affirming that the judges' houses, homes, friends, and families lay under her malediction. "May they live in misery that never ends," was her Christmas wish. "I curse you all. May you rot in hell."[69]

VI

The Discontented

*In which are discussed all those for whom Christmas is a
dreadful trial about which they must alert their neighbors
and the world*

IN THE HOLIDAY season of 2002, drivers on the Pat Bay Highway near
Victoria, British Columbia, were treated to the following greeting; in huge
black letters on red, a billboard spelled out the message: "Gluttony. Envy.
Insincerity. Greed. Enjoy Your Christmas." This was the festive wish of
Valerie Williams, a thirty-two-year-old student of women's studies at the
local university, and her partner, Trevor. Fed up with what they perceived
to be the annual hell of a "white, middle-class, heterosexual, patriarchal,
Christian Christmas," they spent $1200 to alert their friends and rank
strangers to their pent-up rage and followed it with a mass e-mailing of
their manifesto: "In response to the growing onslaught of manufactured
consumeristic Christmas cheer, we have decided to actively reject the
capitalist ideology of Christmas. We refuse to spend one cent on buying
into the consumer machine this year—no tinsel, no tree, no shiny balls,
no Christmas cards, no presents, no wrapping paper, no turkey, no cran-
berry sauce, no candy canes, and no icicle lights.... Christmas will not be
coming to this house.... Join us in our Christmas rebellion!" Should one
have been so bold as to have telephoned this merry couple during that
month, one would have heard the strains of "White Christmas" suddenly
interrupted by this dialogue.

VALERIE: "My God, who put that music on?"
TREVOR: "It's awful, get it off."
VALERIE: "Oh.... Jesus. Oh. Oh. Doesn't that just drive you insane?"

For years the couple had manifested their dislike of the season by sending
anti-Christmas cards festooned with pictures of homeless Santas and

battered child angels, informing the recipients that in lieu of presents donations would be made to charity; but they decided in 2002 to ramp their message up a notch.[1]

This couple and many others like them are an inescapable feature of the modern Christmas. In the words of Minneapolis journalist James Lileks: "There's a new staple in modern newspapers: the tale of the Holiday Crank. In the past these people would be ignored, but nowadays no coverage of the season is complete without a dissenting voice. You don't lose any points in a modern Western newsroom suggesting that the paper run profiles on people who hate Christmas. Float the notion of profiling lapsed Muslims who hold Ramadan in bemused contempt, and I suspect people would react as though you had pushed a ball of tinfoil into one of their dental fillings."[2]

Consider the number of wits who have attacked the season:

Bah! How hollow it all is! Always on Christmas, though, I feel my heart soften—toward the late Judas Iscariot. (Ambrose Bierce)

Christmas to a child is the first terrible proof that to travel hopefully is better than to arrive. (Stephen Fry)

To perceive Christmas through its wrappings becomes more difficult with every year. (E. B. White)

In the United States Christmas has become the rape of an idea. (Richard Bach)

I detest "Jingle Bells," "White Christmas," "Rudolph the Red Nosed Reindeer," and the obscene spending bonanza that nowadays seems to occupy not just December, but November and much of October, too. (Richard Dawkins)

Bloody Christmas, here again, let us raise a loving cup, peace on earth, goodwill to men, and make them do the washing up. (Wendy Cope)

Orphans, dead parents, lonely children at Christmas, morose spoken word recordings, everything you love about the holidays. Move the turkey over so you can fit your head in the oven. (April Winchell)

In our racist, sexist society, Christmas is the 8 hours when we stop killing each other and gratuitous overeating is encouraged so that the starving and other people in the world can die! (Lloyd Kaufman)

Christmas makes everything twice as sad. (Douglas Coupland)

When folk come to put pen to paper or fingers to keyboard to complain about Christmas, those with the most doleful tales are those who suffer emotionally from the onset of the season. "Many of us wanted desperately to love Christmas, yet, in truth, we dreaded it and loathed it as a dark passage we were forced to endure. Once a year. Every year. For the rest of our lives." So wrote Michelle Miller, coeditor of *Christmas Blues: Behind the Mask,* an anthology of offerings about the dark side of the holiday. Most of their authors were not professional writers, and pathos often lapsed into bathos, but their lack of artfulness only accentuated the anguish they sought to express. (Consider the climax to the poem "The Man Who Hated Christmas": "And we who loved him have/ always wondered — / Did he die of the cancer, or / Was it Christmas?") And as amateur as these writers are, we see their critiques echoed widely in the press.

Loneliness at Christmas is one of the most frequent and plangent themes of those suffering from Christmas blues. It is so common a feeling that the Swiss have invented a word for it—Weihnachtscholer—and it stems from a multitude of losses that are keenly felt when all around seem to be celebrating. One of the most common sources of seasonal sadness is recalling the death of a loved one. One of the deepest meanings of Christmas is family togetherness and reunion, and to look for a missing face or see an empty chair that once held a lover, a child, a grandparent is to experience pangs of grief. For this reason many churches hold Blue Christmas or Longest Night services with special liturgies to comfort the sorrowful, knowing that the season's typically joyful services are often like rubbing salt in the wounds of those who have lost someone.[3]

For many, however, it is the family itself that is the source of Christmas dysfunction and misery. According to controversial psychiatrist R. D. Laing, family reunions at Christmas can drive one mad. Laing claims that families operate on dramatic lines, with each member assigned a part from which he or she cannot escape or deviate. Being forced to abandon adulthood and independence and become a child again creates enormous stress. This pressure is worse for the unmarried, the recently bereaved, the divorced, and those who have lost their jobs.[4] "Some of us don't have conventional families, or we don't like the ones we have—or, because of our sexuality, job, or marriage choice, the ones we have don't like us. Or we experience Seasonal Affective Disorder, and with it the Christmas blues. For gay children, for interracial couples, for unmarried working women, coming home to family at the holidays can be a strain. Or it is a strain because grown children remember unhappy childhoods and cannot stand sentimental cant."[5] Other kinds of separation than death are mourned at Christmas.

> Loneliness is a resilient, persistent little beast. For most of the year, those of us who live alone can rub along pretty well.... But Christmas is a different kettle of seasonal salmon altogether. There is no escaping it or ignoring it. For what seems like months it has been mocking those of us who don't have children, partners or friends close and loyal enough to forsake the bosom of their own families to be with you.... Everywhere you look, you are reminded you are a pariah, that you have failed to even dampen life's litmus test of happiness.

The English journalist Liz Jones, a middle-aged childless vegan divorcée with seventeen cats, reminds us that not only are many single people like her feeling bereft at Christmas but that this is an almost inevitable fate for women, who tend to outlive their menfolk.[6] Pity, too, the mistress who cannot spend the holiday with her married lover and the couple who yearn for a child they can never conceive. Those who have lost their Christian faith can feel empty at Christmas and find it hard to locate the joy any more in the season.

The world of popular music has cashed in on Yuletide depression, with songs such as Elvis Presley's hit "Blue Christmas" and Roy Orbison's "Pretty Paper." One might add "What Do the Lonely Do at Christmas?" by The Emotions, "Christmas Eve Can Kill You" by the Everly Brothers, Stan Rogers's "First Christmas," and "Who Took the Merry out of Christmas?" by the Staple Singers. But nothing ever produced for the Christmas maudlin market by Tin Pan Alley can jerk tears out of listeners' eyes faster than "Christmas Shoes," written by Eddie Carswell and Leonard Ahlstrom. In this chart-topping hit of 2000, a last-minute shopper overhears the plight of a young boy trying to buy a pair of expensive shoes for his dying mother ("Could you hurry, sir, Daddy says there's not much time / You see she's been sick for quite a while") so that she can look her best when she goes to meet Jesus. Sadly, the wee lad has insufficient funds to purchase this footwear, but the narrator steps up to pay for them and thus learns the true meaning of Christmas. Millions love it, millions hate it; it has been named the worst Christmas song of all time and has made into a movie and a novel.

Those without loving husbands or wives complain about such an absence; those with mates who are around the house too much at Christmas are said to suffer from "spouse saturation syndrome." Anger can be generated in this season in the hearts of those who loathe themselves for not being able to supply their family with the right gifts, and guilt can spring from not being as happy as the ideal family depicted on television. Christmas is the season of weight gain and increased consumer indebtedness: both reasons for feeling guilty and under pressure in December and January. Complaints about stress abound, but they differ according to the sexes. It has long been noted that women bear the brunt of domestic labor over the holidays, a burden Canadian social historian Leslie Bella has labeled the "Christmas Imperative." Bella claims that "familism" forces women to try to reproduce the idealized Christmases of their Victorian ancestors, even though the modern woman, employed outside the home, lacks the servant class that would have done the work in the nineteenth century. "But still we persist—partly because we are trapped by a resurrected familist ideology that tells us that home-based labour is our responsibility, and that we are failures as women if we abandon that labour. But we also persist because we have been convinced that Christmas should be reproduced— that Christmas itself is good. This message comes to us from those who merchandise....To neglect Christmas is to be a "Scrooge" and to fail in our responsibilities to community and family."[7] A Gallup survey in 2006 indicated that though the majority of respondents did not feel stressed-out at Christmas, a large minority did. This was particularly true for women and for families with children under eighteen. Overall, 13 percent found holiday shopping very stressful, and 30 percent found it "somewhat stressful"; 34 percent claimed it was "not too stressful"; 23 percent testified to feeling no stress at all. However, 51 percent of those with young children and 51 percent of women professed themselves stressed. When asked about the holidays in general and the pressures generated by them, men of all ages were more relaxed than women. There was general agreement (85 percent) that the season was much too commercialized.[8] What was worse, in the eyes of *Guardian* writer Jessica Valenti, was that in the midst of doing all the work at Christmas—"the holidays bring on a whole new set of gendered expectations that make the season less about simply enjoying fun and family and more about enduring consumerism, chores and resentment so that everyone else can enjoy rockin' around the Christmas tree"—women were expected to seem happy about it.[9]

While women stress over the hard work of the festival, what is it about it that elevates the heart rate of men to dangerous levels and causes them seasonal grief? It is shopping, particularly shopping in the presence of women, a task so onerous that it becomes a health hazard. A British study of consumers in 1999 claimed that peak stress levels for men in crowded shops reached levels experienced by fighter pilots or police going into dangerous situations. The same study found that stress in women was lower when they took their children shopping than when they took their partners. The psychologist who conducted the research urged women "to listen to their partners this year and consider the long-term benefits of not forcing them to help. Not only will their men be less stressed at Christmas, but they will be too."[10] A shopping center in Scotland has the perfect solution for both men and women who face this dilemma: surrogate boyfriends to accompany women on their rounds. "The Shopping Boyfriend is the ultimate retail therapist: enthusiastic, attentive, admiring and complimentary," claimed a spokesman, "He will browse with the girlfriend for hours on end. He'll even say her butt looks small."[11]

"It's impossible to 'do' Christmas without running into one patriarchal construct after another." Thus opines Canadian feminist Latham Hunter. "Pity the poor mother who wants to enjoy the holiday season and pass along the delight and warmth of various yuletide traditions but who doesn't particularly want to put the Christ back in Christmas, as it were, or reinforce the notion that men are the foundation of the most important things in the world, like school vacations and presents." Not only is Jesus a prominent figure in this whole holiday thing but other males also take center stage: Frosty the Snowman, Rudolph the Red-Nosed Reindeer, and, of course, Santa Claus. Christmas toys are gendered; Christmas movies are all about guys, and even spunky department store psychologist Doris (played by Maureen O'Hara) in *Miracle on 34th Street* gets domesticity as her Christmas reward—apparently "that fabulous Manhattan career and Central Park West apartment were such a drag."[12] Those who wish to sing along with an attack against a male-centered holiday will salute The Doubleclicks and their song "Sexist Bullshit (Christmas Song)." This sister act intones: "The ability to make sexist assholes disappear / Is all I want for Christmas, it's all I want this year / I'm done with catcalls and with shaming / They've had their chance to learn, but the patriarchy's bullshit / And I want to watch it burn."[13]

Every year millions of families compile a list of notable events from the past year, attach a generic greeting to the top, holiday wishes at the bottom, and reproduce the missive on holly-decorated paper. Dubbed "Christmas letters" or "round robins," they are popped into envelopes for distribution to friends and relatives, most of whom will dutifully read them with gritted teeth. A widespread complaint is about the boasting these letters contain: holidays on the Riviera, promotions, civic awards, and, worst of all, the successes of other people's far-too-talented children. Whereas for some families success is getting little Johnny out of juvenile detention on reduced bail, other families' kids are being honored at the White House, graduating from Yale, or inventing a cure for all known diseases. Awareness of the resentment this causes has led to the invention of the "humblebrag," a devious use of words to convey knowledge of one's greatness while affecting a specious air of humility: "Here is a picture of me at the Nobel Prize ceremony. I didn't realize that gown made me look so dreadfully slender!" So despised are these letters that collections of the worst of them have been made into books, and professional editors now offer tips on how to make yours less likely to be thrown immediately into the rubbish bin.[14]

The fruitcake, a mixture of candied fruit, eggs, flour, and nuts soaked in rum or brandy, has been a Christmas fixture for centuries, but despite its seasonal endurance it has long been the butt of jokes and complaints. Its density and indestructible nature have led some to assert that there exists in the world only a single fruitcake, which has been passed uneaten among recipients for generations. They are deemed to be perfect gifts for distant relatives because the postal service is unable to damage them. Since they are legendarily inedible, suggested uses for them have included their employment as paving stones, air-dropped weaponry, or replacements for broken furniture legs. What other holiday food can be made into a projectile and the subject of an annual town festival entitled "The Great Fruitcake Toss of Manitou Springs, Colorado"? Answering the age-old question "How do I get rid of this *$&*@#! fruitcake?," the cakes can be thrown by hand, shot out of a catapult, or propelled by giant slingshot. Extra points for accuracy.[15]

"My mother-in-law has come round to our house at Christmas seven years running. This year we're having a change. We're going to let her in."

Thus spoke the British comedian Len Dawson, who made a career out of jokes about his wife's mother, but for many the arrival of such a figure at Christmas means only trouble. These women are held to be interfering, unforgiving, and vicious. "The Mother-In-Law Song," set to the tune of "Away in a Manger," offers this verse: "I don't like to gossip, but look at Jim's date / Are twins in the picture or did she gain weight? / That mop on his forehead—no, I shouldn't talk / But throw a leash on it, I'm sure it would walk."[16] In 1999 an Italian lawyer, Paola Mescoli Davoli, created a seminar titled "The Mother-In-Law School" to help the generations understand each other better. One participant complained that on the occasion of her first married Christmas her mother-in-law told her that she had thought of giving her a mink coat but decided a better gift would be a pre-paid burial plot.[17] The *Daily Mail* published "10 Ways to Avoid Mother-in-Law Meltdown This Christmas" with advice such as sympathizing with the woman who was once central to her son's life, not reading too much into her presents, and taking deep breaths in a darkened room. Should mental serenity not be achieved, the paper cautioned against hitting the bottle and urged hostesses to remember the magic phrase "She'll go home eventually."[18]

Martha Stewart has a lot to answer for, in the eyes of many Christmas complainants. The celebrity decorator's elaborate table settings, menus, centerpieces, and holiday knickknacks seem to have driven many a home-maker to fits of perfectionism that drive the rest of her family to desperation. The first verse of "We Must Have a Perfect Christmas: Homage to Martha" is sung to the tune of "We Wish You a Merry Christmas": "We must have a perfect Christmas, / We must have a perfect Christmas / Or I'll slit my wrists!"[19] Cranberries for the sauce must be picked fresh from the bog, hours must be spent in the mall choosing the exactly right gifts, which must be wrapped in cloth-of-gold, with name tags written by a professional calligrapher. No specks of dust nor errant toys must mar the pristine cleanliness of the home, and heaven help the family member who fails to appreciate all that has been done in the name of his or her happiness.

"Yes, it's bloody Christmas music in every shop and bar, / Playing on the radio, playing in the car, / TV jingles swell with it, radio's just as bad, / Bloody Christmas music, it's going to drive me mad!"[20] Since the 1920s businesses have been piping in prerecorded music to enhance worker productivity, alter the work-place mood, mask unpleasant industrial noise, or encourage shoppers to linger and spend more. This type of sound has been labeled "elevator music," or Muzak, after the company that pioneered the practice. During late November and December this music seems to be overwhelmingly Christmas-themed and inescapable, so one imagines that the same version of "The Little Drummer Boy" is played in every store. Surveys indicate that a fair chunk of listeners abhor the presence of this sort of noise, with the most adamantly opposed being people with hearing disabilities and retail employees who must not only listen to the same looped songs again and again but must also field complaints about them from irate customers. Parliamentary legislation has been introduced to ban it, unions have declared it a health and safety issue, and antinoise activists claim that it suppresses the immune system.[21]

Christmas music commits other sins than ubiquity. In an era of microaggressions and supersensitivity, it was inevitable that popular holiday songs were parsed for offensive content and found to be loaded with objectionable lyrics. One list of the "Top Five Creepy Christmas Songs" lambasted the Mariah Carey hit "All I Want for Christmas Is You" for promoting the nasty notion that all a woman needs is a man. Is it any better if a man sings it? No, for then "it borders on stalker territory." "I Saw Mommy Kissing Santa Claus" is interpreted as the trauma of a child watching his mother commit adultery, while "It's Beginning to Look a Lot Like Christmas" fails the grade for singing about inappropriate child gift choices. Warbling over "a pair of hopalong boots and a pistol that shoots/ Is the wish of Barney and Ben/ Dolls that will talk and will go for a walk/ Is the hope of Janice and Jen" commits gender stereotyping and "severely limits the development of all young people." Eartha Kitt's "Santa Baby" is, of course, guilty of recycling the tired trope of women's basic materialism and shallowness, but the most opprobrium is heaped on "Baby It's Cold Outside." This "Christmas date rape song" lauds manipulative male courtship practices that may even involve drugging the woman's drink. It is "a perfect example of the way men pressure women into experiences that they don't want, aren't ready for or aren't interested in." A more nuanced approach is found in "The Fairytale of New York: Some Thoughts on Homophobia and Heteronormative Christmas Soundscapes," in which the author questions the use of an antigay slur in the lyrics. Censorship is repugnant to him, but he wants a discussion about the proper response "when an aesthetic object, art practice, or cultural tradition becomes institutionalised and runs in danger of oppressing minority groups and reinstating white, masculine, heterosexual hierarchies."[22] In a blog post entitled "10 Christmas Carols even an Atheist Could Love," Greta Christina, the cofounder of Godless Perverts, took a leap of theological imagination and found "O Come O Come Emmanuel"—the Advent carol that celebrates the Jewish heritage of Jesus—to be anti-Semitic, while "O Holy Night" is criticized for its "guilty self-loathing."[23]

Among those looking askance at Christmas are many in the psychiatric business. Inspired by their founder, who made much of the Oedipus story and who put Moses on his figurative couch, Freudians have long been interested in myths as expressions of deep psychological truth. This belief led psychoanalyst Bryce Boyer to claim that the source of Christmastime depression is found in unresolved sibling rivalries. The worship of the Christ Child, adored by his mother, Mary, awakens a frustration of never being as good as the favorite child, and he concluded that his female patients sought to obtain penises, which they hoped would win their mother's love that had previously been given to other siblings. However, it is not the Baby Jesus who attracts most of the attention of these analysts: it is Santa Claus. The Dutch psychiatrist Adrianus de Groot, for example, claims that the folk customs surrounding St. Nicholas represent all the stages of the human reproductive cycle from courtship to the production of offspring. The chimney, the fireplace, the outflow of sweets and presents, the shoes waiting to be filled, are all archetypes that signal loudly to the keen-eyed psychoanalyst, who can discern that the treasure St. Nicholas distributes represents semen and the tale of the three murdered students whom St. Nicholas revives from the barrel is the story of the "male triumvirate"; their death is the "death of the phallus."[24] Other psychiatrists have opined that Santa Claus is expected to cure penis envy; "he is a father figure; a grandfather figure; a sexually ambiguous figure; a fear of death ritual; an Oedipal symbol; a totemic symbol; a fire-mastering shaman; a union of Gaia and Uranus; a myth that relieves the infant's fear of its mother; a burdensome transaction between the generations; and a poor second to Barney the purple dinosaur."

Naturally, such a potent figure of our subconscious must be tied to dysfunction and psychological disorder at Christmastime. James Caltrell noted that the holiday season and the presence of one's father, God, Christ, Santa Claus, and Father Time produces a syndrome marked by "diffuse anxiety, numerous regressive phenomena including marked feelings of helplessness, possessiveness, and increased irritability, nostalgia or bitter rumination about holiday experiences of youth, depressive affect, and a wish for magical resolution of problems."[25] Renzo Sereno claimed that children were dragooned into the Santa myth against their will and ended up feeling "cheated, swindled or lied to by parents," and J. T. Proctor, based on his work with children undergoing psychoanalysis, claimed that such kids were often angry and resentful at having been deceived about Santa. The psychiatrist who was most critical of St. Nick was Brock Chisholm, a high-ranking Canadian civil servant and founding director of the World Health Organization who came to be known in the news media as "The Man Who Killed Santa Claus." Though a war hero and a Conservative voter, Chisholm held many radical ideas, espousing eugenics, euthanasia, voluntary sterilization, and masturbation. His dislike of Santa Claus was grounded in his work as a mental health specialist. "A child who believes in Santa Claus, who really and literally believes, because his daddy told him so, that Santa comes down all the chimneys in the world on the same night has had his thinking ability permanently impaired if not destroyed." In 1945 his remarks to parents' groups on the dangers of Santa Claus erupted into a major political scandal, with calls for his resignation from the civil service. Though busy on the global stage, he found time to continue his war on imaginary Gift-Bringers. Said Chisholm: a child who believes in Santa grows up to be "the kind of man who will develop a sore back when there is a tough job to do and refuse to think realistically when war threatens." A businessman with an ulcer and nervous problems could blame his middle-aged ailments on the foolishness he believed as a child. Chisholm announced in 1951 that he was going to bring the case of Santa Claus before the United Nations as a means of denouncing all such local and national fictions that sapped the children of the world of that universal spirit necessary for mankind to solve the planet's problems.[26]

Given the baleful influence that the magical Gift-Bringer is said to exert, many call for a Santa-free Christmas.[27] Believing that the Santa cult instilled only guilt and anxiety in the service of a greedy materialism prompted Jenny Phillips Goodwin and her husband to ponder whether to eschew St. Nick. The decision came easily as she beheld her eighteen-month-old son: "My husband's and my profound respect for truth and for our precious wonderchild were more than principle. How could we deceive our own flesh? What other lies would follow? How could we teach honesty if we had practiced so gross a deception?"[28] Steve Benson, an eight-year-old child of a Mormon family, had been doubting the existence of Santa Claus, and his worst fears were confirmed when he read in a parenting manual that Santa was a myth. He confronted his mother with his findings, and after a brief resistance she caved in and told him the real story. At that moment he realized: "You can't trust adults to tell you the truth. As I look back on that experience, I realize that losing faith in both 'the big fat man with the beard' and in adults who vouched for his existence played a pivotal role in the development in my own mind of a certain degree of skepticism and distrust of authority figures—ranging from Mormon prophets, to parents, to God himself."[29] For David and Nancy French, the decision to avoid perpetuating the Santa story was largely a religious one.[30]

The Christmas story is this:

God gave us the perfect gift even when we did nothing to deserve it. (And, in fact, deserved a lot worse than a lump of coal.) Instead of looking at us in our sin and putting us away, God was overcome with love for us. He didn't hold our wrongdoings against us. Instead, at great cost, He gave us a way to be forgiven and reenter into communion with Him. That gift was His son, in the form of a baby.

The Santa story—other than the tales associated with the historical St. Nick, who's simply a footnote in this commercial age—is this: There's a jolly, wonderful, magical being called "Santa" who is watching you. If you do something wrong, your name will be crossed off the "nice list" and put on the "naughty list." Want good presents? You had better behave.

Which story is actually better and more comforting? The one that has the added benefit of being true.

Valerie Williams of angry billboard fame is definite in her linkage of Santa's sexual orientation, weight, and race: "Who is Santa? He is the mall's puppet.... Children are taught to worship this white, heterosexual man who overeats. I mean, it's wrong."

Others, too, have taken up the feminist critique of Yuletide symbols. Snowmen have long been deemed to be part of the holiday season, appearing on wrapping paper, Christmas cards, advertisements, and front yards, but have you considered their contribution to the sum total of racism and sexism in the world? Professor Patricia Cusack, an art historian of Birmingham University, has. According to her five-year study of the problem, reported in "The Christmas Snowman: Carnival and Patriarchy," snowmen are "rotund relics of Bacchanalia that reinforce traditional gender stereotypes." It is no coincidence, surely, that snowmen are always white or that their placement outdoors "reinforces a spatial-social system marking women's sphere as the domestic-private and the men's as the commercial-public." Snowmen's popularity on Christmas cards heralds the yearning for a return to a conservative, patriarchal order. What is called for is a more equitable distribution of snowperson gender and an increase in the number of snowwomen on cards. Cusack hailed the dwindling appearance of the traditional pipe in the mouths of snowbeings as a sign of a culture less friendly to smoking. (Taking this message to heart was an Australian deli selling "organic, genderless, vegan gingerbread figures.")[31]

But what do children actually think of Santa Claus? Have they joined the legions of jaded critics? If you judge the question by the reactions of tots taken to sit on Santa's knee at a shopping mall, you might think that they should be the first to send the old guy straight back to the North Pole. This was the conclusion reached by John Trinkaus of the City University of New York. He recorded the reactions of 330 children as they were taken to meet Santa in New York shopping malls and department stores. To his dismay, few of the tots were happy about the experience. In his estimation none seemed "exhilarated," 1 percent were "happy," 82 percent were rated "indifferent," 16 percent were termed "hesitant," and 1 percent registered as "terrified." However, he observed that nearly all the parents were visibly quite happy and excited.[32]

And speaking of department store Santas, all is not well in their world. Once the focus of parades, the endearing protagonists of seasonal movies and proud pharaohs of consumerism on their thrones or in their grottoes, they are now an endangered species, dwindling in number and subject to the strictures of a paranoid age. "When the last gig of the season is *finito*," says Victor Nevada, sixty-one, a professional Santa Claus in Calgary, Canada, "I have a bottle of rye whiskey and some Diet Coke by the bed, and a couple of novels, and I'll phone in for pizza, and I won't get out of bed for two days, and if I don't see another child again till next Christmas—*that's OK with me.*"[33] The stresses facing the men in the red suits are piling up: charges of sexual harassment are now part of the challenges they face and must be countered with police background checks, fingerprinting, and liability insurance. Fear of accusations of pedophilia means that children are now seated beside Santa on chairs rather than in his lap. Children whose parents are absent in the military or who are abusive or ill bring emotional requests that Santas find taxing, leading some to file for compensation for job-related depression. The traditional cry of "Ho, ho, ho!" has had to be replaced with "Ha, ha, ha!" lest sensitive ears hear a derogatory term for prostitutes or be frightened by a deep voice.[34] Department stores in Britain are increasingly less willing to devote shopping space to the erection of Father Christmas grottoes and are fearful of censorious parents.[35]

Christmas characters other than Santa have also come in for searing criticism. One such is the Elf on the Shelf, a toy that sits on shelves and is said to monitor the behavior of children reporting back to the North Pole all who have been naughty or nice. The Elf is an early twenty-first-century marketing sensation, selling millions of books and toys. In the words of its creator's website,

> the Elf on the Shelf®: A Christmas Tradition includes a special scout elf sent from the North Pole to help Santa Claus manage his naughty and nice lists. When a family adopts a scout elf and gives it a name, the scout elf receives its Christmas magic and can fly to the North Pole each night to tell Santa Claus about all of the day's adventures. Each morning, the scout elf returns to its family and perches in a different place to watch the fun. Children love to wake up and race around the house looking for their scout elf each morning.[36]

Some parents have expressed unease with the notion of an ever-watching little snitch, but none have gone as far as academics attached to the Centre for Policy Alternatives, a left-wing Canadian think tank. For Laura Pinto and Selena Nemorin, the Elf represents (in sparkling postmodern jargonese) "a capillary form of power that normalizes the voluntary surrender of privacy, teaching young people to blindly accept panoptic surveillance and reify hegemonic power." The two researchers were brought to this conclusion through reflecting on the work of Michel Foucault in his *Discipline and Punish*, where the French philosopher—using the example of the "Panopticon," an imaginary prison designed by Jeremy Bentham—explained the power of the all-seeing state apparatus in schools, factories, hospitals, and other forms of incarceration. The Elf on the Shelf, they say, functions as an unhealthy method of control—"it contributes to the shaping of children as governable subjects...it also sets children up for dangerous, uncritical acceptance of power structures." In response to this elvish avatar of the modern surveillance society, parents and teachers must employ "critical pedagogies alongside the elf's presence in children's play worlds and social lives in 'teachable moments' that cultivate children's ability to identify, question, and resist power."[37]

It would not be Christmas without the often-heard complaint that the season seems to start earlier and earlier every year. In the United States the presence of Thanksgiving in late November works to erect some kind of feeble barrier against pushing the beginning of Christmas back too far, but countries who celebrate the fall harvest at a different time can only watch in horror as advertisements and store decorations make their appearance in October or even September. So hats off to the bold activists who have decided to make a stand against seasonally inappropriate displays. In November 2000 a number of businesses in the Westmount district of Montreal found themselves trashed by splashes of paint, oil, and eggs. Their sin was to have brought out their commercial Christmas decorations too soon, according to their attackers, members of a group styling themselves L'Anti Noël Avant L'Temps (No Christmas Before Its Time). In what is surely the most poetic of all Canadian terrorist manifestoes, the vandals proclaimed:

Halloween has ended. Before Halloween it was autumn, and after Halloween autumn continues. Do you agree? The leaves lie scattered on the soil, the atmosphere is calm and romantic; it is the dead season and many are rejoicing. Right? It is part of a whole season, a beautiful season, and one that does not officially end until the twenty-first of December. Are you listening?

Winter is far off, and Christmas does not exist outside of winter. Christmas = winter. Autumn = tranquility, peace of mind. You see what we want to say, no? We are L'A.N.A.L.T. (L'Anti Noël Avant L'Temps)

We are a group of people who are saddened and frustrated by your ill breeding. We refuse to let you destroy autumn for a reason as pernicious and disgusting as making a little bit of money. Everybody knows that Christmas is coming. You're going to make the same kind of cash! So, if you please, everything has its time. We demand that you take down all of your Christmas decorations without delay, and not put them back up until the first of December. If not, we are going to strike again. N.B. Do not take this lightly. We are SERIOUS.[38]

Sadly, L'Anti Noël Avant L'Temps never reappeared, but their cause was taken up in England by the Movement for the Containment of Christmas, who warned shops in Leeds in the late summer of 2009 against stocking Christmas cards in August and September. Their communication was much more prosaic than the Montreal group's, and they were willing to see Christmas cards sold in November. Their handwritten note read:

> *MOVEMENT FOR THE*
> *Containment OF XMAS*
> *THIS IS A VERY POLITE*
> *BUT:—*
> *VERY SERIOUS REMINDER*
> *NOT TO DISPLAY XMAS*
> *CARDS UNTIL 1ST NOV*
> *WE WILL PUT SUPER*
> *GLUE INTO YOUR*
> *Locks if You DO.*
> *Peace And Goodwill*
> *(The Mind Shop got done*
> *on Sunday)*[39]

Law-abiding Germany has taken a different approach to the problem. Seeing the once sacred period of Advent ignored, with stores opening earlier and earlier and the Berlin government permitting stores to open on all four Advent Sundays, Germans sued. They convinced the Federal Constitutional Court that these Sundays had to remain days of "rest and spiritual elevation." A 2014 survey of attitudes to Christmas revealed overwhelming distaste at commercialization of the holiday, and a third of those asked wanted the government to intervene to prevent the sale of gingerbread cakes and other Christmas goodies before November 30.[40]

Many helpful books have been written about keeping one's sanity and happiness at Christmas. Titles like *Unplug the Christmas Machine, I Saw Mommy Kicking Santa Claus: The Ultimate Holiday Survival Guide, Simplify and Celebrate,* and *Keep Calm at Christmas* offer sensible and humane ideas about where our priorities ought to lie, but there are some who resist the lure of Christmas altogether. To sum it all up, speaking for those who abhor the season, we have "Credo," by "Anonymous Grinch," who announced his repudiation of Christmas traditions, the Virgin Birth, Santa Claus, gift exchange, the cutting down of evergreens, and seasonal altruism. Said this dyspeptic critic: "I reject and dedicate energy to oppose and weaken and discredit the belief system which underlies these traditions.... Ecology, human solidarity and planetary unity all indicate that we should get rid of Christmas. I intend to weaken it a little, by withdrawing my emotional involvement."[41]

VII

The Privatizers

*In which we see that the contemporary "War on Christmas"
is largely an effort to drive religion from the public square
and that the antagonists in this battle are only talking
past each other*

AT THE TURN of the twentieth century Christmas had grown in popularity
and breadth of expression. In the English-speaking world it was a massive
festival of Christian faith, family togetherness, charity, and consumption.
Critics existed, but they lacked critical mass; it was almost unthinkable
that this wonderful holiday, embraced by so many, could have been seen
as in any way harmful to public well-being or be put on the defensive. Yet
that was what was going to happen.

The first great salvo in the American battle over Christmas's place in
the public sphere was fired in 1905 by Jewish parents in New York. In the
nineteenth century many Jewish immigrants had been happy to adopt
aspects of the holiday as a sign of their arrival in a new, tolerant, and prosperous country. Decorated trees, gift buying, enjoying the lighted displays
and shop windows, and exchanging "Merry Christmas" greetings were all
tokens of their settled Americanness. But later waves of eastern European
Jewish newcomers saw things in a different light. Their experience with
Christianity in their homelands had been one of oppression and exclusion, and they were more resistant to their children receiving doses of
the religion through the treatment of Christmas in their public schools.
Matters reached a head in the Brownsville neighborhood of Brooklyn in
1905, where the principal of one school with a large Jewish student population seemed to be veering into open Christian proselytism at a December
assembly by asking all the pupils to be "more Christlike" in their character. Parent groups called for the principal's removal, but the Board of
Education refused. Throughout 1906 Jewish representatives pressed their
case, demanding an end to "the singing of denominational hymns, the

writing of compositions on subjects of religious character, the holding of festivities in which clergymen make speeches and the use of the Christmas tree." When Christmas rolled around and Jewish students were still expected to participate in school end-of-term ceremonies that parents deemed too Christian, they responded by pulling their children from school and boycotting the holiday exercises. Their actions were success-ful; thousands of students were absent, and the press coverage was wide and lively, resulting in a change of heart by the authorities. Within a year, school administrators had agreed to excise the more denominational aspects of Christmas assemblies, though Santa Claus and the Christmas tree would stay. The boycott was not universally popular in the Jewish communities of New York. Many feared a Gentile backlash; others felt that Christmas not only was a harmless celebration but offered a positive good to Jews. Rabbi Maurice Harris of Temple Israel, for example, regretted the discord that now seemed to surround the holiday. Rabbi Judah Magnes of Temple Emanu-El claimed that Jews could benefit from Christmas's call for "Peace on earth. Good will to men; glory to God in the highest...this is a universal thought in which we as Jews could join." Socialist Jewish activists opposed both the boycott and the integrationists, asserting that it was useless to complain about Christian activities in public schools—the real goal should be the establishment of a separate Jewish school system. Nonetheless, the New York example did not go unheeded. In 1914 in Toronto a similar school boycott over compulsory Christmas carol singing succeeded in forcing the school board in that Canadian city to exempt Jewish children from such activities.[1]

Indeed, a backlash was forthcoming. Local non-Jewish parents and teachers were often resentful at such changes and the challenges to their unthinking assumption that America was a Christian country. They could not see any harm in Christmas trees or carols or the overwhelm-ingly Protestant ethos in the public school system. As one teacher said, "Why should *we* give up our religion for the Jews?"[2] Europe and North America saw increased public anti-Semitism in the years after World War I. Ultranationalist parties, including Germany's National Socialists under Hitler and a resurgent Ku Klux Klan in the United States and Canada, blamed Jews for many of the world's problems; these ideas found in famed industrialist Henry Ford a willing publicist. In a series of articles in the *Dearborn (MI) Independent* and in book form, Ford attacked Jews as an alien element out to secularize America and bend it to their will. The proof of this, he said, was their attitude toward Christmas in the public schools: "the Jews began to make such demands as that Christmas carols should be suppressed in the schools, as 'offensive to the Jews'; and that Christmas trees should be banished from police stations in poor neighborhoods as 'offensive to the Jews'; and that the Easter holidays should be abolished as 'offensive to the Jews'; and that the phrase 'a Christian gentleman' should be protested everywhere, as 'offensive to the Jews.'" He went on to say:

> Not only do the Jews disagree with Christian teaching—which is their perfect right, and no one dare question it—but they seek to interfere with it. It is not religious tolerance in the midst of religious difference, but religious attack that they preach and practice. The whole record of the Jewish opposition to Christmas, Easter and certain patriotic songs shows that.
>
> When Cleveland and Lakewood arranged for a community Christmas, the Cleveland Jewish press said: "The writer of this has no idea how many Jews there are in Lakewood, but if there is only one, there should be no community Christmas, no community religion of any kind." That is not a counsel of tolerance, it is a counsel of attack. The Christmas literature of American Judaism is fiercer than the flames of the Inquisition. In the month of January, the Jewish press has urged its readers to begin an early campaign against Christmas celebrations the next Christmas—"Only three hundred and sixty days before Christmas. So let us do our Christmas arguing early and take plenty of time to do it."[3]

Despite the fervor of Ford's rhetoric, most Americans abjured political anti-Semitism between the world wars, and after 1945 the exposure of Nazi atrocities drove the topic underground. (This did not mean that linking Judaism to an attack on Christmas entirely disappeared: marginal figures, including fascist-sympathizing Gerald L. K. Smith, continued to attribute opposition to the holiday to international Communism, the United Nations, and Jews.)[4] Meanwhile, Jewish families continued to ponder the role of Christmas in their lives and in their schools. Some chose to ignore it; some chose to adopt Hanukkah as a sort of religiously acceptable form of midwinter holiday, not as "a protest or critique of Christian culture so much as an effort to fashion an alternative to it"[5]; and others embraced Christmas, despite the pleadings of their religious leaders. In a 1939 article titled "The Jew Celebrates Christmas" Rabbi Louis Witt explained:

For years, I, as a rabbi, like all rabbis, denounced with all the rhetorical fervor and fury at my command this celebration of Christmas by my own people. I called it a shameful aping of alien gods. I stigmatized the Jew who was guilty of it as a renegade....I drew the picture of Jewish brethren in fanatic lands through the centuries enduring horror and massacre on the very day on which Christ was born and cursing the day in the madness of their despair, and I asked with dramatic climax: "How can any Jew even in blessed America celebrate such a day?"[6]

Arguments about the proper role of Christmas entered a new forum after 1945: the courtroom. The American War of Independence in the late eighteenth century had produced a new sort of nation on the earth: a republic whose structure was determined by a written constitution and a bill of rights. No longer would political issues be determined by folk customs, tradition, tribal or dynastic law, or religious dicta but by adherence to an abstract set of principles. Fearful of the sorts of tyranny they saw in Europe, the founders of the new nation had divided their institutional spheres so that the application of power proceeded through tugs-of-war between the executive, the legislative, and the judicial branches of the government. Intractable political disagreements could be solved by reference to the courts, who would be guided in their practical decisions by the lofty principles laid out in the Constitution. This had the effect of making America a highly litigious culture and one in which court precedents featured prominently in the conduct of public life. This would inevitably be the case when disagreements arose over how Christmas could appear outside of the home or church.

Only after World War II did the courts turn their eyes to questions of religion in the public sphere, particularly in schools. The hitherto unchallenged notion that America was a Christian country where expressions of the majority faith would naturally be made when citizens gathered for civic occasions, sports events, educational purposes, or festivals was now going to be tested by the legal system. When judges debated the issue, they turned to the Constitution's First Amendment, which says in part: "Congress shall make no law respecting an establishment of religion, or prohibiting the free exercise thereof." Whatever the founding fathers, in the innocence and optimism of the Age of Enlightenment, thought they were doing in writing that clause, they would surely have been surprised by the twists and turns of the arguments over it in the twentieth century.

A case involving the contribution of a state government toward the costs of transportation of students to a religious school (*Everson v. Board of Education*, 1947) brought forth from US Supreme Court justice Hugo Black this famous flight of rhetoric:

> The "establishment of religion" clause of the First Amendment means at least this: Neither a state nor the federal government can set up a church. Neither can pass laws which aid one religion, aid all religions, or prefer one religion over another. Neither can force nor influence a person to go to or to remain away from church against his will or force him to profess a belief or disbelief in any religion. No person can be punished for entertaining or professing religious beliefs or disbeliefs, for church attendance or nonattendance. No tax in any amount, large or small, can be levied to support any religious activities or institutions, whatever they may be called, or whatever form they may adopt to teach or practice religion. Neither a state nor the Federal Government can, openly or secretly, participate in the affairs of any religious organizations or groups and vice versa. In the words of Jefferson, the clause against establishment of religion by law was intended to erect "a wall of separation between church and State." ... That wall must be kept high and impregnable. We could not approve the slightest breach.[7]

Could Christmas breach that high and impregnable barrier? A number of decisions on the permissibility of a public face for the holiday show that legal thinking on the subject was seldom clear or consistent. Take for example the case that erupted in 1956 over the setting up of a Christmas crèche by a group of Catholics, Protestants, and Jews on the lawn of a high school in Ossining, a New York City suburb (*Baer v. Kolmorgen*). Some residents objected to the Nativity scene on grounds of church-state separation. A judge refused a motion to bar the crèche before a full trial was held, saying:

> The constitutional prohibition relating to separation of church and State does not imply an impregnable wall or cleavage completely disassociating one from the other. While it is necessary that there be a separation of church and State, it is not necessary that the State should be stripped of all religious sentiment. It may be a tragic experience for this

country and for its conception of life, liberty and the pursuit of happiness if our people lose their religious feeling and are left to live their lives without faith.... The Constitution does not demand that every friendly gesture between the church and State should be discountenanced; nor that every vestige of the existence of God be eradicated.

In the 1958 trial itself, Judge Elbert T. Gallagher of the Westchester County Supreme Court upheld the display—it was erected only when classes were over and involved no public expense—and went so far as to object to the notion of any inviolable church-state separation: "If such accommodation [as the plaintiff demanded] violates the doctrine of absolute separation between church and State, then it is time that that doctrine be discarded once and for all. Absolute separation is not and never has been required by the Constitution."[8] So much for ideas of impregnability or an easy solution to the problem.

Though it did not deal directly with Christmas, the 1971 decision in *Lemon v. Kurtzman* took on the question of the funding of private schools (many of them religiously established) by the state and for a time seemed to provide a reliable set of principles for dealing with religion in the educational system. The so-called Lemon Test set out three conditions that would rule any church-state association as unconstitutional. First, the statute must not result in an "excessive government entanglement" with religious affairs. (This came to be known as the Entanglement Prong.) Second, the statute must neither advance nor inhibit religious practice (the Effect Prong), and last, the statute must have a secular legislative purpose (the Purpose Prong).[9] The Lemon recipe was put to the test in 1978 in Sioux Falls, South Dakota, when an atheist parent complained about the Christmas carol program his child was forced to be involved with at school. Though the school district responded with a new set of guidelines that stressed the cultural and nonsectarian content of their Christmas programming, the offended atheist contacted the American Civil Liberties Union (ACLU), who took the board to court in *Florey et al. v. Sioux Falls School District*. The court, using the Lemon precedent, found that the carols were in fact constitutional, in that the guidelines of the district were framed for a secular purpose: to educate students about the history and significance of Christmas.

The rules guarantee that material used has secular or cultural significance: Only holidays with both religious and secular basis may be observed; music, art, literature, and drama may be included in the curriculum only if presented in a prudent and objective manner and only as part of the cultural and religious heritage of the holiday; and religious symbols may be used only as a teaching aid or resource and only if they are displayed as part of the cultural and religious heritage of the holiday and are temporary in nature.

Since all programs and materials authorized by the rules must deal with the secular or cultural basis or heritage of the holidays and since the materials must be presented in a prudent and objective manner and symbols used as a teaching aid, the advancement of a "secular program of education," and not of religion, is the primary effect of the rules.[10]

In Pawtucket, Rhode Island, Daniel Donnelly objected to the city erecting a Christmas display that included not only a Santa Claus house, a "Seasons Greetings banner," a clown, and a decorated tree but also a crèche. Though the site was on private property, the materials were owned and stored by the city, which expended about $20 a year setting it up and taking it down. When Dennis Lynch, the mayor, defended the practice (the Nativity scene had been erected annually without controversy since 1943) he was taken to court by, among others, the ACLU, in a celebrated case known as *Lynch v. Donnelly*. Lower courts agreed with the contention that the display was an unconstitutional violation of the First Amendment's prohibition of an established religion. The city's inclusion of the Nativity scene "tried to endorse and promulgate religious beliefs" and "had the real and substantial effect of affiliating the City with the Christian beliefs that the crèche represents." This "appearance of official sponsorship," the District Court concluded, conferred "more than a remote and incidental benefit on Christianity." However, when the US Supreme Court heard the appeal, it reversed the lower courts' decisions and in a five-to-four ruling came down on the side of the city—to the astonishment of many legal scholars, one of whom called the decision "the most extreme accommodationist position taken by the Burger Court," one that "stood more than three decades of Establishment Clause jurisprudence on its head."[11] Again, Justice Black's high and impermeable wall of separation between church and state had been breached and, in fact, was now reduced to a mere catchphrase. The court opined that the "concept of a 'wall' of separation is a useful figure of speech probably deriving from the views of Thomas Jefferson. The metaphor has served as a reminder that the Establishment Clause forbids an established church or anything approaching it. But the metaphor itself is not a wholly accurate description of the practical aspects of the relationship that in fact exists between church and state." The fact that the same Congress that enacted the establishment clause of the US Constitution in 1789 (and every Congress since) employed paid chaplains to offer prayers demonstrated that religious beliefs could be accommodated by the state. Furthermore, governments have operated galleries that contained religious art, the national motto is "In God We Trust," court buildings contain copies of the Ten Commandments, presidents have long proclaimed days of thanksgiving and celebration, and the Supreme Court itself has ruled that "we are a religious people whose institutions presuppose a Supreme Being." This means that no hard-and-fast rule can be applied to cases of the establishment clause. Rather than an impenetrable wall, the clause sets up a "blurred, indistinct, and variable barrier depending on all the circumstances of a particular relationship." In the case of Pawtucket, the secular purpose of the Nativity scene "to celebrate the Holiday and to depict the origins of that Holiday" legitimated its presence in the display. In an important concurring statement, Justice Sandra Day O'Connor set out a sort of clarification to the Lemon tests when she added what came to be known as the Endorsement Test—whether a government action signals to nonadherents that they are outsiders and sends an accompanying message to adherents that they are insiders. She also noted that it was possible to infer the city's secular purpose for the Christmas display from the "purely secular symbols" that surrounded the crèche.[12] Perhaps because the Court considered a case where the crèche was surrounded by nonreligious elements and found its presence constitutional, popular thinking about Lynch v. Donnelly seemed to conclude that the secular parts of the display had "whitewashed" the religious items and that some sort of "Reindeer Rule" had been established. The notion spread that the Court had decided that the presence of plastic reindeer or candy canes or snowmen could make palatable any otherwise offensive Christian content in a Christmas display. More important, what Lynch v. Donnelly expressly did was to demolish the "high and impenetrable wall" and replace it with a "blurred, indistinct, and variable barrier," making further litigation about Christmas in public places almost inevitable.

Since 1981 the Allegheny County courthouse, in Pittsburgh, had erected at the head of a staircase a holiday display that involved a Nativity scene and an angel holding a banner proclaiming "Gloria in Excelsis Deo." At City Hall, nearby, a giant menorah stood beside a forty-five-foot

Christmas tree and a sign reading: "During this holiday season, the city of Pittsburgh salutes liberty. Let these festive lights remind us that we are the keepers of the flame of liberty and our legacy of freedom." In 1986 the local ACLU chapter sued to force the removal of the crèche and the menorah, claiming that both violated the establishment clause. Lower courts differed, and in 1989 the dispute reached the US Supreme Court. In a puzzling five-to-four decision, the majority decided that the Nativity scene was unconstitutional but the menorah was not. To add to the bafflement, Justice Stevens, who wanted the menorah to go, declared that the Christmas tree (which had not been included in the litigation) was also too overtly religious to be allowed.

The impermissibility of the Nativity scene was clear in the mind of Justice Harry Blackmun: "When viewed in its overall context, the crèche display violates the Establishment Clause. The crèche angel's words endorse a patently Christian message: Glory to God for the birth of Jesus Christ. Moreover, in contrast to Lynch, nothing in the crèche's setting detracts from that message. Although the government may acknowledge Christmas as a cultural phenomenon, it may not observe it as a Christian holy day by suggesting that people praise God for the birth of Jesus." But how could the menorah, a reminder of a divine miracle in the Temple in Jerusalem and one of Judaism's defining symbols, be considered secular? For Blackmun and the majority, it was a question of setting:

> Its combined display with a Christmas tree and a sign saluting liberty does not impermissibly endorse both the Christian and Jewish faiths, but simply recognizes that both Christmas and Chanukah are part of the same winter-holiday season, which has attained a secular status in our society. The widely accepted view of the Christmas tree as the preeminent secular symbol of the Christmas season emphasizes this point. The tree, moreover, by virtue of its size and central position in the display, is clearly the predominant element, and the placement of the menorah beside it is readily understood as simply a recognition that Christmas is not the only traditional way of celebrating the season.[13]

A discussion of one final case, *Capitol Square Review and Advisory Board v. Pinette*, is necessary to understand the scope of legal decision-making on religious expressions of Christmas in the public sphere. In 1993, a grand titan of the Ku Klux Klan, Vincent Pinette, wished to erect a cross during the holiday season on the lawn of Capitol Square in Columbus, Ohio. This was an area given over on many occasions to demonstrations, meetings, and displays of Christmas trees and menorahs; to use it required only filling out a form that required no information on the speech content of the user. The Advisory Board, however, turned down the request on the grounds that the large, unattended cross violated the Endorsement Test. When the Klan appealed and the case reached the Supreme Court, the justices ruled, seven to two, that "religious expression cannot violate the Establishment Clause where it (1) is purely private and (2) occurs in a traditional or designated public forum, publicly announced and open to all on equal terms." The majority tartly noted that pornography and cursing were protected speech and that religious speech under the Free Exercise Clause of the First Amendment was worthy of even more protection.[14] The cross could stay.

At this point, a comparison with the issue in Scandinavian countries may be instructive. Norway and Sweden are, in daily life, much more secular than the United States, yet both have Lutheran state churches, and neither objects to traditional religious activities in schools during the Christmas season. In Sweden, for example, the December 13 Luciatåg (St. Lucy's Day) ceremonies are major events in schools, with processions of girls and boys carrying candles and singing carols. In Norway and Sweden it is also common, despite efforts by local atheist groups and activists, for students to attend church for Christmas Mass with the support of the government. Decisions about such attendance are taken locally and include opt-out provisions.[15]

By the 1990s, therefore, there was a considerable body of judicial decision-making in the United States that seemed to set out the rules for the permissibility of Christmas displays in public spaces and the educational system. Schools could not be venues for proselytism, but Christian and Jewish seasonal holidays could be the occasion for instruction about the art, music, and significance of these festivals. Public spaces could be used for Christmas and Hanukkah displays if there was a mixture of secular and religious content and nothing to suggest that a government body endorsed these messages. Even a purely religious symbol, as in the case of the Klan cross in Columbus, could be erected in the right circumstances. Yet the use or threat of litigation to keep religion out of the public sphere has not abated in the past quarter-century but has accelerated. This "lawfare" is perceived by the holiday's supporters to be part of "the war on Christmas" and even, in the eyes of some, a war on Christianity itself. It has engendered counter-battalions of lawyers to organize themselves as the opponents of an ACLU-led attack on a harmless American tradition. The noise and alarm of these cases has persuaded a generation of bureaucrats, school principals, and commentators that Christmas (and, to some extent, Hanukkah) enthusiasts are attempting to tear down the wall of separation between church and state and violate the Constitution. The dread word "theocracy" has been bandied about when discussing the motives of those who want a public face for these religious holidays. The commentariat is overwhelmingly of the position that no such "war on Christmas" exists. Media Matters for America, a watchdog group "dedicated to comprehensively monitoring, analyzing, and correcting conservative misinformation in the U.S. media," surveyed coverage of the issue in 2005 and found 18 articles supporting the notion of a war and 106 rejecting it. Moreover, the higher prestige papers, including the *Washington Post*, the *New York Times*, the *Boston Globe*, the *Los Angeles Times*, and the *San Francisco Chronicle*, were on record as denying it.[16] Most television and internet coverage was in the deniers' camp, with Fox News opposed by the *Daily Show*, the *Huffington Post*, and CNN.[17]

Examination of the legal battles and local controversies of the past twenty years in three areas—public schools, public spaces, and private businesses—should make it clear that the brouhaha is not all manufactured, phony, cynical, "psycho talk," or a ratings ploy. It is a genuine social struggle between those who wish to clear the public sphere of the presence of—not just Christmas or not just Christianity—but of all religion and those who wish to oppose this movement.

A number of organizations devote a considerable amount of time and money to keeping the public sphere clear of any religious presence. Americans United for Separation of Church and State was established in 1947 largely to oppose government funding of religious private schools. Since then it has fought battles against "faith-based initiatives," school prayer, and blasphemy charges against a boy who simulated a sex act with a statue of Jesus. Though it numbers Christian clergy among its leadership and claims to be nonpartisan, it has a particular animus against the religious right. The Freedom from Religion Foundation believes that the "history of Western civilization shows us that most social and moral progress has been brought about by persons free from religion." Among the accomplishments of which it boasts are bringing an end to religious postal cancelations, stopping a Nativity pageant, overturning a law making Good Friday a state holiday, and halting a government chaplaincy to minister to state workers. It is the ACLU, however, that is most associated with legal battles on the Christmas front, though the organization denies it is leading the charge in the war on Christmas.[18] Claiming a membership of half a million and a budget of over $100 million, it clearly has considerable clout in achieving its missions, among which it includes confronting questions of religious liberty.

When the ACLU or another similarly minded group spots what it believes to be a violation of the establishment clause, it usually begins by firing off a letter or phone call warning the alleged perpetrator of the constitutional misdeed. Often this is enough to achieve the goal, as the legions of lawyers at the command of these organizations conjure up nightmares of expensive litigation. Thus an article from 1990 in the *Titusville (PA) Herald* reads: "A nativity scene at the Beaver County Courthouse was removed Wednesday when county commissioners decided they couldn't afford a potential lawsuit by the American Civil Liberties Union. . . . Litigation of this matter could cost the county tens of thousands of dollars."[19] Twenty-five years ago this sort of warning shot seemed to be singularly effective, with no further action required. A history of the New Jersey chapter of the ACLU boasted: "During the 1992–93 holiday season, for example, the ACLU-NJ wrote a dozen local and county governments after receiving complaints about crèches and menorahs on public lawns or steps. All dismantled their displays, or removed them to private property."[20] When cases did go to court the process itself was the punishment—involve Christmas supporters in expensive litigation, and they, or those like them, will more easily fold next time. In 1991, for example, the ACLU succeeded in getting Vienna, Virginia, to remove a crèche display erected on public property by the Knights of Columbus. The town had heeded the lesson of *Lynch v. Donnelly* and had added plastic reindeer, Santas, and snowmen to the Nativity scene, but the ACLU claimed that in spite of the secular elements, the display was objectionable because the crèche was the primary focus of the display and thus unconstitutional. A district court judge agreed, and the display was banished to privately owned land three-quarters of a mile away. The unhappy mayor complained, "My feeling is that it's really an unfortunate, sad commentary on the level of public tolerance we're experiencing in this country. This is a major holiday, but it has been dragged into litigation and the court system, setting up an adversarial relationship among the people of a community." When in the next year the ACLU objected to the singing of religious carols at an official town celebration, no lawsuit was required before the city capitulated on the advice of their lawyers and banned such carols from being sung. In protest, the town's choral society withdrew from the program, and a crowd of carol singers staged a counter-celebration complete with religious songs. One protestor brought along a banner reading: "The ACLU is jealous of manger scenes because it doesn't have three wise men or a virgin in its organization."[21]

By the mid-90s, however, there was a sense that such easy victories were not always going to be the norm. Journalists had begun to speak of a "war against Christmas," and some civic politicians were angry or stubborn enough to fight back against what they conceived to be bullying tactics.[22] Such was the case in Jersey City in 1994, when the ACLU wrote to object to the menorah and crèche display that had been erected for decades on public property. The city's first reaction was to claim that it commemorated a number of ethnic and religious festivals over the course of the year, including Ramadan and the Hindu New Year. It erected a sign beside the Nativity scene that read: "Through this display and others throughout the year, the City of Jersey City is pleased to celebrate the diverse cultural and ethnic heritages of its peoples." The resulting legal brouhaha, known popularly as *ACLU of NJ v. Schundler* (after Bret Schundler, the local mayor), wound its way through the courts for years with many a twist and turn. In 1995 a district court banned the city from erecting its traditional display. Schundler and the city appealed that decision but took pains to add a number of secular elements, including images of Santa Claus and Frosty the Snowman, to the crèche and menorah, believing, as a judge would later state, that they had "sufficiently demystified the [holy],...sufficiently desanctified sacred symbols, and...sufficiently deconsecrated the sacred." The ACLU again protested, claiming these additions were but a mask, "a ploy designed to permit continued display of the religious symbols." Finally in 1999 an appeals court ruled that the original display had been unconstitutional but the amended site that mixed the secular and the religious was permissible.[23] The city had been backed in its legal fight by the Becket Fund for Religious Liberty, one of a number of organizations that would now work to counter the efforts of the ACLU, Americans United for Separation of Church and State, and the Freedom From Religion Foundation in the question of a public face for religion. Other such groups included the American Center for Law and Justice, established in 1990 as an advocacy group for religious freedoms, and the Alliance Defending Freedom, founded in 1994 by prominent evangelical clergy as the Alliance Defense Fund.

Toward the turn of the century the ACLU launched two more attacks on public religious displays, with mixed results. In Somerset, Massachusetts, a local atheist activist, Gil Lawrence Amancio, backed by the ACLU, challenged the constitutionality of a Nativity scene in a park. Though civic officials had tried to make the site secular enough to pass judicial scrutiny, a judge ruled that the addition of a Christmas tree, a wreath, lights, and a plastic Santa Claus was insufficient to detract from the centrality of the Nativity scene and thus conveyed "to a reasonable viewer the constitutionally forbidden message that the Town of Somerset officially supports Christianity."[24] *Amancio* was a case where religious and secular elements were presented together and the decision rested, as the judge remarked, on an aesthetic rather than "cerebral" assessment. In *ACLU v. City of Florissant* a similarly mixed site yielded a different sort of result. Scott Weiner, a non-Christian resident of Florissant, Missouri, declared himself offended by the presence of a Nativity scene amid the holiday display at his local civic center. With the help of the ACLU he won an injunction against any exhibition "containing a crèche or other religious symbols at the Florissant Civic Center or any other public property." The city fought on, and the judges of the US Court of Appeals, Eighth Circuit, considered the mélange of roofed stable, bales of hay, figures of the Holy Family, candy canes, Christmas tree, snowman, Santa Claus, reindeer, wrapped gifts, and signs bearing the messages "Seasons Greetings," "City of Florissant," "Joy-Love-Peace," and "Happy Holidays" before deciding that the site had passed constitutional muster after all. The legal kerfuffle had attracted the participation not just of the ACLU but also of the National Legal Foundation, the Rutherford Institute, Americans United for Separation of Church and State, the Anti-Defamation League, the American Jewish Congress, and the Baptist Joint Committee on Public Affairs.[25]

The ad hoc, "context is everything" nature of legal rulings on Christmas displays and the relentlessness of the secularist drive ensured that the twenty-first century would continue to see objections to the presence of Nativity scenes and menorahs in public places. In Denver in 2001 a court upheld the constitutionality of a display that included a crèche, tin soldiers, Christmas trees, snowmen, reindeer, and Santa Claus, also allowing the city to exclude a "winter solstice" sign that the Freedom From Religion Foundation had twice asked the city to include in its annual holiday display. The sign was more than a little argumentative:

At this season of
THE WINTER SOLSTICE
may reason prevail.

There are no gods,
no devils, no angels,
no heaven or hell.
There is only
our natural world.
THE "CHRIST CHILD" IS A RELIGIOUS MYTH.
THE CITY OF DENVER SHOULD NOT
PROMOTE RELIGION.
"I believe in an America
where the separation of church and state
is absolute."
John F. Kennedy—1960 Presidential campaign
PRESENTED BY THE FREEDOM FROM
RELIGION FOUNDATION

The city declined to accept the sign, and the matter went to court, where the issue turned on whether the city had to accept speech it did not agree with in its own proclamations. The Court of Appeals decided that the refusal to erect a menorah and an atheist sign was legitimate—the city owned and operated the site and need not be compelled to include messages that were not in accord with its purposes. An earlier ruling permitting a ban on Ku Klux Klan sponsorship on National Public Radio was considered pertinent. A similar attempt by the Freedom From Religion Foundation to erect a counter-crèche sign in Warren, Michigan, was shot down by an appeals court in 2013.[26]

One of the more media-worthy attempts to restrict Christmas displays appeared in *Jocham v. Tuscola County* in 2003, where two atheist women, Anonka and Tammra Jocham, who ran a witch museum in Caro, Michigan, announced that they were "offended, affronted, intimidated, and distressed" when encountering a town Christmas display that included a crèche or, as they put it, "lifelike religious idols." Their protests to the local government received short and hostile shrift, so they took the matter to court, demanding the dismantling of the crèche along with "similar religious idols." The display contained the usual mixture of religious and secular holiday symbols, including toy soldiers, wreaths, and a "Season Greetings" message, but the mother and daughter atheists perceived in it a demonstration of intolerance for non-Christian religious views. Moreover, they claimed the subsequent controversy had made them an object of ridicule in the town and resulted in a boycott of their museum, whose purpose, according to its proprietor was "to dispel the Christian myth that there are witches that are evil, can fly on brooms and turn people into toads. We have a dungeon that takes you back into the bloody history of the Christian church, exposing the churches [sic] terrorism and money racketeering in hideous, factual detail."[27] Though the Jochams lost in court (largely through the application of the Lemon Test) they became the stars of a 2007 documentary movie, *The Separation on State Street,* which recounted their battle against hostile townsfolk.[28]

It must take a heart of stone not to be moved by a Christmas display containing fifteen pink flamingos with Santa hats, but Grace C. Osediacz (supported by the ACLU) found it within herself in December 2003 to object to such a spectacle in Cranston, Rhode Island. She discerned in the presence of a Nativity scene and menorah on the grounds of City Hall a violation of the establishment clause and in the mayoral policy on which it was based an attack on free speech. She was untouched by the presence of the flamingos, an inflatable snowman, a seven-foot Santa Claus, and signs proclaiming "The Public Holiday Displays Are Strictly From Private Citizens Or Groups. They In No Way Represent An Official View Of The City Of Cranston Nor Are They Endorsed By The City" and "Happy Holidays from the Teamsters Union." It was Osediacz's opinion that the nonreligious elements were merely camouflage for the crèche and the candlestick, but the appeals court ruled that there was no endorsement of religion in the display, though it was unhappy with the city's policy guidelines, which seemed to give too much discretion to the civic officials. The city, which had been backed in its legal struggles by the Alliance Defense Fund, could keep its display but had to come up with more objective grounds for judging possible participation.

In 2009 an artificial Christmas tree in the Orange County, California, Superior Court building was removed after a complaint from a member of the public. Though the tree served as a charitable outreach, decorated with tags seeking toy donations to "Operation Santa Claus," court spokeswoman Gwen Vieau defended the expulsion: "It's a public building and we have to serve the diversity of our community." Courthouse employees petitioned to have the tree returned, saying: "That tree holds the cards that contain the wishes and needs of those less fortunate than we are and shame on those who want to take that away from those of us who wish to give. Now at the court's darkest hour, our symbol of hope has been taken away from us."[29] It may be instructive to see how Canada, as multicultural as the United States but with a much less litigious culture and little history of constitutional wrangling over church-state issues, handled the issue of a zealous functionary fulminating at a Christmas tree in a public place. In December 2006 Judge Marion Cohen ordered a Christmas tree removed from the entrance to a Toronto courtroom. She explained that she didn't think it was appropriate that when people entered the courthouse, the "first thing they see is a Christian symbol." For her, the presence of the tree told non-Christians that they were "not part of this institution." Poor Judge Cohen. Aside from a statement of support from an atheist group, the hammer of public opinion came down hard on her. The premier of Ontario called the incident "unfortunate"; he said the province was trying to build a pluralistic society and that meant celebrating all traditions, not asking some to abandon them. "It doesn't offend anyone when we celebrate Diwali at Queen's Park or celebrate Hanukkah at [the provincial legislature]," he said. "It's part of who we are."[30] Cohen's decision was also condemned by her employees, editorialists, religious and ethnic groups, and, as far as can be determined by call-in shows and reader feedback, the general public. Perhaps most damning was the letter of the Ontario Bar Association to the province's attorney general. Its understanding of what constitutes true inclusiveness might be a lesson, not just for Judge Cohen, but for all of those interested in the place of Christmas in the public sphere:

> I read with some concern that the Christmas tree that traditionally greets visitors and staff at the Ontario Court of Justice at 311 Jarvis Street has been removed from the public's view.
>
> I encourage you to put in place a policy that promotes a greater understanding of the diverse religions and cultures in Ontario by allowing displays and symbols, such as Christmas trees, in our court houses.
>
> Inclusiveness and understanding are core values of Canadian society and our justice system, which are only enhanced by the sharing of religious symbols between members of ethnically and religiously diverse communities. Barring Christmas trees and all other religious displays from the public's view in our court houses does exactly the opposite. This controversy only serves to weaken the public's faith in our legal system, which must always be viewed as fair, just and reasoned.
>
> The fact is that cultural and religious displays are found at almost all government institutions in Toronto and across the country. You

can find a towering Christmas tree in Nathan Phillips Square, a Menorah on the front lawn of Queen's Park celebrating Hanukkah and displays of other faiths at public sites across the country. It seems only fitting that our justice system should join in this celebration of diversity.

In closing, please accept my best wishes for a happy and enjoyable holiday season.

Sincerely,

James Morton

President

Ontario Bar Association[31]

In the United States, however, when legal defense organizations are not doing battle over Christmas, solitary public-spirited citizens can be found taking up the cudgels and attempting to privatize the celebration of the holiday. Chief among these was lawyer Richard Ganulin of Cincinnati, who for years has fought in the courts to have Christmas stripped of its status as a legal holiday. "As a matter of law, it cuts me out, it excludes me, I'm an outsider, I'm an observer," he has said of the nineteenth-century federal law mandating a December 25 holiday. "It's a sectarian celebration." For Ganulin the principle of separation of church and state is paramount, and he has compared his struggle to that of the anti-Nazi underground during the Hitler regime. Unfortunately, Ganulin has not only been rebuffed by a series of court decisions but has been mocked by a judge in faux-Seuss rhyme:

> Plaintiff's seasonal confusion
> erroneously believing Christmas merely a religious intrusion
> Whatever the reason constitutional or other
> Christmas is not an act of Big Brother!
> Christmas is about joy and giving and sharing
> it is about the child within us it is mostly about caring!
> One is never jailed for not having a tree
> for not going to church for not spreading glee!
> The court will uphold seemingly contradictory causes
> Decreeing "The Establishment" and "Santa"
> Both worthwhile "Claus(es)"!
> We are all better for Santa the Easter Bunny too
> and maybe the Great Pumpkin to name just a few!
> An extra day off is hardly high treason

it may be spent as you wish regardless of reason.
The court having read the lessons of "Lynch"
refuses to play the role of the Grinch!
There is room in this country and in all our hearts too
for different convictions and a day off too![32]

In the prose portion of her decision, District Court judge Susan Dlott said: "Ganulin and his family have the freedom to celebrate, or not celebrate, the religious and secular aspects of the holiday as they see fit. The court simply does not believe that declaring Christmas to be a legal public holiday impermissibly imposes Christian beliefs on non-adherents in a way that violates the right to freedom of association.... The court has found legitimate secular purposes for establishing Christmas as a legal public holiday."[33] Dlott delivered her poetic put-down in 1999; a year later Ganulin was back in an appeals court pressing his case. The Becket Fund for Religious Liberty was there, too, representing federal employees who were arguing for the holiday, and again Ganulin was unsuccessful in purging the calendar of a December 25 day of rest named Christmas. Undaunted, Ganulin petitioned the US Supreme Court in 2001 for a hearing of his case, presenting it as a matter of national significance. Claiming to speak for 40 million non-Christian Americans, he began his argument by stating: "All Christian children in the United States grow up learning that they are preferred by their government. All non-Christian children grow up learning that they are not."[34] Despite the passion of his argument, the Supreme Court refused to act on it. December 25, Christmas Day, remains a public holiday in the United States.

The argument over how much Christmas children were going to be exposed to in public was much more an issue in the schools than in tussles over the legality of a federal holiday or the presence of an artificial tree in a hallway. This was also where feelings were much more heated as proponents of a religion-free educational environment sought either to banish the holiday from classrooms and auditoriums altogether or to render it a value-neutral recognition of the approach of winter. The stock characters in this seasonal drama are Dismayed and Outraged Parents, bewildered by the regulations forbidding the expression of their particular Christmas cultures; Confused Administrators, fearful of lawsuits, uncertain of the law but wishing to be "inclusive"; and the umbrage industry, composed of activists on all sides, quick to take offense at either the very mention of the C-word or any hint that Christianity might be under attack. Decades of legal wrangling about Christmas in public places convinced many school boards and principals that the holiday was a minefield that was best avoided by adhering to the path of political correctness, but the judicial precedents for Christmas in the schools were actually much simpler than for city hall crèches. The guiding light was still *Florey et al. v. Sioux Falls School District*, which permitted religious content, not as worship but if presented as part of the cultural and religious heritage of the holiday. During the Clinton administration in 1995, the Department of Education sent an explanatory pamphlet to every school superintendent in the country, outlining what Christmas practices courts had found acceptable. In an attempt to set out its own take on the rules for these seasonal tiffs, the Anti-Defamation League in 2000 produced a handout for distribution to schools entitled "The December Dilemma: Guidelines for Public Schools during the December Holiday."[35] The Catholic League responded with a satire of that material, "The December Celebration," which outlined what it thought was permissible in acknowledging the Christmas season within public schools. Since then the ACLU has come out with its own letter to school officials, which states:

> We welcome holiday celebrations that teach children about a variety of holidays. We believe, however, that holiday celebrations that focus primarily on one religious holiday can result in indoctrination as well as a sense within students who do not share that religion of being outsiders to the school. Similarly, we welcome holiday celebrations that share secular symbols such as Santa Claus or dreidels but we believe that holiday celebrations that focus on religious symbols can likewise result in indoctrination and the exclusion of students. The families of your students trust that you will work to ensure that this does not happen.... During the holiday season, it is especially important that we all embrace the constitutional guarantees of the First Amendment in order to ensure that religious freedom flourishes. We ask that if you hold holiday celebrations at your schools, please make sure that they are inclusive and that all students can participate in them.[36]

The Alliance Defense Fund responded in their submission to Tennessee schools:

> In recent years, certain groups, such as the ACLU, have spread misconceptions about the legalities of celebrating Christmas in public

school. As a result, many school officials have removed nearly all religious references to Christmas and replaced them with secular symbols. While many do so unknowingly, school officials have begun a new "tradition" of violating the constitutional rights of students and teachers to seasonal religious expression in our public school system.

And our Constitution acknowledges that people of faith have a right to openly express their beliefs in the public square but many school officials attempt to prohibit students and teachers from expressing any religious aspect of Christmas.... *No court* has ever ruled that the Constitution demands school officials to censor Christmas carols, eliminate all references to Christmas, or silence those who celebrate Christmas.[37]

Despite this plethora of explanation, activists and courts continued to find much to argue about, partly as a result of innocent ignorance and misunderstanding and partly out of a clear desire to push religion out of the public square and back into homes, churches, and synagogues. Examples of the Christmas wars in schools are legion, but the following examples from the past decade and a half should give a sense of the scope of the phenomenon and the different motives behind the outbreaks.

In 1999 in Covington, Georgia, the local school board attempted a daring act: they moved to change the name of the annual year-end break from "Winter Holidays" to "Holidays—Christmas." Unsurprisingly, certain concerned elements in the community detected a religious intent—and they were probably right. "This is a Christian country and it is founded on Christian values with God in mind," said one board member, explaining why he had voted against the advice of the board's lawyer. The head of the local ACLU termed the wording unconstitutional and felt that the board was trying to assert that theirs was a Christian school system. The Anti-Defamation League complained of "a blatant disregard for the diversity of religious faiths represented by the students of Newton County." The next year the board capitulated, citing ACLU pressure, and voted to label the winter hiatus "Semester Break." Similar quarrels over using "Christmas" to describe a seasonal break have taken place in Colorado and Indiana, with the inclusion of "Christmas" winning both times. Probably no one took this trend as seriously as the California man who in 2006 set himself and a Christmas tree on fire to protest a San Joaquin Valley school district's decision to change the names of winter and spring breaks to "Christmas" and "Easter" vacation.[38]

In 2002 the question in *Skoros v. City of New York* was whether the city's school system could bar a Christian Nativity scene in a public school winter holiday display while continuing to allow a Jewish menorah, a Christmas tree, and a Muslim crescent and star. Andrea Skoros, a Roman Catholic parent with two school-age children, claimed that this policy violated both the First Amendment and the Fourteenth (guaranteeing equal protection). School policy had been set out in a memorandum making the following points about holiday displays:

1. The display of secular holiday symbol decorations is permitted. Such symbols include, but are not limited to, Christmas trees, Menorahs, and the Star and Crescent.
2. Holiday displays shall not appear to promote or celebrate any single religion or holiday. Therefore, any symbol or decoration which may be used must be displayed simultaneously with other symbols or decorations reflecting different beliefs or customs.
3. All holiday displays should be temporary in nature.
4. The primary purpose of all displays shall be to promote the goal of fostering understanding and respect for the rights of all individuals regarding their beliefs, values and customs.

It was the school board's opinion, which they claimed had been determined by Supreme Court precedent, that a crèche was a religious symbol and therefore forbidden to be displayed. It was Skoros's view that barring the Nativity scene and allowing other equally religious symbols was to privilege the Jewish and Muslim faiths and interfere with the Christian rearing of her children. Courts ruled against her, finding no endorsement of a particular religion in the diversity of symbols, only an attempt to promote pluralism. Performing a nifty theological tap dance around the various images, the majority ruled:

A nativity scene undoubtedly qualifies as the depiction of a deity, with the infant Jesus usually being worshiped as God-made-man by adoring angels, shepherds, and wise men. While a menorah is understood to commemorate a miracle performed by God, it does not itself depict a deity. Nor does the star and crescent. This is not to suggest that the menorah (or the star and crescent) is a less religious symbol than the crèche.... It simply recognizes that the crèche conveys its religious message more representationally and less symbolically than the menorah and the star and crescent. For this reason, the religious significance of a crèche may be more obvious to the average schoolchild than that of the menorah and the star and crescent.[39]

Though the menorah and the star and crescent had religious overtones and could not therefore be allowed to be displayed in isolation, their collective presence rendered them sufficiently secular. The mathematical formula for this reads *religious symbol + religious symbol + religious symbol = secular display.*

While a Nativity scene, star and crescent, and menorah are clearly religious and thus capable of giving offense by their presence in a public school, what of less obvious tokens of the Christmas season? Parents in Newport Beach, California, were told to pull down strings of colored lights they had put up at a local elementary school. An offended parent threatened to sue over the display, and the school board wished to avoid litigation. While most seemed to find the lights a harmless holiday custom, others were convinced of a more sinister purpose. Said Rabbi Mark Miller: "It's a provocative act to put the lights up—it disenfranchises and marginalizes non-Christian students who are attending the public school."[40] What of marine birds and their status as forbidden symbols? In Port St. Lucie, Florida, the school presentation of *A Penguin Christmas* was deemed too religious by the principal and pulled from the holiday program. Though the little play contained nothing of a religious nature, the use of the word "Christmas" and a Santa Claus character were found worrisome in light of a previous complaint. "Any reference to a religious holiday has the potential to offend anyone who is not part of that particular persuasion," said a board spokeswoman. A gobsmacked parent complained: "What do penguins have to do with the gospel? I don't even think penguins could survive in Nazareth." The mother of a disappointed student who was to have played Mrs. Claus vowed to fight for her constitutional rights. "Kayla's not going to be little for long, and that principal is taking way our memories and our pictures. She thinks I'm going to be quiet and go away, but she's wrong." Other parents complained that their children could not bring Santa cupcakes to school or wrap canned goods for the poor in Christmas wrapping paper lest the wall between church and state be breached. The Becket Fund for Religious Liberty had nominated the principal, Bernadette Floyd, for their 2006 Ebenezer Award. The Ebenezer Award is a Christmas stocking filled with lumps of coal given each year to the individual responsible for the silliest affront to the Christmas and Hanukkah holidays. (Alas for Ms. Floyd, she was beaten out for the prize by Chicago mayor Richard Daley, whose sins against Christmas are discussed later.)[41] Other seasonal dramas supposedly deemed to be constitutionally unhealthy when consumed by schoolchildren are *A Charlie Brown Christmas* and Dickens's *Christmas Carol*. The former was attacked by an Arkansas atheist group when a parent complained about it. "We're not saying anything bad about Charlie Brown," Arkansas Society of Freethinkers vice president Anne Orsi was quick to state. "The problem is that it's got religious content and it's being performed in a religious venue and that doesn't just blur the line between church and state, it oversteps it entirely."[42] It was reported that the Dickens work was canceled in Kirkland, Washington, on the grounds that it was too religious—this won Mark Robertson, the Kirkland school principal, the 2004 version of the Ebenezer Award—but the principal claimed the cancelation was because the event had been improperly booked.[43] Whatever the truth of the matter, the controversy was widely reported both in local and national media, interpreted (depending on one's predispositions) either as part of the war on Christmas or part of the religious right's faux news campaign. In a Beverly, Massachusetts, public school, Doctor Seuss's *How the Grinch Stole Christmas* was reimagined as a play titled *How the Grinch Stole the Holidays*, in which the eponymous villain, disguised not as Santa Claus but as "the holiday fairy," complete with wings and a tutu, made off with Kwanzaa and Hanukkah as well as Christmas. Superintendent James Hayes said the adaptation exposed students to different religions while still enjoying a favorite story. "It allows us to celebrate the holidays and at the same time learn about other cultures."[44]

In the United Kingdom, a similar sensitivity to "other cultures" has led to a decline in school Nativity plays. A 2007 survey reported that only 20 percent of schools were staging the traditional sort of presentation. Where such entertainments are put on, they are often amended to take the religious sting out of them by adding novelty songs, new plot twists, or bizarre characters, for example the Bossy King, Whoops-a-Daisy Angel, or Hoity-Toity Angel. A Birmingham school with a predominantly Muslim student body, said: "We're reluctant to have a lot of music and acting because it goes against the religion of a lot of our pupils. We will stick to discussing the things we can take out of the festivals. So instead of the three men bringing gold, frankincense and myrrh, they will bring, for example, peace and co-operation." This sort of behavior has aroused the ire of British politicians and the archbishop of Canterbury, the highest ranking cleric in Britain, who has complained: "The weary annual attempts by right-thinking people in Britain to ban or discourage Nativity plays or public carol-singing out of sensitivity to the supposed tender consciences of other religions fail to notice that most people of other religions and cultures both love the story and respect the message."[45]

The singing of carols is an even more contentious issue for many than the increasingly rare school religious play. A child singing "Angels We Have Heard on High" or "Little Town of Bethlehem" seems to be making dogmatically Christian statements: "Come, adore on bended knee, / Christ the Lord, the newborn King," or "O holy Child of Bethlehem / Descend to us, we pray / Cast out our sin and enter in / Be born to us today." Who could blame non-Christian parents for preferring "Frosty the Snowman," "Here Comes Santa Claus," or "Suzy Snowflake" or criticize the nervous school officials for wishing the whole Christmas thing would go away? As a California school spokeswoman said to the *Los Angeles Times*: "People do get super-paranoid about this time of year, and, over the years, we have neutered the holidays. Schools are so fearful that they will be attacked...that they'd rather stick to singing 'Jingle Bells' than risk a problem."[46] Others might claim that singing these songs is not a religious rite, an act of worship, or a state endorsement of religion any more than an art student's assignment to examine Botticelli's *Birth of Venus* is pressure to convert to Roman paganism or a drama club's presentation of *Romeo and Juliet* champions teen sex and suicide. Religious Christmas songs are cultural artifacts, and when choir directors lead their students in them they are teaching music, not theology. Still, the battles continue. In Montana in 2013, the ACLU and the Freedom From Religion Foundation both attacked the idea of school choirs singing at a carol event. Choral groups from schools in Glacier, Flathead, and Whitefish had agreed to sing at the "Peace on Earth Community Christmas Celebration" held at a Mormon church. To the ACLU and the Freedom From Religion Foundation, this was tantamount to participating in a worship service and the schools endorsing the Christian religion. The fact that the performances took place in a church made it even worse. "There is no way to get away from the sheer religiosity of the place," said one of the opponents. They recognized that students who did not wish to participate could opt out, but this, they claimed, might result in informal pressure on the children.[47] The choirs, backed by the school superintendent, went ahead with their appearance at the carol festival. That same year saw a number of other

Christmas music controversies across the country. In Rock Hill, South Carolina, news that the band might be playing "Joy to the World" and "O Come, All Ye Faithful" drew threats of legal action against York Preparatory School. In Wausau, Wisconsin, it was alleged that a district attorney had suggested that the Master Singers, an advanced choir at a local high school, would need to exclude all religious Christmas songs from their holiday performances or perform four other types of songs for every religious Christmas song included in their concerts. As a result, the Master Singers temporarily disbanded, and a number of elementary choir concerts were postponed until the spring. In Bordentown, New Jersey, the school superintendent banned all religious music in the December concerts that the district's elementary schools normally held. The Alliance Defense Fund, which had already sent out thirteen thousand advisory letters to school boards, learned of these cases and persuaded the three schools that had decided that religious carols were forbidden to reconsider their decisions. The organizers of the winter festival in Corringham, England, deemed that the carols "Once in Royal David's City" and "Silent Night" were too religious and did not "dovetail" with the festival's theme. The chairman of the Corringham Town Festival Partnership stated that the carols had been banned because the winter festival was meant to be "upbeat."[48]

It is not only the defenders of religious carols who can raise a stink over holiday presentations. Consider the case of the parents in Missoula, Montana, who in 2012 felt that the programming in their school's holiday music was unfair, unconstitutional, and bullying. A letter sent anonymously and signed by "concerned parents" complained: "With many of the children in our neighborhood up here being Jewish and Buddhist, as well as a few Muslim and atheist students, we were assured that this year it would be a secular program.... We have no problem with it being called a Christmas concert, it's just the fact the material should be secular. Frosty the Snowman, Santa Claus, Rudolph the Red-nosed Reindeer. These are things that offend no one, but when the children are singing about their lord and savior, Jesus Christ...public school is not the place." Of the seventeen pieces presented in two concerts, only three were explicitly Christian carols (and one of those was in Polish), and there were two Hanukkah songs.[49]

The desire to be tender toward others' feelings can lead to some head-scratching behavior. Police in Riverside, California, were called to stop a high school choir from singing Christmas carols during an ice skating show featuring Olympic medalist Sasha Cohen, presumably out of concern that she might be offended because she is Jewish. Cohen had finished performing and was signing autographs when the Rubidoux High School Madrigals launched into "God Rest Ye Merry Gentleman." They were told to stop by a city employee, backed up by a policeman. City officials called the incident "unfortunate."[50] Cohen was not offended by the song nor the season—the performance was part of her Christmas Tree Lighting Tour.[51] Some schools have tried to overcome the poison of religious terminology in Christmas carols by removing the offending words and replacing them with something harmless like meaningless sounds. Thus one school's students sang "Silent Night, mmm, mmm, mmm, / All is calm, all is bright, mmm, mmm, mmm," and so on. Even a nonreligious seasonal song like "Silver Bells" can be dangerous unless the C-word is excised thus: "Ring-a-ling, hear them sing; Soon it will be a festive day." A school principal in Ottawa explained: "The choir teachers are trying to be as inclusive as they can be because not everybody is celebrating either Christmas or Hanukkah....The idea in public schools is that everybody feels welcome and has a sense of comfort with the celebrations. I think it's being sensitive to not only the students in the choir, but also to the general population."[52]

How sensitive to holiday slights is the population? Extremely quick to take offense, if we judge by the case of Medina Elementary School in Bellevue, Washington. There parents and children had decided to help the less fortunate by setting up a tree decorated with mittens and bearing the wishes of gift recipients. Already attuned to the sensitivities of the easily offended, they did not call this a "Christmas" tree but a "Giving Tree." One blushes in embarrassment at their innocence—a complainant quickly alerted the principal to the fact that the tree (a coil of silver topped by a star) "represents some part of Christianity." So the Giving Tree had to go, to be replaced by the "Giving Counter," on which the mittens could be inoffensively placed.[53] Lest you think this was an isolated case of a single individual being taken aback by the existence of a "Giving Tree," we learn of a high school that had to change its donation tree to a "Giving Snowman," a term that (of course) was quickly deemed to be sexist and changed to a "Giving Snowperson."[54] Sometimes no complaint is even necessary before amendments are made. A Seattle area school had to spend $494 in reprint costs because a new employee included the phrase "Merry Christmas" on a cafeteria menu. When seventh-grader Bryan Lafond went to a school party in Hampton, New Hampshire, dressed as Santa Claus, principal

Fred Muscara said he told the boy he couldn't get into the dance because of the costume he was wearing. "It was a holiday party," said Muscara. "It was not a Christmas party. There is a separation of church and state. We have a lot of students that go to Hampton Academy Junior High that have different religions. We have to be sensitive to that." Bryan's mother was baffled as to how Santa could be viewed as religiously offensive. "The last time I checked, Christmas was the celebration of the birth of Christ and not Santa Claus," she said. "He didn't go as Baby Jesus."[55] What Bryan's mother did not understand was how dangerous a creature some people in the school systems perceive Santa Claus to be. Good old St. Nick has often been banned from schools for a number of reasons. In Minnesota a twenty-five-year-old tradition of Santa appearing at a Head Start program to distribute gifts to preschool kids was axed lest children of different cultures be made uncomfortable. Jacqueline Cross, director of Anoka/Washington County Head Start, said the program didn't want to force "cultural traditions" down the throats of such kids. In Baldwin City, Kansas, the ACLU accused Santa of proselytizing, causing his school visits to be canceled. In Saugus, Massachusetts, the annual visit by firefighters in Santa costumes delivering coloring books was ended because of "church-state" worries. And on and on, from St. Peter, Minnesota, to Fort Worth, Texas, to Vienna, Austria, to Sydney, Australia.[56]

Controversies such as these have led some states to enact "Merry Christmas" legislation. In 2013 Texas passed the following legislation:

AN ACT

relating to a school district's recognition of and education regarding traditional winter celebrations.

BE IT ENACTED BY THE LEGISLATURE OF THE STATE OF TEXAS:

SECTION 1. Subchapter Z, Chapter 29, Education Code, is amended by adding Section 29.920 to read as follows:

Sections 29.920. WINTER CELEBRATIONS. (a) A school district may educate students about the history of traditional winter celebrations, and allow students and staff to offer traditional greetings regarding the celebrations, including

(1) "Merry Christmas";

(2) "Happy Hanukkah"; and

(3) "happy holidays."

(b) Except as provided by subsection (c), a school district may display on school property scenes or symbols associated with traditional winter celebrations, including a menorah or a Christmas image such as a nativity scene or Christmas tree, if the display includes a scene or symbol of:

 (1) more than one religion; or

 (2) one religion and at least one secular scene or symbol.

(c) A display relating to a traditional winter celebration may not include a message that encourages adherence to a particular religious belief.[57]

Similar legislation was proposed or passed in ten other states, despite the claims of many that the bills were unnecessary. Texas ACLU spokesman Terri Burke said that First Amendment rights were already sufficient protection and that "right-wing advocacy groups raise of a lot of money this time of year by hyping a fake war on Christmas."[58]

Universities are not immune from allergy to Christmas displays that might reveal the Christian content of the holiday. At the School of Law of Indiana University–Purdue University at Indianapolis, a tree was erected in the atrium. Though it was devoid of any Christian symbolism and was decorated only with maps meant to express "diversity and the identification of peoples everywhere," keen minds, such as Professor Florence Wagman Roisman's, detected an unacceptable exclusionary message, and Dean Anthony Tarr ordered the tree removed. Law professor Jennifer Drobac admitted that the tree and its decorations were perfectly legal but supported its eviction on ethical grounds. "Because ours is a state school and, to a great degree, a majoritarian society, Dean Tarr quietly replaced the Christmas tree rather than further discomfort those non-Christians who felt excluded. Under Supreme Court precedent, the tree could remain, but we are a moral community as well as a legal one, an inclusive society. Dean Tarr gave life to the concept of equal protection, as well as to the First Amendment. I agree with the prophet who said, 'blessed are the peacemakers.' I hope we can now rejoice in our peace and new understanding." The offending tree was replaced by two smaller trees and a sleigh filled with poinsettias as the dean proclaimed that a "denominational tree" had been replaced by "a normal Indiana scene." To no one's surprise, Professor Roisman remained offended and stated that she found the pair of new trees to be equally representative of a Christian holiday; they must go as well. This time the dean refused to act, and the revised display remained.[59] In 2014 an administrator at the University of Maine sent out a warning e-mail: "Just wanted to remind everyone that Auxiliary Services is not to decorate any public areas with Christmas or any other religious themed decorations. Winter holiday decorations are fine but we need to not display any decoration that could be perceived as religious." Banned items included "xmas trees, wreaths, xmas presents, menorahs, candy canes, etc." Permitted symbols included "snowmen, plain trees without presents underneath, decorative lights, but not on trees, snow flakes, etc. If you are unsure, best to not use or ask me for clarification." (After a few days of public outrage, the university backtracked and said that the official in question, though a "really solid manager," had acted out of "an excess of caution" and that religious Christmas decorations were, in fact, welcome.)[60] Cornell University's 2015 "Guidelines for the Display of Religious Symbols" urged an inclusive approach that either focused "on the winter season rather than a particular holiday" or that included "the holidays of several religions in combination with secular decorations of the season." To be more specific, snowflakes and trees (decorated with snowflakes but no religious decorations) were permitted. Caution (in the form of a "dialogue within unit or living area") was required for the display of trees decorated with bows, garlands, and lights; wreaths with bows; holly; or a combination of snowflakes, Santa Claus figure, and dreidel. On the utterly naughty list were any Nativity scene, menorah, angel, star at the top of a tree, cross, Star of David, or mistletoe. Why the latter was banned remains a mystery; perhaps the presence of the plant might lead to promiscuous kissing or offend non-Druids. At the University of Tennessee-Knoxville, the "Best Practices for Inclusive Holiday Celebrations in the Workplace" policy advised against dreidels, the phrase "Secret Santa" (though "secret gift exchange" was permitted), and having a holiday party that was just a Christmas party in disguise. Celebrations should be carried out with "no emphasis on religion or culture," and "holiday cards" sent to fellow workers should be nondenominational. Political reaction to these guidelines was furious, with legislators calling for the resignation of university officials and a reduction in diversity funding for the school. The "Inclusive Holiday Practices" of Ohio State University went so far as to discourage the use of red or green bows in decorating.[61] It is clear that there is nothing "inclusive" in these dictates and that the expulsion of religion from the public space is deemed necessary to avoid offense every December.

When one moves off of the city hall lawn or out of the school classroom, one still finds Christmas in an embattled state and the subject of emotional debate. Some clear trends in the twenty-first century are a continuing discomfort on the part of minor officials with religious expressions of Christmas, a belief that minority groups are harmed by manifestations of the dominant culture, a reflexive desire to remove potential offense, and a conviction by the religious right that the controversies surrounding Christmas are an attack on Christianity. A selection of incidents that have drawn public attention over the past fifteen years should illustrate these themes.

The terroristic attacks of 9/11 made Americans more aware of the contributions of their military forces, police, and firefighters and intensified patriotic feelings generally. The event also made national traditions such as Christmas customs seem more precious and connected to the American way of life. Therefore when the town council of Kensington, Maryland, moved by complaints from two local families, called for the removal of Santa Claus from his accustomed spot riding a fire truck to the annual lighting of the town's Christmas tree, it is not surprising that a volcano of criticism erupted. Coming scant months after 9/11, this declaration that the presence of Santa, played by a volunteer fireman at a ceremony to honor the country's men in uniform, was "offensive" struck many as an outrageous provocation. Word of the banishment flashed across the internet, and social media mercilessly mocked the hapless politicians who had voted for the ban; town officials received more than two thousand hostile e-mails. Community volunteers organized a "Million Santa March" on the day of the ceremony; dozens of men dressed as St. Nick marched, rode motorcycles, or waved to the crowds from the backs of pickups. The collective of Clauses sang carols, patted children on the head, and distributed candy canes. Protestors chanted "No Santa, No Peace!" Some carried signs proclaiming "Grinch for Mayor," "Mean Spirited Arrogant Santa Hating Liberals," "Yes, Kensington, There Is a Santa Claus," and "PC = Stupid." One pair, acting on the rumor that the complaining families were Jewish, carried a sign that read "If Jews can ban Santa, why can't we ban Jews?" but they were booed by the crowd, and their banner was ripped from them. Though the mayor performed the tree-lighting ceremony herself, fire engines with sirens blaring accompanied the official Santa through the town to the cheers of the townsfolk. Hoping to soothe injured feelings, town officials agreed to present Santa Claus with a special proclamation, and a local merchants association planned to give him a key to the city.[62]

The Kensington council aroused a town with its misstep; the arousal was far greater when millions of members of the religious right were called on in 2004 and 2005 to respond to an insidious campaign to undermine their belief system, beginning with the right to hear the words "Merry Christmas" on the lips of retailers. It is one thing to be angry with public schools shoving Christmas to the back burner or to see Nativity scenes banished from town halls—these are, after all, matters of constitutional debate, and while one might rant against "liberal judges" there is little individual citizens could do on their own. But to hear political correctness on the lips of store clerks and to be told that "Merry Christmas" might be offensive was too much.[63] Awoken by conservative cultural critics, a considerable chunk of Middle America reacted with alarm. The battle was declared in 2004. The Committee to Save Merry Christmas, a California-based pressure group, announced that it had been observing that a "covert and deceptive war has been waged on Christmas to remove any mention of it from the public square...a consistent and relentless move to culturally pressure merchants, businessmen and individuals to remove the words 'Merry Christmas' from their advertising, decorations and promotional materials." The group claimed this replacement of a time-honored expression "with substitute un-celebratory phases is thoughtless, condescending and hurtful." The Committee's solution, after failing to bring the Federated Stores chain to a negotiating table, was to organize a boycott of the chain, which they accused of deliberately obliterating "Merry Christmas" from its decorations and advertising. Since the company's chain included Bloomingdale's and Macy's, the Committee was taking on a high-profile target, attracting considerable media attention.[64] The company denied it had meant to slight anyone, stating that "phrases like 'Season's Greetings' and 'Happy Holidays' embrace all religious and ethnic celebrations that take place in November and December and are more appropriate for the many diverse cultures in America today," but by November 2005 the company came out with a more conciliatory approach, which was hailed by the Committee as the required surrender. A Macy's executive announced: "I understand your concerns about our use of 'Merry Christmas.'...We hope that you and your committee will be pleased with Macy's Christmas campaign to include Merry Christmas." He promised that Macy's advertising and in-store signage would include the C-word in its television advertising jingle, on gift cards, and in print ads; the windows in Macy's flagship store in New York City would be themed "Christmas Time in the City." The Committee advised its followers to shop once again at Federated Stores. By this time the use of "Merry Christmas" had become a national issue, stoked by Fox News's Bill O'Reilly, John Gibson's *War on Christmas,* the Catholic League, and the American Family Association and involving other retail chains as well.[65]

Nor should we forget the role played by "Kirby," the mysterious functionary at Wal-Mart who answered a complaint about the store's use of "Happy Holidays." Combining the maximum of historical inaccuracy with a healthy dose of snark, Kirby informed his complainant: "Walmart is a world wide organization and must remain conscious of this. The majority of the world still has different practices other than 'christmas' which is an ancient tradition that has its roots in Siberian shamanism. The colors associated with 'christmas' red and white are actually a representation of the aminita mascera mushroom. Santa is also borrowed from the Caucuses, mistletoe from the Celts, yule log from the Goths, the time from the Visigoth and the tree from the worship of Baal. It is a wide wide world."[66] Hopefully the world was wide enough for Kirby to find another job because Wal-Mart soon cut him loose for his impudence and apologized for his poor communication skills. The Liberty Counsel, a Christian activist group, launched a "Friend or Foe" campaign to help consumers identify those merchants who used "Merry Christmas" and those who did not. Sears, Wal-Mart, Lowes, Best Buy, Gap, and Home Depot were all caught up in the controversy and forced to defend their particular approach to seasonal advertising terminology. For the religious right, the battle over "Merry Christmas" greetings was twofold. On its surface was the offense taken by shoppers unhappy with a generic phrase that seemed to marginalize their Christian-American culture. Deeper down, such shoppers were told, this was but one part of a covert war on Christianity by secularist progressives who wished to diminish the majority religion so that their left-wing stances on abortion, gay rights, euthanasia, and drug use would triumph.[67] Counter-blasts came from the head of Americans United, an association of left-wing journalists and academics, who deplored the tone of the debate.[68] For these critics, this "War on Christmas," at least in this campaign over store greetings, was a cheap marketing ploy by Fox News and a reflection of Christian fundamentalists' desire to exercise religious hegemony over their fellow citizens—"some Christians are so insecure about their place in American culture that they are demanding the rest of the culture pander to them." More excitable observers trotted out the word "theocracy." A lighthearted moment amid all of this debate was provided when the online retailer Amazon, in a brief lapse of consciousness in

2008, came up with the less than brilliant marketing slogan "The Twelve Days of Holiday." When a customer wrote in to complain about this vapid phrase, someone at company headquarters hit the reply button to send a form letter that said: "Please accept our sincere apologies if you were offended by the use of the word 'Christmas' on our website. Our intention in referring to Christmas is to give specific ordering guidance for a specific holiday, not to exclude other faiths."[69] In 2014 Bill O'Reilly, who had been alerting his viewers to this issue for years, announced victory in the war against Christmas. "This is the only year we have not had a store that commanded its employees not to say 'Merry Christmas,'" he said. "It's over. We won."[70]

Or had they? Since 1997 the Starbucks coffee company has issued a different red cup design every holiday season; ornaments, sleighs, Santa, abstract designs, and reindeer have been among the decorative themes. In 2015 the cups appeared in a plain red that, according to the press release, mimicked a blank canvas—"a purity of design that welcomes all of our stories," because after all, "creating a culture of belonging, inclusion and diversity" was, the corporation assured the world, a core value of Starbucks. Typical sanctimonious corporate blather, one would have thought, scarcely worth a moment's attention, but that was to reckon without the hypersensitivity the Christmas wars had brought to social media. In the absence of images on the red cups, certain conspiracy-minded folk detected yet another attack on Christians and their most cherished customs. Ignoring the fact that Starbucks had never included any religious imagery on their beverage containers, politicians and preachers weighed in on the perceived slight. English member of Parliament David Burrowes said: "The Starbucks coffee cup change smells more of political correctness than a consumer-led change. The public has a common sense grasp on the reality that at Christmastime, whether you have a Christian faith or not, Britain celebrates Christmas." Andrea Williams of Christian Concern, a group of British activists focusing on religion in the public sphere, said: "This is a denial of historical reality and the great Christian heritage behind the American Dream that has so benefitted Starbucks. This also denies the hope of Jesus Christ and His story told so powerfully at this time of year." A spokesman for the Christian Institute complained: "What is it about Christmas that Starbucks are afraid of celebrating? Haven't they heard it's the most wonderful time of the year, and the season of good will to ALL men? They should get involved and stop being scrooges." In the United States controversial Facebook evangelist Joshua Feuerstein claimed: Starbucks "removed Christmas from their cups because they hate Jesus." Presidential hopeful Donald Trump mused that perhaps one should boycott Starbucks. After this first rush of commentary, sanity quickly returned to the internet: the overwhelming sentiment, especially from disgusted Christians, was that this was an issue of no importance.[71] Nonetheless, while suspicion of anti-Christian corporations might have weakened, it was not dead.

"Not to exclude other faiths" seems a noble enterprise in principle, but it proceeds from the assumption that some cultural expressions of the majority faith are inherently harmful. One might well object to female genital mutilation, slavery, or human sacrifice if they were the cultural products being thrust forward in December, but gifts to hospitalized veterans? Christmas carols in a lobby? Handmade children's cards? Delicacy toward the feelings of others has led to these activities being treated as toxic. In 2013 Jordan McLendon of Montgomery, Alabama, made up a hundred goodie bags to give to veterans in a local hospital. This was to honor her grandfather and because some veterans did not get family visits at Christmas. To her surprise a Veterans Administration official refused to allow her to distribute any material with a religious message such as "Merry Christmas." The hospital's acting director cited regulations meant to protect a diverse patient list whose differing beliefs had to be respected. He also mentioned that in past years some patients had told him they did not want to hear carolers. For similar reasons, a Georgia veterans' hospital prevented a high school choir from singing carols with a religious content; only songs from a list of twelve seasonal ditties would be allowed. "Military service veterans, male and female, represent people of all faiths," a hospital spokesman said. "It is out of respect for every faith that the Veterans Administration gives clear guidance on what 'spiritual care' is to be given and who is to give it." In Iowa, Texas, and Alabama, VA hospitals refused to distribute cards or gifts if they contained the words "Merry Christmas" or "God Bless You," even on the wrapping. (The VA later admitted that the correct policy was that a multidisciplinary staff team should have reviewed the cards to screen out the religious ones and then distributed the nonreligious ones. After this "review is complete, the holiday cards that reference religious and/or secular tones are then distributed by Chaplaincy Service on a one-on-one basis if the patient agrees to the religious reference in the holiday card donation.") Veterans Administration officials were even prepared to make theological judgments—in 2015 executives at the Salem, Virginia, facility announced that "trees (regardless of the types of ornaments used) have been deemed to promote the Christian religion and will not be permitted in any public areas this year." This diktat produced employee protests and won the administrators the 2015 Ebenezer Award; officials were reminded that in *Allegheny County v. Greater Pittsburgh ACLU* (1989) the Supreme Court had ruled that a Christmas tree was not a religious symbol. The Salem VA got a tree after all, when hospital officials decided that such objects were permissible "so long as they were accompanied by the respective symbols of the two other faiths that celebrate holidays during this holiday season—namely symbols commemorating Hanukkah and Kwanzaa."[72] A cancer treatment center in South Carolina banned the appearance of a volunteer Santa Claus on the grounds that it was a state institution that tended some patients who were not Christians. Citing a "passionate response" from the public generated by local newspaper coverage, the hospital soon changed its mind and said it would "allow holiday traditions of all faiths because of the emotional benefits they provide for patients."[73]

George Orwell's essay "Politics and the English Language" was famous for its denunciation of shifty language meant to cloak truth in "a fog of euphemism, question-begging and sheer cloudy vagueness." Orwell might survey the present cultural scene and ask "When is a Christmas tree not a Christmas tree?" When it is presented as a "Holiday Tree." Or a "Care Tree." A "Multicultural Tree." A "Tree of Lights." A "Community Tree." A "Winter Solstice Tree." A "Grand Tree." A "Special Tree." A "Family Tree." The "Annual Tree." A "Festive Bush." A "Unity Tree." A "Culture Tree." A "Seasonal Conifer." A "Giving Tree." A "Tree of Celebration." A "Magical Tree." "The Finals Tree." In many states, arguments have broken out about what to call that large evergreen standing in front of public buildings that appears to be decorated every December. Naïve bystanders might reply "a Christmas tree," not knowing how dangerous that term is to some of their political masters, who insist that it is something else entirely: usually a "holiday tree." When voters protest this neologism as being contrary to fact, poor politicians must sense which way the wind of public opinion is blowing before acting. In 1917 a munitions ship exploded in Halifax harbor, causing thousands of casualties and dreadful devastation in the city. The citizens of Boston generously came to the aid of Haligonians, and in gratitude the people of Nova Scotia have for decades annually sent an enormous Christmas tree to Boston to be lit on Boston Common. In 2005 press releases in Boston, for some reason, termed the gift a holiday tree, a misapprehension that caused an enormous stink back in Canada. The logger who had chosen and cut the tree said that if he had known what they were going to call it, he would have run it through the wood chipper. The premier of Nova Scotia noted pointedly that when it had left his domain it was still a "Christmas tree." Fortunately for international relations, Boston mayor Thomas Menino announced that in his estimation the tree was, and always had been, a Christmas tree. Two years later in Wisconsin, state representative Marlin Schneider (D-Wisconsin Rapids) put forward a motion before the state legislature's Committee on State Affairs to properly name what had been, since 1985, the holiday tree. Naturally, the Freedom From Religion Foundation objected. "When you call it a Christmas tree, that's a celebration of Christmas, which is a Christian holiday," said Annie Laurie Gaylor, the Foundation's copresident; "So what does the state of Wisconsin need with a Christmas tree? It is a proposal that shows ill will, and it isn't necessary." (A Jewish aide to Representative Schneider said that the term "holiday" was also potentially offensive. "It's not my holiday.") The ensuing debate did change the tree's label—from 2008 to 2011 it was the "Capitol Tree," and then under Governor Scott Walker it became the "Capitol Christmas Tree."[74] Similar tiffs broke out in Washington, DC, California, and Kentucky. Lincoln Chafee, governor of Rhode Island, who won the Ebenezer Award in 2012 for clinging to the name "holiday tree," in 2013 finally yielded and admitted that the object standing in front of the state capitol was a Christmas tree.[75] An interesting variation on this theme occurred in Brussels, which had annually erected and decorated a huge fir tree from the Ardennes Forest in the city's main square, the Grand-Place, where it was the centerpiece of the famous Christmas Market. In 2012 the Socialist mayor, Freddy Thielemans, broke with tradition; the market was to be called "Winter Pleasures 2012," and the conifer was replaced with a giant green abstract lighted sculpture somewhat resembling a tree. This was to show how exciting and modern the avant-garde Belgian capital was. Critics instantly charged that these changes were to appease the city's growing Muslim minority. They pointed out that a recent fatwa from a Belgian imam had forbidden Muslims from having anything to do with a Christmas tree: "So it is not permissible to put up this tree in a Muslim house even if you do not celebrate Christmas, because putting up this tree comes under the heading of imitating others that is *haram* [banned], or venerating and showing respect to a religious symbol of the *kuffar* [a derogatory term for non-Muslims]. What the parents must do is protect their children and keep them away from what is *haram*, and protect them from the Fire as Allah, may He be exalted."[76] In 2013 the real tree and traditional decorations returned to the Grande-Place.

A final couple of examples will show how far the brand value of "Christ" and "Christmas" has declined in the eyes of officialdom. One of the seasonal attractions in Chicago since 1997 has been the Christkindl Market, a Christmas fair meant to imitate similar markets that have existed in Germany since the Middle Ages, an open-air attraction where one might buy gifts, cookies, and crafts, drink beer, and enjoy music. It is not uncommon for the fair to attract a million visitors. In 2006 one of the booths was to have been sponsored by the producers of a big-budget holiday movie, *The Nativity Story*, but when the Mayor's Office of Special Events got wind of this they banned the display lest the city be seen to endorse one religion over another. Moreover, they said, a movie about the birth of Jesus at a fair whose name translates as the "Christ Child Market" would be "insensitive to the many people of different faiths who come to enjoy the market for its good and unique gifts." Inclusivity mandated that the historical facts behind the Christmas story were to be banned from the Christmas market. After threats of a lawsuit by the Thomas More Society, officials climbed down and allowed clips of the film to be shown.[77] Four years later, visitors to Philadelphia's "Christmas Village" were greeted by a sign amended to read "Holiday Village." The offending word had been removed by order of Richard Negrin, the deputy mayor. This act won Negrin the 2010 Ebenezer Award. When Mayor Michael Nutter, having weathered a couple of days of public wrath, reinstated the word "Christmas," the Becket Foundation gave him the inaugural Eggnog Toast Award.

DOES THIS CHAPTER'S array of controversies constitute a war on Christmas? Not if we compare the actions of the hapless Kirby of Wal-Mart, the ACLU, appeals court judges, or atheist owners of witch museums with those of sixteenth-century Scottish Calvinists, Fred Phelps and his clan, or Joseph Stalin. The people we have met in this section exhibit no desire to eradicate utterly plum puddings or Santa Claus; or to shoot or send to hell families with a Nativity scene in their home. But this is a war nonetheless—not of abolition but of diminishment, of exile. A Christmas that is barred from public celebration is not like any Christmas for the past thousand years or more. The supposedly countless incidents of secularist hostility to Christmas expressions are not nothing; they are not, as readers of *Salon* have been told, a self-fulfilling myth, "assembled out of old reactionary tropes, urban legends, exaggerated anecdotes and increasingly organized hostility to the American Civil Liberties Union."[78] The contretemps show that in the United States, and some other parts of the industrial world, an uncivil war about the place of religion in the public square is taking place. It is an important one that entangles citizens in their homes, offices, courts, shopping malls, legislatures, and public buildings. Its roots lie in a culture war that is already under way, in deeply held presuppositions about society, in mutual misunderstanding, and in a shift in what constitutes the highest public virtues.

That a cultural war between left and right exists in the United States and, to varying degrees, in other countries is no secret. The battle lines of this war are drawn along issues that reveal stark differences of opinion: abortion, immigration, multiculturalism, sexual mores, climate change, the scope of government action, and the place of religion.

When we set the debate on Christmas in its national religious context, we find that some religious and irreligious groups are not all that fond of each other. A Pew Foundation survey of 2014 asked Americans to express their opinions about various faith groups on a "feeling thermometer." A "temperature" of 100 would signal total approval; 0 would denote total dislike; 50 would express neither negative or positive feelings about the group. The US public expressed its warmest approval for Jews, Catholics, and evangelicals, and Buddhists and Hindus were rated slightly favorably; Mormons, Muslims, and atheists were in the negative zone. When one examines what each group thinks of the other, one finds interesting variations. Jews do not have a high opinion of evangelical Christians, but evangelicals rate Jews highly. Atheists are disliked most by Protestants and Catholics; Jews slightly favor atheists. Atheists hate all kinds of Christians (they give evangelicals a temperature of 28, the lowest score registered next to evangelicals' view of atheists, at 25) but tend to like Buddhists, Jews, and Hindus. Nonevangelical Christians prompt as much strong dislike as they do warm feelings. Christianity is most prevalent among older Americans, and those with no religion are more likely found among the young (32 percent of whom describe their religion as "none"). Politically, there are more distinctions. Democrats have a higher view of atheists than Republicans, and nonevangelical Democrats favor atheists over evangelicals.[79]

What this means for the Christmas debate is that holiday arguments do not take place in a vacuum. Sincere Christians know that many of their compatriots dislike their faith beliefs and may well conclude that this animus accounts for attacks on Christmas. Non-Christians might suppose that Christmas is a tool Christians use to enforce their cultural dominance. Throw in other divisions I will discuss, and any debate on social issues will find the battleground already full of combatants lined up in their accustomed places.

Once such area of disagreement is over whether religious liberty, guaranteed by the First Amendment, is currently under threat. A slight majority of Americans (54 percent) believe that this is so, but opinions on this vary with political affiliation, age, and religious affiliation. Twice as many Republican voters as Democrat voters say that religious freedom is being threatened (80 percent v. 40 percent). A majority of Democrat voters (55 percent) do not believe that religion is under threat in the United States; and Independent voters are more closely divided, with 51 percent opining that religious liberty is under threat and 43 percent saying it is not. Unsurprisingly, white evangelical Protestants strongly believe that religious liberty is being threatened in the United States today (83 percent), compared to 55 percent of Catholics, 53 percent of white mainline Protestants, and 50 percent of minority Protestants. Less than one-third (31 percent) of religiously unaffiliated Americans believe religious liberty is being threatened, while twice as many (62 percent) say it is not. Of seniors, 61 percent believe it is, while most (54 percent) younger Americans do not.

The same poll asked respondents about the problems posed by the place of religion in public life. Thirty percent say the removal of religion from public places is the most serious problem, while 25 percent say government interference with free religious practice is the most serious threat. One-quarter think that the real question is religious groups attempting to pass laws that force their beliefs on others, while a small minority (9 percent) say the lack of protection for smaller faith groups is the biggest headache. White evangelical Protestants (43 percent) are more likely than other religious groups to be vexed about the removal of religion from public places. Thirty-six percent of white mainline Protestants agree, but Catholics (28 percent) and the religiously unaffiliated (16 percent) are less likely to identify removal of religion from public places as a major problem.[80]

It is also clear that those who are on separate sides in the culture wars and sectarian differences are also on separate sides in the arguments over Christmas. At first this seems strange. After all, the overwhelming majority of Americans celebrate Christmas. A 2013 Pew poll shows that of those who identify as Christian (73 percent of the country's population)

96 percent celebrate the holiday, but so do most of the rest of the country—81 percent of non-Christians observe Christmas in some way. Of the unaffiliated (atheist, agnostic, "none"), 87 percent celebrate the holiday; 76 percent of American Buddhists, 73 percent of American Hindus, and even some Muslims mark the holiday. Some also celebrate other December feasts, including Hanukkah, Kwanzaa, or the winter solstice; only 5 percent mark no observances at all in that period. However, an important difference is that for most Christians it is primarily a religious season, while for most of the others it is a secular or cultural event.[81] But even within Christianity there are important distinctions. White evangelical Protestants are more likely to treat the holiday in a strongly religious fashion (71 percent) than any other group, while Protestants from racial minorities, Catholics, and white old-line Protestants are less wedded to that approach. (The elderly are twice as likely as young adults to treat Christmas as a religious holiday.) More than other Americans, white evangelical Protestants are likely to attend religious services on Christmas Eve or Christmas Day; they are much more likely to read the Christmas story from the Bible (68 percent v. 36 percent) and much more likely to believe that the Christmas story as told in the New Testament is historically accurate. White evangelical Protestants spend more on Christmas gifts than the average American and are the most likely to volunteer for charitable activities during the season.[82]

When it comes to expressing the good wishes of the season, we also see evidence of the culture war. In two Pew polls of 2012 and 2013, Americans were fairly evenly divided as to the propriety of "Merry Christmas" versus "Happy Holidays," but there was a significant split between Republicans and Democrats. Republicans strongly preferred the Christmas greeting, and when "it doesn't matter" was included as an option, 63 percent of Republicans said they preferred "Merry Christmas," while 5 percent chose "Season's Greetings" or "Happy Holidays," and 32 percent said it doesn't matter. Among those on the leftward side of the political spectrum, 28 percent preferred "Merry Christmas," 17 percent chose the less religious terms, and 55 percent said "it doesn't matter."[83] When it came to the sort of greeting they preferred in stores, a similar split was found, but again with significant political and cultural differences. Republicans (61 percent) favored "Merry Christmas" over "Happy Holidays," while nearly as many (58 percent) Democrats held the opposite view. Again, the age gap is significant. Two-thirds of young adults (ages eighteen to twenty-nine) preferred a nonreligious greeting when shopping, but seniors disagreed. White evangelical Protestants were more likely than the American average to prefer that stores greet customers with "Merry Christmas," as opposed to "Happy Holidays" or "Season's Greetings."

These surveys get us closer to understanding the current North American Christmas fuss. Secularists are right in detecting in their opponents a trace of Christian triumphalism. One does occasionally hear remarks such as those uttered in the Covington, Georgia, school calendar argument: "This is a Christian country and it is founded on Christian values with God in mind" or "Our nation was indeed founded as a Christian nation and we should not deviate from our Christian heritage." But these stem not from any intention to establish a theocracy or challenge constitutional norms on church-state relations but from a sense of unease among Christians who see their share of the religious landscape slowly shrinking (78 percent of the adult American population in 2007 as opposed to 73 percent five years later) and who feel defensive about their Christmas customs, developed in the days of unthinking Christian dominance, being belittled. But to discern in the presence of a Christmas tree in a public building the intention to send threatening signals to minorities is truly unwarranted. The academic who asserted that the *intended* message of a lavishly decorated conifer in a museum is that "you and your children are different, and your traditions are neither known nor welcome. In this country, our national institutions support the majority's symbols. If you don't like that we're sorry, but too bad," was really saying that he did not know either his Christian or non-Christian neighbors very well.[84] John Gibson and Bill O'Reilly are correct in asserting that the Christmas goings-on in courtrooms, schools, and advertising flyers are part of a larger cultural war, but they were incorrect in seeing it largely as an attack on American Christianity.[85] The symptoms they note are real: important parts of the American state and media are in retreat from a reasonable and even-handed approach to Christmas. A well-meaning but ill-conceived attitude toward social underdogs has preconditioned many officials, lawyers, reporters, and opinion leaders to distrust any expression of the dominant culture. These folk, immersed in the need for sensitivity, have fallen under the spell of minoritarianism, which asserts that the outnumbered possess the moral high ground on any issue and their rights automatically trump the views of the majority. "Inclusivity" has become the argument by which the claims of the majority are to be excluded. Here is a typical statement from a school spokesman as to why the customs of the great majority of his students' families are to be ignored: "We have people of different races and religions and to them this particular time of year may not be celebratory. Because of their religious beliefs, they may not choose to celebrate anything at this time of year." Here is a highly educated librarian explaining why there will be no Christmas tree in her bailiwick: "We strive in our collection to have a wide variety of ideas. It doesn't seem right to celebrate one particular set of customs." A human rights gadfly recently objected to his city's transit system carrying a "Merry Christmas" message among ten preprogrammed displays that included "Happy Holidays," "Lest We Forget," "Bus Full Another Coming Soon," and "Help Your Neighbour Clear the Snow." He said he was complaining on behalf of recent immigrants who had told him that Christmas messages "make them feel like they need to convert to Christianity to be first-class citizens." His city councilor offered to have the bus company recognize other cultures' holidays as well, but the activist declined, saying that there were too many groups to mark their festivities, so it was best that the city celebrate none of them. I have spoken of the Washington atheists who objected to a Christmas charity in City Hall on the grounds that those precincts should be "a place where everybody feels welcome. It is impossible for everybody's religious belief to be displayed and non-religious belief to be displayed, so therefore, no religious beliefs [should] be displayed." It seems perfectly righteous in this new moral dispensation to show no respect to the lived experience of the greater number in order to not expose the minority to something outside their culture, no matter how harmless on the surface a Santa hat, a decorated tree, a friendly greeting, or a reindeer cookie might appear.

Suspicion of the majority culture is multiplied when religion enters the scene. As an ACLU spokesperson explained in arguing for the restriction of Christmas displays to home and church, "religion belongs where it prospers best: with individuals, families, and religious communities."[86] This is the heart of the matter: the desire to make no space in public for religion. This is a tragic misunderstanding of the binding roles religion plays in the larger life of the community and fosters an atomistic view of society according to which social life is conducted only within one's own group. It leads to identity politics and perpetual claims of victimization. Everyone is poorer if Handel's *Messiah,* Mozart's *Requiem,* or "Silent Night" are considered threats to schoolchildren, if St. Patrick's Day parades or Diwali celebrations or Carnival are kept off the public thoroughfares. Religion is already out on the streets, not just in spectacle and music but in the hospitals, homeless shelters, soup kitchens, sports leagues, afterschool programs, homes for the elderly, and so on in which various faiths mandate their followers serve their communities.

As North American and European societies become less homogenous and more multicultural, an old virtue has been lost. Tolerance, once the mark of a cultured citizen, is now seen to be condescending and judgmental. To merely abide with one's fellow citizen's choices is no longer sufficient—what is required now is "affirmation" and celebration of different minoritarian positions. An end to many of the privatizing tussles around Christmas in the twenty-first century could be avoided if tolerance were again socially acceptable. Pro-Christmas advocates could tolerate the slights from corporate advertisers and the umbrage industry, knowing that Christmas is secure in the hearts of their compatriots and will never disappear. They could channel their irritations into heightening their religious appreciation of the season and showing their neighbors a joyful face. Those who dislike or fear religion could set aside their trepidation over Christmas by realizing that for most people it is a secular celebration of enormous value, injecting goodwill and magic into a cold and barren part of the year.[87]

A Brief Epilogue

*In which readers are reminded about what they have learned
in reading this book and of the likely fate of Christmas and
its discontents*

SO IS THERE such a thing as a "war on Christmas"? If you have read this far, you will know what to reply when asked this question. The answer is yes, and over the many centuries, one or two or more assaults on the season have always been going on at any time. Christmas looms far too large in our moral, religious, economic, and social landscapes for one to expect a tranquil uniformity of position.

For Christians, it is the second highest festival and one that makes extraordinary religious claims. Getting its theology and modes of celebration right has always seemed to be worth arguing about. Should one celebrate the birth of the Son of Man? If so, when? If so, how? Then follows the fight, perpetually renewed, to keep the elements of pagan midwinter festivals out of the Feast of the Nativity: the battles against crossdressing, dancing, rude social inversion, ostentatious gift-giving, and ribaldry. When particular battles are deemed unwinnable, the objectionable content is Christianized and made a sanctified part of the season. Meanwhile, the Church is giving Christmas new rituals and adorning it with art, music, and drama. In the High Middle Ages, the holiday becomes more deeply entrenched in the hearts of the common people with the invention of the St. Nicholas cult, opportunities for seasonal charity, and the Franciscans' crèche and carols, while the Church continues to battle the innovations of unruly clergy, such as the Feast of Fools.

Christmas is dealt sharp blows in the early modern period by the Triumph of Lent, with its crackdown on popular customs, and by the Protestant Reformation. St. Nicholas disappears from some lands, as does Christmas itself, in Scotland, New England, and the Puritan Commonwealth.

The holiday is condemned as riotous, papist, pagan, without basis in scripture or history, and simply too much fun to be moral. When the smoke clears new magical Gift-Bringers have emerged, but Christmas is in sore repair in the English-speaking world, discredited, abandoned by the decent classes, and associated with rustics, servants, and boors. It is in worse condition on the Continent, where it is attacked by Enlightenment thinkers and abolished for a time by the French Revolution.

The nineteenth century opens with Christmas in low repute. In the new American republic it is most often a raucous outdoor celebration, fueled by alcohol, and in the cities of the Northeast it is a time for mob violence and disorder. Similar scenes of riot and mayhem are recorded in Canada, Australia, Newfoundland, and Britain. The season is saved by its revival and reinvention in England and New York. Members of the American upper-middle class seek to wrench Christmas from the hands of the liquored-up mob and bring it indoors as a family festival. The fashioning of Santa Claus out of the European St. Nicholas and his rough, fur-clad helpers is decisive in this movement, as it coincides with a new child-centeredness and the wider prosperity the Industrial Revolution brings. In England, carol collectors save the great forgotten songs, Anglican clergy welcome back Christmas rituals, and Charles Dickens reminds his country of the connection between Christmas and charity. In both countries, parents (including the English royal family) and merchants conspire together in the creation of a greatly furbished season focused on love and generosity. This success, however, does not mean that opposition to Christmas ceases—the battle is taken up in the United States by Protestant sects who have not forgotten the objections of the Puritans, in England by antiritualists, and on the Continent by left-wing political groups. Social critics emerge to argue that Christmas is hard on women, makes children greedy, and abuses shop-workers; seasonal charity is derided as merely a means to keep the poor in their place. Atheist and anti-Christian arguments now emerge, and some thinkers propose that a new godless midwinter festival must replace Christmas.

In no century is the war on Christmas waged with such ferocity as the twentieth, as new totalitarian states confront the challenges posed by the cradle in Bethlehem. Marxist-Leninist tyrannies that take root in Europe after the world wars are avid promoters of atheism and attempt to root out Christianity and Christmas with it. Midwinter festivities are moved to New Year, religious Gift-Bringers are replaced by Grandfather Frost, and December 25 is made a work day. Communists in Latin America and China mimic the Soviet example. The fascist governments of Nazi Germany and Mussolini's Italy take a different approach, trying to make Christmas part of the state apparatus. In Germany, Hitler's party tries to paganize and make warlike a festival of peace based on the birth of a Jewish baby. Hitler replaces the Christ Child as the object of veneration. This policy is intensified after the outbreak of World War II, when Nazis attempt to turn Christmas into a military death cult.

In the late twentieth century a surprising similarity is found between atheists and Calvinist Protestants: both despise Christmas and wage war against it in tracts, on billboards, in public speech, and on the internet. Though it has been predicted that the century will see the triumph of freethinking and the death of religion, faith groups continue to thrive, and attempts at state atheism are abandoned. A variety of unfaith called the New Atheism arises in the Western democracies, more aggressive than previous versions. Its adherents claim the right to openly mock the religious and take particular glee in attacking Christmas. Their mockery is no fiercer than that wielded against their fellow Christians by neo-Calvinists who preserve the Puritan distaste for Christmas but have added a biting sense of humor to their arsenal. There are many Christians who wish not to abolish Christmas but to radically reform it—anticonsumerists, ecologists, foes of an Americanized Santa Claus who wish to revive native Gift-Bringers, and those worried about the loss of a Christian core in the celebrations. Christmas is also the target of Muslims who are worried about the infiltration into their cultures of Santa Claus and his holiday.

There is also a war, or rather dozens of them, to appropriate Christmas—to grab a piece of its powerful meanings. Some at the margins of society seek to borrow the season's respectability and magical glow to advance their cause, just as politicians and merchants have. The Ku Klux Klan, African American radicals, gays, terrorists, ecosaboteurs, antismoking activists, vegans, antiobesity crusaders, pagans, Occupy Wall Street, bare-chested FEMEN activists, Palestinians, pacifists, and conceptual artists all have climbed on the Christmas bandwagon and attempted to steer it in their directions.

Then there are those who just hate the season and who must tell the world all about their seasonal dyspepsia. Some have termed them "Holiday Cranks," and the media is full of their whining each December. Their numbers include those suffering from loneliness, the bereaved, the exiled, and those afflicted with spousal saturation syndrome. Those who work too hard or shop too hard labor under a burden of stress; those who receive

Christmas letters from boastful correspondents are driven to anger; the visits of mothers-in-law drive husbands out of the house. Neighbors who dazzle with their Christmas lights or hospitality, holiday Muzak, and the problem of telling a fib to children about Santa also cause distress. Stores who mount Christmas displays too early are subject to vandalism; pictures of snowmen cause an eruption of academic criticism of patriarchy; the woes of department store Santas are increasingly publicized.

Finally, there are those who claim to be no foes of Christmas but wish to drive it out of the public sphere and back into homes and churches. The war to privatize the holiday threatens lawsuits, pursues court cases, and provides employment to legions and counter-legions of lawyers. We learn of a Million Santa March, the constitutional importance of plastic reindeer, the machinations of the umbrage industry, and the forgotten virtue of tolerance.

Will there ever be an end to struggles against, for, and around Christmas? Almost certainly, no. Christmas is simply too important in countless ways: in the intimate lives of families, in the industrial economy, in its spiritual challenge, in art, music, and cinema. It has proved to be bigger than Oliver Cromwell, Adolf Hitler, Mao Tse-tung, Fred Phelps, PETA, and the ACLU. Humankind will be loving it, hating it, and arguing about it for centuries to come.

Notes

CHAPTER I: THE INVENTORS

1. Origen, *Contra Celsum*, bk. 1, chaps. 28 and 32. *The True Word*, the original work of Celsus, the earliest known intellectual attack on Christianity, seems to have been written c. 177 but survives only in Origen's refutation of 248.
2. The *Protoevangelium of James* dates from about 150 A.D.
3. Joseph F. Kelly, *The Origins of Christmas* (Collegeville: 2003), pp. 58–77; Susan K. Roll, *Towards the Origins of Christmas* (Kampen: 1995), pp. 81–83.
4. *Homily on Leviticus*, 8.3, and *On Matthew*, 14.6. See Matthew 14:6–11 and Mark 6:19–28.
5. Brent Landau, *Revelation of the Magi* (New York: 2010), pp. 24–25.
6. Maximus of Turin, sermon 60, *The Sermons of St. Maximus of Turin*, trans. Boniface Ramsey (New York: 1989), p. 144.
7. Translated by Roll, *Towards the Origins of Christmas*, p. 84; she notes that the first reference is problematical because the day of the week and the consuls listed are incorrect.
8. Thomas J. Talley, *The Origins of the Liturgical Year* (Collegeville: 1991), pp. 86–87, 91.
9. A good summary of the historical arguments can be found in C. P. E. Nothaft, "The Origins of the Christmas Date: Some Recent Trends in Historical Research," *Church History* 81, no. 4, December 2012, pp. 903–911. See also Nothaft, "From Sukkot to Saturnalia: The Attack on Christmas in Sixteenth-Century Chronological Scholarship," *Journal of the History of Ideas* 72, no. 4, October 2011, pp. 503–521.
10. Gary Forsythe, *Time in Roman Religion: One Thousand Years of Religious History* (Abingdon, UK: 2012), p. 153.
11. Quoted in Roll, *Towards the Origins of Christmas*, p. 151.
12. Steven Hijmans, "Sol Invictus, the Winter Solstice and the Origins of Christmas," *Mouseion*, ser. 3, 3, 2003, pp. 377–398.

13. Jaime Alvar, *Romanising Oriental Gods: Myth, Salvation and Ethics in the Cults of Cybele, Isis and Mithras* (Leiden: 2008), p. 410.

14. Arnobius, *Adversus Nationes*, 7:29–33, mocks the sacrifices, games, and celebrations in honor of the pagan gods; Tertullian, *De Idolatria*, chap. 14, warns Christians away from Roman festivities.

15. *De solstitia et aequinoctia conceptionis et nativitatis domini nostri iesu christi et iohannis baptistae,* quoted in Andrew McGowan, "How December 25th Became Christmas," Bible History Daily, http://www.biblicalarchaeology.org/daily/biblical-topics/new-testament/how-december-25-became-christmas/. The work was once erroneously attributed to John Chrysostom.

16. Luke 1:39–56 recounts the Visitation; the Baptist refers to Jesus in John 3:30.

17. Thomas J. Talley, "Constantine and Christmas," in *Between Memory and Hope: Readings on the Liturgical Year,* ed. John Francis Baldovin and Maxwell E. Johnson (Collegeville: 2000), p. 267, argues that the Eastern churches counted nine months from April 6, rather than March 25.

18. John Chrysostom, "Concerning Blessed Philogonius," in Wendy Mayer and Pauline Adam, *John Chrysostom* (London: 2000), p. 191.

19. Epiphanius of Salamis, *The Panarion of Epiphanius of Salamis: De fide. Books II and III,* trans. Frank Williams (Leiden: 2013), p. 51: "Greeks, I mean idolaters, celebrate this day on the eighth before the Kalends of January [December 25], which Romans call Saturnalia.... For this division between the signs of the zodiac, which is a solstice, comes on the eighth before the Kalends of January, and the day begins to lengthen because the light is receiving its increase. And it completes a period of thirteen days until the eighth before the Ides of January [January 6], the day of Christ's birth."

20. Gregory Nazianzen, "Homily on the Nativity of Christ," in *Religions of Late Antiquity in Practice,* ed. Richard Valantasis, trans. Nonna Verna Harrison (Princeton: 2000), pp. 444–445.

21. John Chrysostom, *In Kalendas* [On the Kalends of January], trans. Seumas Macdonald, http://www.tertullian.org/fathers/chrysostom_in_kalendas.htm.

22. Asterius of Amasea, "On the Festival of the Calends," *Ancient Sermons for Modern Times,* trans. Galusha Anderson and Edgar Johnson Goodspeed (New York: 1904), pp. 125–126.

23. Saint Augustine, sermon 198, in *Sermons on the Liturgical Seasons,* trans. Mary Sarah Muldowney (New York: 1959), p. 56.

24. Peter Brown, "Aspects of the Christianisation of the Roman World," Tanner Lectures (Cambridge: 1993), p. 129.

25. Alexander Tille, *Yule and Christmas: Their Place in the Germanic Year* (London: 1899), 103.

26. Judith Herrin, "'Femina Byzantina': The Council in Trullo on Women," in *Homo Byzantinus: Papers in Honor of Alexander Kazhdan,* Dumbarton Oaks Papers 46 (Washington, DC: 1992), pp. 97–105.

27. Quinsext Council, Canon 62, *A Select Library of Nicene and Post-Nicene Fathers of the Christian Church: The Seven Ecumenical Councils*, trans. Henry R. Percival (New York: 1900), p. 393.

28. Herrin, "'Femina Byzantina,'" pp. 104–105.

29. In Ramsey MacMullen, *Christianity and Paganism in the Fourth to Eighth Centuries* (New Haven: 1997), p. 18.

30. Boniface, "Boniface to Pope Zacharias on His Accession to the Papacy," in *The Letters of Saint Boniface*, trans. Ephraim Emerton (New York: 2000), p. 59. To see the lingering memory of the Kalends on Christmas celebrations, one has only to look at the name for the holiday in many European languages. Lithuanians call it Kalėdos, and their Santa Claus is Kalėda; the Russians say Kolyáda, and it is Koleda in other Slavic languages; in Provence, folk say Calèndo; in Dauphiné the Yule log is the *chalendal*.

31. Bruce Forbes, *Christmas: A Candid History* (Berkeley: 2008), pp. 6–13.

32. Gregory the Great, "Letter to Abbot Mellitus," trans. James Barmby, in *Nicene and Post-Nicene Fathers, Second Series*, vol. 13, edited by Philip Schaff and Henry Wace (Buffalo: 1898), revised and edited for New Advent by Kevin Knight, http://www.newadvent.org/fathers/360211076.htm.

33. Clement Miles, *Christmas in Ritual and Tradition, Christian and Pagan* (London: 1912), p. 183.

34. In the twenty-first century we continue to leave out food on Christmas Eve, but we now say it is meant for Santa Claus and his reindeer or, in some countries, for the Three Kings and their camels.

35. The initials stand for Kasper (or Gaspar), Melchior, and Balthazar, the names by which the Magi have been known since the sixth century.

36. See Gerry Bowler, "Devils and Evil Spirits at Christmas," in *The World Encyclopedia of Christmas* (Toronto: 2000), p. 68.

37. William Blake's poem "Jerusalem," which begins with the lines "And did those feet in ancient time / Walk upon England's mountains green," refers to this voyage. Since 1929, the queen's Christmas table has been decorated with blossoms from what are said to be offshoots of the original Glastonbury Thorn.

38. Even a king could be raked over the coals for giving gifts on January 1, as was Carloman of the Franks in 742. Brigitte Buettner, "Past Presents: New Year's Gifts at the Valois Courts, ca. 1400," *Art Bulletin* 83, no. 4, December 2001, 599.

39. Tille, *Yule and Christmas*, pp. 95–96.

40. Modern voices who criticize the commercialization of Christmas might be surprised at the extent of the toy industry in the Middle Ages. Karl Ewald Fritzsch and Manfred Bachman, *An Illustrated History of Toys* (London: 1966), pp. 13–26, and Nicholas Orme, *Medieval Children* (New Haven: 2001), pp. 167–174.

41. Richard C. Trexler, *Journey of the Magi: Meanings in History of a Christian Story* (Princeton: 1997), p. 51.

42. Attributed to John Wyclif, "The Ave Maria," in *The English Works of John Wyclif Hitherto Unprinted* (London: 2005), p. 206.

43. "Richard III's Raucous Christmas Parties," December 21, 2012, Medievalists .net, http://www.medievalists.net/2012/12/21/richard-iiis-raucous-christmas-parties/.

44. Trexler, *Journey of the Magi*, p. 52; John F. Haldon, *The Social History of Byzantium* (London: 2009), pp. 248–252.

45. Luke 46–53; from the Douay-Rheims Version.

46. Miles, *Christmas in Ritual and Tradition*, pp. 303–304.

47. Miles, *Christmas in Ritual and Tradition*, and E. K. Chambers, *The Medieval Stage* (Oxford: 1903), are of the pagan remnant opinion, while genuine piety in these ceremonies has been detected by Max Harris, *Sacred Folly: A New History of the Feast of Fools* (Ithaca: 2011).

48. In D. B. Wyndham Lewis, *A Christmas Book: An Anthology for Moderns* (London: 1951), p. 191.

49. Stuart Clark, *Thinking with Demons: The Idea of Witchcraft in Early Modern Europe* (Oxford: 1999), p. 18.

50. December 26, "Boxing Day," also known as St. Stephen's Day, was the traditional time for distributing certain types of charity and for the serving class to solicit gifts from their masters, their masters' tradespeople, and people on the street. English surgeons found it prudent to pay the hangman an annual "Christmas box" to ensure a steady supply of corpses for dissection. A number of English laws attempted to muzzle this annoying begging, but it persisted as an irritating custom until late in the nineteenth century.

51. The term was taken from the medieval Shrovetide figures of Carnival and Lent and was coined in a scholarly context by Peter Burke, in his classic *Popular Culture in Early Modern Europe* (Farnham, UK: 1978). Burke was inspired by Pieter Brueghel's painting *The Combat of Carnival and Lent.*

52. Neil Mackenzie, *The Medieval Boy Bishops* (Kibworth Beauchamp, UK: 2011), pp. 1–4.

53. *Tudor Royal Proclamations,* ed. Paul L. Hughes and James F. Larkin, 3 vols. (New Haven: 1964–69), vol. 1, p. 302.

54. The Church of England and the Catholic Church in Spain have recently revived the idea, and boy bishops can now be found again in a number of monasteries and cathedrals.

55. The concern of Protestant reformers with the propriety of images has a long history in the Church. The Orthodox Byzantine Empire banned their use in worship in the iconoclastic controversies of the eighth and ninth centuries, and Palestinian Christians under Islamic occupation also were uneasy with images. Leslie Brubaker and John Haldon, *Byzantium in the Iconoclast Era, c. 680–850: A History* (Cambridge: 2011), p. 114.

56. The best source for the legend of St. Nicholas and the way it was handled across Europe is Charles W. Jones, *Saint Nicholas of Myra, Bari and Manhattan* (Chicago: 1978).

57. Martin Luther, who is often blamed for the abolition of St. Nicholas as Christmas Gift-Bringer, seems to have been able to accommodate both the saint and his replacement. In 1532 he wrote: "This is what we do when we teach our children to fast and pray and hang up their stockings that the Christ Child or Saint Nicholas may bring them presents. But if they do not pray they will get nothing or only a switch and horse apples [manure]."

58. Gerry Bowler, *Santa Claus: A Biography* (Toronto: 2005).

59. Arthur C. Cochrane, ed., *Reformed Confessions of the Sixteenth Century* (Philadelphia: 2003), p. 292.

60. "Of Doctrine," in *The First Book of Discipline* (1560), Still Waters Revival Books, http://www.swrb.com/newslett/actualNLs/bod_ch03.htm.

61. Margo Todd, *The Culture of Protestantism in Early Modern Scotland* (New Haven: 2002), p. 188.

62. Edward's government (1547–1553) upheld Henry VIII's abolition of the practice of the boy bishop; after Bloody Mary (1553–1558) reinstituted it, Elizabeth I (1558–1603) reabolished it. Protector Edward Somerset tried vainly to prohibit gift-giving at court during the Christmas season of 1548, but he was ignored by most of his fellow aristocrats. David Starkey, *Elizabeth: The Struggle for the Throne* (New York: 2001), p. 85.

63. Philip Stubbes, *An Anatomie of Abuses,* sig. S1v, from the critical edition edited by Margaret Jane Kidnie, http://etheses.bham.ac.uk/4435/1/Kidnie96PhD_redacted.pdf.

64. Nashe's play *Summer's Last Will and Testament* was probably written in 1592 but was not published until 1600. The mention of "crabbes" refers to crab apples, which would be roasted and placed in ale for the Christmas drink called "lamb's wool."

65. Ronald Hutton, *Stations of the Sun: A History of the Ritual Year in Britain* (Oxford: 2001).

66. James VI and I, *Basilikon Doron* (London: 1603), in *The True Law of Free Monarchies; and, Basilikon Doron,* ed. Daniel Fischlin and Mark Fortier (Toronto: 1996), p. 128. The Latin tag is from Horace: "He who has mixed usefulness and pleasure has carried every vote."

67. An English proverb meaning that everything goes well when the old ways are respected.

68. Ben Jonson, "The Masque of Christmas," *The Works of Ben Jonson* (New York: 1879), 717. An excellent summary and explanation of the play can be found in Leah Marcus, *The Politics of Mirth* (Chicago: 1986), pp. 78–84.

69. In Robert Chambers, *Domestic Annals of Scotland: From the Reformation to the Revolution* (Edinburgh: 1874), p. 506.

70. English Broadside Ballad Archive, University of California, Santa Barbara, http://ebba.english.ucsb.edu/ballad/30037/image.

71. Edward F. Rimbault, *Notes and Queries*, 3rd ser., 2, December 20, 1862, p. 481.

72. Stuart Gillespie and Neil Rhodes, eds., *Shakespeare and Elizabethan Popular Culture* (London: 2006), p. 49.

73. William Prynne, *Historio-Mastix: The Players Scourge or Actors Tragedie* (London: 1633), pp. 757–760. Prynne's book weighs in at over eleven hundred pages, with thousands of notes and references. An anonymous critic termed it "the most verbose, tiresome mass of invective that the sinful world ever drew down upon itself." "Christmas Past," *Harper's New Monthly Magazine* 70, December 1884, p. 16.

74. David Cressy, *Travesties and Transgressions in Tudor and Stuart England: Tales of Discord and Dissension* (Oxford: 1999), pp. 218–219; David M. Bevington and Peter Holbrook, *The Politics of the Stuart Court Masque* (Cambridge: 1999), p. 302. The fact that the unpopular Queen Henrietta, a French Catholic, had appeared on the stage led the government to perceive Prynne's book as an attack on the royal family.

75. Diane Purkiss, *The English Civil War: Papists, Gentlewomen, Soldiers, and Witchfinders in the Birth of Modern Britain* (New York: 2006), p. 238.

76. A good introduction to this controversy is Chris Durston, "Lords of Misrule: The Puritan War on Christmas 1642–60," *History Today* 35, no. 12, 1985, pp. 7–14.

77. John Taylor, *The Complaint of Christmas and the Teares of Twelfetyde* (London: 1646), p. 7.

78. Anon., *Mercurius Religiosus: Faithfully communicating to the whole Nation, the Vanity of Christmas* (London: 1651), p. 2.

79. Joseph Hemming, *Certain Quaeries touching the rise and observation of Christmas* (London: 1648).

80. Anon., *Mercurius Religiosus*, p. 4. The reference to the Roman goddess Diana comes from Acts 19, where an Ephesian mob protests the anti-idolatry preaching of the apostle Paul.

81. *Christ-Mas Day, the Old Heathens Feasting Day* (1656), p. 9.

82. Old Christmas claims to have urged "friendly Thrift to be there Caterer, and Temperance to carve at the board, and be very watchful that obscenity, detraction and scurrility be banisht the table"; Josiah King, *The Examination and Tryal of old Father Christmas* (1686).

83. Edward Fisher, *A Christian Caveat to the Old and New Sabbatarians or A Vindication of Our Gospel-Festivals* (1649), sig. D.

84. King, *Examination and Tryal of old Father Christmas*, p. 26.

85. T.H., *A Ha! Christmas, This Book of Christmas is a sound and good Perswasion for Gentlemen, and All Wealthy Men, to Keepe a Good Christmas* (1647), p. A7.

86. Ezekias Woodward, *Christ-Mas Day* (1656), p. 25.

87. *Women will have their will or, Give Christmas his due* (1649), pp. 7–9.

88. *The Merry Boys of Christmas or The Milk-Maids New-Years Gift* (1660). The Oliver referred to is the Puritan lord protector Oliver Cromwell (1599–1658).

89. Martin Ingram summarizing the theories of Peter Burke in "Ridings, Rough Music and the 'Reform of Popular Culture' in Early Modern England," *Past & Present*, 105, November 1984, p. 79.

90. J. M. Golby and A. W. Purdue, *The Making of the Modern Christmas* (Stroud: 1986), p. 35.

91. William Bradford, *Of Plymouth Plantation: Sixteen Twenty to Sixteen Forty-Seven*, ed. Samuel Eliot Morison (New Brunswick: 1952), p. 97.

92. Stephen Nissenbaum, *The Battle for Christmas* (New York: 1997), pp. 18–19.

93. In Ivor Debenham Spencer, "Christmas the Upstart," *New England Quarterly* 8, no. 4, 1935, pp. 503–504.

94. Katharine Richards, *How Christmas Came to the Sunday-Schools* (New York: 1934), p. 54.

95. Hugh Cunningham, *Leisure in the Industrial Revolution: c. 1780–c. 1880* (London: 1980), p. 61.

96. Jan de Vries, *The Industrious Revolution: Consumer Behavior and the Household Economy, 1650 to the Present* (Cambridge: 2008), p. 91.

97. Owen Chadwick, *The Popes and the European Revolution* (Oxford: 1980), pp. 18–63.

98. Mona Ozouf, *Festivals and the French Revolution* (Cambridge, MA: 1991), p. 3.

99. Margaret C. Jacob, *Living the Enlightenment: Freemasonry and Politics in Eighteenth-Century Europe* (Oxford: 1991), p. 153.

100. Dennis L. Bark, *Americans and Europeans Dancing in the Dark: On Our Differences and Affinities, Our Interests, and Our Habits of Life* (Stanford: 2007), p. 36.

101. Stanley Loomis, *Paris in the Terror* (New York: 1964), p. 279.

102. Two hundred years later, Americans, angry at France's refusal to join their coalition in the invasion of Iraq, would change "French fries" to "Freedom fries."

103. Ozouf, *Festivals and the French Revolution*, 269.

104. Matthew Shaw, *Time and the French Revolution: The Republican Calendar, 1789–Year XIV* (Woodbridge, UK: 2011), p. 104.

CHAPTER II: THE REVIVERS

1. Drawing nos. 1866,1114.632; 1877,1013.902; 1861,0518.1008, British Museum, Department of Prints and Drawings; J. M. Golby and A. W. Purdue, *The Making of Modern Christmas* (Stroud: 2000), pp. 36–37.

2. *The London Magazine, Or, Gentleman's Monthly Intelligencer* 41, 1772, p. 579.

3. Samuel L. Macey, *Patriarchs of Time: Dualism in Saturn-Cronus, Father Time, the Watchmaker God, and Father Christmas* (Athens, GA: 2010), p. 157.

4. *Massachusetts Mercury*, December 20, 1793, from J. L. Bell, "Boston 1775," December 25, 2006, http://boston1775.blogspot.ca/2006/12/christmas-anticks-bah-humbug.html.

5. "New Year's Amusements," *New York Gazette*, January 5, 1823, in Paul A. Gilje and Howard B. Rock, eds., *Keepers of the Revolution: New Yorkers at Work in the Early Republic* (Ithaca: 1992) pp. 64–65.

6. Susan G. Davis, "'Making Night Hideous': Christmas Revelry and Public Order in Nineteenth-Century Philadelphia," *American Quarterly* 34, no. 2, 1982, p. 85; John Humphries, *The Man from the Alamo* (Gretna, LA: 2004), p. 262; Frank Cusack, ed., *The Australian Christmas* (Adelaide: 1966), p. 44.

7. Stephen Nissenbaum, *The Battle for Christmas* (New York: 1997), p. 98; *Weekly True Sun*, December 31, 1837.

8. Davis, "Making Night Hideous," p. 185; John R. Gillis, *A World of Their Own Making: Myth, Ritual, and the Quest for Family Values* (Cambridge, MA: 1997), p. 99; James H. Barnett, *The American Christmas: A Study in National Culture* (New York: 1954), p. 6; Thomas Hervey, *The Book of Christmas* (London: 2000), p. 31; "Christmas Festivities," *Gentleman's Magazine* 144, December 1828, p. 505.

9. The account that follows of the changes wrought to Christmas in New York is largely drawn from the second chapter of Stephen Nissenbaum's *Battle for Christmas*, which is now the standard view.

10. The poem is found in Nicoline van der Sijs, *Cookies, Coleslaw, and Stoops: The Influence of Dutch on the North American Languages* (Amsterdam: 2009), p. 251. The second poem is found in Charles W. Jones, "Knickerbocker Santa Claus," *New-York Historical Society Quarterly*, October 1954, reprinted on website of St. Nicholas Center, http://www.stnicholascenter.org/pages/knickerbocker/.

11. This is where I part company with the history of the transition from St. Nicholas to Santa Claus as expounded by Jones and Nissenbaum, both of whom doubt the continued existence in colonial New York of a Dutch Sinterklaas legend. See my *Santa Claus: A Biography* (Toronto: 2005) for more.

12. Anon., *The Children's Friend: A New Year's Present, to Little Ones from Five to Twelve,* (New York: 1821).

13. A long-standing debate has been carried on over the possibility that another, Major Henry Livingston Jr., was the author of the poem. See Dan Foster, *Author Unknown: Tales of a Literary Detective* (New York: 2000).

14. The sharp-eyed reader will note that the reindeers "Dunder" and "Blixem" are now known as "Donder" (or "Donner") and "Blitzen." The poem went through a number of minor variations before a definitive version was established.

15. William Washabaugh, *Deep Trout: Angling in Popular Culture* (Oxford: 2000), p. 62, makes many of these points but asserts that St. Nicholas came down the chimney wearing red clothes, the symbol of authority; in fact, the poem gives no particular color to the furs.

16. Leigh Eric Schmidt, *Consumer Rites: The Buying and Selling of American Holidays* (Princeton: 1995), p. 132.

17. "The Editor's Easy Chair," *Harper's New Monthly Magazine*, December 1856, p. 265.

18. Joseph M. Hawes and Elizabeth F. Shores, eds., *The Family in America: An Encyclopedia*, vol. 1 (Santa Barbara: 2001), p. 481; Lyman Cobb, *The Evil Tendencies of Corporal Punishment* (New York: 1847), p. 8.; David M. Lubin, *Picturing a Change: Art and Social Change in Nineteenth-Century America* (New Haven: 1994), p. 214; Teresa Michals, "Experiments before Breakfast: Toys, Education and Middle-Class Childhood," in *The Nineteenth-Century Child and Consumer Culture*, ed. Dennis Denisoff (Aldershot: 2008), p. 32; Howard Chudacoff, *Children at Play: An American History* (New York: 2007), p. 74.

19. David Goss, "New Brunswick's First Santa Claus: The Story of Fredericton Confectioner Charles A. Sampson," *New Brunswick Reader*, December 15, 2001.

20. American Temperance Union, *Journals of the American Temperance Society* (New York: 1840); Scott C. Martin, *Killing Time: Leisure and Culture in Southwestern Pennsylvania, 1800–1850* (Pittsburgh: 1995), p. 208; Neil Armstrong, *Christmas in Nineteenth Century England* (Manchester, UK: 2010), pp. 112–114; Nissenbaum, *Battle for Christmas*, p. 99.

21. Mark Connelly, *Christmas: A History* (London: 2012), p. 66, is doubtful that carol singing was quite as endangered as has been thought, but he does believe that the English middle class feared its extinction.

22. The publication of "Good King Wenceslas" created a firestorm among scholars of Christmas hymns and carols that continues unabated to this day. No other carol has been met with such scorn by the musical elite, who mock its marriage of sentimental words and springtime dance tune.

23. E. David Gregory, *Victorian Songhunters: The Recovery and Editing of English Vernacular Ballads and Folk Lyrics, 1820–1883* (Lanham: 2006).

24. Susan P. Casteras, "'Weary Stitches': Illustrations and Paintings for Thomas Hood's 'Song of the Shirt' and Other Poems," in *Famine and Fashion: Needlewomen in the Nineteenth Century*, ed. Beth Harris (Aldershot: 2005), p. 21.

25. Geoffrey Rowell, "Dickens and the Construction of Christmas," *History Today* 43, no. 12, December 1993.

26. Penne L. Restad, *Christmas in America* (New York: 1995), p. 63.

27. Martyne Perrot, "Noël, de l'Enfant Quêter à l'Enfant Gâté," *Ethnologies* 29, 2007, p. 286.

28. "The Season," *Friends' Intelligencer*, January 3, 1846, reprinted in Alfred Lewis Shoemaker, *Christmas in Pennsylvania: A Folk-cultural Study* (Mechanicsburg, PA: 1959), p. xviii.

29. Katharine Lambert Richards, *How Christmas Came to the Sunday Schools* (New York: 1934), pp. 68–69; Alfred Lewis Shoemaker, *Christmas in Pennsylvania: A Folk-Cultural Study* (Mechanicsburg, PA: 2009), p. 8; Loyal Jones, "Christmas and Old Christmas in Appalachia," in *A Kentucky Christmas*, ed. George Ella Lyon

(Lexington, KY: 2012), p. 34; Cindy Dell Clark, *Flights of Fancy, Leaps of Faith: Children's Myths in Contemporary America* (Chicago: 1998), p. 24; Restad, *Christmas in America*, p. 41.

30. "Christmas Day," *Sabbath School Visiter* (Massachusetts Sabbath School Society, Boston) 7, 1839, pp. 277–278.

31. Tommy R. Thompson, "Angels and Dollars: One Hundred Years of Christmas in Sioux Falls," *South Dakota History* 26, no. 4, 1996, p. 198.

32. Richards, *How Christmas Came to the Sunday Schools*, p. 145; Thomas Eggleton, "The House of Santa Claus," *Indiana School Journal* 23, no. 12, December 1878, p. 516.

33. "Christmas," *Evangelical Repository and United Presbyterian Worker*, February 1875, pp. 385–391; "A Note from a Correspondent," *Evangelical Repository and United Presbyterian Worker*, March 1879, p. 462.

34. Richards, *How Christmas Came to the Sunday Schools*, p. 220.

35. Gerald Parsons, ed., *Religion in Victorian Britain: Traditions*, vol. 1 (Manchester: 1988), p. 6; Neil Armstrong, "The Christmas Season and the Protestant Churches in England, c. 1870–1914," *Journal of Ecclesiastical History* 62, no. 4, October 2011, p. 745.

36. Edmund Gosse, *Father and Son* (Oxford: 2004), p. 69.

37. Denis G. Paz, *Popular Anti-Catholicism in Mid-Victorian England* (Palo Alto: 1992), p. 132; P. L. Wickins, *Victorian Protestantism and Bloody Mary: The Legacy of Religious Persecution in Tudor England* (Bury St. Edmunds: 2012).

38. Nigel Yates, *Anglican Ritualism in Victorian Britain: 1830–1910* (Oxford: 1999), pp. 170, 218, 316, 364.

39. "Christmas Tide," *New York Times*, December 25, 1853, p. 3; Gillian Avery, *Behold the Child: American Children and Their Books 1621–1922* (Baltimore: 1994), p. 68; Elizabeth Hafkin Pleck, *Celebrating the Family: Ethnicity, Consumer Culture, and Family Rituals* (Cambridge, MA: 2000), p. 50.

40. "Santa's Dying Note," *Life*, December 23, 1897, p. 555.

41. George Bernard Shaw, "No Music at Christmas," December 20, 1893, in *Music in London 1890–94* (London: 1950), p. 119.

42. *Ladies' Home Journal*, December 1891, p. 19.

43. Armstrong, *Christmas in Nineteenth Century England*, p. 18; Bowler, *Santa Claus*, pp. 65–67; Thomas Hine, *I Want That: How We All Became Shoppers* (New York: 2002), p. 177.

44. Susan J. Matt, "Children's Envy and the Emergence of a Modern Consumer Ethic, 1890–1930," *Journal of Social History* 36, no. 2, Winter 2002, pp. 283–302; Ellis P. Butler, "Something for the Kid," *Cosmopolitan*, January 1911, quoted in William B. Waits, *The Modern Christmas in America* (New York: 1993), pp. 126, 172–173; Stephen Leacock, "The Errors of Christmas," *Puck*, December 2, 1916, p. 17.

45. Waits, *Modern Christmas in America*, p. 71.

46. Bowler, *The World Encyclopedia of Christmas* (Toronto: 2000), p. 206; William L. O'Neill, *The Woman Movement: Feminism in the United States and England* (Abingdon, UK: 2013).

47. John R. Gillis, *A World of Their Own Making: Myth, Ritual, and the Quest for Family Values* (Cambridge, MA: 1997), pp. 99–101.

48. T. R. Right, "Positively Catholic: Malcolm Quin's Church of Humanity in Newcastle-upon-Tyne," *Durham University Journal* 75, June 1983, p. 17.

49. Jacqueline Lalouette, "Noël: Une fête humaine et païenne pour les libres penseurs," in *La Nativité et le temps de Noël (XVIIe–XXe siècle)*, ed. Régis Bertrand (Paris: 2003), pp. 170–173; Elinor Accampo, *Blessed Motherhood, Bitter Fruit: Nelly Roussel and the Politics of Female Pain in Third Republic France* (Baltimore: 2006), p. 224.

50. There were many Chartists who took both Christianity and social reform seriously. While some remained in their traditional denominations, others started overtly Chartist churches. "Christian Chartist Churches," *Chartist Circular*, October 17, 1840, p. 226.

51. Gregory Claeys, *Citizens and Saints: Politics and Anti-politics in Early British Socialism* (Cambridge: 2002), p. 91; Barbara Taylor, *Eve and the New Jerusalem: Socialism and Feminism in the Nineteenth Century* (London: 1983), p. 43.

52. Linda K. Hughes, *The Cambridge Introduction to Victorian Poetry* (Cambridge: 2010), pp. 72–73.

53. Ian Heywood, "The Retailoring of Dickens: *Christmas Shadows*, Radicalism and the Needlewoman Myth," in Harris, *Famine and Fashion*, p. 67.

54. S.M., "Hymn Fourth," in *The National Chartist Hymn Book* (Rochdale, UK: 1845), p. 5, https://www.calderdale.gov.uk/wtw/search/controlservlet?PageId=Zoom&DocId=102253&PageNo=4.

55. *Northern Star*, May 21, 1842, quoted in Mike Sanders, *The Poetry of Chartism: Aesthetics, Politics, History* (Cambridge: 2009), p. 161; Taylor, *Eve and the New Jerusalem*, p. 136.

56. Eileen Yeo, "Robert Owen and Radical Culture," in *Robert Owen, Prophet of the Poor: Essays in Honour of the Two Hundredth Anniversary of His Birth*, ed. Sidney Pollard and John Salt (London: 1971), pp. 95–100.

57. Edward Royle, *Radicals, Secularists, and Republicans: Popular Freethought in Britain, 1866–1915* (Manchester, UK: 1980), p. 140, http://www.leicestersecularsociety .org.uk/hymns.htm#S31. This particular hymn does not seem to be of atheist origin, as it appeared in British and American newspapers earlier in the decade.

58. Edward Bellamy, "Christmas in the Year 2000," *Ladies' Home Journal*, January 12, 1895, p. 6.

59. "Christmas Day: A Hundred Years Hence," *Chicago Sunday Tribune*, December 23, 1900.

CHAPTER III: THE TYRANTS

1. V. I. Lenin, "The Attitude of the Workers' Party to Religion," in *Lenin Collected Works*, vol. 15 (Moscow: 1973), p. 402; Alexander N. Yakovlev, *A Century of Violence in Soviet Russia* (New Haven: 2002), p. 157.

2. Dmitri Volkogonov, *Trotsky: The Eternal Revolutionary* (New York: 2007), p. 227; Beryl Williams, *Lenin* (London: 2014), p. 153.

3. William B. Husband, "Soviet Atheism and Russian Orthodox Strategies of Resistance, 1917–1932," *Journal of Modern History* 70, no. 1, 1998, p. 99.

4. In the Orthodox Church, Christmas is celebrated on December 25, but according to the Julian calendar; the Soviet state (and most of the rest of the world) followed the Gregorian calendar, which in the twentieth century differed by thirteen days.

5. Michael Burleigh, *Sacred Causes: The Clash of Religion and Politics from the Great War to the War on Terror* (New York: 2007), p. 50.

6. James von Geldern, *Bolshevik Festivals* (Oakland: 1993), p. 217; Glennys Young, *Power and the Sacred in Revolutionary Russia: Religious Activists in the Village* (College Park: 1997); Richard Stites, "Bolshevik Ritual Building in the 1920s," in *Russia in the Era of NEP: Explorations in Soviet Society and Culture*, ed. Sheila Fitzpatrick, Alexander Rabinowitch, and Richard Stites (Bloomington: 1991), p. 297.

7. Daniel Peris, *Storming the Heavens: The Soviet League of the Militant Godless* (Ithaca: 1998), pp. 39–40; Felicity Anne O'Dell, *Socialisation through Children's Literature: The Soviet Example* (Cambridge: 1978), pp. 12–13.

8. Nicholas Slonimsky, "Soviet Music and Musicians," *Slavonic and East European Review* 22, December 1944, p. 5.

9. Ironically, the Christmas evergreen had been banned by the Russian Orthodox Church in 1916 in the midst of World War I for being a "Germanic" symbol.

10. Catriona Kelly, *Children's World: Growing Up in Russia, 1890–1991* (New Haven: 2007), p. 75.

11. Peris, *Storming the Heavens*, p. 87; Karen Petrone, *Life Has Become More Joyous, Comrades* (Bloomington: 2000), 86.

12. Jukka Gronow, *Caviar with Champagne: Common Luxury and the Ideals of the Good Life in the Soviet Union* (Oxford: 2003), p. 36; Peris, *Storming the Heavens*, p. 84; Robert C. Tucker, *Stalin in Power: The Revolution from Above 1928–1941* (New York: 1992), p. 327; Jeffrey Brooks, *Thank You, Comrade Stalin! Soviet Public Culture from the Revolution to Cold War* (Princeton: 2000), xv.

13. Sigrid Rausing, *History, Memory and Identity in Post-Soviet Estonia* (Oxford: 2004), p. 65.

14. Jan Tomasz Gross, *Revolution from Abroad: The Soviet Conquest of Poland's Western Ukraine and Western Belorussia* (Princeton: 2002), pp. 132, 328–329.

15. "Santa's Sub," *Washington Post*, December 18, 1949, p. B4.

16. Sabina Pauta Pieslak, "'Lenin in Swaddling Clothes': A Critique of the Ideological Conflict between Socialist State Policy and Christian Music in Cold War Romania," *Current Musicology* 78, Fall 2004, pp. 7–30.

17. Andrew Roberts, *From Good King Wenceslas to the Good Soldier Švejk: A Dictionary of Czech Popular Culture* (Budapest: 2005), p. 32; Nike K. Pokom, *Post-socialist Translation Practices: Ideological Struggle in Children's Literature* (Philadelphia: 2012), p. 47; Edwin E. Jacques, *The Albanians* (Jefferson, NC: 1995), pp. 564–564; Vivian H. H. Green, *A New History of Christianity* (London: 2000), p. 365; "East Bloc's Santa Exiled by Russian," *New York Times*, December 25, 1952, p. 20.

18. Dunja Rihtman-Augustin, *Christmas in Croatia* (Zagreb: 1997), p. 203.

19. Joe Perry, *Christmas in Germany: A Cultural History* (Chapel Hill: 2010), p. 276.

20. Perry, *Christmas in Germany*, pp. 259–261; Judith Breuer and Rita Beuer, *Von wegen Heilige Nacht! Das Weihnachtsfest in der politischen Propaganda* (Mühlheim an der Ruhr: 2000), pp. 195–199.

21. Rihtman-Augustin, *Christmas in Croatia*, p. 201.

22. Fenggang Yang, *Religion in China: Survival and Revival under Communist Rule* (New York: 2011), pp. 99–101.

23. Steve J. Stern, *Shining and Other Paths: War and Society in Peru, 1980–1995* (Durham: 1998), pp. 175–176.

24. Elizabeth F. Ralph, "The World War on Christmas: Five Places Where Santa Really Does Have to Watch His Back," *Foreign Policy*, December 24, 2012, http://foreignpolicy.com/2012/12/24/the-world-war-on-christmas/; Gustavo Coronel, "Chavenomics: The Chávez Answer to Milton Friedman," November 19, 2006, https://espanol.groups.yahoo.com/neo/groups/UPLA-VEN_Opinion/conversations/messages/31174; Paul E. Sigmund, *Liberation Theology at the Crossroads: Democracy or Revolution?* (New York: 1990), p. 125; for the Spanish text and translation of the carol, see http://www.sfbach.org/text-cristo-de-palacagüina.

25. H. James Burgwyn, *Mussolini Warlord: Failed Dreams of Empire, 1940–1943* (New York: 2012), p. 132.

26. Victoria De Grazia, *The Culture of Consent: Mass Organisation of Leisure in Fascist Italy* (Cambridge: 2002), p. 214; "The Forbidden Tree," *Catholic Herald*, December 20, 1935, p. 10.

27. Michael R. Ebner, *Ordinary Violence in Mussolini's Italy* (Cambridge: 2011), p. 225.

28. R. J. B. Bosworth, *Mussolini's Italy: Life under the Dictatorship, 1915–1945* (London: 2006), p. 291.

29. Joe Perry's *Christmas in Germany: A Cultural History* (Chapel Hill: 2010) is a penetrating look at how "German Christmas" was seen, particularly by the middle class, to be an essential part of the national soul.

30. Perry, *Christmas in Germany*, 182–183; Breuer and Breuer, *Von wegen Heilige Nacht*, p. 57.

31. "Deutsche, kauft nur bei Juden!," in *Der Angriff. Aufsätze aus der Kampfzeit* (Munich: 1935), pp. 331–333, German Propaganda Archive, www.calvin.edu/academic/cas/gpa/angrif10.htm.

32. "Weihnacht 1931," in *Wetterleuchten. Aufsätze aus der Kampfzeit* (Munich: 1939), pp. 241–242, German Propaganda Archive, http://www.calvin.edu/academic/cas/gpa/angrif14.htm.

33. Bowler, *Santa Claus: A Biography* (Toronto: 2005), p. 263; Esther Gajek, "Christmas under the Third Reich," *Anthropology Today* 6, no. 4, August 1990, p. 4; Rainer Stollman and Ronald L. Smith, "Fascist Politics as a Total Work of Art: Tendencies of the Aesthetization of Political Life in National Socialism," *New German Critique* 14, Spring 1978, p. 43.

34. Brian Moynahan, *The Faith: A History of Christianity* (New York: 2002), p. 681. Horst Wessel was a pimp and a Nazi storm trooper who was murdered in 1930 in mysterious circumstances. He was the author of a famous National Socialist anthem and was treated as a martyr by the party; Lionel Gossman, *Brownshirt Princess: A Study of the "Nazi Conscience"* (Cambridge: 2009), p. 154, n. 8.

35. Perry, *Christmas in Germany*, p. 193.

36. Doris L. Bergen, *Twisted Cross: The German Christian Movement in the Third Reich* (Chapel Hill: 1996), pp. 34–35, 50.

37. Roger Moorhouse, *Berlin at War* (New York: 2010), p. 541.

38. Nicholas Lewin, *Jung on War, Politics and Nazi Germany: Exploring the Theory of Archetypes and the Collective Unconscious* (London: 2009), p. 198; Perry, *Christmas in Germany*, p. 251.

39. "National Socialist Christmas," *Tablet*, December 25 1937, p. 14.

40. Richard Bonney, *Confronting the Nazi War on Christianity: The Kulturkampf Newsletters, 1936–1939* (Berne: 2009), p. 473; Ralph Thurston, "Under the Nazi Christmas Tree," *New Republic*, December 25, 1935, p. 193.

41. Richard Evans, *The Third Reich in Power* (Harmondsworth: 2006), p. 252.

42. Hannes Kremer, "Neuwertung 'überlieferter' Brauchformen?," in *Die neue Gemeinschaft* 3, 1937, pp. 3005a–c, translated as "New Meanings for Inherited Customs," German Propaganda Archive, http://www.calvin.edu/academic/cas/gpa/feier37.htm; Wilhelm Beilstein, "How We Celebrate Christmas," December 1939, translated in German Propaganda Archive, http://www.bytwerk.com/gpa/christmas1939.htm.

43. Fritz Weitzel, *Die Gestaltung der Feste im Jahres und Lebenslauf in der SS Familie* (1938), translated as "Celebrations in the Life of the S.S. Family," http://web-zoom.freewebs.com/spiritualwarfare666/The%20SS%20Family.pdf.

44. Hauptkulturamt in der Reichspropagandaleitung, *Deutsche Kriegsweihnacht* (Munich: 1941), p. 47; and Oberkommando der Wehrmacht Abteilung Inland, *Soldatenblätter für Feier und Freizeit* (Leipzig: 1940–44); Hauptkulturamt in der Reichspropagandaleitung, *Vorweihnachten* (Munich: 1942–44), p. 18a.

45. Helmut Krausnick, "*Soldatenblätter* und Weihnachtsfest: Ein Briefweschel," *Vierteljahrshefte für Zeitgeschichte* 5, no. 3, July 1957, pp. 297–299.

46. Joe Perry, "The Madonna of Stalingrad: Mastering the (Christmas) Past and West German National Identity after World War II," *Radical History Review* 83, Spring 2002, pp. 7–27.

47. Earl R. Beck, *Under the Bombs: The German Home Front 1942–1945* (Lexington, KY: 1986), pp. 18, 104–105.

48. Götz Aly, *Hitler's Beneficiaries: Plunder, Racial War, and the Nazi Welfare State* (London: 2008), p. 133.

49. Elizabeth Harvey, *Women and the Nazi East: Agents and Witnesses of Germanization* (New Haven: 2005), p. 270.

CHAPTER IV: THE GODLY AND THE GODLESS

1. Phil Zuckerman, *Society without God: What the Least Religious Nations Can Tell Us about Contentment* (London: 2008), p. 148. Berger has since come to recant that opinion. Steve Bruce, "The Curious Case of the Unnecessary Recantation: Berger and Secularization," in *Peter Berger and the Study of Religion*, ed. Paul Heelas, David Martin, and Linda Woodhead (Abingdon, UK: 2013), p. 86.

2. David C. Bailey, *Viva Cristo Rey!: The Cristero Rebellion and the Church-State Conflict in Mexico* (Austin: 2013).

3. Phil Zuckerman, ed., *Atheism and Secularity*, vol. 2 (Santa Barbara: 2009), p. 55.

4. Numbers range from 20 million to 150 million. Gary Sigley, "A Chinese Christmas Story," in *Discourse as Cultural Struggle*, ed. Shi-xu (Hong Kong: 2007), pp. 91–104; Tom Phillips, "China on Course to Become 'World's Most Christian Nation' within 15 Years," *Daily Telegraph*, April 19, 2014, http://www.telegraph.co.uk/news/worldnews/asia/china/10776023/China-on-course-to-become-worlds-most-Christian-nation-within-15-years.html.

5. Barbara Bradley Hagerty, "A Bitter Rift Divides Atheists," *Morning Edition*, National Public Radio, October 19, 2009, http://www.npr.org/templates/story/story.php?storyId=113889251.

6. Sam Harris, "Science Must Destroy Religion," *Huffington Post*, May 25, 2011, http://www.huffingtonpost.com/sam-harris/science-must-destroy-reli_b_13153.html.

7. "I think we should stop talking of 'parental rights' at all. In so far as they compromise the child's rights as an individual, parents' rights have no status in ethics and should have none in law." Nichols Humphrey, "What Shall We Tell the Children?," Amnesty Lecture, Oxford, February 21, 1997; PZ Myers, "It's a Frackin' Cracker," July 8, 2008, http://scienceblogs.com/pharyngula/2008/07/08/its-a-goddamned-cracker/; PZ Myers, "The Great Desecration," July 24, 2008, http://scienceblogs.com/pharyngula/2008/07/24/the-great-desecration/; Rob Copper, "Forcing a Religion on Your Children Is as Bad as Child Abuse,

Claims Atheist Professor Richard Dawkins," *Daily Mail,* April 22, 2013, http://www.dailymail.co.uk/news/article-2312813/Richard-Dawkins-Forcing-religion-children-child-abuse-claims-atheist-professor.html; http://www.the-brights.net.

8. See "The New Atheists," https://web.archive.org/web/20160106121854/http://newatheists.org/.

9. Jim Gilliam, "The War on Christmas Escalates," December 5, 2005, http://www.jimgilliam.com/2005/12/the_war_on_christmas_escalates.php.

10. Ian Urbina, "Approaching Holidays Prompt Atheist Campaign," *New York Times,* December 1, 2009, http://www.nytimes.com/2009/12/02/us/02atheist.html?_r=0.

11. Tom Flynn, *The Trouble with Christmas* (New York: 1993); see also Flynn, "The Real War on Christmas," *Point of Inquiry* (podcast), December 22, 2006, http://www.pointofinquiry.org/tom_flynn_the_real_war_on_christmas/.

12. Flynn, *Trouble with Christmas,* p. 147.

13. See http://www.festivusbook.com; http://festivusweb.com/festivus-songs-carols.htm.

14. Stephanie Merritt, "O Come All Ye Non-faithful, and Rejoice in Science," *Guardian,* December 6, 2009, http://www.theguardian.com/culture/2009/dec/06/robin-ince-comedy-christmas/print.

15. Rod Gompertz, *Chrismukkah: Everything You Need to Know about the Hybrid Holiday* (New York: 2006).

16. See http://www.Humanlight.org.

17. In Linda LaScola, "12 Days of Atheist Christmas Extravaganza—Day 1," Rational Doubt, Atheist Channel, Patheos, http://www.patheos.com/blogs/rational-doubt/2014/12/atheists-love-christmas-too/#sthash.zShJDzNP.dpuf.

18. "Atheist Christmas Carol Winners, Blag Hag (blog), November 2, 2010, http://freethoughtblogs.com/blaghag.com/2010/11/atheist-christmas-carol-contest-winners.html. The "Jen" referred to is atheist Jen McCreight, whose blog featured the winners. "Harris" is philosopher Sam Harris, author of *The End of Faith.*

19. "God Rest Ye Unitarians" (1997), http://rationalwiki.org/wiki/Unitarian_Universalism.

20. "Atheists Upset at 'A Charlie Brown Christmas' Church Field Trip," *Digital Journal,* November 21, 2012, http://www.digitaljournal.com/article/337410#ixzz2dDfJHip7.

21. Molly Shen, "Christmas Tree Controversy," *Free Republic,* December 16, 2004, http://www.freerepublic.com/focus/news/1303003/posts?page=35; Michael Dorstewitz, "School Cancels Christmas Toy Drive over Anti-religious Group's Lawsuit Threat," November 16, 2013, BizPac Review, http://www.bizpacreview.com/2013/11/16/school-cancels-christmas-toy-drive-over-anti-religious-groups-lawsuit-threat-87245;http://americanhumanist.org/HNN/details/2013-11-legal-victory-south-carolina-public-school-cuts-ties.

22. Adam Harrington, "Furor Erupts over Atheist Display at State Capitol," December 23, 2009, Pluralism Project, http://pluralism.org/news/furor-erupts-over-atheist-display-at-state-capitol/.

23. Lara Brenckle, "Chambersburg Bans Town-Square Displays over Non-Christian Request," PennLive, December 25, 2009, http://www.pennlive.com/midstate/index.ssf/2009/11/chambersburg_bans_town-square.html.

24. Guy Adams, "Santa Monica's Angry Atheists Declare a Real War on Christmas," *Independent*, December 15, 2011, http://www.independent.co.uk/news/world/americas/santa-monicas-angry-atheists-declare-a-real-war-on-christmas-6276970.html; Kathleen Miles, "Santa Monica Nativity Scene Ban Results from Atheist Controversy," *Huffington Post*, June 13, 2012, http://www.huffingtonpost.com/2012/06/13/santa-monica-nativity-scene_n_1595031.html.

25. Raven Clabough, "Atheists Continue War on Christmas," December 13, 2011, New American, http://www.thenewamerican.com/culture/faith-and-morals/item/1074-atheists-continue-war-on-christmas; "FFRF Places 'Natural Nativity,' Winter Solstice Sign in Wisconsin Capitol," December 2, 2013, Freedom From Religion Foundation, http://ffrf.org/news/news-releases/item/19547-ffrf-places-'natural-nativity'-winter-solstice-sign-in-wisconsin-capitol.

26. "'Good without God': Nebraska Atheists Take Over Nativity to Promote Tolerance," *Guardian*, December 12, 2015, http://www.theguardian.com/us-news/2015/dec/12/nebraska-atheists-humanists-nativity-lincoln-christmas.

27. Dan Kedmey, "Atheist Organization Decks Billboards with Christmas Jeer," *Time*, December 18, 2012, http://time.com/3635817/atheist-billboards-christmas-jeer/; David Roach, "Atheist Billboards: Christmas a 'Fairy Tale,'" *Baptist Press*, December 9, 2014, http://www.bpnews.net/43885/atheist-billboards-christmas-a-fairy-tale; Kimberly Winston, "Newest Front in 'Christmas Wars': Billboards," *Sojourners*, December 18, 2012, http://sojo.net/blogs/2012/12/18/newest-front-christmas-wars-billboards.

28. "Missing Jesus 2," December 19, 2008, https://www.youtube.com/watch?v=fHCS3JFYKF8.

29. Bill Donohue, "Los Angeles Christmas Billboard," December 3, 2014, Catholic League for Religious and Civil Rights, http://www.catholicleague.org/los-angeles-christmas-billboard/; Amy Unrau, "Wadena Rallies with over 1000 Nativity Scenes after Council Removes One from Park," December 8, 2015, WDAY, http://www.wday.com/news/3899427-wadena-rallies-over-1000-nativity-scenes-after-council-removes-one-park.

30. The online marketer cafepress.com claims to have 5,980 atheist Christmas designs.

31. Valerie Richardson, "Yes, Virginia, There Is a 'War on Christmas': Atheists Unveil Anti-Christmas TV Specials," *Washington Times*, December 17, 2014, http://www.washingtontimes.com/news/2014/dec/17/war-christmas-atheists-unveil-anti-christmas-tv-sp/.

32. Christopher Hitchens, "The Horror of Christmas in a One-Party State," December 20, 2005, *Slate*, http://www.slate.com/id/2132806/?nav=ais. To be fair to Hitchens, he was a multidenominational hater of religious holidays. For his scorching attack on Hanukkah, see Christopher Hitchens, "Bah Hanukkah," *Slate*, December 3, 2007, http://www.slate.com/articles/news_and_politics/fighting_words/2007/12/bah_hanukkah.html.

33. See chapter 2.

34. Anti-Trinitarians, including Jehovah's Witnesses, the Restored Church of God, and the followers of Garner Ted Armstrong's International Church of God, have a theological problem with celebrating the nativity of Jesus.

35. Brian Schwertley, "The Regulative Principle of Worship and Christmas," Still Water Revival Books, http://www.swrb.com/newslett/actualNLs/christmas.htm.

36. Kevin Reed, "Christmas: An Historical Survey Regarding Its Origins and Opposition to It," Still Water Revival Books, http://www.swrb.com/newslett/actualNLs/Xmas_ch2.htm. The quote is from George Gillespie, *A Dispute Against the English Popish Ceremonies Obtruded Upon the Church of Scotland*, sec. 1 (1637).

37. A. W. Pink, "Xmas," Still Water Revival Books, http://www.swrb.com/newslett/actualNLs/christmas-awpink.htm.

38. Robin Main, *Santa-tizing* (Maitland, FL: 2008). The reliability of Main's self-published scholarship may be in some doubt, as she cites Dan Brown's novel *The Da Vinci Code* as one of her sources.

39. Lorraine Day, "Christmas: Is It 'Christian' or 'Pagan'?," http://www.goodnews-aboutgod.com/studies/holidays2.htm. Dr. Day also rips the veil of paganism from the celebration of Easter, Valentine's Day, and Halloween.

40. "Volume Five of the X-Mas Files," Truth on the Web Ministries, http://www.truthontheweb.org/xmasvol5.htm.

41. *Balaam's Ass Speaks: A Journal* (blog), balaams.com/journal/balaam.htm, accessed January 8, 1999.

42. James Dodson et al., *Protestant HoHo (i.e. Christmass Carols)* (Edmonton: Still Water Revival Books, 1995).

43. Gary Greenberg, "Just Say Nothing," *Legal Affairs*, May/June 2004, http://www.legalaffairs.org/issues/May-June-2004/story_greenberg_mayjun04.msp.

44. Michael Schneider, "Is Christmas Christian?," Invisible Church, http://www.theinvisiblechurch.ca/miscellany/Is_Christmas_Christian.html.

45. Martin Gardner, *The Annotated Night before Christmas* (New York: 1991), p. 34.

46. "Santa Claus Is Satan," Messianic Evangelicals, http://www.nccg.org/595Art-Santa.html.

47. "Santa Claus Hanged in Effigy," *Daytona Beach Morning Journal*, December 19, 1980, A6; "Church Burns Easter Bunny," *Washington (PA) Observer-Reporter*, April 21, 1981, A9.

48. "Danish Church Hanged Santa to Forsake the Devil," News That Matters, December 9, 2010, http://ivarfjeld.com/2011/11/28/danish-church-hanged-santa-to-forsake-the-devil/; "Danish Priest Hangs 'Elf' from Gallows outside His Church, Saying They Must Not Be Associated with Christmas as They Serve Satan," *Daily Mail*, December 19, 2013, http://www.dailymail.co.uk/news/article-2526438/Priest-HANGS-elf-gallows-outside-church-saying-not-associated-Christmas-serve-Satan.html.

49. Anonymous, "The Light before Christmas," website of Still Water Revival Books, http://www.swrb.com/newslett/actualNLs/HoHoSong.htm.

50. To see a children's chorus belt out this heartwarming ballad, visit "Westboro Baptist Church: Santa Claus Will Take You to Hell," posted by "UnreportedResistance," December 23, 2008, http://www.youtube.com/watch?v=o-l8iqevaoU.

51. http://www.godhatesfags.com/featured/epics/20051221_junction-city-ks-epic .pdf (link no longer live), accessed January 18, 2006.

52. The first sentence of their manifesto gives an indication of their rejection of the rest of Christendom: "In this hour of general apostasy—when the brethren of our Lord (on every hand) are committing themselves in unholy unions with infidels, when the table of the Lord is turned into the table of devils and the temple of God to a house of idols, when pastors, churches and professors define (and approve of) salvation and church behavior different from the book of Acts and the epistles of the New Testament, when there is more leaven in the church than there is sincerity and truth, when the faithful are scattered upon the desolate hills of hopelessness as sheep without a shepherd, when the wicked lift their unholy hands in our assemblies to praise a holy God, and no one thinks twice, no one considers their way—in this hour, I say, it is meet for those whom God has risen up as salt and light, so to salt the corruptions of their generation, and to turn the lights on in that great bedroom of adulteries (*i.e.* the professing church), if perhaps God would be pleased indeed to stem the tide, seal the breach, and resurrect His standard of righteousness which has long lain without a Church to bear it." "Our Manifesto," Church of Wells, http://www .thechurchofwells.com/our-manifesto.html.

53. Sean Morris, "The Abominable Sacrifice to Santa Clause," Church of Wells, http:// www.thechurchofwells.com/the-abominable-sacrifice-to-santa-clause.html.

54. Sean Morris, "Xmas Day Wake Up Call," Church of Wells, http://www .thechurchofwells.com/xmas-day-wake-up-call.html.

55. Jordan Fraker, "Xmas," Church of Wells, http://www.thechurchofwells.com/ xmas.html.

56. See Sean Morris, "Seven Lessons—Ten Sins—Three Threats—Many Dead," A Case against Christmas, http://www.xmasexposed.com/uploads/5/9/9/1/5991751/ a_case_against_xmas.pdf, pp. 8–29.

57. Sean Morris, "The Pagan Origins of Christmas," A Case against Christmas, http://www.xmasexposed.com/uploads/5/9/9/1/5991751/a_case_against_xmas.pdf, p. 32.

58. Morris, "Pagan Origins of Christmas," p. 34.

59. "Christmas," Israel United in Christ, http://israelunite.org/christmas/.

60. Elder Nathanyel, "Megan Kelly's Views Are Typical of Racist America," http://israelunite.org/megyn-kellys-views-are-typical-of-racist-america/. The same webpage notes that Jesus was olive-colored and that olives "come in three colors green, brown and Black, please pick one."

61. "Pagan Holiday," http://www.israelitesunite.com/pagan-holidays.html. Grammatical infelicities as in the original.

62. Izarya-Nathan, "What's the Real Reason for the Season?," Israelite Church of God in Jesus Christ Inc., http://www.theholyconceptionunit.org/main/modules.php?op=modload&name=News&file=article&sid=57.

63. "Holidays or Holy Days" (2001), United Church of God, http://www.ucg.org/bible-study-tools/booklets/holidays-or-holy-days-does-it-matter-which-days-we-observe. Atheist Tom Flynn, the archenemy of Christmas, would be delighted to learn that he is a prime resource cited by this pamphlet.

64. J. Gordon Melton and Martin Baumann, eds., *Religions of the World: A Comprehensive Encyclopedia of Beliefs and Practices* (Santa Barbara: 2010), p. 2211.

65. Leigh Eric Schmidt, *Consumer Rites: The Buying and Selling of American Holidays* (Princeton: 1995), pp. 188–189.

66. "Santa Now a 'Sugar Daddy,' Not Saint, Catholic Editor Says," *Washington Post*, December 16, 1949, p. 1. Jupiter and Baal were ancient pagan gods; Harvey was an imaginary eight-foot rabbit in a movie starring Jimmy Stewart; and the fairy godfather was a character in "Barnaby," a popular comic strip by Crockett Johnson.

67. Mark Connelly, *Christmas at the Movies: Images of Christmas in American, British and European Cinema* (London: 2000), p. 166.

68. "Burn Santa in Effigy," *Milwaukee Journal*, December 24, 1951, p. 2; Claude Lévi-Strauss, *Le Père Noël Supplicié* (Paris: 1952), p. 11; Martyne Perrot, *Noël* (Paris: 2003), p. 49.

69. "Des jeunes catholiques brulent le père Noel," http://www.dailymotion.com/video/xg4pce_des-jeunes-catholiques-brulent-le-pere-noel_webcam#.UNSf5HenNF9; Benedict XVI, "Angelus," December 11, 2005, http://www.vatican.va/holy_father/benedict_xvi/angelus/2005/documents/hf_ben-xvi_ang_20051211_en.html.

70. Rowan Williams, "Advent Video," http://rowanwilliams.archbishopofcanterbury.org/pages/advent-video.html; "Reclaim Christmas," Operation Noah, http://operationnoah.org/resources/reclaim-christmas/.

71. Martyn Percy, "The Church in the Market Place: Advertising and Religion in a Secular Age," *Journal of Contemporary Religion* 15, no. 1, 2000, p. 98.

72. Gary Miedema, *For Canada's Sake: Public Religion, Centennial Celebrations, and the Re-making of Canada in the 1960s* (Montreal: 2005), p. 50.

73. Ari L. Goldman, "A Christmas Plea on the 'Lords' of Commerce," *New York Times,* November 29, 1992, http://www.nytimes.com/1992/11/29/us/a-christmas-plea-on-the-lords-of-commerce.html.

74. Richard John Neuhaus, "The Couture of the Public Square," *First Things,* December 1993, http://www.firstthings.com/article/1993/12/the-couture-of-the-public-square.

75. Ray Lilley, "Controversial Billboard of Joseph and Mary in Bed: God 'A Hard Act to Follow,'" February 9, 2010, Progressive Christianity, http://progressivechristianity .org/2010/02/09/controversial-billboard-of-joseph-and-mary-in-bed-god-a-hard-act-to-follow/; "Virgin Mary's Surprise Pregnancy Test in Billboard a Shocker," *Toronto Star,* December 16, 2011, http://www.thestar.com/news/world/2011/12/16/ virgin_marys_surprise_pregnancy_test_in_billboard_a_shocker.html; "Jesus was 'Gay'! Church Sparks Outrage with Claim Son of God 'Should Come Out,'" *Daily Mail,* December 17, 2012, http://www.dailymail.co.uk/news/article-2249387/ Jesus-gay-Church-sparks-outrage-claim-son-God-come-out.html#ixzz2lJhH4Xhr; "Christmas Billboard Portrays God's 'Selfie,'" *Scoop,* December 19, 2013, http:// www.scoop.co.nz/stories/CU1312/S00386/christmas-billboard-portrays-gods-selfie.htm; Micheal Sergel, "Church Shocks with Controversial Refugee Billboard," December 5, 2013, Newstalk ZB, http://www.newstalkzb.co.nz/news/national/ church-shocks-with-controversial-refugee-billboard/.

76. Christina Rossetti, "In the Bleak Midwinter" (1872), lines 17–20, http://www .poetryfoundation.org/poem/238450.

77. Bill McKibben, "Christmas Unplugged," *Christianity Today,* December 9, 1996, http://www.christianitytoday.com/ct/1996/december9/6te18a.html.

78. "Ten Tips for a Simpler, More Meaningful Christmas," http://simpleliving.start-logic.com/indexoth.php?place=xb/PromoKit.php. Note the gender-sensitive use of "Wise Ones" instead of "Wise Men."

79. Bill McKibben, *Hundred Dollar Holiday: The Case for a More Joyful Christmas* (New York: 1998), p. 11.

80. McKibben, "Christmas Unplugged."

81. See adventconspiracy.org.

82. Aiden Enns, "Why Christians Should Resist Black Friday," *Washington Post,* November 24, 2011, http://buynothingchristmas.org/media/washpost-enns.html.

83. Erica Avery (lyrics), "Buy Nothing Christmas 2005" (song sheet); hear it sung by Santas at http://funnygiftsformen35.blogspot.com/2012/02/santas-against-excessive-consumption.html.

84. "What do you have against capitalism?," FAQ, About Us, Buy Nothing Christmas, http://buynothingchristmas.org/about/index.html#7.

85. See the website revbilly.com; *What Would Jesus Buy: Fabulous Prayers in the Face of the Shopacalypse* (New York: 2006), p. 172.

86. Joanna Moorhead, "Move Over Jesus, Santa's Coming to Town," *Guardian,* December 20, 2000, http://www.theguardian.com/lifeandstyle/2000/dec/20/

familyandrelationships.joannamoorhead; "Jesus Gets Jealous of Santa Claus" was written by Keith Urban and Vernon Rust; "The Night Jesus Met Santa Claus" was written by Rob Saranpa; see performance by Ricky Traywick, posted by "nohawkrob," April 5, 2011, https://www.youtube.com/watch?v=dbJAKpIFmBc.

87. "The Kneeling Santa," http://www.catholicsupply.com/christmas/kneelsanta.html.

88. Chris Hastings and Danielle Demetrious, "Church Backs St Nicholas in Move to Give Santa the Sack," *Telegraph*, December 17, 2000, http://www.telegraph .co.uk/news/uknews/1378547/Church-backs-St-Nicholas-in-move-to-give-Santa-the-sack.html; St. Nicholas Center website, stnicholascenter.org.

89. "Assen Won't Begin to Look a Lot Like Western Christmas," *Reading (PA) Eagle*, November 16, 1993, p. 4.

90. Perrot, *Noël*, p. 10.

91. Kathleen Stokker, *Folklore Fights the Nazis: Humor in Occupied Norway, 1940–1945* (Madison: 1995), pp. 93–95. For much more on the use of magical Christmas Gift-Bringers in wartime, see "Santa the Warrior," in Bowler, *Santa Claus: A Biography* (Toronto: 2005), pp. 113–146.

92. "Natal Made in Brazil," *Revista de História*, September 9, 2007, http://www .revistadehistoria.com.br/secao/almanaque/natal-made-in-brazil; Rainer Gonçalves, "Papai Noel Brasileiro," http://brasilescola.uol.com.br/curiosidades/papai-noel-brasileiro.htm; Rod Gonzalez, "Vovô Índio," Os Primieros Super-Heróis do Mundo (blog), December 1, 2010, http://primeirossuperherois.blogspot.ca/2014/ 06/vovo-indio.html.

93. "Trials of St Nick," *New York Times*, December 22, 1946, p. 101; Natalia Gomez Quintero, "El año de Quetzalcóatl le robó la Navidad a Santaclós," *El Universal*, December 18, 2010, http://www.eluniversal.com.mx/; Helen Delpar, *The Enormous Vogue of Things Mexican: Cultural Relations between the United States and Mexico, 1920–1935* (Tuscaloosa: 1995), p. 13; Daniel F. Solomon, *Breaking Up with Cuba: The Dissolution of Friendly Relations between Washington and Havana, 1956–1961* (Jefferson, NC: 2011), p. 206; Georgie Anne Geyer, *Guerrilla Prince: The Untold Story of Fidel Castro* (New Orleans: 2011), n.p. Malange is a root vegetable often made into fritters.

94. "Who Wants to Be a Caganer?," November 10, 2010, In the Garlic, http:// inthegarlic.com/2010/11/who-wants-to-be-a-caganer/.

95. "The Man Who Once Replaced Santa Claus," December 31, 2014, Slovenia Revealed, http://www.rtvslo.si/news-in-english/slovenia-revealed/the-man-who-had-once-replaced-santa-claus/354671.

96. Anna Lubecka, "Polish Ritual Year—A Reflection on Polish Cultural Policy," http://www.folklore.ee/pubte/eraamat/eestipoola2/anna.lubecka.pdf; Robert Strybel, "Santa—The Real 'Grinch' Who Stole Christmas," Polish Art Center, http://www.polartcenter.com/Articles.asp?ID=143.

97. Hilda Hoy, "Better Watch Out, Better Not Cry," *Prague Post*, December 13, 2006, https://web.archive.org/web/20070120090521/http://www.praguepost.com/ articles/2006/12/13/better-watch-out-better-not-cry.php.

98. See the website antisanta.cz; "Santa Claus je nežádoucí!" [Santa Claus is unde-sirable!], posted by "antisantaczech," December 21, 2012, https://www.youtube.com/watch?v=-6oMNolZY9c.

99. "'Santa, Go Home!' Cry Campaigners for Preserving Czech Christmas Customs," Česká poziche, January 5, 2012, http://ceskapozice.lidovky.cz/santa-go-home-cry-campaigners-for-preserving-czech-christmas-customs-120-/tema.aspx?c=A111216_144937_pozice_48823.

100. Fiona Govan, "Santa 'Mistreats Elves and Tricks Children,'" *Telegraph*, December 24 2007; "El Rap de los Reye Magos" (The rap of the Magi), http://www.yosoydelosreyesmagos.com.

101. Ironically, another German group, with a poorer grasp on history, has claimed that their secular Gift-Bringer, *der Weihnachtsmann*, should be preserved from Santa encroachment. In fact, *der Weihnachtsmann* is an offshoot of the American invention. David Crossland, "Germany Lays Claim to Father Christmas, Warns Traditional Holiday Character 'Under Threat' from Santa Claus," *National Post*, December 16, 2012, http://news.nationalpost.com/2013/12/16/germany-lays-claim-to-father-christmas-warns-traditional-holiday-character-under-threat-from-santa-claus; "Papá Noel versus los Reyes Magos: La pelea del año," December 22, 2007, Infobae, http://www.infobae.com/2007/12/22/355538-papa-noel-versus-los-reyes-magos-la-pelea-del-ano; "Guadalajara Church Calls Santa Claus a Fat Drunk," *Chicago Tribune*, December 7, 1999, http://articles.chicagotribune.com/1999-12-07/news/9912080289_1_santa-claus-st-nicholas-drunk.

102. "Santa Claus: Deda Mraz, Djed Bozicnjak or Saint Nicholas?," http://www.belgraded.com/santa-claus-deda-mraz-djed-bozicnjak-or-saint-nicholas (link expired), accessed December 12, 2012.

103. Mike O'Connor, "Is the Grinch Running Bosnia's Government?," *New York Times*, January 1, 1997, http://www.nytimes.com/1997/01/01/world/is-the-grinch-running-bosnia-s-government.html; "Alija Izetbegovic Generating Extremism," December 31, 1997, AIM, http://www.aimpress.ch/dyn/trae/archive/data/199801/80109-015-trae-sar.htm; Paul Beaumont, "Nationalists Triumph as 'Grandfather Frost' Banned in Sarajevo Infant Schools," *Observer*, December 21, 2008, http://www.theguardian.com/world/2008/dec/21/balkans-christmas-school.

104. "Russia Prohibits Denial of Santa," *BBC News*, December 27, 2007, http://news.bbc.co.uk/2/hi/europe/7161468.stm; Marcus Warren, "Russia's Grandfather Frost in New Cold War," *Telegraph*, December 23, 2000, www.telegraph.co.uk/news/worldnews/europe/russia/1379285/Russias-Grandfather-Frost-in-new-cold-war.html.

105. "Santa Claus and the Magic of Christmas," Rovaniemi, http://www.visitrovaniemi.fi/get-inspired/santa-claus; Mark Lohez, "Santa Claus: Planner of the 'Pole,'" Metropolitics, December 19, 2012, http://www.metropolitiques.eu/spip.php?page=print&id_article=435; Luke Simcoe, "Santa a Canadian, Declares Citizenship

Minister," Canada.com, December 2014, http://www.canada.com/life/santa+canadian+declares+citizenship+minister/1108430/story.html.

106. "Four Faces of Nicholas—Who Is He in His Hometown?," St. Nicholas Center, http://www.stnicholascenter.org/pages/demre-statues/.

107. "Santa Claus of Anatolia Discussion in Antalya," *World Bulletin*, Turkey Press Scan, December 23, 2008, http://www.worldbulletin.net/index.php?aType=haber&ArticleID=33677.

108. "A Muslim Defence of the Christmas Tree," *National Post*, December 15, 2006, http://www.nationalpost.com/news/story.html?id=1922c436-2a9c-4036-b8bc-04985468b6d2; Robert Winnett, "Baroness Warsi Urges Muslims to Celebrate Christmas," *Telegraph*, November 12, 2012, http://www.telegraph.co.uk/news/religion/9671262/Baroness-Warsi-urges-Muslims-to-celebrate-Christmas.html.

109. "Lebanese-Born Cleric Abu Musaab Wajdi Akkar: Saying "Merry Christmas" Is Worse Than Fornication, Alcohol, or Killing Someone," November 6, 2011, Middle East Media Research Institute, http://www.memri.org/clip_transcript/en/4080.htm.

110. Jenny White, "Anatolian Youth Stabs Santa," December 30, 2010, Kamil Pasha, http://kamilpasha.com/?p=3974; Robert Spencer, "Macedonia and Turkey Muslims Slug Santa," December 27, 2013, Jihad Watch, http://www.jihadwatch.org/2013/12/macedonia-and-turkey-muslims-slug-santa-claus; "Turkish Imam Says Santa Claus Dishonest," December 28, 2011, Sputnik, http://en.ria.ru/strange/20111228/170538693.html; Alex MacDonald, "Turks Protest against 'Creeping Christmas,'" December 23, 2015, Middle East Eye, http://www.middleeasteye.net/news/turkey-christmas-not-happy-1848737240.

111. "Muslim Extremists Kill Santa Claus," *Tablet*, January 14, 2012, http://archive.thetablet.co.uk/article/14th-january-2012/30/muslim-extremists-kill-santa-claus-a-group-of-susp.

112. "Christmas Carols in Homes Only 'If Authorized by the Police' Christians Protest," December 15, 2011, News.Va, http://www.news.va/en/news/asiamalaysia-christmas-carols-in-homes-only-if-aut; "A Christian, in Prison because 'Converted,' Has Been Released," January 30, 2014, Agenzia Fides, http://www.fides.org/en/news/35133-ASIA_IRAN_A_Christian_in_prison_because_converted_has_been_released#.U_QMaUs48oo; "Even Two Christian Women among the Prisoners Released," September 19, 2013, Agenzia Fides, http://www.fides.org/en/news/34326-ASIA_IRAN_Even_two_Christian_women_among_the_prisoners_released#.U_QNFos48oo; Azian Othman, "Muslims Prohibited from Celebrating Christmas: Imams," *Borneo Bulletin*, December 15,2015,http://borneobulletin.com.bn/muslims-prohibited-from-celebrating-christmas-imams/; Prashanth Parameswaran, "Brunei Explains Its Christmas Celebration Ban," *Diplomat*, December 31, 2014, http://thediplomat.com/2014/12/-explains-its-christmas-celebration-ban/; http://www.reuters.com/article/us-christmas-

season-somalia-idUSKBN0U61NT20151223; "Somali Government Bans Christmas Celebrations," Reuters, December 23, 2015, http://www.theguardian .com/world/2015/dec/23/tajikistan-bans-christmas-and-new-year.

113. "Celebrating Christmas Confidently," December 1, 2010, Christian Muslim Forum, http://www.christianmuslimforum.org/index.php/news/285-celebrating-christmas-confidently; "'Christmas Is Evil': Muslim Group Launches Poster Campaign against Festive Period," *Daily Mail*, December 23, 2010, http://www .dailymail.co.uk/news/article-1340794/Muslim-group-launches-poster-hate-campaign-festive-period.html#ixzz3Atkq3x52; "A Group of Radical Muslims Is Planning to Use St Paul's Cathedral to Protest against the Sins of British Society and the Fallacy of the Bible," @NewDayStarts, December 25, 2012, http://newdaystarts.wordpress.com/2012/12/25/a-group-of-radical-muslims-is-planning-to-use-st-pauls-cathedral-to-protest-against-the-sins-of-british-society-and-the-fallacy-of-the-bible/.

114. David Smith, *Hinduism and Modernity* (Malden: 2003), p. 189; "Sorry Kids, but VHP Just Told Santa Claus Not to Give You Chocolates!," *Times of India*, November 26, 2014, http://www.indiatimes.com/news/india/sorry-kids-but-the-vhp-just-told-santa-claus-not-to-give-you-chocolates-this-christmas-228620.html; Rajat Pandit, "National Shame President Pranab Mukherjee Meets Santa Claus," *Bharata Bharati*, October 17, 2014, https://bharatabharati .wordpress.com/2014/10/17/national-shame-president-pranab-mukherjee-meets-santa-claus-rajat-pandit/.

115. Thomas D. Williams, "Chinese Authorities Ban Christmas, Call It 'Western Spiritual Pollution,'" December 27, 2014, Breitbart, http://www.breitbart.com/ national-security/2014/12/27/chinese-authorities-ban-christmas-call-it-western-spiritual-pollution/; "Christmas Banned by Chinese University, Says It Is 'Kitsch,'" Reuters, December 25, 2014, https://ca.news.yahoo.com/christmas-banned-chinese-university-says-kitsch-023358427.html; Saibal Dasgupta, "Chinese City, University Ban Christmas Celebrations," *Times of India*, December 25, 2014, http://timesofindia.indiatimes.com/world/china/Chinese-city-university-ban-Christmas-celebrations/articleshow/45643951.cms; "Xi'an University Claims Shanghai Stampede Justifies Its Decision to Cancel Christmas," January 5, 2015, Shanghaiist, http://shanghaiist.com/2015/01/05/xian_university_justifies_ xmas_ban.php.

116. Morten Berthelsen, "Rabbis versus Christmas: Religious Rivalry in Jerusalem Benefits No One," *Haaretz*, December 17, 2009, http://www.haaretz.com/news/ rabbis-versus-christmas-religious-rivalry-in-jerusalem-benefits-no-one-1.1917; "Ban Christmas and Christian 'Vampires,' Says Far-Right Israeli Leader," *Middle East Eye*, December 24, 2015, http://www.middleeasteye.net/news/ban-christ-mas-and-christian-vampires-says-far-right-israeli-leader-1200122012; "Head of Extremist Jewish Group Calls Christians 'Blood-Sucking Vampires,'" *Times of*

Israel, December 22, 2015, http://www.timesofisrael.com/head-of-extremist-jewish-group-calls-christians-blood-sucking-vampires/.

CHAPTER V: THE APPROPRIATORS

1. Leigh Eric Schmidt, *Consumer Rites: The Buying and Selling of American Holidays* (Princeton: 1995), is an excellent introduction to this topic. For the use of St. Nick in commercials over the past two hundred years, see the chapter "Santa the Adman" in my *Santa Claus: A Biography* (Toronto: 2005).

2. Christine Agius, "Christmas and War," in *Christmas, Ideology and Popular Culture,* ed. Sheila Whitely (Edinburgh: 2008), pp. 144–147.

3. See, for example, David Domke and Kevin Coe, *The God Strategy: How Religion Became a Political Weapon in America* (Oxford: 2008). Timothy W. Luke, "Xmas Ideology: Unwrapping the American Welfare State under the Christmas Tree," in *Sexual Politics and Popular Culture,* ed. Diane Christine Raymond (Madison: 1990); David Kuo, *Tempting Faith: An Inside Story of Political Seduction* (New York: 2006); Scott C. Lowe, ed., *Christmas—Philosophy for Everyone* (Chichester: 2010); Michael J. Perry, *Religion in Politics: Constitutional and Moral Perspectives* (Oxford: 1999).

4. Christopher Morris, "Shopping for America, Or How I Learned to Stop Complaining and Love the Pemberton Mall," *Reviews in American History* 29, no. 1, 2001, p. 103.

5. Rory McVeigh, *The Rise of the Ku Klux Klan: Right-Wing Movements and National Politics* (Minneapolis: 2009), pp. 164–165; Kenneth T. Jackson, *The Ku Klux Klan in the City: 1915–1930* (Lanham: 1992), p. 150; Shawn Lay, *Hooded Knights on the Niagara: The Ku Klux Klan in Buffalo* (New York: 1995), p. 138; Shawn Lay, ed., *The Invisible Empire in the West* (Champaign: 2003), p. 143; John Shlien, "Santa Claus: The Myth in America," *ETC: A Review of General Semantics,* Summer 1959, p. 393; Kathleen M. Blee, *Women of the Klan: Racism and Gender in the 1920s* (Berkeley: 2008), p. 142.

6. Ted Ownby, *American Dreams in Mississippi: Consumers, Poverty, and Culture, 1830–1998* (Chapel Hill: 1999), p. 152.

7. Patrick D. Jones, *The Selma of the North: Civil Rights Insurgency in Milwaukee* (Cambridge, MA: 2009), p. 205.

8. "Selective Buying Campaign—1968–69," Durham Civil Rights Heritage Project, http://durhamcountylibrary.org/exhibits/dcrhp/selective.php; "Durham's Civil Rights Heritage," *Herald-Sun,* December 23, 2013, http://www.heraldsun.com/durhamherald/heritage/x1866992354/Durham-s-Civil-Rights-Heritage.

9. Roger Bruns, *Jesse Jackson: A Biography* (Westport: 2005), p. 60; "I'm Dreaming of a Black Christmas," *Ebony,* November 1969, pp. 115–116; "'Soul Saint' Sits at 'Soul Pole' for Black Christmas," *Jet,* January 1, 1970, p. 24.

10. The dating of Kwanzaa was also cleverly situated amid the post-Christmas sales period, when hard-pressed black consumers could take advantage of discount prices.

11. Keith Mayes, "A Holiday of Our Own," in *Black Power Movement: Rethinking the Civil Rights–Black Power Era,* ed. Peniel E. Joseph (New York: 2013), pp. 80–81; Keith A. Mayes, *Kwanzaa: Black Power and the Making of the African-American Holiday Tradition* (New York: 2010), pp. 242–243; Elizabeth H. Pleck, "Kwanzaa: The Making of a Black Nationalist Tradition," in *Contemporary Consumption Rituals: A Research Anthology,* ed. Cele C. Otnes and Tina M. Lowrey (London: 2004), p. 62.

12. "Why We Are Calling for a Boycott on Christmas and Holiday Shopping This Year!," More Videos by Minister Louis Farrakhan, https://www.facebook.com/OfficialMinisterFarrakhan/videos/847359228704684; Pam Key, "Farrakhan Calls on Blacks to Boycott Christmas: 'Bonanza for White Business,'" Breitbart, September 10, 2015, http://www.breitbart.com/video/2015/09/10/farrakhan-calls-on-blacks-to-boycott-christmas-bonanza-for-white-business/.

13. Pat Hopkins and Helen Grange, *The Rocky Rioter Teargas Show: The Inside Story of the 1976 Soweto Uprising* (Cape Town: 2001); Gail M. Gerhart and Clive L. Glaser, *From Protest to Challenge: A Documentary History of African Politics in South Africa, 1882–1990* (Bloomington: 2010), p. 85; Bernard Spong, *Sticking Around* (Pietermaritzburg: 2006), p. 283.

14. Graeme Kidd, "Maastricht Schools Latest to Drop Blackface from Sinterklaas Parties," *NL Times,* October 20, 2015, http://www.nltimes.nl/2015/10/20/maastricht-schools-latest-to-drop-blackface-from-sinterklaas-parties/; Janene Pieters, "Ash to Replace Blackface Zwarte Piet at Sinterklaas Arrival," *NL Times,* October 14, 2015, http://www.nltimes.nl/2015/10/14/ash-to-replace-blackface-zwarte-piet-at-sinterklaas-arrival/; Janene Pieters, "Meet Gouda's Multicolored (and) Zwarte Pieten," *NL Times,* October 14, 2014, http://www.nltimes.nl/2014/10/14/meet-goudas-multicolored-zwarte-pieten/.

15. Audrey Graanoogst, "UN Investigator Pleads for Abolishing Sinterklaas," *NL Times,* October 23, 2013, http://www.nltimes.nl/2013/10/23/un-investigator-pleads-for-abolishing-sinterklaas/; "Why Black Pete (Zwarte Piet) Is Racist," October 26, 2013, posted by "HeWillBeFree Soon," https://www.youtube.com/watch?v=AMuQtkoReqo.

16. Bruno Waterfield, "UN Drops Black Pete 'Racism' Charge against the Dutch," *Telegraph,* October 24, 2013, http://www.telegraph.co.uk/news/worldnews/europe/netherlands/10402662/UN-drops-Black-Pete-racism-charge-against-the-Dutch.html.

17. "Madrid Ends Blacking Up of Characters in Post-Christmas Tradition," *Guardian,* September 17, 2015, http://www.theguardian.com/world/2015/sep/17/madrid-ends-blacking-up-post-christmas-tradition.

18. Bootlyg, "Insurrectionary Mexico Celebrates Black Christmas," *Earth First! Journal,* http://chipuco.co.tv/earthfirstjournal (URL expired), accessed November 19, 2013.

19. "Genova, Italy—30 December, Christmas Tree Lights Sabotaged in City Centre," Angry News from Around the World (blog), January 6, 2011, http://sysiphus-

angrynewsfromaroundtheworld.blogspot.ca/2011/01/genova-italy-30-december-christmas-tree.html, accessed November 19, 2013. The curious neologism "pennyaliner" refers to the members of the media (where hack writers were once paid "penny a line") who uncritically support the status quo.

20. "Riot Police Forced to Guard Christmas Tree in Athens after Protesters Attack It," *Daily Mail*, December 20, 2008, http://www.dailymail.co.uk/news/article-1099150/Riot-police-forced-guard-Christmas-tree-Athens-protesters-attack-it .html; "Anarchists Torch Coca-Cola Christmas Tree in Mexico City," Earth First! Newswire, December 21, 2013, http://earthfirstjournal.org/newswire/2013/12/ 21/anarchists-torch-coca-cola-christmas-tree-in-mexico-city/; "Argentina— Government Christmas Tree Burned in Plaza de Mayo," Angry News from Around the World (blog), January 8, 2012, http://sysiphus-angrynewsfroma roundtheworld.blogspot.ca/2012/01/government-christmas-tree-burned-in.html.

21. "Police Hunt Anarchist Who Vandalized Bristol Cathedral," *Western Daily Press*, December 30, 2013, http://www.westerndailypress.co.uk/Anarchists-cathedral-attack-claim/story-20378854-detail/story.html.

22. Paul Irish, "Santa Claus Quits Smoking in New Twas the Night before Christmas," *Toronto Star*, September 19, 2012, http://www.thestar.com/enter tainment/books/2012/09/19/santa_claus_quits_smoking_in_new_twas_the_ night_before_christmas.html.

23. "All Children Really Want This Christmas Is Their Parents to Quit Smoking," Department of Health, Gov.UK, https://www.gov.uk/government/news/all-children-really-want-this-christmas-is-their-parents-to-quit-smoking--2.

24. "An Urgent Message from Santa," Greenpeace, December 5, 2013, posted by "HDAnuncios," https://www.youtube.com/watch?v=CCQJuzSqj6s.

25. "Polar Bears Dream of a White Christmas," Greenpeace, November 28, 2004, http://www.greenpeace.org/international/en/news/features/polar-bears-dream-of-a-white-c/.

26. Anthony Watts, "The Worst Kind of Ugly Climate Propaganda: David Suzuki Targets Kids at Christmas in the Name of Climate Change," WUWT, November 30, 2011. The ad also features Suzuki dressed as an elf, holding a hockey stick, probably a reference to the infamous "hockey stick curve" graph that purported to show a sharp rise in global temperatures in the late twentieth century.

27. Larry West, "The Hidden Cost of Christmas," About.com, http://environment .about.com/od/greenchristmas/a/christmascost.htm.

28. Nathan Grills and Brendan Halyday, "Santa Claus: A Public Health Pariah?," *British Medical Journal* 339, no. 7735, December 19–26, 2009, pp. 1424–1426.

29. Nancy Ross Ryan, "A Politically Correct Carol," http://freshfoodwriting.com/ writing/vegetarian.links/xmascarol.htm.

30. "Stand Up for Turkeys," http://www.viva.org.uk/stand-up-for-turkeys; VIVA!, http://kathrynandnick.com/news-snapshot-can-stop-carvery/.

31. "Santa Can't Come This Year," What's Next, http://www.whatsnextblog.com/peta_santa_cant_come_this_year/; Sarah Estrella, "Sexy Food: UK Reality TV Star Chantelle Houghton for PETA, 'Fight Impotence: Go Vegetarian,'" Examiner.com, June 4, 2010, http://www.examiner.com/article/sexy-food-uk-reality-tv-star-chantelle-houghton-for-peta-fight-impotence-go-vegetarian; "28 British Celebrities Who Won't Be Eating Turkey This Christmas," PETA UK, http://www.peta.org.uk/blog/28-celebrities-wont-eating-turkey-christmas-2/; Rex Hall Jr., "PETA Billboard of Mary Nursing Baby Jesus Aimed at Judge Who Called Out Breastfeeding Mother," MLive, November 21, 2011, http://www.mlive.com/news/kalamazoo/index.ssf/2011/11/peta_taking_to_task_judge_who.html; "Londoners React to PETA's Christmas Ads," PETA UK, http://www.peta.org.uk/blog/londoners-react-to-petas-christmas-ads; Marlise Simons, "For Abused Saint: The Last Straw: Santa Weighs In," *New York Times*, December 11, 1996, http://www.nytimes.com/1996/12/11/world/for-abused-saint-the-last-straw-santa-weighs-in.html.

32. Fiona McRae, "Is This Crude Ad Really the Best Way to Tackle Unwanted Pregnancies at Christmas?," *Daily Mail*, November 28, 2008, http://www.daily-mail.co.uk/femail/article-1090080/Is-crude-ad-really-best-way-tackle-unwanted-pregnancies-Christmas.html; "'12 Days of Contraception': Planned Parenthood Releases Alternative Carol," Fox News, December 24, 2013, http://nation.foxnews.com/2013/12/24/'12-days-contraception'-planned-parenthood-releases-alternative-carol; "Opt's 12 Days of Contraception," posted by Options for Sexual Health, December 21, 2012, http://www.youtube.com/watch?v=ljaf-qDhTOA.

33. "Kakumei-teki Himote Doumei: The Revolutionary Grouping of Men That Women Are Not Attracted To," Spoon and Tamago, February 9, 2015, http://www.spoon-tamago.com/2015/02/09/kakumei-teki-himote-doumei-the-revolutionary-grouping-of-men-that-women-are-not-attracted-to/; Mark Schreiber, "Christmas in Japan Is Not for Faint of Heart," *Japan Times*, December 20, 2014, http://www.japantimes.co.jp/news/2014/12/20/national/media-national/christmas-japan-faint-heart/#.VnWMGDY4nUo; "Angry Single Men Stage Anti-Christmas Rally in Tokyo, Claim They Are Discriminated Against," *Japan Times*, December 19, 2015, http://www.japantimes.co.jp/news/2015/12/19/national/angry-single-men-stage-anti-christmas-rally-in-tokyo-claim-they-are-discriminated-against/#.VnWQSjY4lp8.

34. Mike Nichols, "Midwinters Night's Eve: Yule," http://www.sacred-texts.com/bos/bos022.htm.

35. The best history of the neopagan phenomenon, and not an unsympathetic one, is Ronald Hutton, *The Triumph of the Moon: A History of Modern Pagan Witchcraft* (Oxford: 1999); Wolf LittleBear, *A Wolf in the Shadows* (Sterling Heights, MI: 2008), p. 26.

36. Ellen Reed, "Glory to the New Born King," Pagan Library, http://www.paganlibrary.com/music_poetry/glory_new_born_king.php, accessed June 1998.

37. "Dancing in a Wiccan Wonderland! by Alexander and Aarcher," Witches of the Craft, December 18, 2012, http://witchesofthecraft.com/2012/12/18/dancing-in-a-wiccan-wonderland-2/.

38. Celtic Music, Wiccan Wonderland (blog), http://walkinginawiccanwonderland .blogspot.ca/p/celtic-music.html.

39. Steven Posch (lyrics), "Mother Berta's Coming to Town," Yule Songs for Wiccans and Pagans, December 16, 2009, website of Cernowain Greenman, http:// www.cernowain.com/pagansongbook/yule/yule.html#Mother; Morven, Jennifer, Roger, Chip, and BG (lyrics), "Faunus, the Roman Goat God," Yule Songs for Wiccans and Pagans, December 16, 2009, website of Cernowain Greenman, http://www.cernowain.com/pagansongbook/yule/yulelyrics.html.

40. Selena Fox, "Celebrating Winter Solstice," Circle Sanctuary, https://www .circlesanctuary.org/index.php/celebrating-the-seasons/celebrating-winter-solstice.

41. "Whose Christmas Is It Anyway?," *BBC News*, December 20, 1997, http://news .bbc.co.uk/2/hi/special_report/for_christmas/_new_year/pagan_christmas/ 37276.stm.

42. Mary Jo Neitz, "Queering the Dragonfest: Changing Sexualities in a Post-patriarchal Religion," *Sociology of Religion* 61, no. 4, 2000, p. 381.

43. Laurence Watts, "Santa Claus Exclusive: 'I'm Gay and I'm Quitting the North Pole,'" *Huffington Post*, December 19, 2011, http://www.huffingtonpost.com/ laurence-watts/santa-claus-gay-comes-out_b_1119330.html. Watts followed up this exclusive with another, equally penetrating scoop a few weeks later: "When Jesus Met Santa Claus," *Huffington Post*, January 2, 2012, http://www.huffing tonpost.com/laurence-watts/when-jesus-met-santa-claus_b_1166116.html.

44. As sung by the Cherry Poppin' Daddies on the album *Kevin & Bean: Santa's Swingin Sack*, KROQ (1998).

45. Iris Mann, "Dishing the Dirt on Santa," *Jewish Journal*, December 7, 2011, http:// www.jewishjournal.com/arts/article/dishing_the_dirt_on_santa_20111207/; *Scrooge and Marley*, Sam I Am Films (2012), http://www.imdb.com/title/tt2262073/? ref_=fn_al_tt_6; "PC Nativity Sets Hit England," *Sojourners*, December 17, 2000, http://sojo.net/sojomail/2000/12/22 (URL expired).

46. John de Graaf, David Wann, and Thomas H. Naylor, *Affluenza: How Over-consumption Is Killing Us—and How to Fight Back* (Oakland: 2014), n.p.

47. "Celebrate Buy Nothing Day," Adbusters, https://www.adbusters.org/ campaigns/bnd.

48. Occupy Christmas, https://www.facebook.com/pages/Occupy-Christmas/ 236907349699891. To upcycle is to repurpose a used object for something new and useful.

49. "Occupy My Heart: A Revolutionary Christmas Carol," December 21, 2011, Daily Kos, http://www.dailykos.com/story/2011/12/20/1047468/-.

50. "It's an Occupy Christmas," December 1, 2011, Funny or Die, http://www .funnyordie.com/videos/ffc27b8ae1/it-s-an-occupy-christmas.

51. Stephen R. Holmes, *The Politics of Christmas* (London: 2011), p. 11.

52. The group's name is a German pun implying both "come into the alleys" and "get things going." "Advent Activism: Hamburg Protest Group Counts Down Days to Christmas," *Spiegel*, December 1, 2010, http://www.spiegel.de/international/zeitgeist/advent-activism-hamburg-protest-group-counts-down-days-to-christmas-a-732674.html.

53. According to the group's website, "FEMEN is an international women's movement of brave topless female activists painted with the slogans and crowned with flowers. FEMEN female activists are the women with special training, physically and psychologically ready to implement the humanitarian tasks of any degree of complexity and level of provocation. FEMEN activists are ready to withstand repressions against them and are propelled by the ideological cause alone. FEMEN is the special force of feminism, its spearhead militant unit, modern incarnation of fearless and free Amazons," http://femen.org/about-us/.

54. Adam Withnall, "Topless Christmas Day Femen Protest in Cologne Cathedral Slammed as 'Unnecessary Disturbance,'" *Independent*, December 28, 2013, http://www.independent.co.uk/news/world/europe/topless-christmas-day-femen-protest-in-cologne-cathedral-slammed-as-unnecessary-disturbance-9028426.html; "Topless FEMEN Activist 'Kidnaps' Baby Jesus from Vatican Nativity Scene," RT, December 25, 2014, https://www.rt.com/news/217703-femen-topless-jesus-christmas/; "California Man Sets Himself, American Flag, Christmas Tree on Fire to Protest Religious Names," Fox News, December 23, 2006, http://www.foxnews.com/story/2006/12/23/california-man-sets-himself-american-flag-christmas-tree-on-fire-to-protest/.

55. Simon Caldwell, "Catholic Church to Replace Nativity Scene with Replica of Israeli Wall," Catholic News Service, December 12, 2006, http://archbishop-cranmer.blogspot.ca/2007/12/nativity-scene-now-includes-israeli.h, http://www.demotix.com/photo/974397/bethlehem-activists-stage-christmas-protest-against-israeli-occupation; "'Hijacked by Hatred': British NGOs Use Christmas for Anti-Israel Attacks," *NGO Monitor*, December 23, 2008, http://www.ngo-monitor.org/article/_hijacked_by_hatred_british_ngos_use_christmas_for_anti_israel_attack; Ron Kampeas, "London Church Hosts Anti-Israel Carols," Jewish Telegraphic Agency, December 5, 2008, http://www.jta.org/2008/12/05/news-opinion/world/london-church-hosts-anti-israel-carols#ixzz3AxTa9zI7s; Daphne Anson, "Open Season's Greetings—Taking the Jew Out of Jesus and Other Tricks of the Israel-Delegitimising Trade," Daphne Anson (blog), December 8, 2010, http://daphneanson.blogspot.ca/2010/12/open-seasons-greetings-taking-jew-out.html.

56. Anne Sewell, "Protestors in Santiago de Compostela Steal a Christmas King," *Digital Journal*, December 24, 2013, http://www.digitaljournal.com/news/world/protesters-in-santiago-de-compostela-steal-a-christmas-king/article/364577.

The Nativity display in question had been the site of an earlier kidnapping of the Baby Jesus to protest homelessness in Spain.

57. Billy Kangas, "Remember That Jesus Was an Undocumented Refugee Child," Patheos, July 19, 2014, http://www.patheos.com/blogs/billykangas/2014/07/remember-that-jesus-was-an-undocumented-child-refugee.html; "Don't Forget to Hate Refugees as You Setup Your Nativity Scene…" uploaded November 2015, Imgur, http://imgur.com/aRHWEqp; "Nativity," imgflip, https://imgflip.com/i/uhhmg.

58. "Record 17,000 Join 'Pinstripe Nazi' Anti-Islam March in Germany," *Guardian*, December 23, 2014, http://www.theguardian.com/world/2014/dec/22/anti-islam-march-germany-sing-christmas-carols.

59. "Christmas Postcards in Russia," https://commons.wikimedia.org/wiki/Category:Christmas_postcards_in_Russia; the Pinterest site "Ukrainian Partisan Army" features a number of UPA Christmas cards: https://www.pinterest.com/michaelboh07/ukrainian-partisan-army/.

60. Kathryn Kish Sklar, Anja Schüler, and Susan Strasser, eds., *Social Justice Feminists in the United States and Germany* (Ithaca: 1998), p. 299; "Blacks Urged to Boycott War Toys This Christmas," *Jet*, December 6, 1982, p. 5; Roger Chapman, ed., *Culture Wars: An Encyclopedia of Issues, Viewpoints, and Voices* (Armonk: 2009), pp. 596–598.

61. "'Toy War' Debates Misunderstand the Causes of Domestic Violence," *Conversation*, December 4, 2014, http://theconversation.com/toy-war-debates-misunderstand-the-causes-of-domestic-violence-34963.

62. Glosswitch, "Secret Santa Sexism: Why Are We So Keen to Reinforce Gender Roles for Adults at Christmas?," *New Statesman*, December 5, 2014, http://www.newstatesman.com/society/2014/12/secret-santa-sexism-why-are-we-so-keen-reinforce-gender-roles-adults-christmas.

63. "Santa 'Shot Jesus Out of Saddle,'" *Times Colonist*, December 7, 2006, http://www.canada.com/topics/news/national/story.html?id=235722b6-d4d7-48fc-b73a-a24dff1f4792&_federated=1. Smith may have been inspired by a Boise man who made a similar crucifixion protest in 2002.

64. Sue Leeman, "Billboard Questioning Santa Claus Is Scrapped," *Seattle Times*, April 30, 2005, http://www.seattletimes.com/nation-world/billboard-questioning-santa-claus-is-scrapped/; Darren Cullen, "Santa Gives More to Rich Kids Than Poor Kids," Spelling Mistakes Cost Lives, http://www.spellingmistakescostlives.com/santa/billboard/01billboard.htm.

65. "Christmastime Means Snow, Gifts and Artist Keith McGuckin Offending People," Chronicle Online, December 3, 2008, http://chronicle.northcoastnow.com/2008/12/03/christmastime-means-snow-gifts-and-artist-keith-mcguckin-offending-people/.

66. Zombie nativity scene, https://www.facebook.com/Zombie-nativity-scene-365944350233282; Sarah Kaplan, "God Frowns upon This Manger Scene," *National Post*, December 8, 2015, http://news.nationalpost.com/news/world/

god-frowns-upon-this-manger-scene-ohio-man-faces-500-a-day-fine-for-zombie-nativity-display; Kimberly Winston, "Zombie Nativity: An Irreverent Addition to Holiday Pop Culture," Religion News Service, December 1, 2015, http://www.religionnews.com/2015/12/01/zombie-nativity-irreverent-addition-holiday-pop-culture/.

67. Jason Silverstein, "Maine Residents Call Cops over Apparent Pro-ISIS Christmas Display, Didn't Notice the Urinating Santa Claus," *Daily News*, December 13, 2015, http://www.nydailynews.com/news/national/maine-residents-confused-isis-display-peeing-santa-article-1.2464432.

68. "Nativity Displays at Claremont UMC over the Years," http://www.claremontumc.org/clientimages/48436/a-history-of-cumc-nativities/pastdisplays.html; http://www.claremontumc.org/clientimages/48436/thewindow/the%20window%202015-01-07.pdf, accessed January 15, 2016; http://www.claremontumc.org/clientimages/48436/thewindow/the%20window%202015-12-16.pdf, accessed January 15, 2016; "Claremont Church Opts Out of Anti-violence Nativity Scene Depicting Guns Pointing at Baby Jesus," KPCC, December 23, 2015, http://www.scpr.org/news/2015/12/23/56463/claremont-church-opts-out-of-anti-violence-nativit/.

69. Peter Lattman, "Holiday Greeting Cards and the Law," pt. 1, *Wall Street Journal*, December 21, 2006, http://blogs.wsj.com/law/2006/12/21/holiday-greeting-cards-the-law-part-i/.

CHAPTER VI: THE DISCONTENTED

1. Mark Hume, "Couple Launches Attack on 'Christmas Hell,'" *National Post*, December 13, 2002, Free Republic, http://www.freerepublic.com/focus/news/805854/posts?page=9.

2. James Lileks, "Lileks Takes on Christmas Haters," December 21, 2002, Free Republic, http://www.freerepublic.com/focus/f-news/810417/posts.

3. "Blue Christmas Services Help with Grieving during Holidays," *USA Today*, December 21, 2012, http://www.usatoday.com/story/news/nation/2012/12/21/blue-christmas-grief/1785833/.

4. Oliver James, "Watch Out When You Go Back Home," *New Statesman*, December 18, 1998, p. 44.

5. Eric Rauchway, "Santa Only Brought Me the Blues: Family Holidays, Old and New," *Reviews in American History* 30, no. 1, 2002, p. 102.

6. Liz Jones, "Wish Me a Lonely Christmas and Spare a Thought for the Millions of Women like Me," *Daily Mail*, December 21, 2009.

7. Leslie Bella, *The Christmas Imperative: Leisure, Family and Women's Work* (Halifax: 1992), p. 231.

8. Lydia Saad, "Christmas Shopping Brings Holiday Cheer: Majority of Americans Are Not Highly Stressed by the Season," December 8, 2006, http://www.gallup.com/poll/25816/Christmas-Shopping-Brings-Holiday-Cheer.aspx.

9. Jessica Valenti, "No, I Will NOT Wrap All the Presents," *Guardian,* December 10, 2014, http://www.theguardian.com/commentisfree/2014/dec/10/wrap-presents-women-holiday-chores.

10. "Official: Shops Are Bad for Men How Stress Is in Store," *Herald Scotland,* December 2, 1998, http://www.heraldscotland.com/sport/spl/aberdeen/official-shops-are-bad-for-men-how-stress-is-in-store-1.316403.

11. Leland Gregory, *Stupid Christmas* (Kansas City: 2010), p. 68.

12. Latham Hunter, "It's a Holly Jolly Feminist Minefield," *Hamilton Spectator,* December 20, 2014, http://www.thespec.com/opinion-story/5214308-opinion-it-s-a-holly-jolly-feminist-minefield/.

13. Sophie Kleeman, "Hilarious Christmas Song Is the Feminist Rally Cry You've Been Waiting For," http://mic.com/articles/106728/hilarious-christmas-song-is-the-feminist-rally-cry-you-ve-been-waiting-for#.VwGxowpzW.

14. Simon Hoggart, "Glad Tidings We Bring," *Guardian,* December 11, 2004, http://www.theguardian.com/books/2004/dec/11/society1.

15. "Fruitcake Toss," Colorado Springs Convention & Visitors Bureau, http://www.visitcos.com/fruitcake-toss.

16. John Boswell and Lenore Skenazy, *The Dysfunctional Family Christmas Songbook* (New York: 2004), p. 27.

17. Olivia Slaughter and Jean Kubelun, *Life as a Mother-in-Law: Roles, Challenges, Solutions* (Indianapolis: 2008), p. 122.

18. Fiona Gibson, "Ten Ways to Avoid Mother-in-Law Meltdown This Christmas…" *Daily Mail,* December 21, 2009, http://www.dailymail.co.uk/femail/article-1237400/10-ways-avoid-mother-law-meltdown-Christmas-.html, December 22, 2009.

19. Boswell and Skenazy, *Dysfunctional Family Christmas Songbook,* p. 16.

20. Paul Curtis, "Musak," Peculiar Poetry, http://www.peculiar-poetry.com/max/christmas/40mcp-105-muzak.htm.

21. "MUZAK: Music to Whose Ears?," Noise Pollution Clearinghouse, December 14, 1998, http://www.nonoise.org/library/muzak/muzak.htm; "Complain about Muzak: Orientation," http://kazumitna.com/antimuzak/23-2/.

22. Anita Sarkeesian, "Top 5 Creepy Christmas Songs," posted by "feministfrequency," December 21, 2011, https://www.youtube.com/watch?v=GpDnr2s9yxQ; Kieran Fenby-Hulse, "The Fairytale of New York: Some Thoughts on Homophobia and Heteronormative Christmas Soundscapes," December 22, 2014, website of Kieran Fenby-Hulse http://kieranfenbyhulse.com/2014/12/22/the-fairytale-of-new-york-some-thoughts-on-homophobia-and-heteronormative-christmas-soundscapes/; Stephen Deusner, "Is 'Baby, It's Cold Outside' a Date-Rape Anthem?," *Salon,* December 10, 2012, http://www.salon.com/2012/12/10/is_baby_its_cold_outside_a_date_rape_anthem/.

23. Greta Christina, "10 Christmas Carols Even an Atheist Could Love," Greta Christina's Blog, December 17, 2013, http://freethoughtblogs.com/greta/2013/12/17/10-christmas-carols-even-an-atheist-could-love-2/.

24. Adrianus de Groot, *Saint Nicholas: A Psychiatric Study of His History and Myth* (The Hague: 1965).

25. Russell W. Belk, "A Child's Christmas in America: Santa Claus as Deity, Consumption as Religion," *Journal of American Culture* 10, 1987, pp. 89–90, offers a catalogue of such research. See also Bowler, *The World Encyclopedia of Christmas* (Toronto: 2000), pp. 182–183; and *Santa Claus: A Biography* (Toronto: 2000), pp. 224–228; Paul Thompson, "A Christmas Fairy Tale," *European Journal of Psychotherapy, Counselling and Health* 5, no. 2, June 2002, pp. 415–418; and Warren O. Hagstrom, "What Is the Meaning of Santa Claus?," *American Sociologist* 1, no. 5, 1966, pp. 248–252.

26. J. T. Proctor, "Children's Reactions to Christmas," *Journal of the Oklahoma State Medical Association* 60, 1967, pp. 653–659; Sereno Renzo, "Some Observations on the Santa Claus Custom," *Psychiatry* 14, 1951, pp. 387–396; Allen Irving, *Brock Chisholm: Doctor to the World* (Markham, Ontario: 1998); Brock Chisholm, "The Family: Basic Unit of Social Learning," *Coordinator* 4, no. 4, June 1956, p. 10.

27. Judith A. Boss, "Is Santa Claus Corrupting Our Children's Morals?," *Free Inquiry* 11, no. 4, 1991, pp. 24–27, and "No, Virginia, There Is No Santa Claus. Someone's Been Lying to You," *Free Inquiry* 12, no. 2, 1992, pp. 52–53.

28. Jenny Phillips Goodwin, "Christmas Is Better without Santa," *New York Times*, December 22, 1985, http://www.nytimes.com/1985/12/22/nyregion/long-island-opinion-christmas-is-better-without-santa.html.

29. Steve Benson, "Mormonism and Teaching Your Children the Truth about Santa Claus," Is Christmas Santa Claus a Mormon?, http://www.i4m.com/think/comments/mormon_santa.htm.

30. Nancy A. French, "Why I'm a Santa Truther," December 10, 2013, Rare, http://rare.us/story/why-im-a-santa-truther/.

31. Tricia Cusack, "The Christmas Snowman: Carnival and Patriarchy," *newformations*, iss. 30, Winter 1996, http://www.newformations.co.uk/abstracts/nf30abstracts.html; Meghan Cox Gurdon, "Frosty's Patriarchal Agenda, Unmasked," *National Post*, December 26, 2000, www.fact.on.ca/news/news0012.htm; Thomas Harding, "Snowmen Get Cold Shoulder," *Telegraph*, December 21, 2000, http://www.telegraph.co.uk/news/uknews/1379010/Snowmen-get-cold-shoulder.html.

32. Bruce Ward, "Santa Blahs: The Twinkle Is Gone," CanWest News Service, December 14, 2003.

33. J. R. Moehringer, "Ho! Ho! Is More Like Uh-Oh," *Los Angeles Times*, December 23, 2004, http://articles.latimes.com/2004/dec/23/nation/na-santa23; "The Organic Genderless Gingerbread Debate," *BBC News*, October 22, 2014, http://www.bbc.com/news/blogs-trending-29706778.

34. Renato Costello, "Santa Ho, Ho, Ho Gets Heave-ho," *Sunday Mail*, November 11, 2007, http://www.adelaidenow.com.au/news/south-australia/santa-hohoho-gets-heave-ho/story-e6frea83-1111114848362?nk=a8a663cd112d1612ab998172f bf4dea5.

35. "Santa Out in Cold for Christmas," *BBC News*, November 2, 2004, http://news
    .bbc.co.uk/2/hi/uk_news/3973697.stm.

36. The Elf on the Shelf, http://www.elfontheshelf.com.

37. Peter Holley, "The Elf on the Shelf Is Preparing Your Child to Live in a Future
    Police State, Professor Warns," *Washington Post*, December 16, 2014, https://
    www.washingtonpost.com/news/arts-and-entertainment/wp/2014/12/16/the-
    elf-on-the-shelf-is-preparing-your-child-to-live-in-a-future-police-state-professor-
    says/; Laura Pinto and Selena Nemorin, "Who's the Boss? 'The Elf on the Shelf'
    and the Normalization of Surveillance," *Policy Alternatives*, December 1, 2014,
    https://www.policyalternatives.ca/publications/commentary/whos-boss#
    sthash.zgajlOOY.dpuf.

38. "You Better Watch Out," *Harpers*, December 2001, http://www.opinionarchives
    .com/files/OA_HarpersMagazine-2001-12-0075750_1_.pdf.

39. Mark Hughes, "New Terrorists On the Block," August 29, 2009, Calling England,
    www.callingengland.net/2009/08/new-terrorists-on-block.html.

40. Isabelle de Pommereau, "Germans Join 'War on Christmas'—Pre-Christmas
    Commercialism, That Is," *Christian Science Monitor*, October 5, 2014, http://
    www.csmonitor.com/World/Europe/2014/1005/Germans-join-War-on-
    Christmas-pre-Christmas-commercialism-that-is.

41. Zelda Leah Gatuskin, Michelle Miller, and Harry Willson, *Christmas Blues:
    Behind the Holiday Mask* (Albuquerque: 1995), p. 32.

CHAPTER VII: THE PRIVATIZERS

1. Joshua Eli Plaut, *A Kosher Christmas: 'Tis the Season to Be Jewish* (New Brunswick:
   2012), pp. 28–29; Albert Menendez, *The December Wars: Religious Symbols
   and Ceremonies in the Public Square* (Buffalo: 1993), p. 84; Jeffrey S. Gurock,
   American Jewish Orthodoxy in Historical Perspective (Jersey City: 1996), pp. 148–149;
   Gil Ribak, *Gentile New York: The Images of Non-Jews among Jewish Immigrants*
   (New Brunswick: 2012), p. 94; Ruth A. Frager, *Sweatshop Strife: Class, Ethnicity,
   and Gender in the Jewish Labour Movement of Toronto, 1900–1939* (Toronto:
   1992), p. 35.

2. Diana Selig, *Americans All: The Cultural Gifts Movement* (Cambridge, MA:
   2008), p. 136.

3. Henry Ford, *The International Jew—The World's Foremost Problem* (1920),
   reprinted in Noontide Press: Books Online, https://archive.org/details/The
   InternationalJewTheWorldsForemostProblemhenryFord1920s, pp. 255 and
   348.

4. Gerald L. K. Smith, "The Divine Anniversary," The Cross and the Flag, http://
   www.thecrossandflag.com/articles/divine_anniversary.html; Glen Jeansonne,
   Gerald L. K. Smith, Minister of Hate (Baton Rouge: 1988), p. 53.

5. Elizabeth Hafkin Pleck, *Celebrating the Family: Ethnicity, Consumer Culture, and
   Family Rituals* (Cambridge, MA: 2000), p. 66.

6. Quoted in Tom Flynn, *The Trouble with Christmas* (New York: 1993), p. 163. Ironically, Witt then testified to a change of heart and urged his Jewish readers to adopt Christmas celebrations, in recognition not of Christ's divinity but of the season's universal messages of peace and goodwill. Penne L. Restad, *Christmas in America* (New York: 1995), pp. 158–159.

7. Everson v. Board of Education of the Township of Ewing, http://www.law.cornell.edu/supremecourt/text/330/1.

8. Baer v. Kolmorgen, http://www.leagle.com/decision/1958102914Misc2d1015_1684.xml/BAER%20v.%20KOLMORGEN.

9. Menendez, *December Wars*, p. 111.

10. See http://law.justia.com/cases/federal/appellate-courts/F2/619/1311/200625/.

11. Melvin I. Urofsky, *Religious Freedom: Rights and Liberties under the Law* (Santa Barbara: ABC-CLIO, 2002), p. 95.

12. Lynch v. Donnelly, http://caselaw.lp.findlaw.com/scripts/getcase.pl?court=us&vol=465&invol=668.

13. Allegheny County v. Greater Pittsburgh ACLU, http://caselaw.lp.findlaw.com/scripts/getcase.pl?navby=CASE&court=US&vol=492&page=573.

14. Capitol Square Review Bd. v. Pinette, http://www.law.cornell.edu/supct/html/94-780.ZO.html.

15. "Skolegudstjenester og kirkeasyl," Dagen, October 9, 2013, http://www.dagen.no/Meninger/Skolegudstjenester_og_kirkeasyl-66035; "Six Things Not To Say on Sweden's Lucia Day," *Local*, December 9, 2015, http://www.thelocal.se/20151209/six-things-not-to-say-on-swedens-lucia-day; "Var sjätte skola har bytt jultraditioner efter ny lag," Sverige Radio, December 7, 2012, http://sverigesradio.se/sida/artikel.aspx?programid=3993&artikel=5372806.

16. "Newspapers, Commentators Agree: Virginia, There Is No War on Christmas," December 23, 2005, Mediamatters, http://mediamatters.org/research/2005/12/23/newspapers-commentators-agree-virginia-there-is/134538.

17. Erin R. Brown, "The War on Christmas," December 13, 2011, Newsbusters, http://newsbusters.org/blogs/erin-r-brown/2011/12/13/war-war-christmas.

18. Americans United for Separation of Church and State, https://www.au.org; "What Are the Foundation's Accomplishments?," http://ffrf.org/faq/item/15000-what-are-the-foundations-accomplishments; "Celebrating Christmas in America," https://www.aclu.org/celebrating-christmas-america.

19. "Commissioners Order Manger Removed," *Titusville Herald*, December 21, 1990, http://newspaperarchive.com/us/pennsylvania/titusville/titusville-herald/1990/12-21/page-2.

20. Mary Jo Patterson, *On the Frontlines of Freedom: A Chronicle of the First 50 Years of the American Civil Liberties Union of New Jersey* (Bloomington: 2012), p. 88. In October 2014 the phrase "bowing to pressure from the American Civil Liberties Union" produced 12,200 hits on Google.

21. Lyle Denniston, "Supreme Court Rethinks Debate on Nativity Scenes," *Baltimore Sun*, December 25, 1991, http://articles.baltimoresun.com/1991-12-25/news/

1991359003_1_religious-displays-government-and-religion-government-buil dings; Chuck Colson, "The Reindeer Rules," December 15, 1992, Breakpoint, https://www.breakpoint.org/bpcommentaries/entry/13/10028.

22. A John Birch tract, "There Goes Christmas?!," by Hubert Kregeloh, in 1959 had spoken of "an assault on Christmas" launched by the United Nations. Michael Medved seems to have been the first to use the term "war on Christmas" in a mainstream publication: "Holiday Grinches: Ho Ho, No No," *USA Today*, December 19, 2001, p. A17.

23. ACLU of New Jersey ex rel. Lander v. Schundler, 168 F. 3d 92—Court of Appeals, 3rd Circuit 1999, http://scholar.google.ca/scholar_case?case=34857273443486 29562&q=ACLU+v.+Schundler,+168+F.3d+92+(1999)&hl=en&as_sdt= 2006&as_vis=1.

24. See http://law.justia.com/cases/federal/district-courts/FSupp2/28/677/2531783/.

25. See http://caselaw.findlaw.com/us-8th-circuit/1279463.html.

26. Lowman S. Henry, "ACLU Grinch Steals Christmas in Pittsburgh," Lincoln Online, http://lincolninstitute.org/archives/Commentary/20021207.html; Wells v. City and County of Denver, http://www.leagle.com/decision/20011389257 F3d1132_11272.xml/WELLS%20v.%20CITY%20AND%20COUNTY%20 OF%20DENVER; "Sixth Circuit Censors Criticism of Religion in FFRF Case," February 25, 2013, Freedom From Region Foundation, http://ffrf.org/news/ news-releases/item/16662-sixth-circuit-censors-criticism-of-religion-in-ffrf-case.

27. According to Roadside America, the museum operated for five years, closing in 2005, http://www.roadsideamerica.com/tip/10212.

28. See the listing for this movie at http://www.imdb.com/title/tt1412561/.

29. Rachanee Srisavasdi, "Christmas Tree Removed from Courthouse," *Orange County Register*, November 24, 2009, http://www.ocregister.com/articles/tree-221073-courthouse-petition.html.

30. "Christmas Tree Banned from Courthouse Lobby," *CBC News*, December 14, 2006,http://www.cbc.ca/news/canada/toronto/christmas-tree-banned-from-courthouse-lobby-1.593521.

31. James Morton, president, Ontario Bar Association, to attorney general of province of Ontario, http://ontariobarassociation.org/en/main/home_en/Newsdetails .aspx?no=NEWS12142006-749-1E, accessed October 13, 2007.

32. Buck Wolf, "Weird News: The Wolf File," *ABC News*, December 21, 2000, http://abcnews.go.com/Entertainment/WolfFiles/story?id=94633&page=1.

33. Ganulin v. U.S., https://casetext.com/case/ganulin-v-us.

34. Ganulin petition, http://law.uc.edu/sites/default/files/Ganulin_Petition.pdf.

35. Anti-Defamation League, http://www.adl.org/about-adl/. The Anti-Defamation League bills itself as "the nation's premier civil rights/human relations agency." It "fights anti-Semitism and all forms of bigotry, defends democratic ideals and protects civil rights for all."

36. American Civil Liberties Foundation Union of Tennessee, http://www.aclu-tn .org/pdfs/Superintendent_letter_holidays.pdf.

37. "ADF Offers Tenn. Schools Free Defense against ACLU Christmas Threat," December 13, 2010, Alliance Defending Freedom, http://www.adfmedia.org/ News/PRDetail/?CID=21073.

38. "Newton Schools Defy Lawyer with 'Christmas Break' Name," December 17, 1999, Online Athens, http://onlineathens.com/stories/121799/new_1217990015 .shtml; "ACLU—Christmas Removed from Calendar," *Straight Dope*, December 23, 2004, http://boards.straightdope.com/sdmb/showthread.php?t=236243; Valerie Richardson, "'Christmas' Break Makes Return," *Washington Times*, April 28, 2006; "Around the Nation," *Washington Times*, December 22, 2005, http:// www.washingtontimes.com/news/2005/dec/22/20051222-122614-5099r/ ?page=all; James Joyner, "Man Sets Self on Fire to Protest Christmas Vacation," December 23, 2006, Outside the Beltway, http://www.outsidethebeltway.com/ man_sets_self_on_fire_to_protest_christmas_vacation_video_photos/.

39. Skoros v. City of New York, http://caselaw.findlaw.com/us-2nd-circuit/1351830.html.

40. Jessica Garrison, "School Pulls Plug on Decorations after Objections," *Los Angeles Times*, December 7, 2000, http://articles.latimes.com/2000/dec/07/ local/me-62410.

41. Teresa Lane, "Religion Drama Plays Out in St. Lucie (FL) Schools," *Palm Beach Post*, October 9, 2006; Anne Morse, "And the Ebby Goes To . . . ," December 20, 2006, Breakpoint, http://www.breakpoint.org/tp-home/blog-archives/recent -point-posts/entry/4/6517.

42. Helen Pow, "Atheist Group Attacks Elementary School over Field Trip to See 'A Charlie Brown Christmas' at Local Church Claiming It 'Violates Religious Freedoms,'" *Daily Mail*, December 25, 2012, http://www.dailymail.co.uk/news/ article-2238396/Charlie-Brown-Christmas-play-Atheist-group-attacks- elementary-school-field-trip-A-Charlie-Brown-Christmas-local-church-claim ing-violates-religious-freedoms.html.

43. Gabe Wildau, "Led by O'Reilly, Conservative Pundits Claimed Washington School 'Banned' *A Christmas Carol*," December 13, 2004, *Mediamatters*, http:// mediamatters.org/research/2004/12/23/led-by-oreilly-conservative-pundits- claimed-was/132494.

44. Ben Casselman, "In Beverly, Grinch Steals Holidays, and Talk Radio Doesn't Like It," *Salem (MA) News*, December 8, 2004, Free Republic, http://www .freerepublic.com/focus/f-news/1297075/posts.

45. Julie Henry and Vikki Miller, "School Nativity Plays under Threat," *Telegraph*, December 3, 2007, http://www.telegraph.co.uk/news/uknews/1571187/School- nativity-plays-under-threat.html?mobile=basic; Tim Ross, "Rowan Williams: Stop Political Correctness Taking 'Christ' Out of 'Christmas,'" *Telegraph*, December 8, 2010, http://www.telegraph.co.uk/news/uknews/8186555/Rowan-Williams- stop-political-correctness-taking-christ-out-of-Christmas.html.

46. Erika Hayasaki and Joel Rubin, "School Yuletide Observances Shift into Neutral," *Los Angeles Times*, December 22, 2004, articles.latimes.com/2004/dec/22/local/me-xmas22.

47. Hilary Matheson, "Church-State Battle Envelops School Choirs," *Daily Interlake*, December 4, 2013, http://www.dailyinterlake.com/news/local_montana/article_c51221d4-5d4f-11e3-a221-001a4bcf887a.html.

48. Billy Hallowell, "Charter School Reportedly Bans Students from Performing 'Joy to the World' and 'Oh Come All Ye Faithful,'" *Blaze*, November 21, 2013; "Public Outcry Restores Censored Christmas Carols," October 14, 2013, Alliance Defending Freedom, http://www.adfmedia.org/News/PRDetail/8576; "NJ School District Withdraws Ban on Religious Christmas Carols," November 4, 2013, Alliance Defending Freedom, http://www.adfmedia.org/News/PRDetail/8631; Andrew Levy, "School Choir Forced to Pull Out of Christmas Concert as Carols Were 'Too Religious,'" *Daily Mail*, December 11, 2008, http://www.dailymail.co.uk/news/article-1093791/School-choir-forced-pull-Christmas-concert-carols-religious.html.

49. Betsy Cohen, "Some Missoula Parents Say School's Holiday Program Not Secular Enough," *Billings Gazette*, December 13, 2012, http://billingsgazette.com/news/state-and-regional/montana/some-missoula-parents-say-school-s-holiday-program-not-secular/article_d3bfffe4-2bb8-5b5d-821f-322fb8693159.html.

50. "'Silent Night': Carolers Told to Stop," Fox News, December 14, 2006, http://www.foxnews.com/printer_friendly_wires/2006Dec14/0,4675,CarolersStopped,00.html.

51. Mark Steyn, "God Rest Ye Merry," *New York Sun*, December 18, 2006, http://www.nysun.com/opinion/god-rest-ye-merry/45337/.

52. Jay Nordlinger, "An All-Too-Modern Homecoming," *National Review*, October 29, 2009, http://www.nationalreview.com/article/228493/all-too-modern-home-coming-c-jay-nordlinger; Tony Lofaro, "Choir Drops 'Christmas' from Carol," *National Post*, December 19, 2007.

53. "School's 'Giving Tree' Turns Into 'Giving Counter,'" December 7, 2005, US Message Board, http://www.usmessageboard.com/threads/schools-giving-tree-turns-into-giving-counter.27462/.

54. Jay Nordlinger, "December's C-Word," *National Review*, December 31, 2003.

55. Ted Olsen, "December Dilemma Award Winner," *Christianity Today*, April 13, 2006, http://www.christianitytoday.com/ct/2005/januaryweb-only/42.0.html.

56. "Tongue Tied: Santa & Elves Banned, Christmas Greeters Canned," Fox News, December 24, 2001, http://www.foxnews.com/story/2001/12/24/tongue-tied-santa-elves-banned-christmas-greeters-canned/; Kristen Dymacek, "School Board Examines ACLU Allegations," *Baldwin City (KS) Signal*, December 10, 2003, http://signal.baldwincity.com/news/2003/dec/10/school_board_examines/; "Bah Humbug! Father Christmas Banned at Children's Centre...To Respect

Faith of One Muslim Family," The Patriot (blog), January 3, 2011, http://boltonbnp
.blogspot.com/2011/01/bah-humbug-father-christmas-banned-at.html;
Todd Starnes, "Fort Worth Bans Santa from Classrooms," *Fox Radio News*,
http://radio.foxnews.com/toddstarnes/top-stories/fort-worth-bans-santa-from-
classrooms.html; George Jahn, "St. Nick Ban Causes Stir in Vienna," Fox News,
November 29, 2006, http://www.foxnews.com/printer_friendly_wires/2006N
ov29/0,4675,NoStNick,00.html; Wendy Tuohy, "PM Stands By Father Christmas,"
The Age, November 30, 2002, http://www.theage.com.au/articles/2002/11/29/
1038386312544.html.

57. H.No. 108, Texas Legislature Online, http://www.capitol.state.tx.us/tlodocs/
83R/billtext/html/HB00308F.htm.

58. Anna M. Tinsley, "Santa Trumps the Grinch under Texas' New Merry Christmas
Law," *Fort Worth Star-Telegram*, December 7, 2013, http://www.star-telegram
.com/news/politics-government/article3839101.html#storylink=cpy.

59. Sean Grindlay, "A Christmas Tree of Campaigns at IU," March 15, 2004, Accuracy
in Academia, http://www.academia.org/a-christmas-tree-of-campaigns-at-iu/.

60. Nick McRae and Ryan McLaughlin, "Email Discouraging Christmas-Themed
Decorations at UMaine Causes Uproar on Campus," *Bangor (ME) Daily News*,
December 11, 2014, http://bangordailynews.com/2014/12/11/news/bangor/email-
discouraging-christmas-themed-decorations-at-umaine-causes-uproar-
on-campus/.

61. "Guidelines for the Display of Religious Symbols," Cornell University, 2015,
https://sp.ehs.cornell.edu/fps/fire-code-compliance/Documents/FCC_Fire_
Safety_Guidelines_for_Holidays_Decorations.pdf; Kate Hardiman, "Public University Tells Campus: 'Ensure Your Holiday Party Is Not a Christmas Party in
Disguise,'" *College Fix*, December 4, 2015, http://www.thecollegefix.com/post/
25368/; Adam Tamburin, "Lawmakers Want UT Chief to Resign after Holiday
Post," *Tennessean*, December 4, 2015, http://www.tennessean.com/story/news/
education/2015/12/03/lawmaker-blasts-ut-post-inclusive-holiday-celebrations/
76734956/; the dictates that were once posted on the webpage titled "Inclusive
Holiday Practices" have been removed and replaced with this statement: "The
content of the webpage referenced was an effort to help facilitate celebrating
holiday traditions of all faculty, staff and students. It is not a mandate or university policy. To avoid misinterpretation or confusion, the webpage has been
removed." Office of Diversity and Inclusion, Ohio State University, https://odi
.osu.edu/about/ohio-state-diversity-officers/inclusive-holiday-practices.html.
The original webpage, with "inclusive strategies" that include banning religious
images and green and red ribbons, is preserved at https://web.archive.org/
web/20150103065432/http://odi.osu.edu/about/ohio-state-diversity-officers/
inclusive-holiday-practices.html.

62. "Despite Ban, Santa Claus Comes to Maryland Town," Fox News, December 3,
2001, http://www.foxnews.com/story/2001/12/03/despite-ban-santa-comes-to-

maryland-town/; "Santa Banned/Bill White's Protest," n.d., Vanguard News Network, http://www.vanguardnewsnetwork.com/wolzek/2001_SantaBanned .html; Candace Smith, "Despite Ban, Santa Makes an Appearance at Fireman's Parade," *Fredericksburg (VA) Free Lance-Star,* December 3, 2001, http://news .google.com/newspapers?nid=1298&dat=20011203&id=wy0zAAAAIBAJ&sjid =RAgGAAAAIBAJ&pg=5414,940573.

63. Usually missing in the debate about the phrase "Merry Christmas" is the fact that December 25 is a national holiday and that no one seems to be upset about being wished a happy Independence Day or Labor Day.

64. "Committee to Save Merry Christmas," May 27, 2004, Free Republic, http:// freerepublic.com/focus/news/1143322/posts.

65. See John Gibson, *The War on Christmas: How the Liberal Plot to Ban the Sacred Christian Holiday Is Worse Than You Thought* (New York: 2005).

66. "How We Beat Wal-Mart," December 2005, Catholic League for Religious and Civil Rights, http://www.catholicleague.org/how-we-beat-wal-mart/; Kirby's spelling and grammar as in the original.

67. Bill O'Reilly, "Part 1, Chapter 5: The Battle for Christmas," in *Culture Warrior* (New York: 2006).

68. Barry W. Lynn, *Piety and Politics: The Right-Wing Assault on Religious Freedom* (New York: 2006); Bill Press, *How the Republicans Stole Christmas: The Republican Party's Declared Monopoly on Religion and What Democrats Can Do to Take It Back* (New York: 2005); Stephen A. Klien, "O'Reilly's War on the 'War on Christmas': Diatribe, Culture, and Conservative Ideology," in *Venomous Speech: Problems with American Political Discourse on the Right and Left,* ed. Clark Rountree (Santa Barbara: 2013), pp. 269–297.

69. Don Feder, "The Attack on Christmas: We Wish You a Merry Multicultural, Inoffensive, Inclusive, Secular Seasonal Holiday," December 13, 2009, Restore Free Speech, http://restorefreespeech.blogspot.ca/2009_12_01_archive.html; Why Do Retailers Fear Using the Word 'Christmas'?," *Washington Times,* December 23, 2008, http://www.washingtontimes.com/news/2008/dec/23/ why-do-retailers-fear-using-the-word-christmas/?page=all.

70. Evan McMurry, "Bill O'Reilly: I Won the War on Christmas," December 18, 2014, Mediaite, http://www.mediaite.com/tv/bill-oreilly-i-won-the-war-on-christmas/.

71. "The Story behind the Design of Starbucks Red Holiday Cups," November 8, 2015, Starbucks, https://news.starbucks.com/news/the-story-behind-the-design- of-starbucks-red-holiday-cups-for-2015; Nick Hallett, "MPs, Christian Groups Slam Starbucks 'Scrooges' over Red Cups," Breitbart, November 5, 2015, http:// www.breitbart.com/london/2015/11/05/mps-christian-groups-slam-starbucks- scrooges-over-red-cups/; "Starbucks REMOVED CHRISTMAS from their cups because they hate Jesus…SO I PRANKED THEM…and they HATE IT!!!!" (video), posted November 5, 2015, More Videos by Joshua Feuerstein, https:// www.facebook.com/joshua.feuerstein.5/videos/689569711145714; Kate Taylor,

"Trump Suggests Boycotting Starbucks' Plain Red Holiday Cups," November 10, 2015, Business Insider, http://www.businessinsider.com/trump-boycotting-starbucks-red-cups-2015-11; Jonathan Merritt, "Most Christians Don't Actually Care About Starbucks Cups. Here's What We Do Know," *Washington Post,* November 10, 2015, https://www.washingtonpost.com/news/acts-of-faith/wp/2015/11/10/most-christians-dont-actually-care-about-starbucks-cups-heres-what-we-do-know/.

72. Jenna Zibton and Christina Craig, "After Heated Debate, Salem VA Medical Center Allows Christmas Tree after All," http://wsls.com/2015/11/20/salem-va-bans-christmas-trees-as-holiday-decorations/. Kwanzaa, of course, is a cultural celebration, not a faith.

73. Bryan Henry, "US Rep Roby Seeks Answers after Montgomery VAs Refusal of Christmas Gifts," December 27, 2013, World Now, http://raycomnbc.worldnow.com/story/24316713/us-rep-roby-seeks-answers-after-montgomery-vas-refusal-of-christmas-gifts; Wesley Brown, "Augusta VA Won't Let Carolers Sing Religious Songs," *Augusta Chronicle,* December 23, 2013, http://chronicle.augusta.com/life/your-faith/2013-12-23/augusta-va-wont-let-carolers-sing-religious-songs?v=1387845251; "The 2015 Ebenezer," Becket Fund for Religious Liberty, http://www.becketfund.org/ebenezer/; Alan Noble, "Todd Starnes Sold Us a War on Christianity. We Bought It," Patheos, December 31, 2013, http://www.patheos.com/blogs/christandpopculture/2013/12/todd-starnes-sold-us-a-war-on-christianity-we-bought-it/; Renee Dudley, "Ho Ho Hold On There: Cancer Center Reverses Santa Decision," *Charleston (SC) Post and Courier,* November 16, 2011, http://www.postandcourier.com/article/20111116/PC16/311169922.

74. Hannah Young, "'Holiday Tree' or 'Christmas Tree' in State Capitol?," November 26, 2007, Free Republic, http://www.freerepublic.com/focus/f-news/1930827/posts; Kevin Petersen, "It's a Christmas Tree," n.d., Wisconsin State Legislature, Rep. Petersen, E-Updates, http://legis.wisconsin.gov/assembly/petersen/eup-dates/Pages/Its%20a%20Christmas%20Tree.aspx.

75. Lincoln D. Chafee, "Statement from the Office of Governor Lincoln D. Chafee Regarding the State House Tree," Office of the Governor, December 2, 2013, http://rhodeislandgovernor.blogspot.ca/2013/12/statement-from-office-of-governor.html.

76. "Abstract Christmas Tree Sparks Protests in Brussels," *BBC News,* December 1, 2012, http://www.bbc.com/news/world-europe-20302574; Soren Kern, "Jihad on Christmas Trees," December 4, 2012, Gatestone Institute, http://www.gatestoneinstitute.org/3479/jihad-christmas-trees; "Ruling on Having a Christmas Tree without Celebrating Christmas," Islam Question and Answer, December 17, 2012, https://islamqa.info/en/161539.

77. "'Nativity' Ad Restored to Christmas Festival," WND, December 23, 2006, http://www.wnd.com/2006/12/39408/.

78. Michelle Goldberg, "How the Secular Humanist Grinch Didn't Steal Christmas," http://www.salon.com/2005/11/21/christmas_6/.

79. "How Americans Feel about Religious Groups," July 16, 2014, Pew Research Center, http://www.pewforum.org/2014/07/16/how-americans-feel-about-religious-groups/.

80. Public Religion Research Institute, "Continued Majority Support for Employer Contraception Mandate, Opposition to Allowing Small Businesses to Refuse Services on Religious Grounds," June 11, 2014, http://publicreligion.org/research/2014/06/employer-contraception/.

81. Besheer Mohamed, "Christmas Also Celebrated by Many Non-Christians," December 23, 2013, http://www.pewresearch.org/fact-tank/2013/12/23/christmas-also-celebrated-by-many-non-christians/.

82. "Survey: Americans Shift Preference for 'Happy Holidays' over 'Merry Christmas,'" December 17, 2013, Public Religion Research Institute, http://publicreligion.org/research/2013/12/prri-rns-dec-2013-survey/.

83. Michael Lipka, "'Merry Christmas' or 'Happy Holidays?,'" December 12, 2013, Pew Research Center, http://www.pewresearch.org/fact-tank/2013/12/12/merry-christmas-or-happy-holidays/.

84. See James Ron, "Christmas Isn't for Everyone," *Ottawa Citizen*, December 22, 2008.

85. This is not to say that there is no anti-Christian element in Christmas wars; earlier I have shown this clearly expressed by atheists.

86. "Merry Christmas from the ACLU," December 4, 2013, American Civil Liberties Union, https://www.aclusandiego.org/merry-christmas-from-the-aclu/.

87. Mark Mercer, "The Significance of Christmas for Liberal Multiculturalism," in *Christmas—Philosophy for Everyone: Better Than a Lump of Coal,* ed. Scott C. Lowe (Chichester: 2011), argues persuasively for a tolerance that avoids identity politics and that would find a secular Christmas a wonderful, socially cohesive element of celebration.

Index